D1624183

Therapies
for Adults

Depressive, Anxiety,
and Personality Disorders

Howard L. Millman
Jack T. Huber
Dean R. Diggins

Therapies
for Adults

Jossey-Bass Publishers
San Francisco • Washington • London • 1982

THERAPIES FOR ADULTS
Depressive, Anxiety, and Personality Disorders
       by Howard L. Millman, Jack T. Huber, and Dean R. Diggins

Copyright © 1982 by: Jossey-Bass Inc., Publishers
               433 California Street
               San Francisco, California 94104
                   &
               Jossey-Bass Limited
               28 Banner Street
               London EC1Y 8QE

Library of Congress Cataloging in Publication Data

Millman, Howard L.
      Therapies for adults.

      (Guidebooks for therapeutic practice)
      Includes index.
      1. Psychotherapy. I. Huber, Jack T. II. Diggins,
Dean. III. Title. IV. Series. [DNLM: 1. Anxiety
disorders—Therapy. 2. Depressive disorder—Therapy.
3. Personality disorders—Therapy. WM 172 M655t]
RC480.M54   1982   616.89'14   82-48064
ISBN 0-87589-537-9

Manufactured in the United States of America

The paper in this book meets the guidelines for
permanence and durability of the Committee on
Production Guidelines for Book Longevity of the
Council on Library Resources.

JACKET DESIGN BY WILLI BAUM

FIRST EDITION

Code 8233

The Jossey-Bass
Social and Behavioral Science Series

GUIDEBOOKS FOR THERAPEUTIC PRACTICE
Charles E. Schaefer and Howard L. Millman
Consulting Editors

*Therapies for Children: A Handbook of Effective
Treatments for Problem Behaviors*
Charles E. Schaefer and Howard L. Millman
1977

Therapies for Psychosomatic Disorders in Children
Charles E. Schaefer, Howard L. Millman,
and Gary F. Levine
1979

Therapies for School Behavior Problems
Howard L. Millman, Charles E. Schaefer,
and Jeffrey J. Cohen
1980

*Therapies for Adolescents: Current Treatments
for Problem Behaviors*
Michael D. Stein and J. Kent Davis
1982

Group Therapies for Children and Youth
Charles E. Schaefer, Lynnette Johnson,
and Jeffrey N. Wherry
1982

Therapies for Adults
Howard L. Millman, Jack T. Huber,
and Dean R. Diggins
1982

Preface

The field of adult therapy is marked by a growing mass of literature, a proliferation of systems and methods, and considerable diversity of opinion on basic issues. It is impossible for most therapists to keep up with the mass of literature, the breadth of systems and methods, or even the basic differences of opinion. At the same time, therapists are expressing growing dissatisfaction with the limitations of following specific systems and a concomitant openness to contributions from other systems.

In response to these conditions, this book presents concise digests of professional articles describing a wide array of therapeutic techniques used for specific problems and found to be successful by the therapists we cite. The book is thus intended as a practical sourcebook for professional people who deal with psychological problems in adults. Specifically, the intended readers are psychologists, psychiatrists, social workers, counselors, and nurses. We hope it will be useful to teachers as well as practitioners.

In order to keep the book to a practical, manageable size, we restricted our coverage to thirteen categories: depressive disorder, agoraphobia, social phobia, simple phobia, generalized anxiety disorder, obsessive-compulsive disorder, and seven personality disorders—antisocial, borderline, dependent, histrionic, narcissistic, paranoid, and schizoid. These diagnostic categories, taken with some modification from the *Diagnostic and Statistical Manual of Mental Disorders,* third edition (1980), provide the organizational structure for the book. We chose DSM-III because its specificity in defining the content and boundaries of the diagnostic categories and its generally atheoretical approach with regard to etiology lend it to wide usage by professionals with varying theoretical orientations.

The articles we have chosen are representative of the enormous range of methods found in the literature. Each digest focuses on specific therapeutic practices described in the original article. Our intent is to provide the reader with a practical overview of therapeutic techniques applied to specific problems. Finding a useful idea here, the reader can obtain further details and discussion of research and theoretical frameworks from the original source. Our goal is to alert readers to the many possibilities for therapeutic intervention so that they can make informed decisions when treating specific disorders.

We have used such terms as *the therapist, the client, the patient,* and plurals of these. When these were not possible, we avoided the cumbersome practice of using both feminine and masculine pronouns, as in *he or she,* by reverting at times to the formerly conventional use of the masculine pronouns.

We wish to thank these friends and colleagues for their help: Aaron Beck, Bonnie Berger, Jacob Cohen, Allen Fay, Zenia Fliegel, Edna Foa, Lisa Ford, Cyril Franks, Harold and Alice Ladas, Arnold Lazarus, Robert Spitzer, Dorothy Susskind, Esta Treiber, Sue Rosenberg Zalk, and the reference room staff of Hunter College of the City University of New York.

We are grateful to the authors who gave permission for their articles to be digested and to the American Psychiatric Association for permission to quote definitions of specific disorders from the *Diagnostic and Statistical Manual of Mental Disorders,* third edition (DSM-III).

August 1982   Howard L. Millman
                                                 Scarsdale, New York

                                                 Jack T. Huber
                                                 New York City

                                                 Dean R. Diggins
                                                 New York City

Contents

The Authors

Howard L. Millman is the director of Psychological and Educational Services of Westchester, which provides help for psychological, behavioral, and learning problems. He practices individual, marital, and family psychotherapy in Scarsdale and New York City. For many years he has been the director of psychology and research at The Children's Village, a residential treatment center in Dobbs Ferry, New York. Millman received the Ph.D. degree in clinical psychology from Adelphi University and completed a clinical psychology internship at the Neuropsychiatric Institute at the University of California at Los Angeles. For several years he was the chief psychologist at the Middlesex County Mental Health Clinic in New Jersey. He has taught psychotherapy and supervised doctoral psychology students at the City College of New York and at Rutgers—the State University. For several years he taught group psychodynamics to graduate students at Manhattanville College. Currently he is a member of the Division of Psychotherapy of the American Psychological Association and the New York State Psychological Association. He is past president of the Westchester County Psychological Association.

Millman has published numerous articles in professional journals concerning psychotherapy, treatment outcome, and psychological and behavioral problems related to learning disabilities. He is the coauthor of *How to Help Children with Common Problems* (with C. E. Schaefer, 1981), *Therapies for School Behavior Problems* (with C. E. Schaefer and J. J. Cohen, 1980), *Therapies for Psychosomatic Disorders in Children* (with C. E. Schaefer and G. F. Levine, 1979), *Therapies for Children* (with C. E. Schaefer, 1977), and coeditor (with J. T. Huber) of *Goals and Behavior in Psychotherapy and Counseling* (1972).

Jack T. Huber is a professor at Hunter College of the City University of New York, where he teaches personality and counseling theory, interviewing, and educational psychology. Huber received the Ph.D. degree in clinical psychology from Columbia University. For twelve years he was a professor in the Ph.D. program in clinical psychology and the postgraduate program in psychotherapy and psychoanalysis, and director of psychological services, at Adelphi University. He was for many years a supervisor and a member of the board of directors of the Vocational Advisory Service, where he was also the director of the Psychiatric Clinic for Disturbed and Delinquent Adolescent Boys. Huber is the author of *Report Writing in Psychology and Psychiatry* (1961), *Through an Eastern Window* (1967; also published under the title *Psychotherapy and Meditation*), coeditor (with H. L. Millman) of *Goals and Behavior in Psychotherapy and Counseling* (1972), and coauthor (with D. R. Diggins) of *The Human Personality* (1976).

Dean R. Diggins is an associate professor at Brooklyn College of the City University of New York, where he teaches undergraduate and graduate courses in personality psychology and human motivation. He is currently doing research on human movement and gestures and conducting experiential movement therapy workshops. Diggins received the Ph.D. degree in psychology from the City University of New York. He is a member of the American Psychological Association, the New York State Psychological Association, the Eastern Psychological Association, and the Laban/Bartenieff Institute of Movement Studies. He has written articles in professional journals and is coauthor (with J. T. Huber) of *The Human Personality* (1976).

Therapies
for Adults

Depressive, Anxiety,
and Personality Disorders

Introduction

In this book we give various therapeutic techniques used for specific problems and found to be successful by the therapists we cite. The book is intended as a practical handbook for professional people who deal with psychological problems in adults. Specifically, the intended readers are psychologists, psychiatrists, social workers, counselors, and nurses. We also envision the use of the book in courses and practica in psychotherapy.

In therapy courses the goal is ordinarily to expose students to an array of therapy systems, and there are numerous texts to fill this need. For example, the first two authors of the present volume, Millman and Huber, covered primary source readings in sixteen therapy systems in their *Goals and Behavior in Psychotherapy and Counseling* (Columbus, Ohio: Merrill, 1972).

1

Our intent here is to provide the reader with practical therapeutic techniques. The book does not include lengthy discussions of theory or research. Finding a useful idea here, the reader can then go to the original source for discussion of how the treatment fits into a larger theoretical system and the research covering the treatment.

Therapies for Adults and the series of which it is a part meet a need felt by us and stated by M. R. Goldfried ("Toward the Delineation of Therapeutic Change Principles," *American Psychologist,* 1980, *35,* 991-999):

> Clearly, we need to rewrite our textbooks on psychotherapy. In picking up the textbook of the future, we should see in the table of contents *not* a listing of School A, School B, and so on—perhaps ending with the author's attempt at integration—but an outline of the various agreed-upon intervention principles, a specification of varying techniques for implementing each principle, and an indication of the relative effectiveness of each of these techniques together with their interaction with varying presenting problems and individual differences among patients/clients and therapists. I sense that the time is rapidly approaching when serious, if not painstaking, work on gathering the necessary information for such a text can begin [pp. 997-998].

The urge for specificity is not new. As long ago as 1967, a plea was made for "*what* treatment, by *whom,* is most effective for *this* individual with *that* specific problem, and under *which* set of circumstances" (G. L. Paul, "Strategy of Outcome Research in Psychotherapy," *Journal of Consulting Psychology,* 1967, *31,* 109-119, p. 111; see also J. Marmor, "Common Operational Factors in Diverse Approaches to Behavior Change," in A. Burton (Ed.), *What Makes Behavior Change Possible?,* New York: Brunner/Mazel, 1976, and M. B. Parloff, "Can Psychotherapy Research Guide the Policymaker? A Little Knowledge May Be a Dangerous Thing," *American Psychologist,* 1979, *34,* 296-306). J. D. Frank ("The Present Status of Outcome Studies," *Journal of Consulting and Clinical Psychology*, 1979, *47*, 310-316) introduced still another variable: "differences in world view"; he cited as an example that Indians treated by Peruvian therapists would find that the attainment of mastery as a therapeutic goal would make no sense, since their goal apparently would be "to learn to accept their fate or to restore their harmony with the spirit world" (p. 315). Put another way, Frank seems to be suggesting a widening of the search for criteria of therapeutic success. A. A. Lazarus ("Toward Delineating Some Causes of Change in Psychotherapy," *Professional Psychology*, 1980, *11*, 863-870) adds still another variable: "One possibility is that specific changes in a person's life circumstances, unrelated to the therapy, are all too readily overlooked as the real ingredient of constructive change"; he cites his own training of an agitated woman in relaxation and meditation only to find that her recovery appeared to be the result of new, quieter neighbors (p. 866). Similarly, Diggins and Huber (*The Human Personality*, Boston: Little Brown, 1976) point out the variable of pure chance, or fortuitous events, as a powerful influence in altering human behavior.

What is suggested for the study of psychotherapy, if we review all these statements, is research involving these variables: the specific *therapy* (or what the therapist actually did), the *therapist* (presumably, personality variables), the *patient* (apparently, both the therapy behavior and personality variables), the specific *problem* being treated, *conditions* under which therapy was done, treatment *goals* (such as "world view"), and changes in the patient's life *circumstances*. The current state of the profession is not strong enough to fulfill such an ambitious goal. There are extraordinary difficulties in correlating any of these variables with therapeutic success (M. L. Smith, G. V. Glass, and T. I. Miller, *The Benefits of Psychotherapy*, Baltimore: Johns Hopkins University Press, 1980).

In spite of these difficulties, an excellent start has been made toward these goals. Our book represents a pulling together of specific therapies for specific clients, of what therapists do well with what techniques, the best treatments for specific problems, and so on. Although there are still contradictions, the reader will be able to make informed decisions when treating a specific disorder.

Selection of Psychological Problems

Our task was to select specific adult problems encountered by professional people in clinical and private practice. Once a list of problems was collected from therapists, the next step was to find a category system for these problems that would be useful, convenient, and clearly understood.

Adult problems are primarily situational (for example, marital discord), affective (for example, anxiety), behavioral (for example, inability to get along with superiors), or in the form of behavior troublesome to others (for example, antisocial behavior). We needed a category system that would cover these aspects and would reflect our emphasis on specific problems. We chose, with some modifications, the *Diagnostic and Statistical Manual of Mental Disorders,* third edition (Washington, D.C.: American Psychiatric Association, 1980) (DSM-III), because of its wide usage and its specificity in defining the content and boundaries of the diagnostic categories. It also reflects a generally atheoretical approach with regard to etiology and is therefore used by professionals of varying theoretical orientations.

We were restricted by the fact that the book had to be of manageable size. We covered thirteen problems—depression, agoraphobia, social phobia, simple phobia, generalized anxiety disorder, obsessive-compulsive disorder, and seven personality disorders: antisocial, borderline, dependent, histrionic, narcissistic, paranoid, and schizoid.

Selection of Therapeutic Procedures

S. L. Garfield ("Psychotherapy: A 40-Year Appraisal," *American Psychologist,* 1981, *36,* 174-183) has written, "At the present time psychotherapy is provided to more people by more therapists than ever before in our history, and all kinds of professional and nonprofessional workers are busily engaged in delivering such services. The social and cultural climate in the United States appears to be favorable for the growth and development of all types of psychotherapy and psychotherapists" (p. 175).

Equally cogent to the point of this book is Goldfried's statement that there is a growing dissatisfaction among therapists following specific systems with their own limitations and a concomitant openness to contributions from other systems ("Therapeutic Change Principles," 1980, p. 991).

The field of adult therapy is marked by a growing mass of literature, a proliferation of systems and methods, and considerable diversity of opinion on basic issues. It is impossible for most therapists to keep up with the mass of literature, with the breadth of systems and methods, or in fact even with what the basic differences of opinion are. Our task here was to select the widest array of therapeutic interventions that have been tried for specific problems.

Our criteria for selecting therapies were that they must be discrete (or different from one another), specific, and reportedly successful. The therapies covered are representative of the enormous range of methods found in the literature. The reader should be aware that these methods may or may not have extensive research backing or long clinical use. The reader is urged to consult the original articles for this information. Although this book is a sourcebook of many approaches, no one therapist is equipped to follow all the procedures given here. For example, in the use of psychopharmacological drugs, the assumption is that only a physician with specific knowledge of these drugs is qualified to use them. Our intention is to alert the reader to the many possibilities so that he can judge for himself his abilities and refer clients to others when a procedure is not part of his repertory.

Format of the Book

As in previous books in the series, we have followed the digest format—concise condensations of professional articles. The digests focus on specific therapeutic practices described in the original articles. We have eliminated technical research data and lengthy theoretical discussions. Each of the digests contains a *precis,* which summarizes what kind of treatment is used for what kind of problem, an *introduction,* which is a brief overview of the problem, the *description* of the therapeutic approach itself, a *commentary* in which we highlight indications and contraindications for using the technique, and the *source.* At the end of each section we have included annotated Additional Readings to help readers be aware of additional therapeutic approaches, variations of methods covered in the digests, and guidelines for making treatment more effective.

A Summary of Trends in Therapy

The purpose of this book is to present as full a range as possible of what therapists are doing; our goal is to show therapists the options they have. The vast range given here will require pulling together. Some perspective should give additional focus to therapists' options. The following is our attempt at an overview.

1. *Teaching.* One trend in therapy practice is away from mainly discussing motivation and past influences and toward therapists' teaching people a point of view about life or ways of coping. These include relaxation training, social skills training, instructions on how to be a better parent, sentences to say to oneself, and so on. This trend has dramatically expanded the field of therapy. This expansion, however, brings with it some added burdens for therapists. If teaching is done as part of a professional service, then it must be done professionally. A professional teacher is conversant with a body of knowledge and is skilled at teaching, both of which take time and practice. Thus, a therapist teaching a particular skill to a client would be expected to be both knowledgeable about that skill and good at teaching it.

2. *Individual versus group teaching.* In many instances in this book, a therapist teaches a client individually. This is, of course, costly. The cost may be unnecessary if the teaching could be done in some other way. An alternative is to put more

responsibility on clients. This can be done by presenting materials in groups or asking clients to read material of relevance to the therapy. One writer teaches self-control methods as a college course, and students devise their own therapy programs. Some writers teach a standard program in groups. Others have one or two books on, for example, anxiety or depression, which they find successful in moving a client ahead.

3. *Discussion of conflict.* Most of the psychodynamic therapies involve primarily a discussion of a client's conflicts. That is, if clients are in trouble because they do not know which of various goals they seek, then a discussion of the goals is in order. As we have pointed out, teaching seems to be more frequent than discussion in therapy. Teaching, however, is appropriate when someone is not in conflict but simply needs information and training. Thus, people who want to be more assertive but simply do not know how to assert themselves may be helped with assertion training. This teaching may be useless to someone in conflict about whether to be assertive or not. Some of the failures in therapy recorded here may have resulted in therapists' training people to do something about which the clients were in conflict. Some therapists here have emphasized the necessity for considerable discussion with clients until the clients are sure they want to pursue the therapy. I. M. Marks, for example ("Review of Behavioral Psychotherapy. I: Obsessive-Compulsive Disorders," *American Journal of Psychiatry*, 1981, *138*, 584-592), warned therapists against beginning exposure treatment until a client has been able to talk and think about and then unequivocally choose it.

In addition, there are people who simply want to talk with someone and desire no teaching or training. Various writers here have emphasized the necessity for initially getting clear what the client wants and what the therapist has to offer.

4. *Self-monitoring.* In our opinion, one of the most promising, frequently used, and least heralded techniques in therapy is self-monitoring. Self-awareness has for years been a major goal of therapy. We believe that self-monitoring may be a prime technique for promoting self-awareness (being self-administered, it may also enhance the perception of self-control).

Awareness, for example, of just how much alcohol one drank last week, how often one felt anxiety, or how often one thought of one's mother would seem to be a major way to motivate one to change and to institute a program in that direction. Almost any form of therapy will inspire self-observation, but focused self-monitoring seems likely to produce more self-awareness and perhaps more motivation to change than random, unfocused thinking about problems.

5. *Homework*. Self-monitoring is only one possible assignment of homework. Homework was a rarity in therapy circles when years ago a few therapists, such as Albert Ellis, assigned it regularly. Today it is used much more extensively; for example, clients are told to practice relaxation at home, try out new social skills in new environments, or take on a new role for a week. Like self-monitoring, assigned homework can focus a client on a particular aspect of a problem and give a client a feeling of self-control. It can also help clients use the valuable time between sessions to further the therapy in a specific direction.

6. *Informing clients about therapy*. Clients have probably always been given some information about therapy before it begins. Today, however, therapists seem more to inform clients about the details of therapy before beginning. As will be seen in some of the therapies here, therapists tell clients what they will have to do, how difficult it may be, what the therapist will do, and how it has turned out with other clients. Therapy seems increasingly to be a joint enterprise between client and therapist in which responsibility is on both sides or even more on the client's side—an enterprise of equals. Therapy is designed this way for numerous reasons. It gets away from clients' waiting passively for something to be done to them. Clients can take credit for successes. Being told of other clients' successes may set up an expectancy effect that motivates the client.

7. *Feedback*. Feedback of all kinds is used increasingly. Corrective feedback is given by therapists in assertion training, group feedback is given in social skills training, feedback is part of self-monitoring, and so on. The original enthusiasm for biofeedback has been somewhat dampened by its expense, requirements in space, and less than totally positive results, but it still

seems to hold promise. Some therapists have insisted that both therapist and client give each other constant feedback on how therapy is progressing so that appropriate changes in procedures can be made. Feedback is also used in family and marital therapy.

8. *Family members as helpers.* Numerous therapists here report on the advantages of recruiting family members to help with therapy. In reports digested in this book, family members monitor a patient's taking antidepressant drugs; a dependent male is given tokens by his wife for assertive behavior and he gives her tokens for more sexual responsiveness; the wife of a paranoid client is instructed to exaggerate his worst fears. An important ingredient here seems to be that an atmosphere of openness is established. In the presence of the client, the therapist instructs family members on their therapeutic duties with the client.

Failures of this procedure are also reported; the reasons seem to be that the client or family member did not really approve of the procedure or did not really want the client to change. Careful discussion of the procedure and what it will mean in terms of changes in the family, and no pressure on anyone's part to accept the procedure, seem to be essential for it to be effective.

9. *Expanded view of causes and cures.* The writings here reveal extensive liberalization in ideas of why people are troubled and what might be done to help them. The view that psychological symptoms are caused by intrapsychic conflicts and frustrations and that cure comes only from a discussion of these problems has undergone considerable change. Lazarus, for example, as mentioned earlier, reminds us of the importance of life circumstances to psychological well-being in his brief case study of an older woman whose anxiety disappeared when her noisy neighbors moved away. We are still being reminded that psychological symptoms can be caused by organic disturbances. J. T. Dietch, for example ("Diagnosis of Organic Anxiety Disorders," *Psychosomatica,* 1981, *22,* 661-669), gives specific diagnostic tests to help rule out specific organic disorders that cause or contribute to anxiety. The natural outcome of an ex-

panded view of causes and cures has been increased eclecticism and the use of multiple therapies.

10. *Eclecticism and multiple therapies.* Old antagonisms between schools of therapy are fading away. We will see here increasing eclecticism of individual therapists and more cooperation between therapists of different persuasions. The reasons for this new trend are probably multiple. Reports of success of a new therapy cannot be overlooked. People originally looking askance at behavior therapy, for example, could not blind themselves to reported successes and the good sense of some of the behavioral methods. A major theoretical shift, too, has come about: the idea that symptoms can be treated without getting at causes and without symptom replacement is accepted by many therapists. New ideas open the door for eclecticism and multiple therapies. Among the writings here, we will see, for example, a case study in which a psychodynamic therapist and behavior therapist work jointly with a patient.

This book attests to the way therapies have expanded in scope. Not many years ago, the idea that running, yoga, meditation, and so on can be used by therapists would have been questioned. Eclecticism and the use of multiple therapies put new burdens on therapists. Eclectic therapists must be able to handle a wide range of therapies. Therapists who need help with clients must be willing to refer clients to other therapists for procedures they themselves are unable to give. In perhaps all areas, therapists seem to have a new flexibility.

Part One

Depressive Disorders

We decided to cover "depressive disorders" and to omit manic or mixed manic-depressive episodes. Most important, we had to limit the scope of this book because of the voluminous literature on adult therapy. True manic episodes are reported as rare in the literature, and practitioners report having little or no contact with this disorder. Practitioners have vastly more contact with people whose depression plays a major or minor role in their difficulties. The therapy literature concerns "depression" and rarely discusses the treatment of cyclothymic or dysthymic disorders.

1

Depression

Depression is believed to be the only psychopathological condition that affects not only humans but monkeys and dogs as well, affects all age groups from young children to the aged, and accompanies many other psychological conditions, such as hysteria, obsessive-compulsive disorders, personality disorders, and alcoholism. In a survey of first admissions to the psychiatric facilities of a large institution, neurotic depression (a DSM-II diagnosis) was the most common single disorder, covering almost one third of all inpatients and close to 40 percent of all outpatients (Akiskal and others, 1978, in Additional Readings).

A comparison of DSM-III with DSM-II reveals that the general category of depressive neurosis has been replaced by four new categories, all listed under major depression: single episode, without melancholia; recurrent, without melancholia; dysthymic disorder; and adjustment disorder with depressed mood. The diagnostic criteria for major depression are (1) one or more major depressive episodes, clearly described in DSM-III, and (2) no history of a manic episode. Our problem was to choose a diagnostic category from DSM-III that would capture most clearly the problems which most therapists face and for which there is therapy literature. The choice was between major depressive episode and dysthymic disorder (or depressive neurosis). The diagnoses are very similar. We eventually decided on major depressive episode as having a slight edge over dysthymic disorder in representing the diagnosis addressed by the greater part of the therapy literature.

According to DSM-III (pp. 213-214), the following are diagnostic criteria for major depressive episode:

> A. Dysphoric mood or loss of interest or pleasure in all or almost all usual activities and pastimes. The dysphoric mood is characterized by symptoms such as the following: depressed, sad, blue, hopeless, low, down in the dumps, irritable. The mood disturbance must be prominent and relatively persistent, but not necessarily the most dominant symptom, and does not include momentary shifts from one dysphoric mood to another dysphoric mood, e.g., anxiety to depression to anger, such as are seen in states of acute psychotic turmoil. (For children under six, dysphoric mood may have to be inferred from a persistently sad facial expression.)
>
> B. At least four of the following symptoms have each been present nearly every day for a period of at least two weeks (in children under six, at least three of the first four).
>
> > (1) poor appetite or significant weight loss (when not dieting) or increased appetite or significant weight gain (in children under six, consider failure to make expected weight gains)
> > (2) insomnia or hypersomnia
> > (3) psychomotor agitation or retardation (but not merely subjective feelings of restlessness or

being slowed down) (in children under six, hypo-activity).

(4) loss of interest or pleasure in usual activities, decrease in sexual drive not limited to a period when delusional or hallucinating (in children under six, signs of apathy)

(5) loss of energy; fatigue

(6) feelings of worthlessness, self-reproach, or excessive or inappropriate guilt (either may be delusional)

(7) complaints or evidence of diminished ability to think or concentrate, such as slowed thinking, or indecisiveness not associated with marked loosening of associations or incoherence

(8) recurrent thoughts of death, suicidal ideation, wishes to be dead, or suicide attempt

C. Neither of the following dominate the clinical picture when an affective syndrome (i.e., criteria A and B above) is not present, that is, before it developed or after it has remitted:

(1) preoccupation with a mood-incongruent delusion or hallucination

(2) bizarre behavior

D. Not superimposed on either Schizophrenia, Schizophreniform Disorder, or a Paranoid Disorder.

E. Not due to any Organic Mental Disorder or Uncomplicated Bereavement.

According to surveys in both the United States and Europe, as described in DSM-III, major depressive episodes are experienced by 18 to 23 percent of women and 8 to 11 percent of men. Six percent of women and 3 percent of men require hospitalization. Major depression may begin at any age. Its onset may be sudden or develop over a period of weeks, and its course varies greatly from person to person. Some people experience major depression only rarely over many years; some have clusters of episodes; some have more the older they get. In 20 to 35 percent of people with this diagnosis the symptoms are chronic, and there is a great deal of lasting symptomatic and social impairment. Both social and occupational impairment dur-

ing the episode are common; the degree varies from slight to almost total incapacitation in which the person is unable to feed
or dress himself. The disorder may follow chronic physical illness, alcohol dependence, cyclothymic and dysthymic disorders,
and psychosocial stress. Major affective disorders seem to run
in families. The obvious complication in depression is, of
course, suicide.

The symptoms of dysthymic disorder are very similar,
but it is considered a chronic state, often thought of as depressive personality. It is thought to be common, occurring more in
females than in males.

By far the most frequently used treatment is some form
of antidepressant drug. Electroconvulsive treatment is said to
be helpful and is still frequently used. Psychodynamic therapy,
including psychoanalysis, is included here. Running seems to
hold promise. Because of the interpersonal aspects of depression, social skills training has been used with some success.
Inability to attain one's goals has often been associated with depression and may account for considerable emphasis on assertion training. Similarly, low self-image and esteem are associated
with depression, and various techniques have been devised to
raise self-esteem. Therapists have taught self-control; others
have emphasized deriving pleasure from life. Cognitive correction has been used to alter expectations from life. In the case of
grief, flooding has been employed. The reader will find, as is obvious from the above, a wide array of potential treatments.

Beck's Cognitive Therapy

AUTHOR: Aaron T. Beck

PRECIS: Modifying people's belief systems, expectancies, assumptions, and styles of thinking to relieve depression

INTRODUCTION: Cognitive therapy is similar to behavior therapy in some ways but is markedly different from it and also from psychoanalytic therapy. In both cognitive therapy and behavior therapy, therapists are active, focus on symptoms, set limited goals, and coach patients on how to reach their goals. Both therapies avoid patients' unconscious conflicts, childhood experiences, and defense mechanisms. Both cognitive and behavior therapists help patients to unlearn their troublesome symptoms, with or without insight into the origins of the symptoms. These two systems differ mainly in that cognitive therapists focus on patients' faulty belief systems, expectancies, and assumptions, while behavior therapists center their attention on patients' overt behavior. In some instances, however, actual technical differences are hard to distinguish.

METHOD: The cognitive therapist's first task is to motivate and train a patient to focus on his faulty appraisals of situations, appraisals that are automatic, involuntary, rapidly made, specific to the patient, and plausible to him. The therapist leads the patient to see that certain events trigger specific unpleasant emotional responses. He then guides the patient to find the missing link between the situation and the response—a troublesome thought. For example, a depressed person sees an old friend, thinks, "He won't accept me as he used to," and becomes sad.

The therapist coaches patients in various ways. He helps them to develop objectivity by repeatedly reminding them that their thoughts are not necessarily the same as reality. They are taught to see their arbitrary inferences. For example, a depressed person, noting a frown on a passer-by's face, inferred, "He is disgusted with me." Patients learn to recognize their overgeneralizations, as seen in a person who generalizes from a single failure that "I never succeed at anything." They learn to recognize how they magnify (or as Albert Ellis calls it, "catastrophize") the meaning of an event and, conversely, how they ignore certain important aspects of their life experiences, such as how frequently they behave in a self-defeating way.

The therapist coaches patients to objectify their thoughts, label their particular faulty logic, and consider alternative beliefs, expectancies, and assumptions. Depressed people, for example, are apt to see themselves as helpless and hopeless, and these faulty thoughts (often also in the form of fantasies) are the focus of therapy.

What occurs in this therapy is, first, that for various reasons (for example, the therapist's acceptance) patients quiet down. They then rehearse, through talking or imagining, their disturbing thoughts or fantasies in a safe environment where they can gain some perspective on the difference between what actually occurs and imagined dangers. They come to view their lives more realistically and thus alter their emotional reactions— for example, depression. Through rehearsal in the safe therapy situation, patients become desensitized to their troublesome thoughts and resultant feelings.

COMMENTARY: In our experience, Dr. Beck's Cognitive Therapy is most widely identified as a therapy for depression (see below for reference to Beck's book on depression). When we asked Dr. Beck which article best presented his system, he chose this one. In the original article he shows the applicability of the therapy far beyond depression alone—anxiety, phobias, paranoid states, hysteria, compulsions, and psychopathic behaviors. Readers interested in any of these conditions should consult the original article for examples and specific applications.

Note the similarity between this approach and the problem-solving approaches covered elsewhere in the book. The steps are identifying the problem, discovering causality, and finding alternative methods of solution. Beck employs a wide range of techniques from both cognitive and behavior therapy systems, similar to the multiple-approach systems cited throughout the book.

One should not overlook the sticky problem posed whenever beliefs are focused on with clients. Therapists may want to stay aware that whatever beliefs they themselves hold are simply one person's beliefs, and they may want to be cautious about putting them forth as Truth.

SOURCE: Beck, A. T. "Cognitive Therapy: Nature and Relation to Behavior Therapy." *Behavior Therapy,* 1970, *1,* 184-200. (For a detailed description of Beck's therapy for depression, see Beck, A. T., Rush, A. J., Shaw, B., and Emery, G., *Cognitive Therapy for Depression,* New York: Guilford Press, 1979.)

Brief Psychoanalytic Psychotherapy

AUTHOR: Leopold Bellak

PRECIS: Rules for establishing areas and methods of intervention to be used in brief, emergency treatment of depressed people

INTRODUCTION: Depression is not only widespread but a condition of misery and danger. Since the same psychodynamic factors can be seen in most depressed people, interventions based on these factors can be planned systematically. Emergency psychotherapy may be even more effective than drugs, although drugs may be used adjunctively. Therapy may be with the depressed person alone, with the person and spouse, or with the person and family. Whereas long-term psychoanalysis is aimed at a structural change in the patient's views, particularly through the transference relationship, brief therapy is focused not on profound change but on rapid therapeutic response necessitated by the great distress and anger of depression.

TREATMENT: Ten psychodynamic factors exist in depression, the first nine of which must be considered in brief treatment.

The therapist takes a careful history and appraises which of the factors are playing a role in the person's depression and how they rank in importance. The therapist looks for historical antecedents of precipitating events. With the areas of intervention formulated, the therapist then devises methods of intervention.

The ten areas of depression and appropriate interventions are described below.

Problems of Self-Esteem. The therapist evaluates the person's self-esteem, looks for recent threats to esteem, and relates past events to precipitating events in order to interpret and help the person develop insight. The therapist treats the person with respect, points out events in the person's past relating to high self-esteem, and helps the person get his expectations and reality more in line with each other. He examines carefully all aspects of the person's self-aggression. Last, transference problems relating to the person's self-esteem are interpreted.

A Severe Superego. The therapist investigates the relation between past and present in superego problems impinging on self-aggression. An effective method to use with people with a strong superego and considerable aggression is for the therapist to express the aggression and take responsibility for it or put the responsibility on others. The therapist may use such statements as "Certainly if the foreman had done that to me, I would have kicked him" or "Of course, a conscientious person like yourself would not permit himself to think so, let alone do it, but somebody else might certainly feel like killing the son of a bitch." The therapist points out the person's denial and encourages him to express his feelings. If the patient begins to project onto the therapist, the latter points this out and supports his own neutrality.

Intra-aggression. The therapist tries to uncover who the original target for the patient's aggression was, who the current target is, and how the patient may be distorting the current target or even pitting one side of himself against another. Last, the relation between self-esteem and self-aggression is dealt with.

A Feeling of Loss. The depressed person should be helped to work through the relation between losses precipitating the depression and losses early in life. In addition, the therapist should focus on the person's passivity, dependency, and need for love, particularly from the therapist.

Feelings of Disappointment. Again, the therapist should relate precipitating events with early events, in this case disappointments with people the person loved or loves and anger at them, not overlooking these factors in relation to the therapist.

Feelings of Deception. The patient should be helped to gain insight into early deceptions and their effect on deceptions precipitating the depression. In addition, the accompanying suspicion of people and difficulty in establishing relationships, including that with the therapist, should be gone into.

Orality and Stimulus Hunger. The patient should be apprised of his need for stimulation from the outside and the depression that follows if it is not supplied; this includes love, human contact, light, sound, and so on. In addition, the therapist should help work through the person's needs to devour, to be devoured, and to sleep. The therapist should entertain the possibility that the need for stimulation may be physiological.

Narcissism. The person should be helped to see that he is apt to become depressed when there is insufficient feeling of self-esteem, being loved, and the like. The patient is apt to be torn between overactivity/tension and underactivity/depression, and this dilemma should be dealt with in helping the person plan his life. He should be taught to be aware of signals of disappointment and guard against the letdown that follows experiences of high gratification. Again, the possibility of physiological disturbance should not be overlooked.

Denial. It is essential that the therapist aid the person to get through denial of central events, particularly the event precipitating the depression. This can be helped along by searching for previous denials followed by depression. The patient's new perception of continuity in his life where there had been only discontinuity may well break the depression. Then the person must be helped to expose his rage at the person who precipitated his depression; the event may have entailed either disappointment or deception. The person should be urged to ventilate his feelings, and the therapist can help by expressing the aggression and assigning responsibility elsewhere than onto the patient, as described under "A Severe Superego."

Object Relations. In this factor the therapist examines how some or all of the foregoing nine factors come together in the kinds of relationships the person tends to form and how the people involved touch on the patient's dependency, narcissism, self-esteem, and so on. These also strongly touch on the person's view of the therapist. All the possible things that may happen with the therapist should be openly anticipated—the disappointments, separation, anger, and so on. The therapist should make every effort to end the emergency therapy with good feelings on the part of the patient.

These guidelines have been effective with the vast majority of depressed people this author has treated over almost three decades.

COMMENTARY: The detailed analysis and instructions given here may be useful to all therapists who treat depression, including those who use individual psychotherapy solely and those who use it adjunctively to other measures, such as social skills training. However, it will be obvious to the reader that almost all the suggestions involve constant reference to the past and early memories, a position less and less emphasized in current psychotherapy literature (although, of course, discussions of the past may be more prevalent than is seen in current literature).

Another salutary element in this article is its focus on brief and emergency treatment, a position increasingly discussed in current therapy literature.

SOURCE: Bellak, L. "Brief Psychoanalytic Psychotherapy of Nonpsychotic Depression." *American Journal of Psychotherapy,* 1981, *35,* 160-172.

Drug Guide for Nonmedical Therapists

AUTHORS: Kenneth Byrne and Stephen L. Stern

PRECIS: Suggestions for deciding which depressed clients are appropriate to refer for antidepressant medication

INTRODUCTION: Possibly the most frequent complaint brought to outpatient therapists is depression. While psychotherapy alone may be sufficient for some depressed patients, medication may facilitate psychotherapy for others. Clinical psychologists are apt to be insufficiently trained in the nature of antidepressant drugs and the range of people who respond to them. This survey serves as an introduction to the use of antidepressant medication in therapeutic practice.

METHOD: Nonmedical therapists will be aided by information in the following four areas, briefly summarized here.

Evaluation of Depressed Patients. In trying to evaluate which people are likely to profit from antidepressant medication, the therapist should be trained to observe these aspects in patients: symptoms of depression, previous depressions, family background, and present and past medication conditions.

A therapist should first look for biological disturbances in sleep, appetite, sexual behavior, and physical activity. Common sleep problems cover a wide gamut: early morning or night awakening, inability to go back to sleep, difficulty in falling asleep, and sleeping longer than usual. An accompaniment of sleep difficulties is tiredness and low energy during the day. Patients are apt to have increased or decreased appetite and to lose weight or gain it, all uncharacteristically. They may be less interested in sex and derive less from it; men may be impotent, while women may show menstrual irregularities. Behavior may be either slow or agitated.

Psychologically, depressed people may be unable to get interested in or get pleasure from the things they usually do; they may be bored with life and find it meaningless.

Some patients fail initially to complain of depression, and

the therapist must be acutely aware of the symptoms just mentioned plus background information and medical history. Therapists should inquire about previous periods of unusual psychological highs as well as lows. Patients may have been euphoric, uncharacteristically active and talking, sleeping less, showing poor judgment, having an inflated ego, spending impulsively, and engaging in sexual sprees. Conversely, the patient may previously have had periods of depressive symptoms. In getting historical information, therapists should try to see a family member, as patients are apt to forget manic periods during times of depression. The manic periods are important to detect, as they alter the diagnosis from unipolar to bipolar depression.

Details of family history may give ideas about the patient's possible response to medication. Such factors as family history of depression, mania, alcoholism, favorable response to antidepressant medication may all be helpful in deciding on medication for the patient. Current and past medical status should be asked about in order to help the physician decide on type and dosage of medication. Aspects worth pursuing are the presence of heart disorders, chest pains, high blood pressure, and memory difficulties, and the use of medications, recreational drugs, and alcohol. To rule out the possibility that an organic illness is causing the depression, a physical examination is essential.

Selecting Patients Who May Profit from Medication. Those patients who should be referred for possible medication are those who show moderate or severe depression accompanied by the physical symptoms listed above, a family history of depression, a family member's favorable response to antidepressant medication, or previous benefits from drugs. People with atypical depressions, those showing psychological but few physical accompaniments previously listed, and those with depressed feelings tied to actual events often have a good response to medication. If a patient shows mild or moderate depression without physical symptoms, psychotherapy might be tried alone for a few weeks, after which there should be a reevaluation.

Medications for Depression. (These are covered in some detail in digests on single drugs [Stern, Rush, and Mendels,

1980] and drug combinations [Stern and Mendels, 1981] in this section.)

Referring Patients for Medication. A nonmedical therapist should establish a cooperative relationship with a physician knowledgeable in the use of antidepressant medication, with easy access to communication between the two, so that referrals can be made with most benefit and least difficulties for patients. Obviously, in making a referral, a therapist does not recommend drugs, as this decision is professionally in the hands of the person who gives the prescription.

Questions that may make referral difficult sometimes arise in the minds of both therapists and patients concerning drug treatment. Therapists sometimes worry that if patients are relieved of depression by medication, they will not continue with psychotherapy. There are, however, indications that if these conditions cause patients to quit psychotherapy, they were not good candidates in the first place. Conversely, relief of depression through drugs often makes psychotherapy easier. Patients, too, sometimes have problems accepting the idea of drugs. Some people have an aversion to medication, some are afraid that drugs will be habit-forming, and some wish to handle the problems alone, without medication. In any case, these are problems that can be discussed between therapist and patient.

COMMENTARY: While this highly informative guide seems to have been addressed to clinical psychologists, the information brought together here is, of course, appropriate for a wide range of nonmedical therapists and counselors.

SOURCE: Byrne, K., and Stern, S. L. "Antidepressant Medication in the Outpatient Treatment of Depression: Guide for Nonmedical Psychotherapists." *Professional Psychology,* 1981, *12,* 302-308.

Self-Control

AUTHORS: Carilyn Z. Fuchs and Lynn P. Rehm

PRECIS: Self-monitoring, self-evaluation, and self-reinforcement to eliminate depression

INTRODUCTION: Self-control may be seen as continuing to behave in a desired way even though the behavior is not being reinforced. Presumably, then, a person using self-control, as in dieting or studying, would have to believe that some future reward would come if he followed the regimen he had set for himself. Self-control would appear to rest on a circular set of self-operations: self-monitoring (watching what one actually does), self-evaluation (comparing what one has done to what should have been done), and self-reinforcement (rewarding oneself for doing what one set out to do). Depressed people are apt to behave inefficiently in one or more of these three steps. In self-monitoring, they tend either to look at the short-term effects of their behavior rather than the long-term effects or to focus on negative results rather than positive ones. In self-evaluation, they set almost impossible goals for themselves and then judge themselves harshly and in a general way beyond what they have actually done. In self-reinforcement, depressed people mete out low rewards and high punishments to themselves. This pattern of responses adds up to the passivity and dependency seen in depression. Presumably, this pattern might be altered by training depressed people to act differently, or efficiently, in each of the three steps.

TREATMENT: Twenty-eight moderately depressed women between ages eighteen and forty-eight were selected on the basis of meeting certain criteria for depression determined by test scores and interview, having no history of psychiatric hospitalization, no suicide attempts, and no psychotherapy in the previous month. Eight of the women were trained in self-control methods, ten were in nondirective group therapy, and for controls, ten were put on a waiting list. Selection for groups was random. The two therapy groups met for six weekly sessions of approximately two hours' duration. The two women therapists were Ph.D. candidates in clinical psychology who had finished all requirements except the dissertation and showed no bias for behavior therapy.

The women on the *waiting list* were called after initial testing and told that because groups were filled they would have to wait eight weeks but would definitely be seen at that time.

The women in *nondirective group therapy* were introduced to group therapy procedures of a generally nondirective nature; in the ensuing sessions the therapists encouraged group discussion and reflected and clarified feelings in an empathic way. Therapists avoided both teaching behavioral principles and suggesting any kind of therapy work outside the sessions.

The six-week program of *self-control therapy* was divided into three phases—self-monitoring, self-evaluation, and self-reinforcement. Each phase consisted of two sessions: in the first session, the women were taught relevant self-control principles and given homework, and in the second session, they discussed their homework and reviewed what they had learned in the first week.

In the self-monitoring phase, the therapists taught that mood is a function of one's behavior, and they taught skills aimed at greater control in working toward one's own goals. They emphasized the importance of self-monitoring and the tendency to look only for unpleasant events and short-term effects of behavior rather than long-term effects. The women were provided with log forms to record daily positive activities and moods. In the second session, the women reviewed their homework, and the therapists repeated behavioral principles, encouraged them to look for patterns, and instructed them to continue self-monitoring and to look for activities that had great personal meaning but low frequency in their lives.

In the self-evaluation phase, the therapists stressed the importance of setting goals that one could reasonably attain and of accurately evaluating one's own goal-directed behavior. The women identified goals and then subgoals (or behavior expected to lead eventually to the major goals). Their homework was to refine goals and subgoals on the basis of their continued monitoring. In the fourth session they were asked to give point values to their subgoals on the basis of meaningfulness to them and, as homework, were told to evaluate their daily behavior using their own point systems.

In the self-reinforcement phase, the therapists taught principles of reinforcement—the importance of immediate reinforcement as opposed to delayed reinforcement, kinds of reinforcement, and so on. The instructors showed how self-reinforcement or lack of it was relevant to depression. The women selected rewards for themselves and set "prices" on subgoal behaviors. They were given the homework assignment of continuing all they had learned in the three phases. In the last session, the women reviewed the results of self-reinforcement, and the entire program was reviewed.

All three groups were tested in the seventh week, and the two therapy groups were again tested six weeks later to determine the longer-term effects of therapy.

On tests (self-report) of depression and group interaction measures, given in the seventh week, the self-control group clearly improved more than the other two groups. On six-week follow-up of the two therapy groups, the differences between the two groups were somewhat clouded. However, this dissipation of differences resulting from improvement in some of the nondirective-group members can be explained by the fact that a large majority of this group followed up on referrals for further therapy and received it.

COMMENTARY: The authors point out that there is no irrefutable evidence here that decrease in depression can be accounted for by the use of self-control measures. However, the method is provocative in that it can be administered in groups, focuses on self-control rather than outside control, and emphasizes the individual patient's goals. The reader might wish to compare this system with the other self-control methods digested in this section (Tharp, Watson, and Kaya; Zeiss, Lewinsohn, and Muñoz; Lewinsohn, Sullivan, and Grosscup; and Beck). One of the authors of the present article, Dr. Rehm, has compared this system with the therapy systems of Lewinsohn and Beck; see L. P. Rehm, "A Self-Control Model of Depression," *Behavior Therapy,* 1977, *8,* 787-804, in which she attempts to relate the approaches of Beck, Lewinsohn, and the "learned helplessness" concept of depression. The present study reflects an attempt to demonstrate the effectiveness of her scheme for pulling these ideas together.

It might be helpful to see the self-control method here with slightly different emphases from the three headings the authors use. The patients first were taught self-control principles; this is not unlike an opening statement of the self-control rationale stressed in other systems. They were then taught self-control skills aimed at getting what one wants. They were instructed to look for what had great personal meaning; this is similar in other therapies to looking for what gives one pleasure and going after it. Still more refined emphasis was then placed on goal setting. They evaluated daily how well they were reaching their goals, and finally they were taught how to reward themselves for their efforts.

SOURCE: Fuchs, C. Z., and Rehm, L. P. "A Self-Control Therapy Program for Depression." *Journal of Consulting and Clinical Psychology,* 1977, *45,* 206-215.

===============================

Running as Treatment for Depression

AUTHORS: John H. Greist, Marjorie H. Klein, Roger R. Eischens, John Faris, Alan S. Gurman, and William P. Morgan

PRECIS: Running at least three times per week prescribed for relief of depression

INTRODUCTION: There is evidence that regular exercise, jogging in particular, is correlated with a sense of well-being and reduction of depression. One might plausibly ask how it compares with individual psychotherapy in relieving reactive depression. A study was undertaken to answer this question.

TREATMENTS: The population tested (eliminating dropouts) consisted of twenty-two men and women, aged eighteen to thirty, with prominent depression as the target problem. They were tested for signs of depression and absence of psychoses, "significant risk," need for antidepressant medication, and cardiopulmonary distress. They were randomly assigned to ten weeks of running or ten sessions of either time-limited or time-unlimited individual psychotherapy.

   Running as Treatment. The running leader's goal was to ensure that his clients learned the correct approach to running and became independent runners by the end of ten weeks. The leader gradually diminished his sessions held individually with clients: three or four one-hour sessions per week initially, two sessions in the fifth week, one session in the seventh and eighth weeks. Clients were encouraged to run at least three times a week.

   The leader taught clients to run and walk comfortably and to use their breathing rate and conversation during running as guides to a comfortable pace. Pace and distance were increased gradually and steadily. Pain and fatigue were avoided by interspersing walking with running. Discussion focused on running; discussion of depression was not reinforced either during or after the running session. If patients began focusing on depression, the leader suggested concentrating on separate physical elements of running, which broke through the depressive rumination.

   Results were that running was at least as effective in alleviating depressive symptoms and target complaints as either time-limited or time-unlimited psychotherapy.

CASE STUDY: A twenty-eight-year-old professional student with a master's degree, suffering two years of depression, showed a distinct relief of depression after three weeks of running. Improvement continued until the fifth week, when she hurt her ankle; during the three ensuing weeks, in which she was unable to run, her depression returned. On beginning to run again, her depression rapidly disappeared, and on a three-month follow-up her subjective report of remission persisted.

COMMENTARY: The authors point out the serious limitations of psychotherapist inexperience, single running leader, small sample size, limited age range, and so on. They emphasize the importance of expertise in teaching and individually prescribing for effective and harmless running. Their exhaustive list of possible explanations for the effectiveness of running therapy for depression touches on some of the leading ideas of what relieves depression: the perception that people can change themselves for the better (the self-control idea); improved health and appearance increases self-acceptance (the self theorists' idea); competence in one area generalizes to other areas (a learning theory idea); new sensations (or reinforcements) distract people from their depressive thoughts (learning theory); running decreases anger and anxiety as well as depression (touching on the idea of the close connection between anxiety and depression). The reader will recognize these ideas in other digests in the book.

Certainly the idea of a routine physical activity, offering the above accompaniments, as treatment for depression, or perhaps other disorders as well, is provocative. One may surmise that running might be only one of many possible salutary physical therapies for depression. There is a strong possibility that an absorbing, routinized physical activity in various combinations with other therapies digested here might be a powerful antidote to depression.

SOURCE: Greist, J. H., Klein, M. H., Eischens, R. R., Faris, J., Gurman, A. S., and Morgan, W. P. "Running as Treatment for Depression." *Comprehensive Psychiatry,* 1979, *20,* 41-54.

Tailoring Therapy for an Individual's Specific Depression

AUTHORS: Peter M. Lewinsohn, J. Michael Sullivan, and Sally J. Grosscup

PRECIS: Combinations of daily monitoring and cognitive methods, discussion, assertion training, relaxation, daily planning, time management, and so on, to increase an individual's pleasures in life and decrease displeasures

INTRODUCTION: People become depressed when they receive too few rewards and too much punishment in their lives. Depressed people lack the outlook and skills to get enough pleasure and avoid pain. Treatment must be designed to reverse these conditions. This is done by helping people change their perspective and develop skills to gain more pleasure and cut down displeasure. The overall scheme is to change the events that cause a person to be depressed.

The symptoms and problems behind depression vary from person to person, and so the goals and tactics for treatment must fit the individual. A therapist must first have a theory to explain why a particular individual is depressed, then develop specific treatment goals, and finally plan therapeutic methods to reach the goals.

The therapist's tactics must also fit the patient; for example, directive therapy may be poor for people who hate being controlled. Therapist and patient must work together to develop tactics so that both can do their parts in relieving the depression.

METHOD: To see whether a person can benefit from this treatment for depression, the person takes self-report questionnaires to determine whether depression is the major problem. He then completes another questionnaire to pinpoint key pleasant and unpleasant events in his life. From these diagnostic measures, the therapist develops ideas about the causes of the person's depression and some ways to handle them. The therapist's ideas of causes, goals, and tactics are discussed openly with the patient. From the person's lists of pleasant and unpleasant events, patient and therapist develop a daily activity monitoring schedule, which the patient fills out at the end of the day to rate his mood and check pleasant and unpleasant activities for the day. The person begins to see the relation between moods and events. An essential part of the process is that both therapist and patient watch continuously to see whether the treatment is moving toward the goals and adjust the tactics accordingly—a continuous evaluation of treatment.

In this highly structured therapy, the therapist teaches the depressed person ways to achieve more pleasure and avoid displeasure. The various techniques used include relaxation, assertion, daily planning, time management, parenting skills, and altering perception of events, among others (the authors have developed manuals for dealing with pleasant and unpleasant events). More and more aware of what initiates his depression, the person learns to diagnose it himself and take appropriate action.

The ability of depressed people to carry through with the structured assignments is seldom a problem, partly because the therapist initially spells out the rationale for treatment and the two people work together at all times. Time is always allowed for the patient to discuss important problems of any nature. The therapist sets up various kinds of contracts with patients, one of which allows the patient to earn back as much as 40 percent of treatment fees by sticking to various aspects of the treatment plan. The last sessions are spaced to wean the person from therapy.

Three groups of patients, totaling forty-seven people, showed marked improvement with this therapy. This treatment is for unipolar, nonpsychotic depression, not for bipolar and/or psychotic people.

CASE STUDY: Alice, a thirty-seven-year-old secretary living alone with her nine-year-old daughter and fourteen-year-old son, showed moderate to severe depression on testing. She showed high potential for pleasure in being with people but low actual pleasurable social activities. She reported displeasure with material-financial, parenting, and domestic problems. The therapist offered suggestions for how to cut down the displeasure in each of these areas, both by change of attitude and by concrete actions. Alice also learned to reward herself when appropriate, and gradually negative reactions subsided.

Therapy then shifted to her gaining more pleasure from life, and Alice's previous report led the therapist to focus on social activities. The therapist suggested changes in attitudes, helped Alice become more assertive, and urged her to engage in more social activities.

Unpleasant events stayed low, and pleasant events doubled in frequency; problems in the material-financial and parenting areas decreased, while pleasure in social activities increased. Her monitoring revealed marked improvement in mood, and tests revealed no to minimal depression. At the end of treatment she acknowledged its value and stated that she had developed skills for handling depression.

COMMENTARY: The elements of this system, as well as the underlying rationale, are very useful. The basic idea that the therapist and patient are working together, are frank, and are evaluating and constantly revising the therapy together is seldom so clearly stated in therapy literature. The patient is asked to look for what gives him pleasure in life and is taught skills to get the pleasures he wants (the therapist is prepared to teach a wide range of skills) and to evaluate how successful he is at it. The treatment can constantly be revised if the patient's goals are not being reached. A unique twist is the therapist's offering a cut in fees as an incentive for the patient's following through on treatment plans.

This well-conceived and practical therapy can hardly be faulted in its flexibility and consideration for the patient. The breadth of knowledge of tactics required of the therapist would seem to be formidable. The therapist, for example, should be an expert in teaching parenting skills, relaxation, and assertion, among others. The scoring of diagnostic tests and the statistical procedures used to work with the daily monitoring apparently can be something of a problem but not insurmountable. The therapist's belief in the rationale of the system is pointed out as being crucial to his being able to present it to patients, and this in turn is crucial to the outcome of therapy.

This therapy could conceivably lead the way to a new avenue for psychotherapy—away from systems thought to handle all problems and toward systems flexible and broad enough to tailor tactics to the unique problems of individuals.

Therapists following this system would, it seems, have to be open to the uniqueness of individuals, free in planning with rather than for patients, highly knowledgeable about a host of skills, and expert in teaching skills. This is not a therapy for one to try on for size without considerable thought about basic therapeutic issues (for example, how much to share responsibility with patients) and considerable training.

SOURCE: Lewinsohn, P. M., Sullivan, J. M., and Grosscup, S. J. "Changing Reinforcing Events: An Approach to the Treatment of Depression." *Psychotherapy: Theory, Research, and Practice,* 1980, *17,* 322-334.

Contingency Management

AUTHORS: Robert Paul Liberman and David E. Raskin

PRECIS: Reinforcing adaptive behavior and ignoring depressive behavior demonstrated to increase adaptive behavior and decrease depressive behavior

INTRODUCTION: Depressive behavior can originate under various general conditions of altered reinforcement or loss of reinforcement: having to do too much to get rewarded, getting no reward at all for effort, punishment, or a sudden change in the environment. These sometimes occur all at the same time, as with concentration camp inmates subjected to very little of a positive nature, punishment, and environmental dislocation. These add up to a drop in the amount of reinforcement for adaptive behavior.

In a review of widely diverse theories of depression, there appears to be agreement on two basic ideas: (1) depressive behavior begins when satisfactions from the environment are dramatically lessened, and (2) once begun, the depressive behavior is maintained and even strengthened by people who come into contact with the depressed person. In broader terms, "sick" behavior of many kinds is apt to get attention from others, and so long as it does get attention, the behavior continues. For example, the loss of a loved one may deprive a person of satisfactions of a wide variety, and the person's response may be one or more of a wide variety of depressive behaviors, including withdrawal, sleeplessness, and others. To the extent that depressive behaviors are reinforced by attention, sympathy, and so on, and more adaptive behaviors receive little or no reinforcement, the depressive behavior is strengthened. Similarly, those who are unable to get the attention they desire from those who are significant to them may hit on suicide attempts to get social reinforcement; and so long as the reinforcement is forthcoming, the suicide attempts continue. Family members, and even therapists such as physicians, can inadvertently reinforce the very behavior they would prefer to eradicate. For example, a "thorough" examination by a physician may reinforce the person's idea of illness.

TREATMENT: A solution to this dilemma is active intervention by a therapist or family member, or both, to extinguish the depressive behavior by lack of reinforcement and by reinforcement of behaviors incompatible with depression.

Three case histories illustrate these principles.

Case Study 1. A forty-two-year-old woman became depressed after her children grew up and left home. Because of lack of interest and loss of confidence, she had given up painting, a previous major interest. Her therapist thought her depression might decrease if reinforcement could come from her getting back to painting. After a month of supportive therapy, he planned a visit to her home to see her paintings and talk to her while she painted. Before he even arrived, however, she had begun to paint again. After a few weeks, her depression gradually lessened.

Case Study 2. A fifty-six-year-old factory foreman became depressed while his wife was undergoing a series of operations. With his therapist he endlessly complained of illnesses and his worthlessness. By the third session, the therapist stopped responding to his complaints and instead repeatedly asked about the efforts he was making to cope with his work and keeping his home without his wife. Therapist and client agreed on ten sessions of therapy. As the therapist continued to demonstrate his interest in the client's coping, the client's depression diminished.

Case Study 3. The therapist made a home visit to a thirty-seven-year-old woman who had become depressed by the death of her mother. He observed that her depressive behavior was reinforced by her husband and children with sympathy, concern, and helpfulness. At the same time, her efforts as homemaker were low. In family sessions, the therapist told her husband and children to pay instant and frequent attention to her carrying out her responsibilities and gradually ignore her depressive behavior. The therapist explained that they were not to lower the amount of attention but simply to switch the targets (or contingencies). Within a week, her homemaker behavior increased and her depressive behavior decreased. As an experiment, after the fourteenth day the therapist instructed the husband and children to return to their former reinforcements, and within three days she had returned to her depressive behavior, although at a lower level. The therapist then asked the family to return to reinforcing her homemaker behavior and ignoring depressive behavior, and she quickly improved. On one-year follow-up she was without depressive symptoms and doing well.

COMMENTARY: This rich article gives a moderately extensive history of aspects of behavior theory, particularly reinforcement and contingencies, in relation to depression. The reader particularly interested in theory (as opposed to therapy, the focus of this book) may well want to read the original article, especially for the authors' attempts to show relations between such disparate theories as those of B. F. Skinner and Sigmund Freud.

The reader will readily recognize the ease with which one can criticize the emphasis on the passivity of human beings and the manipulativeness of the environment, a persistent criticism of early behavior theory and therapy. A great deal has happened to behavior therapy since 1971, when this seminal article on contingency management appeared, notably the expansion of behavior therapy methods and the joining of behavior therapy and cognitive therapy, as will be seen in other digests in this section.

Nevertheless, the principles demonstrated are worth keeping in mind, both for the therapist and for the depressed person's family. Therapists might be particularly sensitive to whether they actually reinforce depressive behavior in patients. The reader will see that poor handling of this particular method might be disastrous—if, for example, by ignoring the patient's depressive behavior, the therapist gives the impression of lack of interest in the patient.

SOURCE: Liberman, R. P., and Raskin, D. E. "Depression: A Behavioral Formulation." *Archives of General Psychiatry*, 1971, *24*, 515-523.

Grief-Resolution Therapy

AUTHORS: Frederick T. Melges and David R. DeMaso

PRECIS: Guided imagery for reliving, revising, and revisiting scenes of the loss of a loved one

INTRODUCTION: During ordinary grief at the loss of a close relative or friend, the symptoms usually mirror those of depression. Grief can last as long as two to four years, and during this time a person is highly susceptible to physical and mental deterioration. People often report auditory or visual hallucinations, which in some cases go on for years. Therapists should be aware that people showing classical depressive symptoms may be suffering a grief reaction of years' standing.

Although it is difficult to distinguish clearly between normal and abnormal grieving, the latter is the result of too little grieving right after the loss, too much grieving too long after the loss, or both. In unresolved grief reactions, people want to go back to and redo the past, thus rendering the present and future hopeless. This disturbing reaction can result from one or more of the following obstacles to normal grieving: (1) continuous yearning for the dead person, (2) physical or personality changes that mirror the dead person, (3) the inability to cry or express rage at the loss despite wanting to, (4) anger at the dead person transferred to oneself or others, (5) the awakening of pain at previous losses, (6) unrevealed contracts with the dead person, (7) secrets never told to the dead person and other unfinished business, (8) inadequate current support from others, and (9) holding onto grief because it is rewarding, especially if it helps a person to avoid responsibilities and get taken care of. The therapist's goal is to remove one or more of these roadblocks to grieving.

TREATMENT: In the gaining of rapport, the therapist states how hard it is to let go of a loved one who has died. He gets the patient to relate some positive aspects in the relationship with the deceased, which may give the patient hope that he can find his own identity again.

When the person seems ready, the therapist might ask, "Do you think you can find the courage to grieve and let him go so that you can redirect yourself toward the present and the future?" Before going on, the therapist explains the procedure of guided imagery: the patient will relive events before and after the death, seeing them with his eyes closed and speaking about them in the present tense. A progression of scenes, from shortly before the death to saying "Goodbye" and leaving the grave with feelings of beginning again, is gone over, each for twenty minutes per session. The reliving is followed each time by the patient's revising the scene with the obstacles to grieving removed; revisions might entail, for example, a scene in which the mourner receives forgiveness for some action. The therapist sometimes adds revisions. Next, a revisiting of the scene occurs, with the patient allowing himself to express feelings and conflicts previously hidden; a scene might involve the patient's anger or love, for example. Of crucial importance is the patient's expressing everything in the present tense.

After hearing this explanation of guided imagery, the patient must decide that he wants to proceed; if he does, the guided imagining begins. As the therapy proceeds, the therapist moves the person further and further toward the final "goodbye" to the deceased.

The next phase involves a review of what the person has learned in the therapy and a decision about continuing to talk for more growth. Future-oriented psychotherapy can be used to crystallize choices and the patient's developing his own self.

Whenever possible, the therapist should see the patient's family to prepare them for behavior changes in the patient.

Grief-resolution therapy ordinarily requires six to ten half-hour or hour sessions within the context of other forms of therapy—cognitive, milieu, and/or family therapy. Antidepressant drugs may also be used to mobilize severely depressed people.

The method is contraindicated for manic or schizophrenic people and for those grieving less than one year after a death. It has been tried with well over 100 people, and good—often dramatic—results were obtained, usually after six to ten sessions.

COMMENTARY: While there are methods similar to some of those employed here, such as flooding and V. D. Volkan's Re-Grief Therapy [in B. Schoenberg and others (Eds.), *Bereavement: Its Psychological Aspects,* New York: Columbia University Press, 1975], the current system is perhaps unique in the patient's being required to use the present tense in reliving, revising, and revisiting the circumstances surrounding the death of a loved one. The reader should note that the authors consider it a procedure to be used along with other therapies.

SOURCE: Melges, F. T., and DeMaso, D. R. "Grief-Resolution Therapy: Reliving, Revising, and Revisiting." *American Journal of Psychotherapy*, 1980, *34*, 51-61. See also Melges, F. T. *Time and the Inner Future: A Temporal Approach to Psychiatric Disorders.* New York: Wiley, in press.

Short-Term Interpersonal Psychotherapy

AUTHORS: Carlos Neu, Brigitte A. Prusoff, and Gerald L. Klerman

PRECIS: Focusing on the present social aspects of patients' lives found effective for thirty-two patients, mostly women, in the acute phase of depression

INTRODUCTION: A wide variety of therapies exist for depression, among which is a short-term system focusing on current social, interpersonal problems and deemphasizing unconscious conflicts and early history. This therapy, of course, may not be useful if a patient's depression began with other than interpersonal problems. It is important to constantly keep tabs on how the therapy is going, and this can be done through the two people involved. It can be done fairly systematically by (1) keeping track of the patient's input and (2) tabulating the therapist's use of a carefully categorized set of techniques. With the use of these two kinds of tabulations, a study of this therapy was undertaken to answer the following questions: What exactly is altered in the patient with this therapy? What techniques appear to be used most frequently by therapists? What kind of patient input is most common? Is severity of depression a predictive guide for the kind of input patients will give?

METHOD: Thirty-two outpatients, thirty of them women aged twenty to sixty-five, in the acute phase of moderately severe depression of about thirty-five weeks' duration, on the average, were treated. Eighteen of the thirty-two were using amitryptyline with an average dose of 125.5 mg/day, some prescribed while the study was going on. The patients were nonpsychotic, and none had seen therapists for at least two weeks prior to this study. The thirty-two people were divided into four groups: psychotherapy alone, amitryptyline alone, a combination of the drug and psychotherapy, and a control group who could get treatment when they asked for it. Therapy patients were seen for a minimum of eight sessions and an average of fourteen sessions, once a week for fifty minutes.

Therapist interventions were of three main varieties, described below.

Descriptive techniques comprised various methods ordinarily used at the beginning of therapy. Nonjudgmental exploration is crucial at the beginning and includes simply listening, encouraging the patient to continue with a topic, and supportively acknowledging what the patient says. Elicitation of material, a more active procedure used throughout therapy, consists of exploring with the use of questions or urging the patient to go further. Clarification is a kind of restructuring for the patient in which the therapist rephrases what the patient has said or asks her to rephrase, points out inconsistencies between what the patient said or did and what she apparently meant or felt, and explores with the patient her possible beliefs or themes not actually stated but inferred from ethnic and job status.

Reflective techniques encourage reflection and are designed to bring about change in the client. Direct advice gives methods of handling life situations and is particularly useful with impulsive people. Often simply exploring alternatives is enough. Following these comes decision analysis, particularly appropriate when a person is actually facing a choice. The therapist leads the person herself to consider and compare possible long-term and short-term effects of her actions.

Development of awareness is intended to increase the patient's understanding of herself and can be aided by one of the clarification techniques described above.

The therapist's own emotional response, if given with full consciousness, can aid the patient in being more productive through the therapist's support.

Patients' responses are of two kinds: *descriptive,* which includes explanation with little recognition of behavior, and *reflective,* which reveals awareness of the patient's own or other people's behavior and readiness to change.

To analyze what went on in the therapy done in this study, the therapist recorded both therapist and patient inputs during each session. The overall finding was that this form of psychotherapy effectively lowered patients' depression and improved their social functioning. Therapists mostly used the three *descriptive* techniques described above—nonjudgmental exploration, elicitation of material, and clarification. The therapists seemed unaffected by whether patients were taking drugs, nor did they change how much they used the techniques during the whole treatment. Patients used mostly descriptive input—describing daily events and current problems. The fact that this variety of input seemed to have therapeutic value may mean that reflective input may not be necessary for a positive outcome. However, this finding was true more for patients who had been more severely ill for a longer-time, while those who were less depressed for a shorter time did reflect more.

COMMENTARY: The short-term beneficial effects of this economical therapy were demonstrated by this study, but the authors make no claim for durability or great impact on the enduring makeup of patients. One suspects that many therapists are currently using a kind of talking cure, and this delineation of and sensitizing to exactly what the therapist does may be helpful for therapists using these techniques. A refreshing finding is that relief of depression may not necessarily require either reflective techniques or reflective patient input. It would appear also that the therapist's use of the third category of techniques, the therapist's sharing of his emotional responses, may not be necessary either. Given these considerations, it would appear that the authors are demonstrating the efficacy of descriptive sharing, not necessarily the usefulness of the entire system.

It is difficult to avoid our repeated comment that a discrete system might be enriched by compatible techniques from other systems, especially in this instance. One wonders here what might have been accomplished in an even shorter time and perhaps with more durability if this method had been supplemented by other measures, especially social skills training and assertiveness training in light of the emphasis on current, social, interpersonal problems. The authors point out that their method perhaps is applicable only to depressions with interpersonal antecedents, and so our suggestion might be especially cogent. In addition, it is easy to imagine further supplementation with self-monitoring, flooding, and other behavioral techniques.

SOURCE: Neu, C., Prusoff, B. A., and Klerman, G. L. "Measuring the Interventions Used in the Short-Term Interpersonal Psychotherapy of Depression." *American Journal of Psychiatry,* 1978, *48,* 629-634.

Cognitive Therapy Geared to Patients' Value Systems

AUTHOR: L. Rebecca Propst

PRECIS: Using religious imagery to treat religious college students for depression

INTRODUCTION: People's emotional responses are determined by the structure they impose on their experience. Thus, how a person interprets his experience may produce not only pleasant feelings but intensely unpleasant feelings as well, such as depression. Cognitive therapy was designed to aid people in altering the structure they impose on their experience and consequently alter their feelings.

One way to get at the way people structure their experience is through their imagery, which is related to their assumptions about the world. Depressed people have been found to have both negative, masochistic imagery and negative fantasies in general. If this is true, then modification of imagery might have an effect on depression.

Highly religious individuals have been found to quit therapy or not benefit from it if their therapists do not share their religious orientation or do not encourage it or use it in therapy. If a therapist employed imagery content familiar to a client, this might not only improve the client's trust in the therapist but facilitate imagery modifications as well.

METHOD: From a college introductory psychology class, students were selected who scored in the mild to moderate range of depression on a self-report measure of depression, scored at least moderately high in religiosity on a religiosity scale, and showed the lowest mood scores on recording moods five times daily for two weeks prior to the final selection of subjects. They also had to indicate a real interest in the program, described as training to control "feelings of dysphoria or down feelings."

The students were assigned as follows: ten to training employing nonreligious imagery, seven to training involving religious imagery, thirteen to self-monitoring plus therapist contact, and eleven to self-monitoring only. Therapy was given in groups that met twice weekly for eight one-hour sessions. Treatment was as follows:

Nonreligious Imagery. Therapists told clients to relive depressing situations and describe the accompanying images. The therapists used these examples to illustrate the point that emotion is affected by thoughts and images; they also wanted subjects to become aware of the images that initiated depression. To make subjects even more self-aware, therapists assigned homework of recording moods and accompanying images five times a day.

When subjects appeared to absorb what had been taught, the therapists asked them to select personally meaningful depression-reducing statements and images from each of three components—negative self, negative environment, and negative future (these are given in A. T. Beck, *Cognitive Therapy and the*

Emotional Disorders, New York: International Universities Press, 1976). Therapists instructed subjects to relive their depressive images and to modify them with the use of the coping images and statements, for example, "I see myself in the future coping with that particular situation."

Religious Imagery. The same procedure as above was used, except that therapists specified religious imagery. Beck's list of coping statements and images was given to the subjects, but with religious content. An example of a coping image is "I can visualize Christ going with me into that difficult situation in the future as I try to cope."

Self-Monitoring plus Therapist Contact. Subjects did the mood-recording homework as described above and also recorded items for group discussion. All met in a discussion group, the topics of which were determined by the participants. The therapist said as little as possible.

Self-Monitoring Only. People in this group were given the mood-recording assignment as described above. They were told that they were in a control group that was a very important part of the project.

Participants in all groups were reassessed within the week following the end of treatment and again six weeks later. In these two evaluations, all participants completed a questionnaire battery. They were then assigned randomly to discussion groups, and observers recorded individual participants' behaviors.

Participants in the religious imagery group showed greater reduction of depression on both self-report and behavioral measures than people in the nonreligious or self-monitoring-only group. The self-monitoring plus therapist contact group showed intermediate effects but only on the self-report measures. The findings suggest that therapists' techniques are most effective when the therapists make as much use as possible of their clients' own belief systems.

COMMENTARY: This article may be particularly useful to those who do therapy or counseling with people having a dominant ideological focus in life—for example, religion, such as Catholicism; politics, such as socialism; social orientation, such as mother. The underlying point here may be generalized, of course, to any kind of therapy largely dependent on the client's perception, which most therapies are. The article pinpoints the value of a therapist's making abundantly clear his respect for the client's value system.

SOURCE: Propst, L. R. "The Comparative Efficacy of Religious and Nonreligious Imagery for the Treatment of Mild Depression in Religious Individuals." *Cognitive Therapy and Research,* 1980, *4,* 167-178.

Assertion Training Versus Group Psychotherapy

AUTHORS: Victor C. Sanchez, Peter M. Lewinsohn, and Douglas W. Larson

PRECIS: Group assertion training shown to be more effective than traditional group therapy with depressed adults who are also unassertive

INTRODUCTION: In general, depressed people have been found to be more submissive, to feel less comfortable in interpersonal relations, and to interact less with other people than the nondepressed. It would follow, therefore, that depressed people who are low in assertiveness might particularly profit from assertion training.

METHOD: People seeking treatment in an outpatient psychiatric clinic were accepted for a study of group therapy methods on the basis of interviews and tests that clearly revealed that they were both depressed and low in assertiveness. Men and women in the sample were randomly assigned to one or the other of two treatments: eleven people completed the prescribed group assertion training and eleven completed a course of "traditional" group psychotherapy. All groups met for one and a half hours twice weekly for five weeks.

Assertion Training Group. Two groups were established and the therapist followed a detailed training manual (not specified as being available). Therapists began each session by presenting didactic material on some aspect of assertive behavior. This was followed by patients' reports of progress and then a practice period in which therapists modeled behavior and coached members of the group, and clients rehearsed assertive behavior. The major emphasis was on individual members' specific problem situations. Clients were given verbal rewards and "token feedback" for their performances. At the end of each session, therapists handed out cards to each member, specifying homework involving rehearsal of modeled behavior or use of didactic material. Although medication was available to clients, the assertion therapists spoke against it except as a second choice. No clients used medication. The two therapists were advanced Ph.D. students in clinical psychology who were oriented toward behavior therapy.

Traditional Group Psychotherapy. The therapists established the goal of helping group members to change through insight into their problems with little or no advice or training from the therapists. Therapists followed procedures given in a manual in which traditional psychotherapy was distinguished from behavior therapy. These therapists made no objection to clients' use of available medications, and the majority used them (including tranquilizers, hypnotics, antidepressants). The two therapists were advanced Ph.D. candidates in clinical psychology who espoused insight therapy.

Testing of clients was done before treatment, after treatment, and on follow-up one month later with self-report measures of depression and assertiveness. At the end of treatment, the assertion groups had improved more on all measures than the psychotherapy groups, although differences were not highly significant. However, on follow-up, significant differences appeared: the assertion groups continued to improve, while the psychotherapy groups did not. The assertion group members reported less depression, more comfort with assertiveness, and more assertive behaviors than the psychotherapy group members. Since antidepressant medication is reported to relieve depression, the differences in use of medications between the two groups makes the results of this study even more impressive.

COMMENTARY: The results of this fifteen-hour treatment are impressive, especially in that it was done in groups. In addition, only one form of therapy was used, and this means that the skills required of the therapist are more feasible than those required in systems in which therapists are expected to be able to teach numerous skills (see, for example, Lewinsohn, Sullivan, and Grosscup, 1980, digested in this section). A detail is noteworthy here: clients had to report their progress in front of the group. This would reasonably be expected to inspire them to do their homework seriously.

The reader will note that this is a study of depressed people specially chosen for the secondary quality of nonassertiveness. The study suggests some refinements that might be made in choosing therapies for specific depressed individuals. Since assertion training alone was shown to be effective with depressed, nonassertive people, it stands to reason that social skills training might be effective with depressed, nonsocial or socially awkward people. Further distinctions might be worthwhile—between people with low assertion skills and low assertiveness and between people with low social skills and low social contact. Skills training might be found to be more effective with those lacking the skills, whereas some other form of therapy, such as group psychotherapy, might be more effective with people who have the skills but do not use them.

The authors conclude that, in light of the heralded efficacy of antidepressant drugs, the result showing that clients using no drugs improved more than those who took drugs is especially noteworthy. However, their drug group took not only antidepressants but tranquilizers, hypnotics, and presumably other unspecified drugs. We cannot conclude, therefore, that this study in any way deflates the current enthusiasm for careful prescriptions of specific single or combinations of antidepressant drugs. In addition, the reader should not overlook the fact that the assertion leaders spoke against the use of drugs, therefore perhaps communicating their belief in their clients' ability to recover on their own.

SOURCE: Sanchez, V. C., Lewinsohn, P. M., and Larson, D. W. "Assertion Training: Effectiveness in the Treatment of Depression." *Journal of Clinical Psychology,* 1980, *36,* 526-529.

Antidepressant Drug Combinations

AUTHORS: Stephen L. Stern and J. Mendels

PRECIS: Combining drugs for people who do not respond to single drugs

INTRODUCTION: Although antidepressant drugs have been shown to be highly effective for the treatment of depression, some patients do not respond. An alternative lies in trying combinations of drugs. In general, studies showing successful results with drug combinations have not shown either more or worse side effects than when single drugs are used. However, the studies have usually been done with only small numbers of inpatients and often have not been adequately controlled. Therefore, these therapies should be viewed with caution.

TREATMENTS: The following combinations have been tried.
    Tricyclic Antidepressants with Monoamine Oxidase Inhibitors (MAOIs). Even though almost all tricyclics and MAOIs have been used together safely, the combination has been known to produce serious negative results, even death. The safest combination appears to be amitriptyline with either phenel-

zine or isocarboxide. Most therapists who have used it successfully suggest its use with people who fail to respond to other
treatments. The two should be started at the same time, or the
MAOI a few days after the tricyclics, in which case lower dosages
should be used.

In one study, ten of twelve patients showing atypical
endogenous depression (accompanying anxiety, fear of being
left alone, and bodily complaints) and not responding to either
of the two kinds of drugs individually, or showing rapid relapse
after electroconvulsive therapy, responded well to a daily dosage of amitriptyline 75 mg and phenelzine 45 mg. However,
seventeen patients unresponsive to single drugs responded much
better to electroconvulsive therapy than to amitriptyline 71 mg
plus phenelzine.

Tricyclics with Triiodothyronine. Supporting reports that
small doses of L-triiodothyronine (T_3) quicken depressed wom-
en's response to tricyclics, a group of forty-nine women suffering unipolar or bipolar depression but not responsive to two
weeks of daily doses of amitriptyline 72-200 mg were put on
one of two other kinds of treatment. Twenty-three of thirty-
three women responded extremely well to the same dosage of
amitriptyline along with daily T_3 20-40ug. In contrast, only
four of sixteen women treated only with daily amitriptyline increased to 300-350 mg improved markedly. In another study,
men responded to this combination of drugs better than wom-
en, but limitations in the study do not lead to any safe conclusions. In general, this combination is not yet well established.

Tricyclics with Methylphenidate. Methylphenidate seems
to be useful for refractory depression in at least three important
ways: it appears to increase the effectiveness of tricyclics by increasing plasma levels; it elevates mood; and it seems to cut the
lag before people on tricyclics begin to feel better. Dosages
cited are methylphenidate 20 mg daily combined with imipramine 150-225 mg daily. Methylphenidate should probably not
be used with tricyclics, which decrease therapeutic benefit when
plasma concentrations go over a certain level.

Tricyclics with Lithium. Although it is reported that lithium increases the effectiveness of tricyclics, results are inconclu-

sive. However, for bipolar depression, the combination or lithium alone is recommended over a tricyclic alone, which may bring on a manic episode.

Tricyclics with L-Tryptophan. Although this combination has been tried, current evidence is that L-tryptophan does not increase the effectiveness of imipramine, amitriptyline, or perhaps most other tricyclics, with the possible exception of chlorimipramine.

Tricyclics with Reserpine. This combination appears to hold considerable promise. With one or two intramuscular or intravenous injections of reserpine, range 2.5-10 mg, a good proportion of patients resistant to various tricyclics used alone showed improvement.

Tricyclics with Neuroleptics. A neuroleptic, usually perphenazine, has been tried in combination with tricyclics for depressed patients also suffering delusions, a group reported to respond poorly to tricyclics, and the outcome was successful. Because these trials were uncontrolled, the reader should be cautious in employing this combination.

MAOIs with L-Tryptophan or DL-Tryptophan. This combination has shown some impressive results with endogenous depression. It is likely, however, that only those people who develop a suboptimal degree of enzyme inhibition will find the addition of L-tryptophan beneficial, while no further benefits will come from this addiction in people with atypical depression (showing anxiety, phobic, and hypochondriacal symptoms) who respond well to MAOIs alone. The possibility of side effects (drowsiness, nausea, and others) must be entertained.

L-Tryptophan with Allopurinol. The good results obtained with this combination in a study of eight male outpatients with endogenous depression must be looked at cautiously owing to the small sample, no controls, and side effects.

In summary, drug combinations should probably be reserved for people who do not respond to single drugs. What we still need to know is (1) whether people respond to the combination or whether some people respond to one drug while others respond to the second drug and (2) for which kinds of clinical and/or biochemical aspects of depressed people these combinations of drugs are most effective.

COMMENTARY: The point in this clear summary of drug combinations is, as the authors point out, that if patients do not respond to single drugs, certain combinations seem promising. The authors remind readers, however, that the single most effective treatment for severe endogenous depression is electroconvulsive therapy and that there are numerous provocative psychotherapies, as is evidenced in this section.

It is worth repeating here that combinations not only of drugs but of various available therapies might always be considered, particularly for people who do not respond to one form of drug or one form of any kind of therapy.

The reader should also note the authors' statement that many of the combinations cited here were tried with inpatients, so that their use with outpatients may not be warranted until further research is done with outpatients.

SOURCE: Stern, S. L., and Mendels, J. "Drug Combinations in the Treatment of Refractory Depression: A Review." *Journal of Clinical Psychiatry*, 1981, *42*, 368-373.

Antidepressant Drugs

AUTHORS: Stephen L. Stern, A. John Rush, and Joseph Mendels

PRECIS: Aids in making choices of drugs and dosages for specific depressive conditions

INTRODUCTION: Despite the years that drugs have been used for depression, prescribing for individuals is still highly personal and sometimes arbitrary. A study of the literature on the three major groups of antidepressant drugs—tricyclic antidepressants, monoamine oxidase inhibitors (MAOIs), and lithium carbonate —helps to provide a more rational pharmacotherapy. Following are brief instructions for the specialized use of each of the three groups.

TRICYCLIC ANTIDEPRESSANTS: If a patient (or even a relative of the patient) has responded to these drugs, a good chance exists for the next favorable response, but this is apt to decrease with each episode. Good response is predicted for people with the symptoms of unipolar endogenous depression and traits of extreme orderliness, conscientiousness, and dependency; but there is a lack of agreement on what other traits bode well. Whether the onset should be precipitous or not is still open to question. Response of people with neurotic depression, for example, has been varied. Urinary MHPG (3-methoxy-4-hydroxyphenylglycal) level has not yet been found unequivocally to be a sign of good response. Therapists should measure CSF 5-HIAA (cerebrospinal fluid 5-hydroxyindoleactic acid) concentration as an indicator of which specific tricyclic to prescribe. In addition, a diagnostic measure of amphetamine response, activity of COMT (catechol-O-methyltransferase), and sleep EEG may suggest what response specific tricyclic drugs will initiate.

Determination of which tricyclic drug to use and in what dosage will probably be greatly aided by determination of plasma levels, although current evidence is complex. The therapist should use a predictive test so as to get a patient's dosage up to optimal level, at the same time cutting down risks of side effects or overshooting the mark. Only a careful study of the intricacies of research in this area (summarized by the authors) will suffice to give the therapist some feeling of assurance in knowing which tricyclic to use and how much.

MAO INHIBITORS: Complete agreement does not exist on whether the patient's (or a relative's) previous response to these drugs augurs well for a good current response. People with atypical depressions, particularly those with chronic fluctuating depressed mood, seem to respond well, while those with uni-polar endogenous depression are predicted generally not to be helped.

Studies to help in prescribing dosages are absent except in the case of the MAOI phenelzine. For this drug, it looks as if testing for acetylator status might be a predictor, but this is not firmly established. Response to phenelzine appears to be direct-ly related to the degree of platelet MAO inhibited. Research suggests that therapists who have no way of knowing the inhibi-tion of platelet MAO may get a better response to phenelzine by prescribing 60 mg per day and, if necessary, gradually in-crease the dosage.

LITHIUM: Conflicting reports exist on predictors for success of lithium from family history. Current evidence on personality factors suggests the following: good response in people with normal premorbid personality; poor response in bipolar de-pressed people with higher scores on interpersonal sensitivity, paranoid ideation, and psychoticism on a self-report checklist; prediction of success from certain subscales of the MMPI for women and other subscales for men; poor response for people with low depression and psychasthenia scores on the MMPI. Rapid and frequent alternations of mania and depression appear to predict poor response to lithium prophylaxis and perhaps to lithium as a curative. Evidence exists that lithium is effective with bipolar patients, and perhaps with unipolar, who have a manic family history or some manic traits themselves.

Efforts to determine biological characteristics predicting lithium response have so far not been successful, though numer-ous studies have been done. However, prophylactic benefit has been shown to exist in both unipolar and bipolar patients with a given serum lithium level. A test exists that may aid the ther-apist to raise a depressed person's serum level more quickly and safely into the therapeutic range, and this may hasten the be-ginning of relief from depression.

COMMENTARY: The reader should be especially aware here that what has been presented is a digest, much shortened, of an original article of considerable length and detail. It seems certain, however, that the authors would not suggest using even their summary as anything more than an overview. The reader should consult our additional readings for more complete coverage of this complex subject. The authors, however, have presented what appears to be an excellent overview that may serve as an introduction to the topic for those unfamiliar with the literature. Their emphasis on selecting specific drugs for specific patients is particularly laudable.

SOURCE: Stern, S. L., Rush, A. J., and Mendels, J. "Toward a Rational Pharmacotherapy of Depression." *American Journal of Psychiatry*, 1980, *137*, 545-552.

Self-Made Therapy

AUTHORS: Roland G. Tharp, David Watson, and Janice Kaya

PRECIS: Four women college students devise therapy programs for themselves

INTRODUCTION: In devising self-change methods, therapists have suggested that such private feelings as depression might be altered by self-observation and self-control. Four college students, who had done projects on self-change methods for behaviors less complicated than depression, decided to devise their own individual programs to overcome their depressive feelings. A fifth undergraduate met with each of the four alone and instructed her to examine carefully the things that occurred just before her feelings of depression.

Following are the four successful self-help programs they devised.

CASE STUDY 1: This young woman recorded her usual activities and rated them as producing either good or bad feelings. As a result, she began to pay special attention to her happy feelings. This device appeared to stop the gradually rising feeling of depression. This simple method should not be construed as being broad enough for many people.

CASE STUDY 2: In observing what preceded her depressions, this student discovered that unfortunate interactions with other people led to her self-deprecating feelings such as unworthiness. She therefore set about paying less attention to what others said about her and relying more on herself. She used engaging in a favorite hobby as self-reward when she was successful in overcoming morbid ruminations, thus increasing self-reliance.

CASE STUDY 3: This young woman tried to stop her thought of suicide by changing to neutral or happy thoughts, but this did not seem to do the trick thoroughly. After two months of trying, she hit upon using a happy fantasy as soon as her depressions began, thus stopping the escalation of depression. In unhappy situations she stopped her depressive feelings and for fifteen minutes thought only about her happy fantasy. Seven days of this lowered her depression dramatically. On a three-month follow-up she reported that her self-control method was still working well.

CASE STUDY 4: After looking at herself carefully, this young woman realized that she strongly rejected the expression of her true feelings and thoughts. She decided to change this about herself but was only partly successful in lowering her depression. After one and a half months she decided to make an important addition to her initial scheme—she would begin rewarding herself for being honest with herself and others. After two months, her initial test scores on depression had lowered greatly.

These examples of self-control of depression suggest that therapists should investigate the possibilities of group methods for teaching self-modification techniques, which may turn out to be economical for people with emotional and behavioral problems.

COMMENTARY: The provocative point of this study is that some people can devise their own self-treatment if taught self-change methods. This is similar to other self-control methods digested in this section (see, for example, Lewinsohn, Sullivan, and Grosscup), but the twist here is that the methods are learned in a class (see Fuchs and Rehm, digested here, for a group method other than classroom), not taught, evaluated, and revised by an individual therapist. The method suggested here is like reading a self-help book, except that a class allows for some discussion and questioning. Certainly the method is preferable in terms of expense, but our guess is that it may be applicable only to a particular group of people—something that could perhaps be said of any therapy. This therapy might be ideally suited for bright, highly motivated people.

SOURCE: Tharp, R. G., Watson, D., and Kaya, J. "Self-Modification of Depression." *Journal of Consulting and Clinical Psychology,* 1974, *42,* 624. An extended report of this study is available from Dr. Roland G. Tharp, Queens College, Toot Balden, Oxon, England.

Social Skills Training

AUTHORS: Karen C. Wells, Michel Hersen, Alan S. Bellack, and Jonathan Himmelhoch

PRECIS: Role playing, verbal instruction, modeling by the therapist, feedback, and social reinforcement for improving social interactions decreases depression in three women

INTRODUCTION: The relation between depression and social

skills is circular; lack of social skills contributes to depression, and depression lowers social skills. Social skills training was used with three females, aged nineteen to forty-five, all suffering uni-polar nonpsychotic depression. The method may be used alone or in conjunction with antidepressant medication. Only one of the patients, however, was under medication.

TREATMENT: Patients were seen weekly for twelve one-and-a-half-hour sessions. Through a structured interview and review of videotapes made of the patient's interactions with a research as-sistant in role-playing situations, deficits in verbal and nonverbal skills were identified in each of four content areas: family inter-actions, work interactions, interactions with friends, and inter-actions with strangers. These content areas were hierarchically arranged to reflect importance to the individual patient. In addi-tion, the patient established for each area a hierarchy of repre-sentative situations in which she found difficulty in expressing her feelings or point of view in a personally satisfying way.

Training began with the least anxiety-provoking scene in the least anxiety-provoking area. Training involved role playing of each scene, instructions about effective behavior, modeling by the therapist, feedback, and positive social reinforcement. After discussing how to handle the scene, the therapist trained the patient in such things as eye contact and smiling. Training continued until both therapist and patient approved of all as-pects of the patient's behavior. Training then began on the next scene in the hierarchy.

Patients were urged to practice their new behaviors when-ever possible and to report to the therapist what occurred and how they rated their behavior on a 1 to 5 scale. Discussion with the therapist might alter the rating. Patients were given social reinforcement and were taught to reinforce themselves for at-tempts and performance.

On various measures, all four patients showed improve-ment in depressive symptoms and increased assertiveness.

COMMENTARY: The distinction between social skills training and assertion training is not pointed out in this report, although the authors do comment on the increased assertiveness in their clients and offer as examples such skills as smiling and the like. Presumably social skills training includes much more than assertion training and might be useful with people who get themselves in social trouble because they are overly assertive and eventually become depressed. This therapy might be limited to people who have deficits of one kind or another in social areas; it may not be applicable to those whose social skills are adequate but who suffer other depressing problems.

Certainly, discussion of and alteration of a wide range of problems, beyond lack of social skills, ordinarily associated with depression (self-reproach, withdrawal, lethargy, agitation, and so on) would appear to be worthwhile for depression. In terms of reinforcement alone, altered social behavior conceivably would bring social reinforcement in the natural environment. One suspects that this therapy might be joined with other therapies for the most rapid alleviation of symptoms.

SOURCE: Wells, K. C., Hersen, M., Bellack, A. S., and Himmelhoch, J. "Social Skills Training in Unipolar Nonpsychotic Depression." *American Journal of Psychiatry*, 1979, *136*, 1331-1332.

Therapies for Different Kinds of Depression

AUTHOR: Joseph Wolpe

PRECIS: Twenty-five people with reactive depression treated with systematic desensitization, training in assertion or relaxation, cognitive correction, flooding, modeling, and/or *in vivo* desensitization, depending on the type of depression displayed

INTRODUCTION: Three kinds of depression exist: normal depression, which is a reality-bound reaction to a specific event and is usually self-limiting; biological (endogenous) depression, which may be unipolar or bipolar in nature and responds well to antidepressant drugs or electroconvulsive therapy; and neurotic depression, or reactive depression, which is a persistent unadaptive habit and can be relieved by various combinations of behavior therapy.

Neurotic depression does not arise from learned helplessness, as has been said, but almost always from conditioned anxiety responses. Anxiety is the person's pattern of autonomic responses to unpleasant situations; so for depression to be relieved, these responses must be deconditioned.

Neurotic depression is seen under four different conditions, although two or more may be combined in any one person: (1) as a result of strong and lasting anxiety that is directly conditioned; (2) as a result of anxiety based on incorrect, self-devaluating ideas; (3) as an accompaniment of an anxiety-based incapacity to control interpersonal relations; and (4) as an accompaniment of strong, lasting responses to bereavement.

METHOD: Twenty-five people with neurotic depression, among a larger group treated in thirty years' practice of behavior therapy, were classified into the above four types. Specific therapies for each type are described here. The therapist must take a careful history in order to put a patient in the correct category and therefore use the correct treatment.

Depression Resulting from Conditioned Anxiety of a Prolonged and Severe Nature. Among these people, the depression fluctuates with the strength of the anxiety; but if the anxiety is pervasive, the depression becomes pervasive. This is treated by systematic desensitization or by other methods found to be appropriate in individual cases, among which are relaxation training, assertion training, and *in vivo* desensitization (see Index).

In the case of a thirty-six-year-old woman with a life history of anxiety, depression, and social inadequacy, numerous suicide attempts, and nine years of unsuccessful psychoanalysis, the therapist used assertion training along with systematic desensitization of inappropriate fears of ridicule and rejection.

After thirty-one sessions she had no depression, and on nine-month follow-up she was still not depressed.

Depression Resulting from Anxiety Based on False Self-Devaluations. The therapist uses "cognitive correction" (presumably employing Beck's system; see Index).

A thirty-five-year-old woman with a ten-year history of irritability and severe depressions, and an unsuccessful psychoanalysis, believed that she was basically incapable of orgasm during intercourse. In the third session, the patient saw (from the therapist's analysis of her behavior) that she easily had orgasms during masturbation and that her inhibition of orgasm during intercourse was based on her fear of trusting people, a result of her father's devious cruelty. She felt great relief and her depression left. She and the therapist spent the next few months talking about making her sex life more satisfactory. In seven years of follow-up, she reported no return of neurotic depression.

Depression Resulting from Submissiveness Because of Inability to Handle Other People, in Turn Resulting from Conditioned Anxiety About Relations with Others. These people inhibit themselves because of the anxiety they feel when they assert themselves, and then they become depressed. Assertion training is the major treatment, sometimes preceded by systematic desensitization when necessary.

A thirty-two-year-old hairdresser became tearful and helpless when criticized by his customers. The therapist gave him assertion training, and all his symptoms, including his depression, disappeared. At a five-year follow-up, he was still free from depression.

Depression as an Exaggerated Reaction to Loss. Some of these people have not only a particular response to an event but a physiological predisposition to depression, in which case appropriate drug or hormonal treatment should be given. If the response to loss leads to self-devaluation, the therapist should use cognitive correction. If depression results from a conditioned anxiety response to loss, the person may respond to systematic desensitization.

(No pure examples of this category of neurotic depres-

sion were included in this report. This category is convention-
ally referred to as *reactive depression,* a term the author uses
synonymously with *neurotic depression.*)

Of the twenty-five people treated, twenty-two are reported to have been lastingly free of depression, two were unim-
proved, and one had subsequent repeated depressions but much
less severe.

COMMENTARY: Wolpe's distinctions between kinds of depression may be very useful in applying different therapies for different depressed people. These distinctions are at least one
answer to a dominant question running through all therapy literature: Which therapy is effective for which kind of person?
His diagnostic distinctions are related basically to four currently
popular general systems: behavior therapy, cognitive therapy,
assertion (and perhaps social skills) training, and grief-resolution
therapy. His recommendations might be supplemented with various methods suggested in this section—for example, goal clarification, monitoring, ongoing evaluation of results, and running.

SOURCE: Wolpe, J. "The Experimental Model and Treatment
of Neurotic Depression." *Behaviour Research and Therapy,*
1979, *17,* 555-565.

Raising Self-Competence

AUTHORS: Antonette M. Zeiss, Peter M. Lewinsohn, and Ri-
cardo F. Muñoz

PRECIS: Interpersonal behavior therapy, focus on pleasant activities, and cognitive therapy were all successful in lowering depression in a group of adults.

INTRODUCTION: Three current treatment approaches designed

to alter behavior in three different areas were used to observe the effects on groups of depressed people. Presumably, an interpersonal approach would affect assertiveness and social relations and subsequently affect mood. A pleasant-activities approach should increase the pleasant events in people's lives and therefore elevate mood. A cognitive approach would apparently decrease negative thoughts and increase positive thoughts, thus improving mood.

TREATMENT: Nine men and thirty-five women aged nineteen to sixty-eight and showing moderate to severe unipolar, non-psychotic depression on testing and interview were randomly assigned to either immediate or delayed treatment in one of three therapy programs. Treatment was free in exchange for their participation in extensive testing. Clients had, on the average, three sessions a week for four weeks and were expected to work between sessions on material covered in the sessions. Some clients began immediately, and some waited one month before beginning therapy. The immediate group was given a pretest, a test at the end of therapy, and one-month and two-months follow-up testing. The delayed groups were tested before and after therapy and one month later. The graduate student and master's degree therapists each saw three clients, one in each kind of therapy. The three therapies are described below.

Interpersonal behavior approach. Three areas of interpersonal behavior were covered: assertion, interpersonal style of behavior, and social activity. For the six weeks of *assertion* training, the therapists offered instruction, modeling, a rehearsal period, and feedback. Clients were expected to read *Your Perfect Right* by R. E. Alberti and M. L. Emmons (2nd ed., San Luis Obispo, Calif.: Impact, 1974) and to practice assertion in real life. To work on *interpersonal style,* therapist and client set specific goals, such as reducing complaining or responding more positively to others. The format of therapist instruction and modeling, rehearsal, and feedback was again followed. Therapist and client monitored progress, and then the client was expected to work on his own. For increase in *social activity,* goals were established and gradually increased, and a manual on the subject

(E. Gambrill and C. E. Richey, *It's up to You: Developing Assertive Social Skills,* Millbrae, Calif.: Les Femmes/Celestial Arts, 1976) was used for instruction.

Pleasant Activities Approach. The goals here were for clients to increase the number and enjoyment of pleasant activities in their lives. They monitored both their activities and their mood on scales developed for these purposes and came to see how mood is affected by activities. They even received computer data on this relationship taken from their self-monitoring. The clients then set about to increase pleasant activities, and therapist and client discussed how to continue this when therapy was over. In addition, therapists taught clients muscle relaxation, and clients were told to use it in their lives to increase pleasure. They were also expected to read a book giving ways to organize time and activities (A. Lakein, *How to Get Control of Your Time and Your Life,* New York: New American Library, 1974).

Cognitive Approach. The goal here was to change the ways the clients thought about reality. An array of current cognitive materials was given to clients, and they largely were left to their own control. Therapists gave instruction on the importance of one's thoughts; helped clients to look at their thoughts and make such distinctions as positive and negative, necessary and unnecessary, constructive and destructive; taught cognitive self-management approaches; and showed how to dispute irrational thoughts. Clients were expected to practice these on their own. In addition, the therapist designed a new role for a client, and the client acted it out for a few days in real life; from this the client was expected to get perspective and develop more adaptive ways of behaving. Clients also wrote a role description of how they would think in order to curb depression.

The results were surprising. All treatments were effective in lowering depression, and none had the expected effects on specific target behavior for which it was designed. Over time, patients did improve on pleasant activities, social skills, and cognitions but not, as expected, depending on the kind of therapy they had. It may be that the content of therapy is relatively unimportant in comparison with the possible increased feeling of self-efficacy or self-competence in clients. All the therapies began with the therapist's instruction that practicing certain skills would lower depression and that the clients should learn them and use them in their lives. In addition, clients began to have more positive experiences, which they attributed to their new sense of self-competence.

A second surprise was the great amount of improvement seen during the waiting period in the delayed-treatment group. Perhaps this group had, because of the extensive assessment, considerable contact with the staff and perhaps positive reinforcement from them for decreased depression.

The results of this study suggest that successful therapy for depression has certain specific elements. Therapy should begin with a rationale and structure that lead clients to believe that they can control their own behavior and thus their depression. Therapists should teach skills that help clients to handle their lives better, arrange that clients can actually learn them, and encourage them to use these skills. Lastly, therapists should encourage the idea that improvement comes from patients' own improved skills, not therapists' skills.

COMMENTARY: From this important study, a few major points are worth restating. All the therapies were specifically geared to self-control. This was initiated by an opening statement of the rationale for each therapy, with emphasis on patients' being able to control their own depression with a given training. In each case, the therapy was set up so that the patients had to do most of the work on their own—read books, monitor their progress, practice new skills, act out a new role, and so on. From the fact that all the therapies lowered depression, it seems that increased sense of control over one's life, rather than any particular therapy for any particular deficit, is the crucial ingredient in alleviating depression. However, one wonders, as do the authors of this study, how much more effective the therapies might have been in economy of time and durability if the specific therapies had been matched to the problems for which they were designed (the procedure in the study was random assignment).

To use these therapies effectively, we believe, therapists must be committed to the idea that clients can take care of themselves, given some skills, and must communicate this unequivocally to the clients. In contrast, the use of ECT or drugs requires no such commitment.

SOURCE: Zeiss, A. M., Lewinsohn, P. M., and Muñoz, R. F. "Nonspecific Improvement Effects in Depression Using Interpersonal Skills Training, Pleasant Activity Schedules, and Cognitive Training." *Journal of Consulting and Clinical Psychology,* 1979, *47,* 427-439.

Additional Readings

Anton, J. L., Dunbar, J., and Friedman, L. "Anticipation Training in the Treatment of Depression." In J. D. Krumboltz and C. E. Thoresen (Eds.), *Counseling Methods.* New York: Holt, Rinehart and Winston, 1976.

Depressed people do not have enough pleasant events in their lives, and they tend to anticipate negative things happening to them. Therapy, therefore, might be directed toward increasing pleasant events and changing the person's anticipations from negative to positive. Nine depressed women were given six sessions of individual anticipation therapy over a period of one month. Each woman first was given a log of her daily activities to fill out within a week and discussed her depression for about half an hour. From the second session on, the therapist's goal was to help the client increase pleasant events in her life and teach her self-control of anticipations. She had to select and plan six pleasant activities to accomplish in the next two weeks —three alone and three with at least one other person. For each of the six events, she chose three positive anticipation statements, each beginning with "I will enjoy . . . ." She was then instructed to close her eyes, relax, and get a mental picture of the first event, rehearse mentally each of the three statements, and create a mental image of the positive anticipations. She was to do this also at home three times a day. In subsequent sessions, the events were reported and discussed and the next ones planned. Seven of the women became markedly less depressed, while two showed little or no change. These latter two had few social skills, were lacking in positive relationships with others, and had very little chance for pleasure from their environments. The authors see the training as a beginning for therapy, especially in light of the brief time it takes.

Arieti, S. "Psychotherapy of Severe Depression." *American Journal of Psychiatry*, 1977, *134*, 864-868.

Although outpatient psychotherapy has long been used for mild or moderate depression, it has seldom been employed for severe or psychotic depression. With severe depression, drugs and electroshock are conventional, but of course they do not always work. Psychotherapy can be used effectively if the therapist employs the right approach.

The approach described here was used on an outpatient basis with nine women and three men, all severely depressed, ten of whom harbored ideas of suicide. They were seen at least twice a week for a minimum of one and a half years. On three-year follow-up, seven had fully recovered with no relapses, four sustained marked improvement, and one failed.

Depressed people suffer an underlying ideology that involves either (1) living for someone else or (2) pursuing a dominant but unattainable goal. They either cannot even imagine other ideologies, see them but cannot imagine their being realized, or see them but consider them worthless. Although Beck has described depressive cognitions (see descriptions elsewhere in this section), the ones he describes can be seen as being used by people to justify their preexisting depression. What the therapist must get to is more basic and intense depressive trends emanating from early life.

Briefly described, therapy should proceed as follows: The therapist is highly active, firm, clear, and sure and invites the patient to lean on him. This often brings immediate relief because the patient sees the therapist as a new love object. The

therapist, however, must clarify his position to that of an un-
ambiguous person who neither makes threatening demands nor
wants the patient to go on living in a sick way. When the therapist collects enough information, he interprets (1) the patient's
own responsibility in his relation with the dominant other or
(2) the reasons the patient accepted a supreme inaccessible goal.
The therapist must then guide the patient to see other possibilities and to become motivated toward them. Other less crucial
issues arise, which are described briefly in the article.

Some patients are given concomitant drug therapy, while
others who have not had success with drugs or ECT are successfully treated with psychotherapy alone.

Avery, D., and Lubrano, A. "Depression Treated with Imipramine and ECT: The DeCarolis Study Reconsidered." *American Journal of Psychiatry*, 1979, *136*, 559-562.

A large and potentially important Italian study comparing electroconvulsive therapy (ECT) with high dosages of imipramine was reported as favoring imipramine. The authors of
the present article obtained the original data and subjected
them to a careful reexamination. Their conclusions differ from
the original conclusions.

The patients, 183 men and 254 women, with a mean age
of forty-seven years, covered a wide range of depressions and
some psychoses. All were started on imipramine dosage of 200
to 350 mg/day. If they did not respond at any time up to thirty
days of drug treatment, they were given eight to ten ECT treatments. Results were evaluated one month after the end of treatment.

The present authors found from the Italian data that ECT
was clearly better for manic-depressive psychosis, endogenous
unipolar depression, and the atypical psychoses. This fits with
seven studies written in English covering 2,000 patients: ECT is
superior to antidepressant medication (no study shows antidepressants superior to ECT). Evidence exists, however, that
dosage is an important factor in the use of antidepressant drugs.
In one study, people given 300 mg/day fared much better than
those on 150 mg/day.

Also noteworthy in the present study is that neurotic and

reactive depressions responded poorly to ECT, but a history of a precipitating event (as in reactive depression) does not completely rule out the use of ECT.

The major thrust of this reexamination of a large body of data for clinicians is that the procedure of automatically putting depressed clients on antidepressant drugs would not appear to be warranted. Careful diagnosing and subsequent selection of drugs or ECT to fit the person will, it seems, save considerable expense and suffering. The present study gives some guidelines to aid clinicians in these pursuits.

Blackwell, B. "Treatment Adherence." *British Journal of Psychiatry,* 1976, *129,* 513-531.

In instances in which patients do not keep up with prescriptions of drugs, Blackwell suggests employing relatives to give the drug and noting in a diary how closely the regimen is followed.

Cammer, L. *Up from Depression.* New York: Simon & Schuster, 1981 (paperback).

The author's major goal in this book, written for relatives of depressed clients, is to furnish them with information that will "knock down the walls of hearsay" about depression and help them to deal with and understand it. The author has found that many depressed patients have improved largely because their families participated in the recovery process.

Part One of the book, "Understanding Depression," discusses what depression is, its seriousness, and "what you should know about" endogenous depressions, reactive depressions (grief), and neurotic depressions. A detailed chart compares these three major types of depression in terms of causes, onset, and various symptoms.

Part Two, "Overcoming Depression," includes chapters on drug treatment, physical treatment, psychotherapy, and psychiatric hospitalization. Accompanying each chapter is a companion chapter discussing the relatives' role in each area (for example, "Your Role in Drug Treatment").

The final chapter focuses on who gives treatment (family doctor, psychiatrists, psychologists, psychoanalysts, and lay therapists) and where treatment can be obtained (outpatient and inpatient facilities, methods of admission for inpatient treatment, types of psychiatric hospitals, the difference between reception and treatment centers, and medical insurance programs for depressive illness).

Chiles, J. A. "A Practical Therapeutic Use of the Telephone." *American Journal of Psychiatry,* 1974, *131,* 1030-1031.

Many therapists and clinics, especially crisis centers where suicide prevention is the goal, employ the telephone as a safety valve for patients. Therapists sometimes encourage patients to call when they are feeling bad. The calls catch the therapeutic urge at its peak and cut down transference to a level manageable for patients. Patients call therapists for numerous reasons, centering largely on a need for contact and expression of feelings.

The telephone can also be used in a totally different way. The therapist can set up a routine of the patient's telephoning, often every day at a specified time to report on specific aspects of the patient's behavior. This routine is designed to increase self-esteem, give patients a place where they can express their disturbing feelings, enable them to concretize vague situations, and aid in zeroing in on problems in a new, more helpful way.

Two case studies are cited, both of women in their fifties suffering depression. The first woman was accustomed to staying in bed until noon, calling around to various doctors and social agencies to complain about her illnesses. She had been both an inpatient and outpatient many times, seeking treatment, with no improvement. Then she was referred to the clinic described in this article. Here she was told to call daily at 8 A.M. to talk about her problems and troublesome feelings, but she was not to call any other agency. If she missed calling at 8 A.M. she was fined, and after two misses she would be discontinued as a patient at the clinic. Surprisingly, she got herself up in time to call, but then she had to fill the four hours she had previously used to call around. She was offered clinic visits twice a week and was told to call the clinic again at 10:30 A.M. each day. After three weeks, she came for joint therapy with her son and lover, the two central and most troublesome people in her life. After a year, she was working, had better relations with her two men, and reported feeling happier. She came for sessions once a month and called every day at 8 A.M. The call took only five minutes, and it sufficed for her to talk to any one of four or five staff members, all of whom she came to know.

In the second case study, a withdrawn, overweight, alcoholic fifty-eight-year-old woman was equally improved. Besides group therapy twice a week and family sessions, she was required to call the clinic each evening at 8:30, a time that had always been worst for her, and talk about her problems and particularly to report on her food and alcohol consumption, which both she and the clinic staff recorded. As with the previous woman, any one of a number of staff members sufficed for the calls. After three months, she had lost fifteen pounds, had controlled her drinking, and was having considerable social contact.

Although inherently the method involves dependency and focus on illness, it also provides therapists with a daily opportunity to point out the patient's growth. The planned use of the telephone can make a useful tool of something that consumes considerable time at a clinic anyway, turning crises into an ongoing therapeutic movement.

Clum, G. A., Patsiokas, A. T., and Luscomb, R. L. "Empirically Based Comprehensive Treatment Program for Parasuicide." *Journal of Consulting and Clinical Psychology,* 1979, 47, 937-945.

The authors propose an interesting set of factors predictive of attempted suicide and proceed to suggest programs for specific kinds of people. (1) When the depressed person perceives suicide as a solution to life changes, a two-phase program should be instituted. First, the person is helped to deal with the life change. Second, cognitive therapy should help the person alter his belief system. (2) For people who use a suicide attempt to produce some change in other people, a problem-solving approach is designed to help the person define the problem, look for alternative solutions, make a decision, and then check it by trying it out (see the digest of D'Zurilla and Goldfried in the section on dependent personality disorder). (3) When suicide is an expression of anger, the person should be taught how to express his anger and assert his rights through assertion training.

Glasser, W. *Reality Therapy: A New Approach to Psychiatry.*
New York: Harper & Row, 1965.

People have two basic psychological needs: to love and be loved and to feel that they are worthwhile to themselves and others. Helping clients to fulfill these two needs is the basic focus of Reality Therapy. Responsibility, a key concept of this approach, is defined as the ability to fulfill these needs in a way that does not deprive others of the ability to fulfill their needs. Conventional diagnostic labels are dispensed with, and clients who are having serious difficulties in their lives are seen as "irresponsible." Thus the term *responsible* is substituted for *mental health* and *irresponsible* for *mental illness.* Reality Therapy is a special kind of teaching designed to accomplish in a relatively short, intense period of time what should have been learned during growing up. The more irresponsible the person, the more he must learn about acceptable realistic behavior in order to fulfill his needs.

The therapist begins by becoming involved with the client —a relationship in which the therapist is firm, sensitive, accepting, and empathic. Once the therapist/client relationship is firmly established, the therapist pushes the client to decide whether his behavior is responsible and whether he should change it. The therapist teaches that true happiness occurs only when people are willing to take responsibility for their behavior. No emphasis is placed on the past or unconscious aspects of behavior. The therapist focuses on what the client is doing now and does not search for reasons why. When the client admits that his behavior is irresponsible, the last phase of therapy begins—a relearning period in which the client learns better, more "responsible" ways of behaving.

The following case study illustrates this approach. A nineteen-year-old college student requested therapy because he was depressed, was failing in his freshman year, had no vocational plans, and felt life was empty. After a year of unsuccessful conventional therapy, he began Reality Therapy. At the initial session, the therapist expressed his belief that the student's problems were not insoluble and in general communicated the idea that he would see the student until he could become better able to fulfill his own needs. The therapist encouraged responsible behavior by asking the student to share the therapy fees with his mother (which he could afford) and then listened sympathetically to the young man's talk of his problems, which was full of self-pity, resentment, and the blaming of others. The therapist did not encourage these topics but instead repeatedly asked the student what "plan" he had. Through continued questioning and discussion, the student was encouraged to clarify his goals about what he really wanted. Therapy continued, with the therapist often discussing his own college experiences, successes, and failures. The assumption was that this was a situation between two people, of whom one had problems because he was irresponsible and the other was a responsible person interested in helping him solve these problems. The therapist became more involved in the student's life, reading his papers, discussing homework, and suggesting that he develop a closer relationship with his stepfather. The student discovered that he wanted to go into medicine and began to pursue that goal. Because of the successful involvement with the therapist, the student could discuss his relationship with his real father, whom he had not seen for years. After approximately three years of therapy, the student graduated and was accepted by every medical school to which he had applied. He handled his real father's sudden suicide with strength and a gained sense of self-worth and had a good relationship with his mother and stepfather.

Jacobsen, E. "The Psychoanalytic Treatment of Depressive Patients." In: E. J. Anthony and T. Benedek (Eds.), *Depression and Human Existence.* Boston: Little, Brown, 1975.

Careful diagnosis of potential psychoanalytic patients is essential in order to anticipate and handle various problems the analyst encounters, especially with severely depressed people. Some patients should be hospitalized because of suicidal danger and be given drugs and perhaps electroshock treatment. For others, the choice may be supportive treatment, psychoanalytically oriented psychotherapy, or psychoanalysis. There are, however, no definite rules one can use. People are not ruled out of psychoanalysis, for example, on the basis of neurotic, borderline psychotic, or psychotic diagnoses. There are, nevertheless, some predictions and guidelines that may aid analysts in treating severely depressed people.

Severely depressed clients tend first to idealize their therapists and then turn against them in disappointment. An analyst should treat depressed people only if he is naturally warm, is not emotionally detached, and harbors no dislike or rejection of patients. The patient should be allowed to develop an early idealization of the analyst, but the analyst should prepare the client for negative transference by early interpretation of the patient's tendency to idealize and then be disappointed in people. With compulsive depressed people, however, any underlying hostility should be interpreted only gradually to avoid the patient's guilt, increased depression, and even suicidal ideas. With paranoid depressive people, an analyst should be wary and not accept them if he has any negative countertransference, as these patients have a knack for getting at therapists' sore spots and inviting anger and rejection in the analyst. A patient's relationship with a current love object is often crucial to the analysis, and the analyst should pay careful attention to this. The change in the affection from a client's partner can alter depression dramatically; for example, a husband's leaving a depressed wife can remove her depression.

Penis envy and castration conflict may be the cause of most depressions in women, and this must be carefully analyzed. The analysis of infantile conflicts, particularly hostility conflicts, must be allowed to surface and can lead to good therapeutic results, even in severe depression of borderline and psychotic people.

Some patients cannot bear to be separated from their analysts and demand extra sessions, but analysts should not yield to these demands. The exception is with psychotically depressed clients, who may be given sixty minutes instead of the usual fifty for an analytic session because of their characteristic slowness.

(For further reading by this author, see E. Jacobsen, *De-*

pression: Comparative Studies of Normal, Neurotic and Psychotic Conditions, New York: International Universities Press, 1971.)

La Pointe, K. A., and Rimm, D. C. "Cognitive, Assertive, and Insight-Oriented Group Therapies in the Treatment of Reactive Depression in Women." *Psychotherapy: Theory, Research, and Practice,* 1980, *17,* 312-321.

Three major approaches to depression are currently used —psychoanalytic, cognitive, and behavioral, each with its own theory and procedures. Very little systematic study has been done, however, to compare the three therapies. Since women are affected by depression in far greater proportions than men, a comparative study of the three therapies was undertaken with women. Selected for treatment were thirty-three women between ages twenty-one and sixty-three, of various work and marital statuses, whose testing and interviewing revealed recurrent, situationally related, moderate depression, the kind that brings women to mental health clinics. The women were divided into groups of three to nine members and assigned to one of the three therapies, given two hours a week for six weeks. At the beginning of each session for all groups, the women were presented with situations of hurt, anger, criticism, disappointment, and positive feedback—all of which could lead to depression— and were asked whether they had been in the situations, told to imagine being in them, and asked how they felt, what they thought, and what they would do. The therapists then followed one of the three therapies. The insight group discussed how they felt and why and discussed past and present reactions to the presented situations. The assertive group discussed what they said in the situations and what stopped them from being assertive, and then they role-played assertive responses to the situations. The cognitive group discussed what they told themselves in the situations and how their thoughts affected their feelings and practiced using nondepressive thoughts. In the second hour of sessions two through six, all group members broke into pairs and practiced what they had learned in the first hour. The authors point out that their forms of the three therapies possibly do not jibe with those of practitioners of the therapies.

After six weeks of treatment, women in all groups showed less depression, less irrationality, and more assertiveness on testing. However, from interview, the women in the assertive and cognitive groups seemed to fare better than those in the insight groups. The women in the first two groups reported better mood, better relations with people, better feelings about themselves, increased ability to cope, and increased energy. The insight group showed more variation in therapy outcome, some women getting better and some getting worse. Two important implications are that more rationality and assertiveness are apparently associated with decreased depression and that women might hold particular irrational beliefs that heighten their depression.

Miller, J. "Helping the Suicidal Client: Some Aspects of Assessment and Treatment." *Psychotherapy: Theory, Research, and Practice,* 1980, *17,* 94-100.

Where suicide is suspected, the clinician must be extremely careful in diagnosing the situation. There are numerous danger signals the clinician can look for: the person's underlying attitude of hopelessness and helplessness, change in sleeping and eating habits, inability to follow through on usual daily chores, weakening of ego, lowering of reality testing, inability to make and keep a relationship with another person, inability to control impulses and hold off their expression, improvement in mood and a new attitude of peace (the decision in favor of suicide is made), previous suicide attempts, the loss of someone or something of crucial importance in the person's life, and the death of a parent in the person's childhood. Careful appraisal of these issues will help the clinician decide on outpatient treatment or hospitalization. People close to the patient should be brought in not only for the clinician to get full information but to help build a support system for the suicidal person. If hospitalization is chosen, it should be as brief as possible in order to minimize the person's becoming dependent on the security, care, and attention of the hospital milieu. While the person is in the hospital, the clinician should try to plan for support in the regular life of the patient. Careful planning should also be done with the patient and those close to him concerning the assured continuance of antidepressant or antipsychotic medication following hospitalization. With potentially suicidal people the clinician should avoid ignoring or pushing aside suicidal statements as insincere ("He doesn't mean it"), disputing the person ("Things can't be as depressing as you make them sound"), and having preconceptions about putting the person in the hospital. It is helpful to discuss openly with the person the possibility of suicide, make decisions with the person rather than for him, tell him openly that we are going to try to arrange things to save his life but that no one can really prevent him if he decides to kill himself, help him get a time perspective by informing him of how acute depression is usually time-limited, enlist the help of those close to him immediately, prompt evaluation for medication, provide for the person's being able to talk things out in individual sessions, and teach him expressive and assertive behavior. Suicide prevention in a clinic or hospital is, of course, much simpler than in the hands of a private practitioner who has few aids at his command. The private practitioner should fortify his position by establishing mutual-help schemes with colleagues.

Ramsay, R. W. "Behavioural Approaches to Bereavement." *Behaviour Research and Therapy*, 1977, *15,* 131-135.

Phobic people have been successfully treated by exposing them to situations to which they have a phobic reaction and have previously avoided. (See digests under "Phobias.") They are, in effect, "flooded" with exposure, and the conditioned emotional reaction is deconditioned. Phobic people and people in grief over the loss of a loved one, wealth, position, or self-esteem are similar in that their behavior is based on avoidance of facing squarely the actual situations that bother them. Thus, grief can be treated much as phobia is treated by "flooding" grieving people with the objects, situations, and so on that evoke extreme emotional response. Finding stimuli that evoke powerful emotional responses for people in grief is, however, generally harder than for phobic people. Once the stimuli are found, the procedure involves repeated confrontation with the emotion-laden stimuli, prolonged exposure, and prevention of any avoidance or escape from facing what needs to be faced.

The therapist gives no interpretations, and people recover in as little as three weeks.

Rosenblatt, S., and Dodson, R. *Beyond Valium: The Brave New World of Psychochemistry.* New York: Putnam's, 1981.

This book, presumably written for the layperson, has four sections: (1) general background and history of the use of tranquilizers, antidepressants, and other mind-altering drugs; (2) a nontechnical explanation that represents current thinking on how drugs work; (3) the current "state of the art" in treating various disorders, including presently approved treatments for depression, schizophrenia, anxiety, panic, phobias, and compulsions; and (4) speculations about the role of drug treatment in the future. The authors also discuss diet and suggest how vitamins, sugar, chocolate, and food additives may be associated with mood changes. Numerous tables present information about various drugs (generic name, brand name, and manufacturer) that may be helpful to nonmedical practitioners. Therapists may want to recommend this book to clients who have questions about drug therapy.

For extensive coverage for professional readers, Rosenblatt and Dodson recommend J. D. Barchas, P. A. Berger, R. D. Ciaranello, and G. R. Elliott, *Pharmacology: From Theory to Practice,* New York: Oxford University Press, 1977; L. S. Goodman and A. Gilman (Eds.), *The Pharmacological Basis of Therapeutics,* New York: Macmillan, 1980.

Rush, A. J. (Ed.). *Short-Term Psychotherapies for Depression: Behavioral, Interpersonal, Cognitive and Psychodynamic Approaches.* New York: Guilford Publications, 1982.

The editor of these primary source readings begins with a chapter on assessment, emphasizing (1) which people are candidates for psychotherapy and which require some other treatment and (2) which psychotherapy might be appropriate for which patient. The body of the book focuses on four therapy approaches: behavioral, interpersonal, cognitive, and psychodynamic. Two chapters are devoted to each system, the first giving the underlying theory of the approach and research supporting the theory, the second giving specific methods of therapy.

Case histories, follow-up data, transcripts of actual sessions, and reasons for failures are also included. The final chapter is an attempt to give an overview of the four systems.

Rush, A. J., Shaw, B., and Khatami, M. "Cognitive Therapy of Depression: Utilizing the Couples System." *Cognitive Therapy and Research,* 1980, *4,* 103-113.

Cognitive therapy has been used successfully in both group and individual format. What has been missing is the use of cognitive therapy in a couples format with the specific goal of altering depression rather than merely the marital relationship. The spouse of a depressed person cannot, after all, be considered neutral. In response to depressive behavior, the spouse is apt to become angry, overly solicitous, or withdrawn, for example, thus reinforcing the depressed person's negative view of the world. As an ally in therapy, however, the spouse can help record what actually happens, serve as an objective reporter of events, provide alternative perceptions and conceptualizations of events, articulate the patient's beliefs or unspoken assumptions, and encourage the patient to work on therapy outside the sessions (for example, do homework assigned by the therapist). In addition, the therapist can directly observe the couple to see the patterns of behavior that are maintaining or increasing the depression.

Specific examples of these principles are given in three very clear successful therapy accounts of three severely depressed married women, ages sixty, thirty-three, and thirty.

Shipley, C. R., and Fazio, A. F. "Pilot Study of a Treatment for Psychological Depression." *Journal of Abnormal Psychology,* 1973, *82,* 372-376.

Depression is seen as a dysphoric reaction to the loss of reinforcement due to (1) an error in discrimination, such as seeing rejection as "playing hard to get" and assuming a friendship existed where none actually did, or (2) an error in responding, such as talking about committing suicide when another person starts a conversation. Therapy should be designed to help a person manipulate his environment more effectively, control himself, and communicate his intentions.

Two therapy studies were undertaken involving twenty-four college students in the first study and twenty-eight in the second, all depressed and interested in a project that might help them overcome their depression. Therapy designed according to the above principles was compared first with no therapy and then with an interest/support-group treatment. The latter simply involved conversations about clients' problems; the therapist offered no interpretations or solutions.

The therapy being tested was as follows. The therapist recommended certain behaviors the client might try in order to improve his life, and the client was to try them between sessions. Therapist and client discussed the results, and new recommendations were made. Responsibility to act or not act on the therapist's recommendations was clearly in the hands of the client; the therapist was supportive and encouraging. To learn control, the therapist suggested to the client that he confine his expressions of depression to "isolated depression"—a special period when he would be neither rewarded nor punished for showing his depression. After this period the client was either to seek out some postponed pleasurable activity or to try to experience anger at his situation in life in an effort to get him off his depression and on to positive action.

Significant improvement, revealed on a self-report questionnaire (MMPI), was shown only in the special therapy group. Clients in both the special therapy group and the interest/support group (in the second study) reported that they were helped by talking with someone, but only the special-group members were able to say how their lives had changed.

The treatment described here was based on a detailed outline given in F. H. Kanfer and J. S. Phillips, *Learning Foundations of Behavior Therapy,* New York: Wiley, 1970.

Todd, F. J. "Coverant Control of Self-Evaluative Responses in the Treatment of Depression: A New Use for an Old Principle." *Behavior Therapy,* 1972, *3,* 91-94.

In proposing to treat a chronically depressed forty-nine-year-old woman with other very serious complaints and a history of over three years of only mildly successful psychotherapy, the therapist felt that a fairly elaborate behavior therapy plan would have to wait until the woman first overcame her severe depression. The therapist began with a technique to change the client's self-evaluative statements. Asked by the therapist to describe herself with single words or short phrases, she gave only negative responses. He told her that he could see how she was depressed if that was the way she viewed herself, and he suggested that they look for positive statements. With much prodding from the therapist, she came up with six positive statements (the therapist would have begun the list for her with honest statements about her if she had been unable to find any on her own). The six statements were printed on a card that was put under the cellophane wrapper of her cigarettes. The therapist explained the use of the Premack principle in her situation: Thinking positively about herself could be increased if it was paired with cigarette smoking (or anything she enjoyed and did often). The rule was that, without exception, she must read one or two of the positive statements before lighting a cigarette. When she put her cigarette package down, she had to put it on a sheet of paper on which the statements were printed in large letters. When she was able, she was to add to the list of positive statements.

Within a week of carefully following instructions, she not only had added eight statements to her list but was feeling considerably less depressed. After another week, she reported feeling better about herself than she had felt in years. She said the positive thoughts came to her even when she was not smoking. At this point, the therapist began his original behavior therapy plan, involving thirty-five individual sessions and six joint sessions with her husband. In a three-year follow-up, she reported no serious depressive bouts and considerable happiness. She occasionally made herself better by thinking good thoughts but long ago had given up any regular use of the Premack rule.

The therapist believes that, in this instance, this technique enabled the patient to go ahead with the successful therapy program. He uses the technique as an adjunct in treatment plans for some patients; it can be used with problems other than depression. (See Additional Readings under "Test Anxiety.")

When the procedure is successful, it can in some cases be followed with the use of a more complex technique for improving self-image (see digest of the Susskind Idealized Self-Image Technique under "Dependent Personality Disorder").

(For a description of a more general application of the technique described here, see L. E. Homme, "Perspectives in Psychology XXIV. Control of Coverants, the Operants of the Mind," *Psychological Record,* 1965, *15,* 501-511.)

Van Der Hart, O., and Ebbers, J. "Rites of Separation in Strategic Psychotherapy." *Psychotherapy: Theory, Research, and Practice,* 1981, *18,* 188-194.

"Strategic psychotherapy" is a brief therapy focused on symptoms that are cured by a fundamental change in the person's social situation, which then frees him to grow and develop. In all people's lives there are transitions, both predictable (for example, marriage) and sudden (for example, death of a spouse), for which redefinitions and alterations of relationships are required. Symptoms come from people's becoming "stuck" and therefore unable to move on. Strategic psychotherapy helps people cope with their symptoms and at the same time make the transition that will help them move on. This is done by therapy that is pragmatic and eclectic; the therapy is "tailor-made" for each patient, and strategies from many sources are used.

The strategy discussed in this paper revolves around rites of passage, used to help people take leave of situations and people from the past. Rituals are devised by the therapist to aid people in making important transitions (such usual rituals in life are funerals, weddings, or puberty rites). Rituals are particularly useful with people who are held up by unresolved feelings about people or situations. Three aspects of rites of passage must be dealt with: separation (as in burials), transition (as in initiation), and incorporation (as in marriage).

Two therapy cases are presented: two depressed, lonely women, ages forty-eight and twenty-four, neither of whom could move on from an unresolved troublesome relationship with a man. In the first case, the therapist instructed the forty-eight-year-old woman to draw one picture a week depicting the most important moments of her life. Each drawing was discussed with the therapist. To say goodbye to these, she took the drawings and all the memorabilia from her husband and, in a secluded place, burned them in the presence of the therapist. She then returned home, took a shower, and threw away the clothes she had worn to the "funeral" (an expression she spontaneously used). That evening she had dinner with a friend, thus completing the ritual, the rite of passage. Contacts with the therapist continued for three months, after which her depression disappeared and her social contacts increased; she began a new life, unburdened by the past. With the second woman, the therapist took a similar tack, with similar results.

Using rites of separation, the therapist recognizes and validates people's suffering, gives their emotions a manageable form or container, protects his clients through his presence during the ordeal of separation, and helps them in redefining existing relationships (the evening meal on the day of the "funeral" is designed as a beginning for this). Through this process a new self-image emerges.

(For further reading about this approach, see R. Rabkin, *Strategic Psychotherapy,* New York: Basic Books, 1977.)

Weakland, J. H., Fisch, R., Watzlawick, R., and Bodin, A. M. "Brief Therapy: Focused Problem Resolution." *Family Process,* 1974, *13,* 141-168.

A brief therapy approach, applicable to a wide range of disorders, is described. Regardless of the nature or severity of the problem, each client has no more than ten one-hour sessions, usually weekly. Treatment is based on the assumption that clients' problems persist only if maintained by the behavior of the clients and others around them. If this behavior is appropriately changed or eliminated, the problem will disappear, regardless of its nature, origin, or duration. The therapist's major task is to take action to change poorly functioning patterns of interaction as powerfully, effectively, and efficiently as possible. Therapists in the Brief Therapy Center follow a six-step sequence in their treatment for each client, who is accepted without screening. First, the therapist explains the brief therapy system to the client, obtains demographic and historical data, and tells the client there will be no more than ten sessions. Second, the therapist determines the specific nature of the problem through discussion with the client and/or family. Third, the therapist attempts to discover what behavior is maintaining the problem, usually repeatedly reinforced through the social interaction between the client and other significant people. Fourth, concrete, observable goals of treatment are set, usually by the second session. Fifth, specific intervention strategies are determined. The general aim is to produce behavior change; little emphasis is placed on working toward "insight." The therapist attempts to discover the client's idiosyncratic characteristics and motivations in order to choose an approach that will appeal to him. The therapist does not hesitate to make requests for direct behavior change and may assign homework exercises. Paradoxical instruction is used in which the client is encouraged to perform the undesirable behavior in order to decrease it or bring it under control. The therapist does not hesitate to involve other people from the client's life and may see family members and/or spouses separately. Sixth, at the end of ten sessions or sooner, the therapist reviews the course of therapy, pointing out gains and unresolved issues.

Significant improvement has been noted in about three fourths of a sample of ninety-seven widely varied cases.

(For a case study illustrating this approach with a depressed client, see P. Watzlawick and J. C. Coyne, "Depression Following Stroke: Brief Problem-Focused Family Treatment," *Family Process*, 1980, *19*, 13-18.)

Whitehead, A. "Psychological Treatment of Depression: A Review." *Behaviour Research and Therapy*, 1979, *17*, 495-509.

Antidepressant drugs have been shown to be effective for depression, and psychological therapies are showing efficacy. The author reviews numerous studies of therapeutic measures and concludes that totally behavioral methods have shown a measurable effect and this is made even larger when cognitive methods are added. However, exactly what it is that produces the effect, how long the effect lasts, and which kinds of people respond to which measures are not yet known.

Of Whitehead's many interesting points, one stands out as

particularly provocative. In reviewing the Ramsay (1977) study (digested in this section), Whitehead points out that to get over grief, forced exposure or flooding has been shown to be effective, as it is in treating phobias. He observes that in both grief and phobia there is a clear focus; accordingly, perhaps in any depression where there is a clear focus, flooding might be used.

For an excellent review devoted entirely to behavior therapy, cognitive behavior therapy, and cognitive therapy, see M. Kovacs, "The Efficacy of Cognitive and Behavior Therapies for Depression," *American Journal of Psychiatry,* 1980, *137,* 1495-1501.

Part Two

Anxiety
Disorders

In DSM-III, there are three major anxiety disorders: phobic disorders (or phobic neuroses), anxiety states (or anxiety neuroses), and posttraumatic stress disorder. An additional category, atypical anxiety disorder, is intended for people who appear to have an anxiety disorder but do not fit any of the above three disorders. We did not cover this category, because therapy literature is not devoted to catch-all categories.

Approximately 2 to 4 percent of the general population has experienced symptoms at one time or another that would be classified in one of the above ways, according to DSM-III.

Under *phobic disorders*, there are four diagnoses: agoraphobia with panic attacks, agoraphobia without panic attacks, social phobia, and simple phobia. We present therapies for the three basic phobias, eliminating the distinction about panic attacks because this distinction is seldom if ever currently made in the therapy literature.

Three disorders are listed under *anxiety states*: panic disorder, generalized anxiety disorder, and obsessive-compulsive disorder (or obsessive-compulsive neurosis). We cover therapies for the latter two disorders. Since the incidence of panic disorder is listed as apparently common, we wanted to cover it. Unfortunately, we did not find in the fairly extensive therapy literature on anxiety enough specifically devoted to panic attacks to warrant coverage. If panic is indeed common or a distinct entity removed from generalized anxiety, it may be that therapies for generalized or chronic anxiety are applicable to panic disorder. We believe the reader will find this generally true.

The symptoms of *posttraumatic stress disorder* include some of the symptoms of anxiety disorders and some symptoms of the depressive disorders. According to DSM-III, the symptoms follow "a psychologically traumatic event outside the range of usual human experience." Among such traumas are rape, assault, military combat, floods, car accidents with serious physical injury, and death camps. No information is given on incidence of this disorder. As the reader might expect, there is some therapy literature for rape but a dearth of therapies devoted specifically to any of the other traumas. Given the size restrictions of this book and our desire to give extensive coverage for a disorder, we decided to eliminate posttraumatic stress disorder. General practitioners facing patients suffering the stress that follows any of the abovementioned disasters have the following outlets for help: special resources set up to handle a special traumatic event (for example, rape clinics) and a discrete, fairly small, and perhaps easily found body of therapy literature covering particular traumas. In addition, if the response to trauma is anxiety, the reader should look at the section on generalized anxiety disorder. If the traumatized person's response is phobic, see the section on phobic disorders. And if the response is depression, consult the section on depressive disorders.

2

Phobic
Disorders

The essential feature of phobias is a persistent and irrational fear of a particular object, activity, or situation. The phobic stimulus is avoided, and the fear is recognized as excessive or unreasonable. Many people have some irrational fears, which have little effect on their lives. A phobic disorder is diagnosed when the fear or avoidance causes significant distress or interferes with functioning. Three types of phobias are discussed—agoraphobia, social phobia, and simple phobia. The reader is urged to review the different therapies in each of the sections, not only the methods covered in the phobia of concern. For example, there may be a method found only in the agoraphobia section that is well suited for someone with a social phobia. Moreover, many of the digests and additional readings involved successful treatment of two or all three types of phobias. Therefore, some of our decisions to list a therapy under a type of phobia were arbitrary. When the method was clearly designed for, or used with, a particular phobia, it was included in that section.

Agoraphobia

According to DSM-III (p. 227), the diagnostic criteria for agoraphobia are as follows:

> *A. The individual has marked fear of and thus avoids being alone or in public places from which escape might be difficult or help not available in case of sudden incapacitation, e.g., crowds, tunnels, bridges, public transportation.*
>
> *B. There is increasing constriction of normal activities until the fears or avoidance behavior dominate the individual's life.*
>
> *C. Not due to a major depressive episode, Obsessive Compulsive Disorder, Paranoid Personality Disorder, or Schizophrenia.*

The most common forms are fears of crowds, tunnels, bridges, elevators, and public transportation. When leaving home, agoraphobics often want a family member or friend to accompany them. This disorder occurs in .5 percent of the population and is more prevalent in women. Some people try to relieve their anxiety with some form of drug and may become psychologically or physiologically dependent on drugs. The most frequent age of onset is late teens or early twenties. Accompanying problems are depression, anxiety, rituals, or rumination (DSM-III).

Analyses of agoraphobia have pointed to absence of security and distance from familiar surroundings without a sup-

portive figure as being more important than the fear of open spaces or walking outside. In a recent analysis of agoraphobia, an overriding importance of the significant other was found (A. Sinnott, B. Jones, and A. Scott-Fordham, "Agoraphobia: A Situational Analysis," Journal of Clinical Psychology, *1981, 37, 123-127). Agoraphobics attempt to secure the anxiety-reducing presence of significant others, who should receive counseling as part of treatment. In a similar vein, a lengthy follow-up of agoraphobics revealed a very high frequency of difficulties and abnormalities in their husbands (R. J. Hafner, "The Husbands of Agoraphobic Women and Their Influence on Treatment Outcome,"* British Journal of Psychiatry, *1977, 131, 289-294). This study supported the view that a proportion of women would not be successfully treated unless their husbands' tendencies toward denial of difficulties were treated.*

    A useful analysis of treatment problems is provided by A. J. Goldstein and D. L. Chambless, "A Reanalysis of Agoraphobia," Behavior Therapy, *1978, 9, 47-59. People whose symptoms are caused by panic attacks produced by drug experiences or physical disorders such as hypoglycemia can be classified as simple agoraphobia, and recovery is rapid. Most cases fall into the category of complex agoraphobia. There is a fear of fear, low self-sufficiency, a misunderstanding of causes of discomfort (anxiety following interpersonal problems is interpreted as fear of being alone on the street), and interpersonal conflict. These people are almost always nonassertive and very fearful and see themselves as incapable of independent functioning. Social anxiety and fear of responsibility are characteristic and should be addressed in treatment.*

Group Psychotherapy for Phobias

AUTHOR: Hassan A. Al Salih

PRECIS: Psychodynamically oriented group treatment of agoraphobic women for nine months

INTRODUCTION: An important first step is to help people with phobias realize that there are others with similar problems. In addition, many phobics have been dependent on one significant person. In individual therapy there is a shift to becoming dependent on the therapist, which interferes with recovery. Therefore, group therapy appears appropriate even though phobics have reportedly not done well in group treatment. Few therapy groups have consisted only of phobic patients, and advantages and disadvantages will be discussed.

METHOD: Patients with a phobic neurosis were seen once for individual therapy and informed of the possibility of being included in a group. Typical reactions were concerns about being accepted by others, being harmed by the experience, and catching others' symptoms. Of twelve candidates, six actually joined the group. They had individual therapy for an average of eight one-hour sessions. The group then met for nine months in weekly one-and-a-half-hour sessions. For the first five months, each person also received weekly one-hour individual sessions. Thereafter, individual meetings were discontinued.

Historical details are given for each woman in the group. Only brief descriptions are presented here. (1) A thirty-year-old housewife had fears of going out and driving alone. If accompanied by her mother, she could be in a crowd or shop in stores. During thirteen years of marriage, there had been several separations. Her husband drank heavily and objected to his wife's being in treatment. In the group, she was the most talkative and depended on group support. (2) A thirty-two-year-old housewife feared driving and being in crowded places. She had an ongoing relationship with an older man who refused to marry her. During group meetings she frequently complained about various things. (3) A thirty-six-year-old housewife was afraid of staying home, going out, strangers, and other things. However, she was active in social organizations and church. In the groups, she was detached but participated well in intellectual conversations. (4) A thirty-four-year-old black housewife had agoraphobia and anxiety attacks. During a seventeen-year marriage she had left her husband to live with a man for two years but then returned. During group sessions she was relatively quiet but did participate. (5) An eighteen-year-old single woman had acute agoraphobia and claustrophobia. She lived with her mother, who constantly argued with her. She engaged in promiscuous sexual activities. In the group, she was very tense and anxious. (6) A twice-married twenty-six-year-old woman had agoraphobia and claustrophobia. Her second husband had moved in with her siblings and mother. During group meetings, she was anxious, listened attentively, and made only brief comments.

There were three group phases. In Phase I, people introduced themselves and described their symptoms at length. Some exaggerated their problems, and some revealed shocking information about infidelity and dishonesty. These unstructured sessions led to disorganization, and the members were dependent on the leader, who was seen as being omnipotent. All members addressed themselves to the leader. The therapist changed tactics and structured and directed the conversations. Since he knew people's backgrounds, he asked for their opinions about specific situations. During individual sessions, all the members thought the others were faking and exaggerating. In Phase II, people began to feel closer (with resulting anxiety) after six sessions. Intimate sexual fantasies and aggressive (even murderous) feelings were discussed. (When one member said she was cured and wanted to quit, the group pointed out that she lacked insight and still had other symptoms. She continued and embarrassedly revealed that she had romantic thoughts about the therapist.) Group members sought to please the leader and overcome their phobias. Shortly thereafter almost all members overcame their phobias. In Phase III, evaluation and discussion of problems and group cohesiveness all improved. The leader was not seen as omnipotent, and members expressed their own points of view. Relationships with friends and acquaintances increased, and dependency on group members decreased.

Phobic people seen for group therapy require good rapport with the therapist. After individual therapy for about three months, combined individual and group therapy enhanced rapport. The individual sessions provided the opportunity for discussing anxiety caused by the group meetings. Dependence on the leader was accepted, and people were encouraged to remain in the group. As fear of criticism decreased, group support increased. In keeping with the dynamics of phobias, sexual and aggressive feelings were discussed. Since the husbands were either heavy alcohol consumers or work addicts, sexual frustration and repressed anger were main concerns. Adding new members to the group did not succeed. New members felt like outsiders and perceived pressure to prematurely eliminate their symptoms.

Group therapy is more effective than individual therapy when treating phobias. Competition for the leader's attention is used to help phobics give up symptoms and become better adjusted. Members help one another through depression and difficult situations. The group helps people try out and develop better social behavior, and there is a clear goal for change. Changes are encouraged and praised, and more social responsibility is promoted. Group identity reduces overdependency on families.

COMMENTARY: Al Salih makes the point that group therapy offers phobics advantages that are not possible in individual therapy. Most impressive is the reasoning related to dependency on maladaptive relationships with spouses. Group support and relationships with others dilute an intense marital interaction. If dependence on an individual therapist is not encouraged, shorter time for treatment may result. Other therapists would likely call for a direct confrontation of marital problems. Either marital therapy or a group for couples would serve the purpose of reducing destructive interactions and increasing positive, more adaptive interpersonal behavior. Recently, behavioral approaches to agoraphobia and other phobias have proliferated. This article represents a psychodynamic approach, in which people discuss their sexual, aggressive, and dependency conflicts.

Group approaches have become much more popular recently because of the demonstrated effectiveness of group pressure for change.

SOURCE: Al Salih, H. A. "Phobics in Group Psychotherapy." *International Journal of Group Psychotherapy,* 1969, *19,* 28-34.

Group Therapy for Agoraphobic Women and Their Husbands

AUTHORS: David H. Barlow, Matig Mavissakalian, and Linda R. Hay

PRECIS: Exposure and cognitive restructuring for six women and the effect on marital satisfaction

INTRODUCTION: Men and women have an equal incidence of simple phobias, but 75 percent of agoraphobics are women. Fear of separation, dependency, and lack of coping skills often keep women locked into difficult marriages. Agoraphobia may serve to lessen the desire to escape and to become more independent, thus making treatment more difficult. Behavioral exposure treatments have cured phobias, but marital problems have frequently been noted in agoraphobia. Spouses have often interfered with treatment, and marital therapy was necessary. The high failure rate with phobics may well be due to interpersonal problems. One follow-up study of agoraphobics found that those with the worst marriages had the most recurrence of symptoms. Husbands of agoraphobics have felt worse when their wives improve and better when their wives relapse.

METHOD: Weekly group therapy sessions were held for two groups of four couples. One group met for ten sessions and the other for thirteen. Data are presented for only six couples because one husband refused to attend and another attended infrequently. The method consisted of cognitive restructuring, covert rehearsal of ways to cope with anxiety, and gradual real-life exposure between sessions. Each client had been helped to list a hierarchy of ten situations that were avoided or caused great difficulty. During the first few sessions, the nature of agoraphobia was explained. Treatment strategies were outlined, including the husband's role in treatment and the danger of encouraging the wife's dependency. Each woman practiced at least one fearful situation for a minimum of three times a week. The husband accompanied his wife at least once but not more than twice each week for the practice sessions. He encouraged adequate exposure to the feared situation and suggested the cognitive coping strategies that had been taught. During the later weekly sessions, progress was reviewed and problems were discussed. The need for adequate exposure and appropriate self-talk strategies was reviewed. When clients did not do an assignment, the problems were discussed and they were encouraged to confront that situation before the next meeting. Occasionally, spouses disagreed on strategies, but marital problems were not discussed.

Before each session, the Marital Happiness Scale was completed independently by each couple. This measures current happiness, with different dimensions such as household responsibilities, social activities, communication, and independence. Each dimension is rated from 1 (completely unhappy) to 10 (completely happy). Additionally, each item on the fear hierarchy was rated from 0 to 8 regarding the degree of anxiety and avoidance. Clients and their husbands completed this rating independently. Clients also completed a diary about fearful situations entered. This was confirmed by checking the husband's ratings.

IMPROVED PHOBIA AND HIGHER MARITAL SATISFACTION: Client number 1 was thirty years old, married eleven years, with one six-year-old child. Shortly after marriage, she panicked while eating in a restaurant. Very soon, she had great difficulty in eating in front of people and leaving home alone. Her husband was quiet, pleasant, and understanding of her problems. Both client and husband reported gradual improvement on phobia and marital satisfaction. Improvement continued as reflected by a six-month follow-up. A sixteen-month follow-up showed a slight worsening of the phobia and marital satisfaction.

Client number 2 was forty-four years old and had two children. She could travel for only a mile unaccompanied, had had moderate agoraphobia for sixteen years, and took tranquilizers. Her husband was understanding, helpful, and quite supportive. Marital satisfaction was relatively high before treatment and improved, as did the phobia.

Client number 3 was thirty years old and had several children. For six years, she had had severe agoraphobia and could only travel two miles with her husband and walk one block from home alone. She took excessive amounts of tranquilizers to cope with her general anxiety. Her husband was sympathetic, and both thought that their marriage was a good one. Phobia and marital satisfaction both improved, but several fluctuations are depicted in graphs.

A thirty-six-year-old, obese woman, married seventeen years with two children, was client number 4. Shortly after getting married, she could not walk unaccompanied more than one block from home. Her husband was intelligent, energetic, and interested. Occasionally, he was critical and impatient with his wife's problems. This couple's ups and downs in their personal lives were directly reflected in ups and downs in both their marital satisfaction ratings and the phobia.

IMPROVED PHOBIA AND LOWER MARITAL SATISFACTION: Client number 5 was forty-two years old with five children and married for twenty-three years. Four years before treatment she had become dizzy and anxious on a sightseeing tour and calmed down on returning to her hotel. Since then she had avoided mainly social situations (more like a social phobia). Her husband was quiet and occasionally supportive. Steady improvement in her phobia was accompanied by a steady decrease in her husband's marital satisfaction. She was very pleased with her greater mobility and independence.

Client number 6 was sixty-two years old, had been agoraphobic for twenty years, and could not walk without assistance owing to a physical handicap. She could not travel by car for more than one mile. Although interested, her husband was annoyed and impatient with her fear. Improved phobia was accompanied by less marital satisfaction reported by both.

Another study is mentioned in which marital satisfaction improved with successful exposure therapy with twelve anxious couples. In a different study, husbands were thought to sabotage treatment efforts, but they were not included in treatment, as were the husbands in the present study. In the two couples with the inverse relationship, the husbands rated their wives' phobias considerably lower than the wives' own ratings. This lack of empathy may contribute to the inverse pattern. There is a discussion of the significance of fluctuations and differences in the ratings of each couple.

COMMENTARY: The methods used (cognitive restructuring, rehearsal of anxiety coping strategies, and exposure to the real feared situation) have been frequently used and are described in detail in other digests in this book. The fears of all the women decreased. An invaluable contribution is the pinpointing and refining of the role of the husband in agoraphobia. His attitude and participation are significant in the course of treatment. Marital satisfaction of both partners may well be influenced in some direction as the phobia diminishes. We believe that the findings of this study make it imperative to provide some form of adequate evaluation of marital satisfaction of both client and spouse. Any sign of marital dissatisfaction should lead to an immediate practical intervention. This might take the form of brief, focused marital therapy or counseling or group sessions focused on marital problems.

SOURCE: Barlow, D. H., Mavissakalian, M., and Hay, L. R. "Couples Treatment of Agoraphobia: Changes in Marital Satisfaction." *Behaviour Research and Therapy*, 1981, *19*, 245-255.

Cognitive Modification Versus
Prolonged Exposure for Agoraphobia

AUTHORS: Paul M. G. Emmelkamp, Antoinette C. M. Kuipers, and Johan B. Eggeraat

PRECIS: Real-life exposure to feared situations as a superior treatment to cognitive restructuring for twenty adults

INTRODUCTION: Exposure to the feared situation is a direct way of dealing with avoidance. Shaping, self-observation, flooding, and prolonged exposure to the fearful situation have been used. "Cognitive restructuring" is based on the belief that anxiety stems from erroneous interpretations of situations. Emotional reactions and avoidance may be changed by changing the cognitive label given to situations. Productive self-statements are substituted for the anxiety-producing labels. Small-animal phobias, test anxiety, public speaking anxiety, and lack of assertiveness of students have been successfully treated with cognitive restructuring. However, controlled studies with patients were not done.

METHOD: Of twenty-four clients, ages twenty-three to sixty years, twenty completed treatment. Two groups had cognitive restructuring and two groups had prolonged exposure. An intermediate test measured the effect, and then each group was given the other treatment and a posttest. Since the effects of individual or group exposure have been equivalent, only group treatment was used. Treatment consisted of five two-hour group sessions within two weeks. Two therapists led each group. Assessment included interviews by a clinical psychologist before and after treatment and measurements pre, intermediate, post, and follow-up. Measures included length of time walking alone from the hospital to town and back, observer rating of anxious mood, and client-completed questionnaires (Fear Survey Schedule, Internal-External Control Scale, Self-Rating Depression Scale, Adult Self-Expression Scale). Using a 9-point scale for phobic anxiety and avoidance, the client and an independent observer rated behavior on a busy street and bus, in a supermarket and restaurant, and walking from the hospital.

COGNITIVE RESTRUCTURING:

1. *Relabeling.* The nature of phobias was explained, and neutral examples as well as client examples were discussed. Situations do not cause anxiety, but maladaptive thoughts do. After the first session, clients were given a rationale of the treatment to study. They were to complete homework sheets every time they became anxious. They had to describe the situation, their anxiety level, irrational thoughts, rational thoughts, and subsequent anxiety level. This homework was to help clients see their anxiety-producing self-statements. By relabeling situations, one reduces anxiety.

2. *Irrational beliefs.* Starting with the second session, two irrational ideas were discussed during each of the four sessions. The eight irrational beliefs were selected from Ellis's theory as being relevant to agoraphobia. The client studied Young's Rational Counseling Primer, which explains Ellis's theory simply. Clients discussed their beliefs that were related to the irrational ideas being discussed.

3. *Self-instructional training.* Clients were taught to make positive self-statements. Beginning with the second session, clients practiced productive statements about preparing, confronting, coping, and reinforcing. They used their imagination to rehearse what to say to themselves to overcome anxiety. The clients vividly imagined what the therapist said, assessed how anxious they were, became aware of their negative self-statements, and then substituted productive statements. Situations rehearsed included walking, traveling, and being in crowded stores.

PROLONGED EXPOSURE: Clients discussed their phobias at the beginning of the first session, and the therapists reviewed the purpose of exposing themselves to fearful situations. Avoidance behavior was explained, and clients were told they would remain in the feared situation until their anxiety lessened. Clients and therapists then walked to town together. Back at the hospital, a brief meeting was held to discuss their ninety minutes of exposure. Each subsequent session followed the same format—fifteen-minute group discussion of the day's program, ninety-minute exposure, and fifteen-minute discussion of the experience. At first two or three clients accompanied each other, but they gradually went on their own. Assigned situations depended on individual fears. Feared situations typically were walking on busy streets, shopping in crowded stores, and riding on buses. The therapists gradually withdrew from the exposure situations and did not accompany the clients during the later sessions.

Detailed tables of results are presented. The main conclusion is that prolonged exposure was clearly superior to cognitive restructuring, as assessed by both the behavior measure and the phobic anxiety and avoidance scales. Neither method improved assertiveness. Cognitive restructuring led to only slight improvement. Other studies reporting success with restructuring have mainly used college students. It is possible that intelligent students are more likely to respond to rational thinking than actual clients will be. Further, cognitive restructuring might work better with low physiological reactors, such as students, and less well with highly aroused clients. The clients found it difficult to use productive self-statements in the feared situations even though they could do so in imagination. During exposure, clients become aware that anxiety lessens and fainting or heart attacks do not occur. Therefore, they may think that nothing bad will happen to them. Several clients reported that their thinking changed more during exposure than during cognitive restructuring. A type of cognitive restructuring may be occurring spontaneously.

COMMENTARY: In conjunction with earlier studies, the authors conclude that group exposure to real feared situations is the most effective treatment for agoraphobia. The use of cognitive restructuring with clinical phobias is seen as inappropriate unless combined with exposure. The procedure described is clear, brief, economical, and effective. Dependency on the therapist is clearly discouraged by the increasingly independent role

of the clients in facing their phobias without the therapists or
other clients. When a group is not available, the same form of
treatment is clearly usable in individual therapy. The therapist
may accompany the client at first or use a family member,
friend, or assistant to accompany the client at the beginning of
treatment.

SOURCE: Emmelkamp, P. M. G., Kuipers, A. C. M., and Eggeraat, J. B. "Cognitive Modification Versus Prolonged Exposure In Vivo: A Comparison With Agoraphobics as Subjects."
Behaviour Research and Therapy, 1978, *16*, 33-41.

===

Multifaceted Treatment of Agoraphobia

AUTHOR: Alan J. Goldstein

PRECIS: Paradoxical intention, muscle relaxation, dealing with
situations, and making connections between interpersonal events
and anxiety reactions with a thirty-two-year-old woman

INTRODUCTION: For nine years, a woman with two children
could not leave home without being very anxious. Treatment by
several psychiatrists had not helped. She could travel with her
husband in relative comfort. Her first anxiety attack was an intense desire to leave work. At that time, she was engaged and
had a conflict because her fiancé was Protestant and she was
Catholic. Her family was against her marrying outside her religion, and there were arguments about the religion of their off-
spring. Other panic attacks occurred at the office and when she
was alone in her apartment. Being alone made her uncomfortable. When the present treatment began, her anxiety attacks followed a pattern. She thought of going somewhere, her chest felt
tight periodically, and she felt better when she reached her destination. Suddenly, a panicky feeling led to heart pounding, a

feeling of extreme vulnerability, and an intense desire to return home. If she could not get home, she thought she would become crazy and have to go to a mental hospital. This history is relatively typical of agoraphobia. She could travel with her husband but not alone and was more uncomfortable going to rather than from someplace. Very typical was the beginning of agoraphobia, when a person feels trapped and under stress.

METHOD: The client's parents had separated when she was fourteen, and she lived with her brother and mother. She had many fears, especially of the dark. There were frequent moves, and she felt excluded and friendless. In high school she was afraid of closed places, thinking that she would faint, and feared having an appendicitis attack. Other childhood experiences were unremarkable. At age eighteen she began a relationship with a man, and she had an abortion four years later. She saw a psychiatrist because of guilt feelings and nightmares and became very anxious whenever she thought about abortions.

During the third therapy session, many marital problems were discussed. She was unable to express herself to her domineering husband, who worked long hours and was rarely home. When she tried to discuss family problems with him, he would get angry, and she would feel guilty for bothering him. Assertiveness training was begun and continued throughout therapy. Scenes were role-played in order to enhance her self-expression. She was worried that being more assertive could result in her husband's leaving her but was told that their relationship would probably improve if she expressed herself accurately. Rather than desensitization to anxiety, she was taught to handle anxiety better. If desensitized to specific fearful places, she could still become anxious for other reasons and become upset and fearful because of this anxiety. Fearful people should be able to tolerate anxiety and not have to feel a loss of control.

The first method of dealing with anxiety was a form of paradoxical intention, in which she practiced increasing symptom intensity. She was to make a tightness in her chest more intense and try to faint when she felt dizzy. Any anxiety symptoms were to be exaggerated, since fighting symptoms tends to magnify them. Anxiety attacks should be allowed to occur, and the physical reaction would be brief. Each exposure to anxiety would result in her feeling more able to handle situations. The second method used was relaxation (used during the fourth through eighth sessions). Relaxing various body parts was taught, and she practiced daily at home. After an anxiety attack she was told to relax for a few minutes. Several increasingly longer trips were successfully completed during the fourth through seventh sessions. Tension headaches diminished with continued use of relaxation.

The eighth session consisted of a detailed discussion of a panic attack that occurred while the client was coming for the appointment. She mistakenly believed that the panic was due to driving (which she had successfully done previously). She felt better when she realized that she was upset about the announced pregnancy of the friend who accompanied her. She felt guilty about asking her for help and not being able to help her in return. Becoming aware of causes of anxiety and expressing her feelings were stressed. Expressing herself to her husband had more and more led to a better relationship. Rather than holding back her disappointment in his lack of attention toward her, she let him know how she felt and what she wanted from him. This included becoming aware of and telling him about several things that concerned her about his behavior. Instead of ignoring his complaints, she was told to discuss them with him. During another session, desensitization took place regarding a feared plane trip. She relaxed and was able to imagine the trip with no anxiety.

COMMENTARY: Goldstein believes that the necessary ingredients for the patient's improvement were tolerance of some anxiety, being able to reverse anxiety, learning the interpersonal causes of fear, and learning to express herself. In keeping with the many instances of combinations of methods, he used paradoxical intention and muscle relaxation to reduce anxiety. It is very striking that "insight" into the interpersonal cause of panic reactions played an integral role in the successful treatment outcome. This multiple, eclectic approach has become more and more popular. Many criticisms have been made about endless unsuccessful insight-oriented therapy for agoraphobia or temporary alleviation of symptoms with strict behavioral approaches. We would speculate that people feel better when they understand their problem and have a method to use when panic occurs. The nature of the understanding may vary, depending on the theoretical model used by the therapist.

SOURCE: Goldstein, A. J. "Case Conference: The Treatment of a Case of Agoraphobia by a Multifaceted Treatment Program." *Journal of Behavior Therapy and Experimental Psychiatry,* 1978, *9,* 45-51.

Exposing Groups of Agoraphobics to Feared Situations

AUTHORS: I. Hand, Y. Lamontagne, and I. M. Marks

PRECIS: Twenty-five adults treated by flooding in structured or unstructured groups for twelve hours over three days

INTRODUCTION: Flooding (rapid exposure to real feared situations) has been successfully used for phobic and obsessive-compulsive disorders. Group exposure has several advantages over individual treatment aside from being more efficient and economical. Anxiety reduction and cooperation may be enhanced by the social cohesion and reinforcement of a group. Real-life examples (modeling) of coping take place in a group. The present study is designed to assess the possibility that modeling of panic may hinder progress. Two groups are also compared as to the effect of different degrees of social cohesiveness.

METHOD: Nine men and sixteen women with chronic moderate to severe agoraphobia (fear of travel) were treated in structured or unstructured groups. Each group had four of five members and met for three sessions during one week. Four hours of exposure took place during each session. Every forty-five minutes there was a fifteen-minute period for completing ratings and discussion (group or with a therapist). There was a half-hour lunch break after two hours. Pre and post self-administered and observer rating scales were used, and a follow-up assessment was completed.

Structured Groups. Before and after each group session, the group met with the therapist for a half-hour discussion of their phobias. During each four-hour session, a fifteen-minute group discussion was held regarding actual problems after every forty-five minutes of exposure. During discussions, the therapist gave a simple explanation of treatment and said that working together as a group was essential. Treatment steps should be discussed with the group, and progress should occur no faster than the slowest person could go. The therapist rarely intervened in the group process and minimized contacts with patients. Group interaction was encouraged, and alternative group action was suggested at times by the two therapists, who always tried to act together. The group met on follow-up days to discuss exercises and achievements and to suggest further individual (not pair or group) exercises.

Unstructured Groups. The same rationale as above was used, but all discussions were individual. Members met briefly before going into the feared situation and were told not to discuss any problems with each other. Problems were discussed individually with the therapist before, during, and at the end of a session. Achievements and exercises were discussed on follow-up days but individually, not in a group.

Treatment Rationale. Members were told that avoidance maintains a phobia, and so they should remain in a fearful situation until their anxiety (no matter how intense) spontaneously lowered. Rather than mentally or physically avoiding anything, they focused on their thoughts and bodily sensations. Lessening anxiety was the signal to move to the next fearful situation. Intense anxiety was brief and tolerable. The therapist explained that phobias should be treated regardless of their cause. Therapists should be thought of as "trainers" who teach exercises, not as expert "doctors." Exposure exercises were practiced daily for an hour for weeks or months until they were not fearful. Anxiety attacks were to be expected but would be less frequent as more exercises were done.

Detailed results are presented. Group exposure was very successful, and group cohesion made treatment easier for the therapists and produced better long-term results. Treatment outcome was as good for all groups as similar treatment carried out previously on an individual basis. The structured groups did show more social cohesiveness than the unstructured groups. Cohesiveness was produced by the task-oriented group discussions. The better follow-up results in the structured group were most likely due to more motivation to do the posttreatment exercises. Prolonged and intense exposure to the real-life feared situation is the key ingredient for change. Members are urged to stay in the most fearful situation until anxiety lessens for at least ten minutes. Reducing phobic avoidance and anxiety in a hospital is not sufficient. In order for enduring improvement to occur, people have to deal with phobias in the natural setting. Most members had to work hard to tolerate much anxiety until fearful responses lessened. Two persons listened to the treatment rationale and then learned to tolerate fearful situations on their own. Free-floating anxiety is dealt with similarly to the phobia. Anxiety is accepted, is observed, and then subsides.

Humor was very helpful in difficult moments. Often a member eased the tension with a joke or humorous remark. An added feature of group exposure is the learning of better social skills and assertiveness. Several examples are given in which members learned to deal better with others during the exposure periods.

COMMENTARY: Clear support is given for treating agoraphobics in cohesive groups. Cohesiveness made treatment easier to conduct and yielded better longer-term results. Another very important feature is the clear gains in social and assertive skills as a result of the group experience. For therapists who see an agoraphobic client individually, exposure may still be the treatment of choice. Feelings of being part of a group may be instilled to some extent by discussion of experiences of other clients who have been "in the same boat" and overcame their fears. The authors caution that interpersonal and marital problems are important to assess and treatment of these difficulties may be necessary. About 60 percent of the patients in this study reported having interpersonal problems, and two thirds of the twenty-one married patients reported that their marriages were unsatisfactory. Seven patients reported increased marital problems after treatment. This finding is in keeping with other reports of agoraphobics' often having problems in relating to others. Exposure and social skills training may be an effective treatment.

SOURCE: Hand, I., Lamontagne, Y., and Marks, I. M. "Group Exposure (Flooding) In Vivo for Agoraphobics." *British Journal of Psychiatry,* 1974, *124,* 588-602.

Treating Agoraphobia at Home

AUTHORS: Leila Jannoun, Mary Munby, Jose Catalan, and Michael Gelder

PRECIS: Programmed practice for reducing anxiety by resolving problems in twenty-eight women

INTRODUCTION: Systematic practice in entering feared situations has been effective in treating agoraphobia. Without contact with a therapist, many patients cease to enter the feared places. Group pressure and positive reinforcement from a family member have been used to motivate patients to continue practicing fearful encounters. Home-based practice reinforced by a spouse was quicker and longer-lasting than treatment at a clinic. The present study is a better-controlled extension of that method and includes a comparison treatment using problem solving to reduce general anxiety.

METHOD: Each of two therapists treated seven patients using programmed practice and seven using problem solving. The therapist spent about three and a half hours with each patient. Sessions were scheduled twice during the first week, once for the next three weeks. The first session was about one and a half hours and the rest about one-half hour. Patient and partner were always seen together, and follow-up visits were made two and six weeks after treatment. The twenty-eight women met the criteria of a main complaint of fear of leaving home and being in public places, no other severe symptoms, a spouse or close friend willing to help ("partner"), and a severity of 4 or more on a 0 to 8 scale. Most patients were taking anxiety-reducing medication and were told that, if necessary, they could take small amounts of the drug before leaving home. All patients were told that this was a "self-help" method. All treatment took place in their homes, and the partner was involved in treatment planning and reinforcing practice.

Both treatment groups received the same "nonspecific treatment components." Each patient read a booklet explaining the causes of agoraphobia and how to cope with it. A graded approach was used in which a hierarchy of fears or problems was constructed for each person. Early success was promoted by having patients deal with situations in ascending order of difficulty. Detailed behavioral records were kept (self-monitoring), including time away from home, nature and destination of trip, and situations causing anxiety. A diary about problems was kept by the problem-solving group.

An instruction booklet describing the rationale and procedures from the earlier study was used by the programmed practice group. Agoraphobia is described as behavior that is learned and can be changed by gradual exposure to feared situations. The method of practice is described in detail, as are ways of coping with panic. Daily practice of going out for at least one hour each day is prescribed. A separate pamphlet provides instructions for the partner, specifically describing ways to reinforce the patient's progress. The booklet for the problem-solving group discusses chronic anxiety and oversensitivity to stress as causing agoraphobia. Therefore, reducing or resolving identified stress lowers anxiety and cures agoraphobia. Instructions are given for appropriately using problem solving. The issue of going out more is not discussed. For at least one hour each day, the patient and partner are to discuss stresses and problems. Instructions are given to the partner to help and reinforce the patient in problem-solving efforts. All booklets were carefully read before the first treatment session.

Assessment was done without knowledge of form of treatment. Patient, partner, and assessor rated phobic severity on a 0 to 8 scale. General anxiety, depression, marital adjustment, and partner's willingness to help were rated by the assessor on a 0 to 8 scale. During the first interview, the assessor constructed for each patient a hierarchy of twelve fearful situations. Patients estimated the anxiety provoked by each situation on a 0 to 10 scale. Each patient completed the Eysenck Personality Questionnaire, the Spielberger State Trait Anxiety Inventory A-Trait, the Fear Questionnaire, and a questionnaire evaluating the treatment.

Results of the different measures are presented in detail, with the conclusion that systematic practice in entering feared situations does reduce anxiety. Results are similar to the earlier study even though therapists spent only half the amount of time with each patient. Amount of change and continued improvement during follow-up were similar. Even though programmed practice was superior to the problem-solving method, the changes resulting from learning to solve problems were significant and comparable to results obtained through much longer behavioral methods. One therapist's problem-solving group did as well as all the patients who used practice. In addition, these patients who learned to solve problems continued to improve after treatment. This group was not instructed to go out more. Therefore, systematic exposure to feared situations is not essential in successfully treating agoraphobia. Phobic behavior can be diminished by instructing patients to enter phobic situations, which leads to a lowering of anxiety. Or patients' general anxiety may be lowered, which permits their entering phobic situations on their own.

COMMENTARY: These findings confirm past reports of the efficacy of gradual practice in entering fearful situations in reducing fears. However, the authors conclude that anxiety reduction, rather than exposure, is the essential ingredient. This lends support to the many cognitively based methods that aim to alter the person's attitude (reducing anxiety), which permits the overcoming of the phobia. The authors also point out that the results were obtained with a select group. People with other major problems, such as depression or marital problems, were screened out. The methods used may or may not be as successful with these people. Once again, we conclude that combined methods often work the best. For example, people with various phobias may be taught problem solving and required to practice entering phobic situations. The brevity of these methods makes them very suitable for therapists in individual practice. Other methods may easily be used for people with additional specific difficulties. For example, physically tense people can be taught muscle relaxation in one or two sessions. People with agitated thinking may be taught how to switch their focus to more positive ideas ("thought stoppage" method) or learn meditation or yoga. These methods would be in keeping with the authors' conclusion that anxiety reduction is a crucial goal in agoraphobia. The reader is urged to consult the fuller account of treating agoraphobia in M. G. Gelder and D. Johnston, *Agoraphobia: Nature and Treatment* (New York: Guilford, 1981).

SOURCE: Jannoun, L., Munby, M., Catalan, J., and Gelder, M. "A Home-Based Treatment Program for Agoraphobia: Replication and Controlled Evaluation." *Behavior Therapy,* 1980, *11,* 294-305.

Psychoanalytic Treatment

AUTHOR: Julian L. Stamm

PRECIS: A seven-year psychoanalysis of a thirty-eight-year-old woman who felt worthless and helpless and feared a loss of identity

INTRODUCTION: This paper demonstrates how an actual infantile trauma leads to an exaggerated narcissistic vulnerability and the symptom of agoraphobia. A thirty-eight-year-old mother of two children began psychoanalysis with a variety of symptoms, including phobias, obsessive thoughts, and conversion ractions. She was unable to leave home alone, afraid of closed places, and afraid of choking. Additionally, she was hypochondriacal, was depressed, and had severe headaches. She was a beautiful, exhibitionistic woman who constantly wanted to be told how beautiful she was. Her parents were lower-middle-class people who valued wealth and social status and did not express loving feelings toward her.

METHOD: In the analysis, the client recalled a complete lack of privacy through adolescence. Family members were frequently nude and observed each other bathing and toileting. Father frequently bathed her, and she watched him bathing. She had many masturbatory fantasies in which she was admired and raped by several men. Father and brother, both tall and effeminate, stressed her beauty, which was seen as the means for her to marry a wealthy man. She was encouraged to be friends with wealthy children. This unfavorable comparison and the frequent sexual exposure to father and brother created narcissistic insults. For her first three years, mother took care of her. A "neurotic" maid was employed when the mother had to go to work. The maid engaged in compulsive rituals, feared robberies and sexual attacks, and told her that sex was disgusting. At school, she did average work, but her main interest was flirting and being admired. At age nineteen she married a very wealthy, handsome young man. He was similar to her father in being slim, uncertain, unemotional, and withdrawn. His family made her feel beneath them, which served as another narcissistic insult.

Her husband soon left for the war. Shortly after his return, she began to have anxiety about leaving home. She became disenchanted with him and more negative about his family's criticisms of her. Her father then died of a heart attack, leaving her with guilt feelings about her many wishes for his death. Psychiatric treatment was sought when she became depressed and obsessed with jumping out of a window. She was told that her marital difficulties were making her ill, and she obtained a divorce after four years of marriage. Following this, a main source of gratification was the flattery and attention of four men who lived together. They wined, dined, and romanced her, but no sex took place. After they discontinued seeing her (another narcissistic insult), she became very lonely and depressed. When she was twenty-four years old, she panicked while on her way to work. She ran home and refused to go out unless accompanied by her mother.

She entered psychoanalysis, where her vanity, orality, need for attention, and penis envy were discussed. After two and a half years of treatment, she was less anxious and her symptoms improved, but she could not leave New York City. She married a man whom she did not really love, and she continued to feel inadequate socially and fearful of traveling. Her older child developed breathing difficulties and a fear of choking and was referred for treatment. She was told that a tense atmosphere and marital problems were causing these difficulties. Her symptoms reappeared, especially her fear of leaving the house. She could leave only when accompanied or by taking Valium, Librium, and Scotch. Hypochondriasis and extreme worry returned, and her marriage worsened.

Analysis focused on her difficult marital situation and her feeling unappreciated and outdone by her richer friends. Many events were sobbingly recalled, such as long, boring summers, constant moving due to unpaid rent, and her father's failures. Dreams related to oral wishes, deprivation, and penis envy occurred. Associations revealed her fear of sexual impulses and her inability to experience an orgasm during intercourse. Her fantasies involved being admired or being sexually attacked. Transference consisted of seductiveness, seeking attention, and complaining about the analyst's lack of praise of her. There were erotic dreams about the analyst, which were related to feelings about her father. These feelings were undone by making derogatory remarks about the analyst. Repeatedly interpreted were her orality, narcissism, penis envy, homosexual yearnings, and longing for the good mother she never had. Her marital relationship improved, and she began to enjoy sexual intercourse more. There were several indications of masculine identification, such as preferring to wear pants, preferring the company of women, admiring women more than men, and dreaming of sucking a large, juicy orange or tomato. The core of her character structure was intense feelings of deprivation, which were related to penis envy, a wish for her mother's breast, and the real childhood traumas she had experienced.

Because of her urging, her husband obtained a very good position, and he also inherited a large amount of money. Lack of symptoms resulted only after repeated working through of exhibitionism and narcissistic need for admiration. She was now able to travel anywhere. However, when she discussed her father, she still sobbed intensely. Penis envy was interpreted in various ways, such as identification with father, guilt feelings about his death, and wish to remain eternally beautiful and pursued by men. Penis envy diminished, and she stopped wearing pants and became less hypochondriacal. She was not depressed, read more, studied art, and developed more solid values.

Despite improvement, she was still vulnerable to any narcissistic insult. A slight business setback to her husband precipitated panicky thoughts about traveling. A key was her helpless feeling and inability to control the situation. This was linked to the many childhood traumas, which instilled feelings of worthlessness and helplessness in her. She could not cope with the feeling of being a nothing. Identifying with her husband, she anticipated becoming sick and helpless again. She identified with her father's castration (leg amputation) and death, which were linked to his arousing her exhibitionism as a child and thwarting her at the same time. When she could not gratify her exhibitionistic fantasies with men, she felt totally unloved, rejected, and inadequate (an overwhelming narcissistic insult). In a sense, she saw herself as a castrated little girl receiving picture postcards from her vacationing rich friends. Her fears symbolized her nothingness and loss of identity. The deep-seated sexual fixation resulted from the bathroom nudity, which excited her voyeurism and exhibitionism. Therefore, the main aim of lovemaking was to be looked at and fondled. Unsatisfied oral cravings resulted from the frequently absent, detached mother.

These early traumas led to lasting defects. She was unable to tolerate frustration and feared losing control of her impulses. Excessive early stimulation prevented the development of a sense of control. There were conflicts between ego, id, and superego as well as a conflict within her superego (between introjects of her mother and father). Her ego ideal (wealthy friends) was at odds with and defused from her superego introjects. Her unrealistic ego ideal prevented the achievement of a stable self-representation. Relief from tension and some happiness came only when her exhibitionistic fantasies were gratified. Her ego was shattered when gratification was not obtained. Agoraphobia was a symbol of her deflated narcissism. This narcissistic vulnerability was the crucial factor in her neurotic development.

She feared being unable to cope. Even when her life greatly improved, she still obtained gratification from fantasies of suffering. This masochism, which had become ego-syntonic, had to be worked through. Her identification with disrespected parents was another narcissistic insult leading to an inadequate self-concept. Her lowered sense of identity prevented her from being able to express and control impulses, evaluate reality, and maintain stable object relationships. She was therefore very vulnerable to feelings of shame and humiliation. All the childhood and adult humiliations further lowered her self-esteem, reinforced her self-defilement and feelings of helplessness, and aroused archaic anxiety, which led to a paralyzing agoraphobia.

COMMENTARY: Psychoanalytic case studies are especially difficult to digest because of the amount of detailed information presented. We hope that this digest will serve as an example of a psychoanalytic approach to phobias. Stamm clearly follows the tradition of using analytic interpretations to free the client to obtain gratification from real life rather than from neurotic goals stemming from childhood fixations. The article is a painstaking step-by-step account of the cause, development, and treatment of the woman's character structure and agoraphobia. In a more recent article (J. L. Stamm, "The Impact of the Deflated Self-Image on the Prolongation of Treatment," *American Journal of Psychotherapy*, 1981, *35*, 276-286) Stamm further comments on this woman's treatment. Her archaic self-image must be dissolved if permanent change is to be achieved. In other cases, he summarizes that the pathology stems from feelings of inadequacy due to a defective self-concept resulting from early ego developmental trauma. These ideas are in the tradition that claims that symptom reduction does not affect the core problem. Other theorists represented in this book would agree that some therapeutic approach is necessary to deal with long-standing characterological problems that accompany phobias. This article represents one method (psychoanalysis) of dealing with the personality structure of a phobic person.

SOURCE: Stamm, J. L. "Infantile Trauma, Narcissistic Injury and Agoraphobia." *Psychiatric Quarterly*, 1972, *46*, 254-272.

===

Contextual Therapy for Phobias

AUTHOR: Manuel D. Zane

PRECIS: Changes in agoraphobic behavior of three adults and changes in group therapy are carefully observed, analyzed, and used in treatment.

INTRODUCTION: Phobic behavior is the automatic occurrence
of overwhelming fear and avoidance of some common situation.
The behavior gets better and worse, and mental, physical, social,
and environmental factors are analyzed. Instead of focusing on
historical origins, phobic behavior is studied as it changes in the
natural context. Almost any body or mind function can be disturbed. Examples are body shaking, dizziness, chills, weakness,
heart pounding, chest tightness, feelings of floating, and changed
perception of events.

METHOD: Tape recordings were made of actual changes that
occurred in treatment. Patients' reactions to their own levels of
distress were obtained and recorded on a scale from 0 to 10 (almost unbearable distress). Two cases of agoraphobia follow.
    1. An agoraphobic woman remained alone in the office
with a tape recorder for three minutes. Her phobic behavior is
presented in a diagram showing sequential changes and level of
distress. There were four instances of increased distress and five
instances of diminished distress. The important factors were her
perception of things as manageable or unmanageable and her
thoughts about being with or separated from the therapist.
Thoughts of unmanageable tasks or being alone led to dramatic
increases in perceived distress.
    2. An agoraphobic man used the tape recorder while at a
large, open area where he had previously panicked. The analysis
showed three intense and rapid rises in stress when he was preoccupied with imagined unmanageable dangers. Fear diminished
twice, when the therapist tapped his arm (occasioning a feeling
of connectedness) and when the patient described his experience.
    These and other cases suggest a "phobogenic process"
that causes fear. Previous disturbing experiences cause automatic
fear reactions to situations or thoughts of situations. Anticipated
dangers raise the level of fearfulness, resulting in intense panic.
The imagined threats feel real, and the real world feels distant
and meaningless, causing a great fear. Avoiding the phobic situation becomes essential. Imagined dangers dominate, and think-

ing about reality is not possible. These imagined dangers lead to increased feelings of disorganization, which can be diminished by interrupting the frightening thoughts. Changing the patient's attention to the phobia may be accomplished by relaxation, thinking about a causal explanation, remembering a therapist's comment, or becoming involved in activities. The change of focus intensifies or impedes the phobogenic process. Fear depends on the ratio of imagined dangers (the extreme being 10) to comforting realities (the lowest distress level being 0). A 5 rating indicates an equal involvement between fearful and comforting thoughts. Contextual therapy is designed to enable the patient to focus on manageable issues and not on unmanageable, imagined fears. The therapist's presence, touch, and conversation are focused on the idea of manageability, which allows the patient to observe, think, and react realistically. People begin to understand the phobic process through guided and positive experiences in the phobic situation.

Therapists should gain experience by studying and treating phobias where they occur. This experience makes for more efficient and effective treatment in the office. In the phobic situation, the change in behavior can be identified, and the therapist's role becomes clear. How to diminish the phobic reaction is apparent to both therapist and patient.

An illustrative case of an agoraphobic woman is presented in detail. She had many fears (elevators, trains, and revolving doors, for example) and would not go farther than four blocks from her apartment. Her continuously changing phobic behavior was treated for three years in the actual feared situations. The first session centered on her fear of closing the bathroom door. She was afraid that she would be trapped and had difficulty breathing and heart palpitations. The therapist encouraged her to open and close the lock, and she gradually was able to lock herself in. This experience illustrates contextual therapy in the following ways. The therapist explains the theory and encourages the patient to manage the phobic experience and stay with it as long as possible. Gradual steps are taken by the patient while accompanied by the therapist. The patient decides which steps to take and when to leave the phobic situation and is helped to understand practical realities (such as the functioning of a lock or elevator). Phobic situations are then faced alone, and the patient is expected to discuss thoughts and feelings when changes occur. Relations between feelings and actions are explained and demonstrated to the patient. Patients receive positive or negative feedback about their performance and learn to deal with phobic feelings rather than avoiding or eliminating them.

The therapist visited her for two hours each week, and a former patient was used as a helper. Gradual steps were taken in walking and traveling by car. She recorded her successes and failures and charted her thoughts and feelings as her phobic behavior changed. The helper assisted her in boarding a bus and rode with her for six blocks. After four months, she fearfully entered an elevator with the therapist and gradually overcame this fear. A significant point was the therapist's discovering that her pulse rate was 192 when she said she was frightened, even though she looked calm. After six months, she still could not leave her neighborhood. While traveling, she could not speak. During the tenth month, she was able to travel up to ten miles from home. She and her husband leased a New York City apartment. The therapist and the helper had to sleep in the apartment with them five times until she could manage alone. An incident is described in which she felt total panic at night and saw the therapist as being unable to help her. The therapist saw this as an alteration of the usual organized and realistic perception of events. It is as if conflicting neuronal patternings caused disturbed functioning.

People with various phobias have been successfully treated with contextual group therapy. Groups meet for one and a half hours a week and review individual experiences of changes in phobic behavior. Members learn that they are not alone, that their apparently illogical experiences are understandable, and that they can learn reliable coping methods. Helpers (former patients), friends, and family members participate in the groups. Eight-week workshops for groups of ten patients have been very successful. Helpers trained in contextual therapy work with the patient for one hour a week in the phobic situation. Self-help groups have been very successful in applying contextual therapy principles without professional leadership.

COMMENTARY: Zane discusses the applicability of contextual therapy to all phobias and presents other cases of an elevator phobia in an adult and elevator and dark phobias in a girl. He clearly highlights the necessity for therapists to become aware of the *changes* that occur in phobic behavior. Recordkeeping by patients is a simple means of assuring that the therapist is aware of this information. Contrary to many therapists' exclusive use of an office, Zane calls for the therapist to accompany the phobic patient to wherever the fear takes place. He also believes that the therapist should be aware of bodily changes (pulse, palmar sweating, and muscle tension) and should note discrepancies between appearance and reported distress. The patient's attention must be directed away from imagined dangers and toward accepting and coping with the situation. Zane's method is very much in keeping with the many reports of successful combinations of specific behavioral approaches and promotion of some type of insight.

SOURCE: Zane, M. D. "Contextual Analysis and Treatment of Phobic Behavior as it Changes." *American Journal of Psychotherapy,* 1978, *32,* 338-356.

Treating Agoraphobia with Group Exposure and Imipramine

AUTHORS: Charlotte Marker Zitrin, Donald F. Klein, and Margaret G. Woerner

PRECIS: *In vivo* desensitization and imipramine used with seventy-six women resulted in significant global improvement and reduced primary phobia and spontaneous panic

INTRODUCTION: Agoraphobia has reportedly been very difficult to treat, with mediocre results when traditional psychotherapy or psychoanalysis has been used. In the last twenty years,
techniques such as systematic desensitization and flooding have
been developed. Desensitization has been superior to individual
or group psychotherapy for specific phobias but relatively less
successful with agoraphobia. Conflicting reports about the efficacy of exposure *in vivo* are reviewed. A distinction is made between gradual exposure *in vivo* and flooding (which purposely
maximizes the amount of anxiety experienced).

Imipramine has been successful in eliminating panic attacks, but considerable supportive therapy has been necessary
to change phobic patterns. Moreover, anxious expectations tend
to reinforce agoraphobia.

METHOD: Imipramine and group exposure *in vivo* are used to
treat agoraphobia. Since spontaneous panic attacks and anticipatory anxiety reinforce each other, both should be treated.
Imipramine prevents panic, and exposure reduces anticipatory
anxiety. Group exposure promotes support and sharing of fears
and goals and is economical.

Because women agoraphobics greatly outnumber men,
this study used only women, from twenty-one to forty-five
years of age. To select participants, a psychiatric interview and
two rating scales (National Institute of Mental Health Early
Clinical Drug Evaluation Unit self-rating symptom scale and the
Brief Psychiatric Rating Scale) were used. Women judged schizophrenic or severely depressed were excluded. Other assessments
included the Hamilton Anxiety Rating Scale, modified Wolpe
Life History Questionnaire, Wolpe-Lang Fear Inventory, Taylor
Manifest Anxiety Scale, Agoraphobia Inventory, and Acute
Panic Inventory. Assessments were conducted before treatment,
immediately after treatment, and six months later. Several de-
tailed tables are presented.

Imipramine was begun with 25 mg at bedtime and increased by 25 mg every second day until 150 mg was taken.
Higher dosages (up to 300 mg/day) were taken if panic attacks
did not diminish. Dosages were decreased if undesirable side ef-

fects resulted. A pilot study had shown that initial drug side effects interfered with treatment. In addition, before group exposure was to begin, medication could be used to prevent panic attacks.

In this study, seven to ten patients were assigned to imipramine or placebo groups. For four weeks, weekly individual visits were conducted to administer and evaluate medication. *In vivo* exposure was begun during the fifth week by psychiatric social workers trained in behavior therapy techniques. Ten weekly sessions of three to four hours followed. A forty-five-minute discussion took place before the group went into some phobic situation. The therapist functioned as a supportive but authoritative group leader. Group members were expected to remain in the phobic situation until their anxiety diminished. Initially, patients walked alone from the hospital to a shopping center six blocks away. They went into a department store, ate lunch in a restaurant, and walked back to the hospital. During later sessions, they drove to distant shopping centers, entered crowded stores, and traveled by bus, train, and subway. Finally, they traveled alone back and forth to New York City, mingling with crowds and going into crowded stores and restaurants. Trips of this type were given as homework assignments. Imipramine or placebo was continued for twelve more weeks after the group exposure sessions were completed. Continuation of imipramine after exposure sessions serves to prevent panic attacks.

The authors note that this procedure is a form of *in vivo* desensitization (not flooding) because exposure to fearful situations is gradual. Flooding would require, for instance, going alone to New York City and being in a crowded store for at least an hour during the initial clinic visit. In the present study, anxiety was not deliberately induced, and patients controlled the degree of anxiety they were exposed to.

Detailed tables examine the results in different ways. Of the seventy-six women participating, twenty-two dropped out of treatment. Imipramine was found to help patients remain in treatment. There was significantly greater improvement among the patients taking imipramine than for the placebo group. There was more improvement at twenty-six weeks than at fourteen weeks. About 20 percent of the patients on imipramine had insomnia, jitters, irritability, and more energy. Reduction and gradual increase in dosages solved this side-effect problem.

Group exposure is an effective treatment for agoraphobia, most patients showing at least moderate improvement. Data are presented confirming that the effectiveness of imipramine is not due to its antidepressant action. Group exposure was compared with individual imaginal desensitization (used in a prior study). The conclusion is that the methods are equally effective overall and that *in vivo* group exposure is more cost-effective (a therapist can treat more patients, and treatment is shorter). However, more patients drop out of group exposure than in the individual desensitization through imagining. Both methods are quite successful when used without imipramine (which enhances effectiveness). Patients found the group to provide very valuable support, encouragement, and helpful suggestions in coping with fear.

COMMENTARY: The authors provide clear and useful data that imipramine enhances *in vivo* group exposure for treating agoraphobia. They call for the development of phobic clinics, where expertise is available for using behavioral methods and medication. When feasible, treating groups of agoraphobics is effective and morale-enhancing. Imipramine would be very useful for private practitioners in coping with patients having panic attacks. Also useful is the finding that desensitization using imagination and group exposure were equally effective. We are moving closer to having specific methods for specific patient problems. In some cases, particularly when time is a crucial factor, a flooding technique may be useful. With various methods available, a practitioner should be successful in alleviating this very incapacitating problem.

SOURCE: Zitrin, C. M., Klein, D. F., and Woerner, M. G. "Treatment of Agoraphobia with Group Exposure In Vivo and Imipramine." *Archives of General Psychiatry,* 1980, *37,* 63-72.

Additional Readings

Benjamin, S., and Kincey, J. "Evaluation of Standardized Behavioral Treatment for Agoraphobic In-Patients Administered
by Untrained Therapists." *British Journal of Psychiatry,*
1981, *138,* 423-428.

Significant reduction of fear in eight of nine adult patients was achieved by nurses and medical students who received no training or supervision. The therapists used a standardized hierarchy of twelve steps gradually exposing the patients
to fearful situations. The only guidelines were a single page of
instructions and explanations. Like other recent studies, this report shows that untrained people can successfully help even
severely phobic patients.

Blount, H. G. "The Existential Psychotherapy of Phobias." *Psychotherapy: Theory, Research, and Practice,* 1979, *16,* 282-
285.

A successful case study is presented of a fifty-four-year-
old, married agoraphobic woman. Psychotherapy with phobias
follows five stages. (1) The patient is assured of the correctness,
integrity, and limited effect of experienced anxiety. (2) The
phobia is seen as intentional. (3) If the person's being in the
world is restructured, power over the phobia is achieved. (4)
Unconscious knowledge and feelings are reclaimed. (5) Constant
attention must be paid to interpersonal processes and the suffering caused by the phobia. Failure of other approaches is due
to not recognizing that the phobic process is intentional and
comes from the person's focused awareness of vulnerability and
loss of awareness of the experience to be avoided.

Hand, I., and Lamontagne, Y. "The Exacerbation of Interpersonal Problems After Rapid Phobia Removal." *Psychotherapy: Theory, Research, and Practice,* 1976, *13,* 405-411.

After successful treatment by group exposure (flooding)
of 25 agoraphobics, an unexpectedly high number of interpersonal crises occurred. Treatment took place in six groups with
about four patients in each for twelve hours in one week. Treatment was easy to conduct and surprisingly easy for patients to

accept, and fifteen improved satisfactorily. Flooding appears to be the most economical method for agoraphobia. Each case is described in detail. Phobic behaviors have reportedly been used as weapons in interpersonal struggles. Two thirds of the twenty-one married patients reported having marital problems. Even when marital therapy was offered, patients always insisted on phobia treatment first. Treatment methods should be flexible, depending on the patients' changing needs.

Mathews, A. M., Gelder, M. G., and Johnston, D. W. *Agoraphobia: Nature and Treatment.* New York: Guilford Publications, 1981.

Major approaches to diagnosing and treating agoraphobia are reviewed. Strengths and limitations of medication, psychoanalysis, paradoxical intention, relaxation, and hypnosis are presented. A behavioral treatment is advocated in which clients are taught to overcome avoidance and deal with social factors that reinforce their symptoms. The roles of family members and significant people are modified. Clients and their families use a home-based programmed procedure. Practical and useful appendixes contain programmed practice manuals for the client and for his or her helper/partner. Summaries, checklists, and assessment materials for therapists are described in detail.

Milton, F., and Hafner, J. "The Outcome of Behavior Therapy for Agoraphobia in Relation to Marital Adjustment." *Archives of General Psychiatry,* 1979, *36,* 807-811.

A six-month follow-up was done with eighteen agoraphobics (sixteen women and two men) who were treated by thirteen and a half hours of exposure to real fearful situations. Those patients with unsatisfactory marriages improved less during treatment and relapsed more. Their progress during treatment appeared very dependent on the therapist's support and encouragement. Patients with satisfactory marriages showed significant further improvement. Symptom improvement in nine patients had negative effects on their marriages. Relapse was associated with two types of marriage. (1) "Compulsory" marriage is the most frequent pattern. Fear of divorce leads to agoraphobia and dependency and to the spouse feeling compelled to support and help the patient. Or a patient would leave the spouse if the agoraphobia was cured; the spouse then panics because the compulsory aspect is diminished. (2) Improvement in agoraphobia reveals the spouse's problems or inadequacies. Symptomatic improvement affects the homeostasis of a family. Finally, eight of the patients showed substantial improvement, and six of them reported that their marriages became more harmonious.

Ross, J. "The Use of Former Phobics in the Treatment of Phobias." *American Journal of Psychiatry,* 1980, *137,* 715-717.

An effective, low-cost approach to phobias is the use of former phobics as aides. The aides guide phobics in the fearful situation and teach them fear-reducing techniques while they are anxious. Methods used include taking one step at a time, making physical contact with a person or object, identifying causes of change in anxiety, delaying panic, substituting positive thoughts for negative ones, doing simple and manageable tasks, and using paradoxical intention. Patients are inspired by former phobics, who are very empathic with their fears. Two cases of agoraphobia are described. Specific methods for panic included counting backward, counting forward (also by threes), counting windows, reciting words to a poem or song, and talking to someone.

Sinnott, A., Jones, R. B., Scott-Fordham, A., and Woodward, R. "Augmentation of In Vivo Exposure Treatment for Agoraphobia by the Formation of Neighborhood Self-Help Groups." *Behaviour Research and Therapy,* 1981, *19,* 339-347.

Eight adult agoraphobics were successfully treated by eleven weekly sessions of exposure to their fears (travel). Discussions for twenty minutes before and after each session were held to promote group cohesiveness. These patients (in contrast to seven others) all lived within a one-mile radius (zoned group). Homework assignments included their meeting each other at "target destinations." The zoned group showed more anxiety reduction than the unzoned group. Their exposure was probably more effective because they encouraged one another. They appeared more cohesive and had superior gains in social range

(number and types of social contacts). The zoned group participated in joint ventures and social activity. Increased mobility of
the unzoned group did not lead to increased social range. For
agoraphobics with social phobias, a program of social exposure
in a zoned group is recommended.

Solyom, L., Heseltine, G. F. D., McClure, D. J., Ledwidge, B.,
   and Kenny, F. "A Comparative Study of Aversion Relief and
   Systematic Desensitization in the Treatment of Phobias."
   British Journal of Psychiatry, 1971, *119,* 299-303.
      In order to avoid some difficulties in the use of system-
atic desensitization, reciprocal inhibition of anxiety by aversion
relief was developed. Ten adult agoraphobics were treated with
each method. Aversion relief was the cessation of finger electrical shock at appropriate times during a tape recording of anxiety-provoking stimuli and responses made by the patients. The
100 percent reinforcement schedule was gradually reduced to
20 percent. Both treatments resulted in a significant reduction
in phobia intensity after twelve hours of treatment, but aversion relief was more effective on more of the assessment measures. Rather than any symptom substitution, improvement
generalized directly in keeping with the amount of decrease in
phobic intensity. Patients having obsessive, hysterical, and hypochondriacal symptoms benefited more from aversion relief,
whereas patients high on the IPAT anxiety scale and some sub-
groups of MMPI scores benefited more from desensitization.
The mildly unpleasant shock was below the pain threshold and
did not result in dropping out. Aversion relief may be very helpful when desensitization is not effective.

Social Phobia

According to DSM-III (p. 228), the diagnostic criteria for social phobia are as follows:

> *A. A persistent, irrational fear of, and compelling desire to avoid, a situation in which the individual is exposed to possible scrutiny by others and fears that he or she may act in a way that will be humiliating or embarrassing.*
>
> *B. Significant distress because of the disturbance and recognition by the individual that his or her fear is excessive or unreasonable.*
>
> *C. Not due to another mental disorder, such as Major Depression or Avoidant Personality Disorder.*

There is a great deal of confusion in the literature concerning this diagnosis. DSM-III discusses social phobia as avoidance of a specific situation, such as fear of speaking, and avoidant personality disorder as avoidance of personal relationships. However, much of the therapy literature defines social phobia as fear of social (interpersonal) situations (see digest of Öst, Jerremalm, and Johansson, 1981, for example). Therefore, we have included social anxiety, fear of speaking, and fear of performing in public in this section. DSM-III also includes fears of using public lavatories, eating in public, and writing in the presence of others under social phobia, but there is little to be found in the literature about these specific fears. We believe that the therapies covered are applicable not only to these spe-

cific fears but also to people who would be classified as avoidant personality disordered. These people are sensitive to rejection and unwilling or very reluctant to enter into a relationship or form close personal attachments. Further, DSM-III cautions that "normal" fear of public speaking or avoidance of social situations that are normally a source of distress should not be diagnosed as a social phobia. Although this diagnostic issue may be agreed on by therapists, we believe that these problems can be effectively treated with the methods covered in this section.

Situations are avoided because the person experiences marked anticipatory anxiety at the prospect of being in a feared situation. There is often a vicious cycle in which the irrational fear causes anxiety that impairs performance and therefore justifies avoidance of the phobic situation (DSM-III). Generalized anxiety, agoraphobia, or simple phobia may coexist with social phobia, which often begins in late childhood or early adolescence and is usually chronic. Social phobia (according to the DSM-III definition) is apparently relatively rare, but we believe that the range of problems that can be treated by the methods presented is relatively frequent. People with social fears are prone to using alcohol, barbiturates, and antianxiety medications in coping with their anxiety. Much of the research on fears of social situations and public speaking was done with college students and then extended to other populations. We believe that the methods used are applicable to adults in general. This is so because techniques such as desensitization, role playing, behavioral rehearsal, and cognitive therapy have been successfully used with a variety of problems in adults, who may well be less intelligent or less motivated than college students.

Systematic Desensitization and Expectancy Effects for Speech Phobia

AUTHORS: Thomas D. Borkovec and J. Krogh Sides

PRECIS: Relaxation found to be more important than expectancy in fear reduction of sixty college students

INTRODUCTION: Research on the contribution of relaxation to the process of desensitizing fear is equivocal. There is some evidence that relaxation aids in the exposure to fearful situations by enabling attention to be paid to those situations by reducing the distractions of anxiety. Relaxation leads to low arousal, which enables exposure to and increased vividness of imagining feared situations. Expectancy effects are seen when positive instructions cause people to display less fearful behavior. Expectancy effects have been absent in fears having strong physiological arousal (such as speech phobias).

METHOD: Geer's Fear Survey Schedule was administered to introductory psychology students. Of the students indicating "very much fear" or "terror" about public speaking, twenty-five males and thirty-five females agreed to participate in treatment. Pre and post three-minute speeches were videotaped and rated for anxiety (using Paul's Timed Behavioral Checklist). Each participant was pre- and posttested with the Anxiety Differential and the Autonomic Perception Questionnaire, which measures anticipatory, subjective anxiety. Instructions regarding treatment were played on audiotape, and electrodes measuring heart rate and galvanic skin response were attached. Participants were seen in groups of two or three, assigned randomly to three treatments with positive or neutral expectancy. There were two no-treatment control groups. The three methods used were (1) desensitization—relaxation followed by hierarchy exposure, (2) hierarchy exposure followed by relaxation, and (3) hierarchy exposure only.

   The general procedure follows. During the first session, the ten-minute taped treatment rationale was played. Progressive relaxation was taught for forty minutes for the two conditions involving relaxation. Pleasant imagery was practiced for five minutes, and a standard sixteen-item speech hierarchy was discussed for fifteen minutes. For those in the hierarchy exposure only, practicing seeing pleasant scenes was used instead of relaxation. Each participant determined the content of pleasant scenes to be imagined, involving his or her active participation. For forty minutes, each image was presented twice for sixty seconds with a discussion of the quality of the image. Each participant ranked the sixteen hierarchy scenes according to his or her own level of anxiety. The average rank determined that group's order of presentation. The scenes were constructed from information gathered from the pretests. Relaxation was accomplished with participant-controlled automated tapes and practiced twice a day. The hierarchy exposure group practiced imagining pleasant scenes twice a day. Positive expectancy participants completed credibility and expectancy of improvement questionnaires at the end of the first session.

During the next four sessions, participants' heart rate was recorded and samples analyzed. Relaxation training was performed lying down. Each scene was described, then visualized for ten seconds, and a sixty-second rest period occurred between scenes. The next scene was presented if no anxiety was signaled after two presentations. For those still anxious, a maximum of six brief presentations were given. If still anxious, two ten-second presentations of the previous scene were given. During the sixty-second rest, each participant rated the vividness of the image (0 to 6) and how fearful he or she was. The relaxation followed by exposure group was told to focus on the sensations of relaxing during the sixty-second rest. All others counted backward from 100 in order to prevent them from focusing on the fearful images. Each session ended when four scenes were completed.

For those in the positive expectancy condition, each session began with a statement that therapy was designed to eliminate their speech anxiety. Those in the positive expectancy no-treatment group were called and told that past research showed that those giving the posttest speech react with much less fear.

Neutral expectancy instructions were that the method used was to investigate the complex relationships between self-report and physiological and behavioral measures of anxiety.

Results are diagrammed and discussed in detail. Relaxation clearly increases the vividness of imagery and maximizes autonomic reactivity to the images. Relaxation also enhances the decrease in autonomic reactivity over repeated exposure. Those participants not receiving relaxation showed generally declining vividness. Assessment methods showed that relaxation followed by exposure led to significant reduction of fear in anticipation and in actual confrontation of the fearful situation. However, there were, surprisingly, no changes in physiological response as had been found in past research. Expectancy did have brief effects, such as greater initial subjective reactions and lower heart rates. But, as predicted, expectancy instructions had no significant effect on treatment outcome.

COMMENTARY: Here is clear evidence supporting the usefulness of relaxation procedures in treating phobias. Many therapists have not used relaxation training because of reports in the literature that relaxation was not a necessary component of fear reduction and because therapists often find the teaching of relaxation to be tedious. Positive imagery is frequently used without relaxation training. This study should signal therapists that relaxation training maximizes fear reduction. The fact that relaxation enhances the vividness of imagination is a very useful piece of information. Treatment can then be briefer and more efficient. Desensitization done individually rather than in groups can be even more flexibly administered and efficient.

SOURCE: Borkovec, T. D., and Sides, J. K. "The Contribution of Relaxation and Expectancy to Fear Reduction via Graded, Imaginal Exposure to Feared Stimuli." *Behaviour Research and Therapy*, 1979, *17*, 529-540.

Skills Training for
Socially Anxious Women

AUTHORS: A. Toy Caldwell, Karen S. Calhoun, Lewis Humphreys, and Thomas H. Cheney

PRECIS: Instructions, modeling, behavioral rehearsal, and audiotaped feedback with two female college students

INTRODUCTION: Communication skills, assertiveness, dating behavior, and social anxiety play a part in the adequacy of social skills. The vast majority of studies have focused on college males, and the present study concerns the effects of social anxiety and weak social skills in females. In most studies, self-report of social anxiety was used to select participants. The present study used self-report and a behavioral measure to select women with social discomfort and poor social skills.

METHOD: The Social Anxiety & Distress Questionnaire and the Social Relations Questionnaire were completed by 195 female undergraduates. The five lowest scorers had conversations with two male confederates. The two women with the poorest target skills (who previously said they were interested in treatment) were selected. Definitions of the three target skills (to improve conversational ability) follow. (1) Minimal Encourages to Talk. A speaker is encouraged to talk by the listener's expressing emotions similar to the speaker's, stating interest, asking questions, and reflecting some words back. (2) Open-Ended Questions. Questions are to be directly relevant to the other person's previous statement. Questions should be phrased so that a yes or no answer is not adequate. Instead, an elaboration should be necessary. (3) Parallel Experiences. Statements are made about personal experiences relevant to the other person's previous topic. Similarities or differences in experiences are appropriate to express.

Before training, three conservations (three minutes each) were held with a therapist and three with a male volunteer in order to get a baseline regarding the three skill areas. The conversations also took place after training in each skill and at the end of treatment. The volunteers had no idea of the purpose of the conversation and were told to become acquainted with the person as they would normally do. After each conversation, each woman completed a self-report (semantic differential scale) on level of social discomfort.

Fifteen sessions were held at a rate of four thirty-minute sessions per week. Minimal Encourages to Talk, Open-Ended Questions, and Parallel Experiences were taught in that order. Each session consisted of the following five steps. (1) Skills Description. A written description of the skill was given to the participants before the appropriate session. In a discussion the therapist made sure that the woman completely understood the skill and why it was important in conversations. (2) Modeling Tapes. Good and bad examples of each skill had been audiotaped (three minutes long) by a male and female volunteer. (3) Behavior Rehearsal I. A three-minute conversation between the participant and her therapist was taped. She had been told to use the skill in question as much as possible. (4) Audio Feedback. While listening to Behavior Rehearsal I, the therapist gave feedback to the client, particularly about the positive aspects of her use of the appropriate skill. (5) Behavior Rehearsal II. Another three-minute conversation was held. Therapist feedback consisted mostly of praise of the client's improved skill and general conversational ability. This conversation was taped and scored for frequency of each skill. Training of each skill ended when that skill was used for at least 45 percent of the session and remained at that level for at least two sessions.

Results are reported and were very similar for both women. The training resulted in dramatic improvement in the specific conversational skills and generalization with other people. Both women reported significant decreases in feelings of discomfort during the social interactions. Some of the skills were used less as a new skill was introduced. To some extent this was due to instructions to use the new skill as much as possible. However, after treatment all three skills were used equally.

COMMENTARY: This study supports the growing use of specific skills training for social phobia or anxiety. Skills are taught, practiced, and then used in real-life situations. Clear success is achieved when the clients report less subjective discomfort, seek social interactions more, and are more skilled in interpersonal relationships. A very helpful aspect of this study is the discussion of social anxiety and poor social skills. The authors purposely selected two women who were very socially anxious and had measurably poor skills. The authors suggest that it may not be necessary to treat anxiety directly, since people appear to become less anxious when their social skills improve. For therapists, this possibility has significant implications. Socially fearful people with poor social skills should receive skill training as a treatment of choice. This treatment may well be the most efficient and economical choice. However, as we see in many other digests, combined treatments are becoming much more widespread. Relatively brief individual or group treatment could include relaxation techniques and specific skills training.

SOURCE: Caldwell, A. T., Calhoun, K. S., Humphreys, L., and Cheney, T. H. "Treatment of Socially Anxious Women by a Skills Training Program." *Journal of Behavior Therapy and Experimental Psychiatry,* 1978, *9,* 315-320.

Cognitive Group Counseling and Skills Training for Social Anxiety

AUTHORS: Jim Gormally, Douglas Varvil-Weld, Ralph Raphael, and Gary Sipps

PRECIS: Group counseling, skills training, and a combination of both found equally effective for forty-six college men

INTRODUCTION: Socially anxious men who rarely date may be viewed in the following four ways. (1) Social anxiety may be seen as a classically conditioned response to social interaction, and treatment by systematic desensitization is appropriate. (2) Socially anxious men's thoughts cause anxiety, or they do not use adaptive coping thoughts. Cognitive behavioral counseling is used to handle setbacks such as rejection more rationally and to learn coping self-statements that reduce anxiety. (3) Poor social skills may cause anxiety. Therefore, modeling and rehearsal of appropriate behavior are used. (4) People who rarely date may, nonetheless, have the necessary social skills. Therefore, men and women have been randomly paired and instructed to go on practice dates. A review of the literature reveals that all these methods have apparently had equal success. However, desensitization alone has not led to improved social skills. The present study was designed to compare different treatments of social anxiety and also to assess the effects on a group of generally withdrawn people.

METHOD: Participants had referred themselves for counseling. Forty-six college males were selected who had long-standing social problems with females. Self-confidence, dating, daily social behavior, and handling a phone conversation were assessed by general outcome measures (Goal Attainment Scale, Survey of Heterosexual Interactions, Behavioral Log, and Phone Call Task). Specific objectives of treatment were assessed with observer ratings of a social conversation (videotaped and rated), the Irrational Beliefs Test, and the Situational Expectancies Inventory. Based on a pilot study, a treatment plan was arrived at comprising nine ninety-minute group sessions and two brief individual sessions.

All three treatment groups used the following common counseling procedures and spent the same amount of time together. The treatment rationale is carefully described in detail. A three-step hierarchy of increasingly anxiety-arousing social situations with women is constructed. Written descriptions are distributed concerning the specific use of the methods taught. The methods taught are practiced during the sessions and then at home. Techniques are used to enhance the group's cohesiveness and feelings of commonality. The leader was assisted by four trained undergraduate female peer counselors. Groups consisted of a male leader, a female peer counselor, and three to five clients. In all groups, the first two sessions were used to explain treatment, build group cohesiveness, and teach relaxation. An individual third sesson was used to obtain an anxiety hierarchy. Training in the method was begun in the fourth session; a fifth individual session concerned the use of the method with the first step in the hierarchy. The sixth through eleventh sessions consisted of practicing the method for the second and third steps. The waiting-list control group completed the pre and post assessment procedures.

COGNITIVE COUNSELING: Anxiety was explained as being due to thinking about negative consequences of interacting socially with women. Clients were to learn to identify unrealistic interpretations of rejection and use a more rational approach. This approach consists of four reevaluation steps. (1) Identify anxiety and thoughts by asking what I am telling myself that makes me feel this way. (2) Evaluate feared consequences and irrational thoughts by asking what it is that I am afraid will occur. (3) Perform rational reevaluation by asking how likely the consequences are and how I cam interpret the fear differently. (4) Make a social overture in order to prove that behaving is not dangerous or that risky. Alternative rational reevaluations (from a woman's point of view) of rejection were suggested by the peer counselor. No suggestions or behavioral feedback was given regarding appropriate social behavior.

Skills Training. Assertion training methods (behavioral rehearsal) were used. It was explained to the group that lack of knowing appropriate behavior caused social anxiety. Social skills would be learned by practice and feedback. (1) Individual goals were set. (2) Participants acted out the hierarchy step with the peer counselor and were given feedback. (3) If necessary, the leader modeled appropriate behavior. (4) Positive reinforcement was given for improved behavior. Faulty thinking was not discussed in any way.

Combined Treatment. The need for rational thinking and social skills was discussed. For each hierarchy step, one session of cognitive counseling and one session of skills training occurred.

Many participants had very little dating experience and doubted that counseling would help them, since they were so shy. Strikingly, all three methods were equally effective and resulted in significant improvement on three of the five outcome measures (attaining individual social goals, more self-confidence, and improved dating behavior). It appears that helping men to practice previously avoided behavior is more important than the type of method used. However, cognitive counseling clearly produced the most improvement of maladaptive thinking. The most withdrawn men dropped out of treatment significantly more than others. This might be due to low self-esteem and lack of confidence in facing social situations. Finally, counseling did not significantly improve telephone conversation, and specific training in this area is probably necessary.

COMMENTARY: Most striking is the equal effectiveness of the three methods in improving social interaction. The authors speculate that shy men probably find a supportive group situation reassuring and helpful. In all three methods some participants rated the group meetings as more helpful than the specific method used. This supports the idea that some form of group experience would be in order for socially fearful men. Also, we can see the importance of attempting to assess an individual's specific problem. Some people may lack social skills, some may think maladaptively, and some may have both problems. Treatment may then proceed accordingly. The use of female peer counselors seems to us to be a valuable idea regardless of the type of method used.

SOURCE: Gormally, J., Varvil-Weld, D., Raphael, R., and Sipps, G. "Treatment of Socially Anxious College Men Using Cognitive Counseling and Skills Training." *Journal of Counseling Psychology,* 1981, *28,* 147-157.

Stress Inoculation for Speech Anxiety

AUTHORS: Matt E. Jaremko, Rob Hadfield, and William E. Walker

PRECIS: Education and/or skills training for twenty-one college students fearful of public speaking

INTRODUCTION: Interpersonal, speech, and test anxiety, anger, and pain have been successfully treated with stress inoculation training. Clients learn the treatment rationale, rehearse ways of dealing with anxiety, and use these skills in coping with real or imaginary situations. Since stress inoculation has several components, this study is an attempt to clarify differential effectiveness, particularly of the educational aspect. Clients are educated about the reason for treatment effectiveness (therapy rationale). Past studies indicate that providing a rationale increases the effectiveness of treatment.

METHOD: Administration of a fear survey schedule resulted in the selection of college students who were afraid of public speaking. Pre- and posttesting was performed with the Multiple Affect Adjective Checklist, a ten-item self-rating scale, and a behavioral assessment of speech anxiety by two raters. Treatment was done in two one-hour group meetings with three to five participants.

Education Only. The first session was a lecture and discussion of anxiety according to an educational rationale model. Stress was described as a self-perpetuating cycle of physiological arousal, seeing situations as anxiety-provoking, and negative self-statements. Using a Socratic method of questioning, personal experiences and examples were obtained. Dating, test taking, and public speaking stress were covered. No methods for coping with stress were given. However, students were told that the anxious cycle could be stopped by using coping skills at the three situations of physical arousal, anxious appraisal, and negative self-statements. A review of this model and a "filler" discussion about stage fright were presented at the second session.

Skills Only. Speaking was described as causing stress that could be coped with by the following three skills, which were practiced during the first session. (1) Physical. Muscle tension is to be identified and reduced, and breathing is done diaphragmatically. Imagining oneself in a peaceful, restful state results in relaxation. (2) Reappraisal. Stress is handled as a sequence of preparation, confrontation, dealing with feeling overwhelmed, and self-reward. Each of these stages requires positive coping statements, which were discussed. Throughout a speech, participants were taught to use these positive thoughts. (3) Replace negative self-statements. Self-statements that increase anxiety and interfere with performance were identified. Participants developed positive coping statements and practiced substituting them for the negative self-statements. Skills were reviewed and a practice speech given during the second session. Each student used the following coping sequence: Relax before speaking. Engage in self-talk, using the reappraisal stages of preparation, confrontation, dealing with overwhelming feelings, and self-reward. Replace negative with positive self-statements. The participants were urged to use the coping sequence when giving a speech.

Combination. The first session consisted of the presentation of the educational rationale and the practicing of the skills. The rationale and skills were reviewed during the second session. The practice speech made in the skills-only group was then made by each participant.

No Treatment. The ten students in this control group were assessed for speech anxiety during the first, second, and final speeches given in the speech class.

The education-only group improved at least as much as the skills-only and combination groups. The implication is that understanding how stress operates plays a significant part in the stress inoculation method. This is in keeping with the literature concerning "perceived control," in which understanding of fear responses increases a person's perception of control over the fearful situation.

COMMENTARY: Psychotherapy has often been called a "reeducative" experience. This study supports the possible importance of educating people about the cause and operation of stress. Many therapists have been influenced by the success of "experiential" approaches, which purposely avoid "intellectual" discussions. At this point it is clear that combinations of methods are appropriate and often successful. It appears worthwhile to explain how stress operates (especially in a lecture or in the media) and follow up with a specific method when necessary. Stress inoculation is becoming more and more popular as a treatment and as a means of prevention of a variety of stress-related problems.

SOURCE: Jaremko, M. E., Hadfield, R., and Walker, W. E. "Contribution of an Education Phase to Stress Inoculation of Speech Anxiety." *Perceptual and Motor Skills*, 1980, *50*, 495-501.

Cognitive Therapy and Desensitization for Social Anxiety

AUTHORS: Norman J. Kanter and Marvin R. Goldfried

PRECIS: Rational restructuring, self-control desensitization, or both for sixty-eight adults

INTRODUCTION: Social anxiety is often accompanied by worry about the reactions of others. Unrealistic self-statements are made about likely negative evaluations by others. Possible rejection leads to intense emotional arousal. Therefore, a more realistic reevaluation of consequences would be helpful. This type of rational-emotive approach was more effective than desensitization for speech anxiety, when there was also more general interpersonal anxiety. However, high-anxious people may be too anxious to think clearly. Therefore, relaxation might be useful before cognitive restructuring is used.

METHOD: People responded to a newspaper announcement for a treatment program for people uncomfortable in groups or anxious, tense, or shy in social situations. Participants were fifty females and eighteen males aged twenty-two to fifty-two years. Forty percent had some prior treatment, and all saw uncomfortable interpersonal anxiety as their main problem. Pre- and posttesting was carried out with three types of measures: (1) Behavioral assessment. Each participant was videotaped while interacting with two trained confederates (one male and one female) for five minutes. Tapes were viewed and rated for fifteen observable behaviors. (2) Self-report measures. Subjective anxiety was measured by the State Anxiety Inventory and the Anxiety Differential. Social-evaluative anxiety was assessed by the Social Avoidance and Distress and the Fear of Negative Evaluation scales. Four hypothetical socially anxious situations (being at a party, being introduced to strangers, giving a speech, and being interviewed) and four nonsocial situations were rated by participants using the S-R Inventory of Anxiousness. Generalized anxiety was measured by the Trait Anxiety Inventory. Changes in beliefs were assessed with the Irrational Beliefs Test. (3) Physiological assessment. Three thirty-second pulse rates were taken.

Therapy took place in groups of eight to ten persons in one-and-a-half-hour sessions for seven weeks. A standard twelve-item hierarchy of anxiety-arousing social situations (each presented for three one-minute imagined scenes) was used in all treatments.

Self-Control Desensitization. Progressive relaxation, imagery training, and desensitization were used. Participants learned to relax when experiencing any anxiety. They recorded when they relaxed and their tension level before and after visualizing each scene. After the third presentation of a scene, participants discussed their experiences. Homework assignments included reviewing the written treatment rationale, practicing tape-recorded relaxation twice a week, and trying to relax in actual nonsocial and social situations. Each session began with a discussion of participants' written record of homework experiences.

Systematic Rational Restructuring. Participants learned to recognize the unrealistic and self-defeating aspect of anxiety-producing thoughts. Reasonable ideas are substituted for unrealistic thoughts. An example of an unrealistic thought is thinking you will say something foolish and others will think you are dumb. The more reasonable thought is "Chances are I won't say anything foolish. Even if I do, it really doesn't mean that I'm a dumb person." After imagery training, the anxiety hierarchy was used. Anxiety was used as a signal that more reasonable thoughts should be substituted for unrealistic ideas. Participants recorded these thoughts and their level of tension before and after visualization. After the third presentation of a scene, a group discussion took place. Homework consisted of reviewing the written treatment rationale and practicing rational restructuring in actual situations. Each session began with a discussion of homework experiences.

Combination. Progressive relaxation, training in rational thinking and imagery, and hierarchy presentation occurred. Tension led to relaxation, identifying any unrealistic thoughts, and substituting reasonable ideas. After each scene, participants recorded their experiences. After the third presentation of a scene, a group discussion took place. Each session began with a discussion of homework (reviewing the treatment rationale, practicing relaxation and rational reevaluation in real-life situations).

All three treatments resulted in significant decreases in anxiety that were maintained or improved at follow-up. Rational restructuring was more effective than desensitization in decreasing state and trait anxiety and irrational beliefs. In general, rational restructuring produced more improvement on more variables, and anxiety was more reduced in nonsocial situations. Past studies are reviewed in which rational restructuring was more effective than desensitization in improving interpersonal difficulties and promoting assertiveness. It appears that rational restructuring improves subjective feelings of anxiety. The degree of initial anxiety had no influence on the effectiveness of the procedures. In sum, the pre- and posttesting showed that rational restructuring and restructuring plus desensitization both significantly improved sixteen variables measured. Desensitization improved only ten of the variables.

COMMENTARY: Kanter and Goldfried speculate that rational restructuring may be superior to desensitization when clients are initially highly socially anxious. Additionally, when people are anxious in many social situations, rational restructuring may be the most effective treatment. Strikingly, many forms of treatment include some type of homework. This is a direct means of countering many clients' tendency to face their problems only in the therapist's office. All three methods used required reviewing the treatment rationale, practicing, and keeping a record for discussion. This is a concrete way of indicating that therapeutic procedures are designed to modify real behavior and are not meant as once-a-week verbal exercises. Finally, rational restructuring is a useful tool as part of a therapeutic repertoire. For example, even if psychodynamic psychotherapy is working very well in dealing with a client's social difficulties, it is likely that rational restructuring would be quite useful periodically in dealing with irrational thoughts as they arise in therapy sessions.

SOURCE: Kanter, N. J., and Goldfried, M. R. "Relative Effectiveness of Rational Restructuring and Self-Control Desensitization in the Reduction of Interpersonal Anxiety." *Behavior Therapy*, 1979, *10*, 472-490.

Fixed-Role Therapy and Rational-Emotive Therapy for Public Speaking Anxiety

AUTHORS: Thomas O. Karst and Larry D. Trexler

PRECIS: Assuming a new role and changing irrational beliefs with twenty-two college students

INTRODUCTION: George Kelly introduced fixed-role therapy, which can be considered a cognitively oriented method. All present interpretations can be revised and replaced (constructive alternativism). Rather than specific or best ways to interpret situations, different ways should be tried in order to find an effective construction. Albert Ellis introduced rational-emotive therapy, in which basic irrational ideas have to be depropagandized. A set of fairly definite rational perceptions is to be learned and used. Both methods focus on cognition, and rather than modifying specific behaviors, general strategies are changed. Clients learn to interpret situations in an alternative way.

METHOD: All of the twenty-two college students were anxious about public speaking but did not totally avoid speaking in public. Assessment measures used were the Temple University Fear Survey Scale (general anxiety), the Social Fear Scale, Paul's shortened version of Gilkenson's Personal Report of Confidence as a Speaker, and a ten-point anxiety scale completed before giving a speech. Behavioral measures were the Timed Behavioral Checklist and the Speech Disruptions Checklist. Participants were given ten minutes to prepare a four-minute speech on one of fourteen topics (how I spent last summer; describe a movie, play, or sports event; and so on). Speeches were given in front of a few other prospective participants, the therapists, and two raters.

Fixed-Role Therapy. The rationale was explained during the first session. Participants were aided in describing their public speaking roles, and alternative roles were discussed. Homework was assigned to observe others in public speaking situations. Participants were to assess the role that public speakers adopted and to guess what the underlying thoughts and feelings were in comparison with their own. This homework was discussed during the second session. Then, situations requiring assertive public speaking were described, and participants wrote what they would ordinarily think, feel, and do. A discussion followed concerning alternative roles that could decrease anxiety. A description of an alternative public speaking role was assigned. This was studied and tried out if possible. These constructions were discussed during the final session and then tried in front of the group. The role and speeches were discussed and summarized by the therapist.

Rational-Emotive Therapy. The rationale was described, and the speaking anxiety of members was discussed. Anxiety ranged from speaking to a friend to speaking in front of large audiences. Basic irrational ideas were described and a more rational approach strongly suggested. A paper describing public speaking anxiety according to rational-emotive theory (internal sentences cause anxiety) was assigned to be read as homework. Homework was discussed during the next two sessions, and irrational ideas were challenged. Members were shown how they could challenge their own irrational thoughts when speaking in public in the future. The following anxiety-creating irrational ideas were emphasized: (1) the desperate need to be approved or loved by others; (2) the perfectionistic need to achieve and be totally competent; (3) seeing failure as catastrophic.

Both treatments were equally effective and significantly better than a no-treatment control group. The fixed-role therapy group improved more than the rational-emotive therapy group on almost all measures, although the difference was not statistically significant. It is possible that three sessions are too brief to overcome irrational beliefs and that role playing may be easier to grasp.

COMMENTARY: Cognitive approaches to fear of speaking are supported in this study. Strikingly, only three sessions resulted in clear improvement in speech anxiety. There appears to be little question that long-term treatment is not necessary in modifying fears. Combining either method with relaxation and/or social skills training would be a powerful, relatively brief treatment. Certainly, combating irrational ideas and considering alternative roles has been, and should be, part of psychotherapy for many fearful clients. Therapists might assess whether particular clients would respond better to either method. Both approaches might be beneficial.

SOURCE: Karst, T. O., and Trexler, L. D. "Initial Study Using Fixed-Role and Rational-Emotive Therapy in Treating Public-Speaking Anxiety." *Journal of Consulting and Clinical Psychology*, 1970, *34*, 360-366.

Cognitive Therapy and Real-Life Exposure for Stage Fright

AUTHORS: G. Ron Norton, Lynne MacLean, and Elaine Wachna

PRECIS: Cognitive desensitization and performing in increasingly stressful situations found effective for a twenty-year-old pianist

INTRODUCTION: Research is reviewed that demonstrated the effectiveness of participant modeling and self-directed mastery for severe phobias. Compared with other methods, this combination resulted in greater fear reduction and more generalization. However, participant modeling is often difficult (such as modeling in front of an audience), and covert modeling (imagining oneself coping with fearful situations) has been used instead.

METHOD: When playing the piano in public, a twenty-year-old woman became extremely anxious, could not remember the music, and shook her pedal foot uncontrollably. Teaching piano, social contacts, or other public performance (singing or speaking) did not cause difficulties. For five years, her piano-playing stage fright had been increasing. It started when she completely forgot her music while playing in front of an audience and music judge. She became more and more anxious that she would forget the music and began to forget even when only playing for her teacher. An upcoming concert competition led her to seek treatment.

Deep muscle relaxation was taught in the first four sessions, and a seventeen-item anxiety hierarchy was constructed. Five categories of anxiety were covered—the time before a concert, playing at a concert or at home, for knowledgeable or less knowledgeable people, for strangers or friends, and for large or small audiences. The client was asked to create several positive self-statements she could make about piano playing. These statements were said to the therapist and then at home while playing.

Cognitive Desensitization. Each anxiety scene was described while the client was lying down and relaxed. Some scenes had her forgetting her music and then remembering and continuing to play by imagining herself relaxed and rehearsing the music. All scenes were presented three times. If she was still anxious during the third repetition, it was presented again while she said positive self-statements to herself and the cue word used for relaxing. However, the last four most anxiety-provoking scenes were presented while she imagined herself as calm and making positive self-statements. Then she imagined herself becoming very anxious but overcoming her panic. Since a competition was scheduled, one- to one-and-a-half-hour sessions were held every weekday for a total of fifteen sessions.

Self-Directed Mastery Training. When cognitive desensitization was almost completed, the client began practicing at home in front of people. The audiences were gradually increased in size and musical sophistication. When desensitization was completed, she performed on several occasions at a university concert theater for small audiences. Before and during performing, she relaxed and made positive self-statements.

During the first four sessions, she learned to relax very well. By the third presentation of most scenes she reported no anxiety. When she was still anxious, a fourth presentation with positive self-statements and coping imagery worked. Home performances and playing at the university theater were accomplished with minimal anxiety and no foot shaking or memory loss. At one university performance broken piano pedals and a musician in the audience caused no difficulties for her. Her competition and subsequent performance were completed with little anxiety and no problems. She felt that learning to relax and make positive comments were both very helpful. The self-directed mastery performance increased her feelings of competency by demonstrating her ability to play with little anxiety and no foot shaking or memory loss. The natural consequences of praise for successful playing could then occur.

COMMENTARY: This case study was intended by the authors to provide alternatives to participant modeling or other real-life procedures. Cognitive desensitization, the alternative used, is a simple, useful method for the therapist. It is possible to include a brief version of cognitive desensitization with all phobias. Clients can imagine progressively more fear-provoking scenes while relaxed and making positive self-statements. Particularly useful is the inclusion of a panic-reaction scene followed by the calm overcoming of the panic. The self-directed mastery training consists in actually performing in increasingly fearful situations while using the learned cognitive skills. Many therapists have successfully used this type of gradual real-life desensitization experience.

SOURCE: Norton, G. R., MacLean, L., and Wachna, E. "The Use of Cognitive Desensitization and Self-Directed Mastery Training for Treating Stage Fright." *Cognitive Therapy and Research*, 1978, *2*, 61-64.

Behavioral Methods for Social Phobia

AUTHORS: Lars-Göran Öst, Anita Jerremalm, and Jan Johansson

PRECIS: Social skills training or applied relaxation for sixteen behavioral and sixteen physiological reactors aged twenty-one to fifty-one

INTRODUCTION: Almost all past studies concern the effectiveness of different treatments on groups of people according to diagnoses. The role of individual response patterns has been largely ignored. There are a variety of patterns possible according to the definition of phobic anxiety as having cognitive/subjective, overt behavioral, and physiological aspects. Although there is some overlapping, methods for treating these aspects may be categorized as follows: cognitive—stress inoculation training, systematic rational restructuring; behavioral—reinforced practice, flooding, modeling, contact/desensitization; physiological—relaxation methods, anxiety management training, systematic desensitization, biofeedback. Past studies are reviewed in detail, and the treatment effects have been modest. No method has been proved superior, physiological anxiety components have rarely been studied, and only self-reports have shown significant positive changes. Individual response patterns have not been studied. Only one study demonstrated that people high in autonomic reactions showed less behavioral improvement in avoiding snakes than did people measuring low in autonomic reactions (heart rate).

METHOD: All participants were adults with the main complaint of debilitating anxiety in a wide range of social situations (work and leisure). Self-report measures of anxiety included the Fear Survey Schedule, the Autonomic Perception Questionnaire, and the Social Situations Questionnaire. A behavioral measure was the rating of a videotape recording of a conversation with an unknown person (confederate) of the opposite sex. Heart rate was recorded during the conversation. For two weeks before and after therapy, participants recorded all social contacts and activities. Pre and post interviews included structured questions and ratings by the participants of their most anxiety-provoking social situations.

Physiological reactions were measured by the difference in heart rate between a baseline resting rate and the average during a conversation test. Physiological reactors had large heart rate reactions and low overt behavioral reactions. Behavioral reactors had large behavioral reactions but little or no heart rate reaction. Only participants fitting these categories were used, and other patients were offered therapy elsewhere. Each group had sixteen patients, eight of whom were randomly assigned to one treatment and eight to the other treatment. Therefore, only one treatment group corresponded to those patients' response patterns. Both patients and therapists were unaware of the identified response patterns. Over three months, ten to twelve sessions (forty-five to sixty minutes) were held approximately once a week.

Applied Relaxation. Each patient's physiological arousal in social situations was specifically analyzed during the first session. The treatment to be used was described, and tensing and releasing of muscles were taught. During the first three sessions, all three muscle groups were covered. At the fourth session, instead of tensing muscles first, a release-only method was taught. Cue-controlled relaxation and differential relaxation were introduced. During the eighth and ninth sessions, the learned relaxation skills were used in role playing. Patients were coached to systematically use the relaxation skills, and a discussion of tension took place after each role-playing event. Extra training (two sessions) was given if necessary. Homework was assigned in which the learned skill was practiced twice a day and recorded on special forms.

Social Skills Training. A combination of personal effectiveness training and social skills training was used. Treatment was described, and problematic social situations were assessed for each participant, during the first session. The second session consisted of a rank ordering of situations to be rehearsed and role-playing a simple situation. The next seven sessions consisted of training the participants in their individual situations. At first, general situations (beginning a conversation, declining unreasonable requests, introducing oneself) were practiced. Then the individual's list of the most anxiety-arousing situations was practiced. New recent situations were added at times. Each situation usually began with the patient playing himself or herself and the therapist acting as another person. The therapist gave feedback (especially about nonverbal behavior) and suggested alternative behaviors. At the patient's request, the therapist modeled the behavior by reversing roles. The patient tried again and was given feedback until the behavior was satisfactory. The situations were discontinued when the patient felt comfortable in the role playing and the therapist thought the training to have been adequate. Homework was self-observation and recording while applying the skills in natural situations. Two extra sessions were available if necessary. The tenth session consisted of a discussion of the use of learned skills in real life, and patients were told to continue using the skills in social situations.

In general, better results were obtained by using a method in keeping with the person's response pattern. Behavioral reactors improved more by learning social skills, and physiological reactors changed more through relaxation training. Detailed results are presented for the different assessment methods used. Most measures showed decreases in anxiety for participants in both groups. Strikingly, participation in social activities increased for all groups. All groups also showed significant improvement on the social interaction test. As predicted, physiological reactors treated with relaxation showed the greatest decrease in behavioral signs of anxiety on this observation of social interaction. However, heart rate during this period did decrease for the physiological reactors and not for the behavioral reactors. But there was no difference in heart rate within the physiologically reactive group who received relaxation training and those who learned social skills.

COMMENTARY: Most striking is the welcome addition to the literature concerning the best method for a specific type of person. Phobic physiological reactors should receive methods that focus on physiological reactions. Simple as this seems, we are still too often applying general methods for specific types of reactions and problems. This study found relaxation effective for physiological reactors and social skills training more effective for behavioral reactors. One hopes that the authors (or others) follow their own call for extending this research to other phobias. Their discussion of the three anxiety components (behavioral, cognitive, and physiological) of phobias should be helpful to therapists. An evaluation of the phobia should include an assessment of each component and a treatment plan for each if necessary. For cognitive problems, stress inoculation and rational restructuring have been used. For the behavioral aspect, flooding and modeling are effective. Systematic desensitization and biofeedback have been successfully used for physiological reactors. This prescriptive approach is very similar to multimodel therapy (A. Lazarus, *Multimodal Behavior Therapy*, New York: Springer, 1976), in which behavioral, affective, sensate, imagery, cognitive, interpersonal, and drug modalities are used to assess and treat problems.

SOURCE: Öst, L.-G., Jerremalm, A., and Johansson, J. "Individual Response Patterns and the Effects of Different Behavioral Methods in the Treatment of Social Phobia." *Behaviour Research and Therapy*, 1981, *19*, 1-16.

Self-Reinforcement for Reducing Social Anxiety

AUTHORS: Lynn P. Rehm and Albert R. Marston

PRECIS: Systematic self-help training (instigation therapy) and nondirective therapy for twenty-four heterosexually anxious college males

INTRODUCTION: An important means of self-control is self-reward of certain behaviors. Problem behavior related to a poor self-concept may be described as a malfunctioning of self-reinforcement. A person may perform some behavior, evaluate it negatively, and feel discomfort. Behavior may be rarely performed because self-reinforcement is lacking. Faulty self-reinforcement may be improved with a resulting better self-concept, lower anxiety, and more contact with fearful situations.

METHOD: Twenty-four college males were recruited who had difficulties in meeting and dating women. They avoided women and were uncomfortable in their presence. Four therapists treated participants in pairs by self-reinforcement or nonspecific therapy; there was also a no-therapy control group. Each participant in the self-reinforcement group arranged an anxiety hierarchy of thirty standard items. The described situations were typed on cards and arranged in increasing order of personal discomfort. Four hierarchy levels (at least four items each) were arranged by participants according to increased levels of discomfort. Examples of items included taking a seat next to a woman, being introduced to a woman, calling to ask for a date, and dancing. Sexual behavior was not included. The most physically intimate situation described was kissing.

Before the first session, participants read the treatment rationale. The self-reinforcement group read about self-reinforcement, hierarchies, and teaching machines. The nonspecific therapy group read material describing efficient short-term therapy and the general principles of nondirective therapy. Participants in the control group read about the positive effect of volunteering for therapy in that their commitment to change could lead to altering their own behavior. Pre and post assessment methods included a discomfort ranking of the hierarchy items (Situation Questionnaire), the Manifest Anxiety Scale, the Fear Survey Schedule, and the Adjective Check List. A situation test was given consisting of ten audiotaped social situations, which the participants spontaneously responded to as they usually would. Also administered were a posttherapy questionnaire and an eight-month follow-up battery.

Self-Reinforcement Therapy. The first session consisted of questions and discussion of the rationale. The therapist explained that participants were to engage in the situations on their hierarchy. They would evaluate their behavior and reward themselves with self-approval, then record their behavior that evening. Each member rated his own behavior (0 points for avoidance, 1 point for minimally participating in the situation, 2 points for positive participation, and 3 points for doing very well). During the first session, the assignment was given to focus on the first (lowest) level for the week. Situations at other levels were to be recorded if they occurred. During each session, participants described their behavior and the points awarded. The therapist expressed verbal approval of the 2- and 3-point awards. For 0- or 1-point awards, the therapist asked them to describe more appropriate behavior they could have done. Behavioral suggestions were not given by the therapist. Level 2 of the hierarchy was focused on during the second week, level 3 for the third and fourth weeks, and level 4 for the fifth week.

Nonspecific Therapy Group. Therapists used nondirective therapy methods but did not suggest that members perform any specific behaviors. Sessions were one-half hour long, and positive or negative evaluations were not made by the therapists. Instead, they used reflection and clarification of feelings, questions, and some low-level interpretations.

No-Therapy Group. Weekly sessions were held to discuss participants' views of their difficulties and any changes in their ideas. They discussed their means of working on their problems and their plans for the following week. Therapists asked questions and encouraged participants to work on their problems. No evaluations or suggestions were given.

Detailed tables are presented demonstrating the greater improvement of the self-reinforcement group. As in past studies, reduction of anxiety was shown by less report of social discomfort, more dates, and more verbal output with women. Some of the significant differences disappeared on follow-up, but the self-reinforcement group was still doing better (particularly on self-report measures). Therapy was designed to increase the probability of self-reinforcement occurring in real heterosexual situations, thereby leading to a self-sustaining positive change in social behavior. Participants were encouraged to engage in more and more difficult graded problem situations. Each was helped to set explicit behavioral goals in keeping with his own standard of success in each situation. Goals such as getting a positive reaction from someone or not feeling anxious were discouraged.

COMMENTARY: Several helpful suggestions for individual or group therapists are contained in this study. Clearly, therapists can use the basic method as a powerful homework assignment for socially fearful clients (regardless of the therapist's theoretical beliefs). A standard or specifically constructed hierarchy may be used. Clients should be told to set minimal achievable goals, not global ones such as getting a date or not being at all anxious. The authors comment on the similarity of changing covert self-reactions to traditional insight therapy. They see the difference as being that their method focused on the one specific category of self-evaluation and systematically increasing positive overt verbalizations. We are reminded of the cognitive behavior modification and rational-emotive methods, which also directly attack negative self-evaluations. The use of self-administered points is in keeping with many current methods stressing accurate self-assessment and administering of self-rewards (self-control). The authors believe that positive self-evaluation may generalize to other behaviors in the same manner that many of the target clients have overly generalized negative self-evaluations.

SOURCE: Rehm, L. P., and Marston, S. R. "Reduction of Social Anxiety Through Modification of Self-Reinforcement: An Instigation Therapy Technique." *Journal of Consulting and Clinical Psychology*, 1968, *32*, 565-574.

Additional Readings

Curran, J. P. "Skills Training as an Approach to the Treatment of Heterosexual-Social Anxiety: A Review." *Psychological Bulletin,* 1977, *84,* 140-157.

    Three major concepts are discussed as causing and maintaining social anxiety—conditioned anxiety, skills deficit, and faulty cognitive-evaluative appraisal. An exhaustive review follows of social skills training in which appropriate responses are learned. The majority of studies reviewed showed a significant increase in social skills and a reduction of anxiety as measured by self-report and behavioral indexes. Details are given on the use of modeling, behavioral rehearsal, self-observation, vicarious learning, coaching, homework assignments, and assertion training. Problems with the studies reviewed include inadequate screening and assessment procedures, lack of transfer and follow-up measurement, and lack of attention to the interaction between treatment procedures and client characteristics.

Hall, R., and Goldberg, D. "The Role of Social Anxiety in Social Interaction Difficulties." *British Journal of Psychiatry,* 1977, *131,* 610-615.

    Among forty-eight adults with social interaction difficulties, social anxiety was the main complaint. High social anxiety impairs social behavior. Two methods were used with thirty socially anxious persons in nine sessions. Systematic desensitization consisted in self-relaxation and imaginal desensitization taught as a self-control method to be applied in real situations. A social skills training program was role playing with feedback. A videotape demonstrated strategies to use in problem social situations. Patients role-played their own social difficulties in increasing order of difficulty. Participants gave each other feedback about verbal and nonverbal behavior and practiced these skills in appropriate situations. Both therapies reduced social anxiety, but social skills training was more effective in reducing problem behavior. However, desensitization led to more generalization of improvement because actual social participation was increased. Therapy to improve social behavior should deal with high anxiety at the behavioral and cognitive levels. Anxiety-reduction and training methods should be combined.

Jaremko, M. E. "The Use of Stress Inoculation Training in the Reduction of Public Speaking Anxiety." *Journal of Clinical Psychology*, 1980, *36*, 735-738.

Two one-hour sessions were held in groups of five to ten college students with public speaking anxiety. Three phases were taught: (1) Education. Stress is discussed as a cycle of physical arousal, automatic appraisal of the situation as tense, and negative self-statements. This vicious cycle can be broken at three points—physical coping skills to reduce physical arousal, appraising stress as a series of stages, and replacing negative self-statements with positive ones. (2) Skills learning. Hypnoticlike relaxation is learned and muscle tension is identified and counteracted. Stress is coped with by using preparation, confrontation, handling of overwhelmed feelings, and self-reward. Negative self-talk is replaced with positive coping statements about public speaking. (3) Application. A short speech is given in front of the group. All the skills learned are used before, during, and after the speech. Self-reported anxiety was significantly reduced and confidence in public speaking was significantly improved by only two group sessions.

Kaplan, D. M. "On Shyness." *International Journal of Psychoanalysis*, 1972, *53*, 439-453.

Like many situational anxieties, shyness is a form of phobia, since it is activated by exposure to an actual physical situation. There is a phenomenological and dynamic resemblance to depersonalization. Social situations are anticipated with dread. Analytic therapy is directed toward altering the narcissistic equilibrium by the taming of aggression and a transition toward internalization of guilt and toward depressive affects. Clinically, the transition toward depressive emotions is shown by the lessening of playful tactics (coyness and teasing) directed at the therapist. Therapeutic process is seen by the patient's depressed sobriety. Social anxiety is a continuity of the person's vivid fantasy life. These people are very frequently preoccupied with conscious daydreaming, have extrapunitive impulses (externalize blame), and ward off guilt. They have often been infantilized by a parent, and a form of oedipal fantasy exists in which the father has been excluded.

Peterson, J., Fischetti, M., Curran, J. P., and Arland, S. "Sense of Timing: A Skill Deficit in Heterosocially Anxious Women." *Behavior Therapy,* 1981, *12,* 195-201.

Socially anxious college women observed a videotape of a male discussing his life. They pressed a switch when they thought a response would communicate understanding or rapport. Results confirm previous research showing that the timing and placement of responses (response synchronicity) is an important aspect of social skills in men. This phenomenon may be more important than the frequency of responses. Currently, social skills training often minimizes the opportunity for response synchronization because the reactivity of the role-playing partner is often restricted. In treating socially anxious people, the acquiring of responses has been emphasized at the cost of cue discrimination and social perception.

Shaw, P. "A Comparison of Three Behavior Therapies in the Treatment of Social Phobia." *British Journal of Psychiatry,* 1979, *135,* 620-623.

Social phobia is an excessive anxiety and tendency to avoid interpersonal situations such as meetings, informal interviews, making complaints, or being watched. Ten weekly treatment sessions were given to social phobics (nineteen males, eleven females —mean age, thirty-two years). Desensitization, flooding, and social skills training were equally effective in reducing social fears. Desensitization was performed using the patient's imagination to visualize increasingly anxious social situations. Flooding involved imagining the most fearful situations. Social skills training focused on listening and expressive skills and role playing of relevant situations for each patient (meals, having an interview, and so on). Patients all practiced between sessions. Since the treatments were equally effective, decisions might be made on the basis of cost or acceptability to the patient. Flooding is low on patient acceptability, and social skills training is very costly. Desensitization may be most appropriate and can be made even less costly through the use of patient manuals.

Trower, P., Yardley, K., Bryant, B. M., and Shaw, P. "The Treatment of Social Failure." *Behavior Modification,* 1978, *2,* 41-60.

Social failure may be primary (poor social skills) or secondary (social phobia). Systematic desensitization to reduce anxiety consisted in graded exposure to imagined situations. Social skills training consisted in coaching, modeling, behavior rehearsal, and video and audio feedback. One of the treatments was given to twenty socially unskilled and twenty socially phobic patients. As predicted, the unskilled patients responded better to social skills training. They reported less difficulty in social situations, went out more, and improved their behavioral inadequacies. However, the social phobics responded equally well to both treatments. Evidently, social skills training reduces anxiety as well as improving behavior. The findings support the idea of a primary form of social failure (social inadequacy). Unskilled people may not benefit from desensitization, since they lack the competence to perform covert behavior rehearsal. They do not have the cognitive resources and knowledge for imagining coping behavior.

Simple Phobia

According to DSM-III (pp. 229-230), the diagnostic criteria for a simple phobia are as follows:

> *A. A persistent, irrational fear of, and compelling desire to avoid, an object or a situation other than being alone, or in public places away from home (Agoraphobia), or of humiliation or embarrassment in certain social situations (Social Phobia). Phobic objects are often animals, and phobic situations frequently involve heights or closed spaces.*
> *B. Significant distress from the disturbance and recognition by the individual that his or her fear is excessive or unreasonable.*
> *C. Not due to another mental disorder, such as Schizophrenia or Obsessive Compulsive Disorder.*

DSM-III notes that simple phobias are sometimes called "specific phobias." The most common phobias involve animals, especially dogs, snakes, insects, and mice. People with acrophobia (fear of heights) and claustrophobia (fear of closed spaces) often seek treatment. When exposed to a phobic situation, people often become overwhelmingly fearful and may have a panic attack. Animal phobias almost always begin in childhood and often disappear without treatment. Simple phobias lasting into

adulthood rarely diminish or are eliminated without treatment. If the phobic object is rarely encountered, impairment is minimal. Impairment may be considerable if the phobic object is common and cannot be avoided. Simple phobias are common (and more frequent in women), but treatment is often not sought unless functioning is markedly impaired.

Expectation of therapeutic gain in fear reduction has been a significant issue in treatment. J. Lick and R. Bootzin ("Expectancy Factors in the Treatment of Fear," Psychological Bulletin, *1975, 82, 917-931) reviewed many studies. They concluded that expectancy of improvement (often called "demand characteristics") significantly contributes to treatment success. Expectancy influences the change process by increasing treatment compliance, increasing the tendency to test reality and give self-reinforcement for improvement, and modifying self-thoughts. Treatment results have been complicated by nonstandard rating forms. I. M. Marks and A. M. Mathews ("Brief Standard Self-Rating for Phobic Patients,"* Behaviour Research and Therapy, *1979, 17, 263-267) call for the widespread use of a simple one-page self-rating form for monitoring change. This would be helpful to practitioners and result in useful comparisons of interventions. The form yields four scores—main, global, and total phobia scores and an anxiety-depression score.*

Another useful finding has been the categorization of fear into three systems—cognitive/verbal, physiological, and motoric (K. Hugdahl, "The Three-Systems Model of Fear and Emotion— A Critical Examination," Behaviour Research and Therapy,

1981, 19, 75-85). Success has been achieved by tailoring the treatment method to the specific system affected. The relative importance of each of the three systems in a particular phobia often varies among patients. Hugdahl suggests that physiological responders would do well with a technique that extinguishes autonomic arousal to the phobic scene (in imagination or in real-life situations). A cognitive responder would be given a cognitive relabeling or restructuring method. For example, stress inoculation teaches patients cognitive coping skills as a substitute for negative self-thoughts. Motoric responders require a technique that makes escape or avoidance impossible. For example, reinforced practice is specifically aimed at interrupting the reinforced avoidance response. This would be particularly appropriate if the phobic person did not show physiological arousal or maladaptive thoughts. However, since all phobias involve avoidance, it is probably appropriate to use the exposure method along with treatment tailored to the person's response systems.

We seriously considered grouping digests and additional readings by type of phobia (snake, tests, heights, and so on). However, a category system would have been cumbersome and misleading. It is very clear that the methods used for one type of phobia are directly applicable to other types. Therefore, we list articles alphabetically by authors and urge readers to consult different therapy methods and not only look for specific treatment of a spider phobia, for example. In fact, many of the articles included phobics of all types in their treatment.

Thought Stopping and Assertive
Statements for Fearful Thoughts

AUTHORS: M. Carole Arrick, Jacqueline Voss, and David C. Rimm

PRECIS: Stopping unadaptive thoughts and making assertive comments to diminish fear of snakes in thirty-six college students

INTRODUCTION: Thought-stopping techniques have been used with obsessions, phobias, deviant sex fantasies, and hallucinations. Usually, thought stopping has been combined with other procedures, and results of several studies do not clearly support its effectiveness. However, a method called "thought stopping and covert assertion" has been clearly effective. Clients are told to imagine being in the problem situation, which usually leads them to try to suppress their thoughts. By initially thinking aloud, they facilitate adaptive thoughts. Thought stopping alone interrupts all thoughts, not just maladaptive ones. Thought stopping with covert assertion encourages adaptive thoughts by means of covert assertions. Clients practice this in an overt way and then covertly, making adaptive thoughts more likely in real-life situations.

METHOD: Thirty-six college students who had a strong fear of harmless snakes participated. Before, after, and at a four- to five-week follow-up, three tests were administered—Fear Survey Schedule, Behavioral Avoidance Test, and the Fear Thermometer (subjective rating of anxiety). Four same-sex persons were treated together in approximately one-hour sessions. All sessions began with an explanation that the therapy was designed to stop unadaptive thoughts, which cause fear or anxiety. The Behavioral Avoidance Test requires the person to approach a snake (a forty-five-inch Yuma king snake in this study) in nineteen graduated steps. The number of steps completed is the score. Each person was to imagine the next two steps beyond the highest one completed and the last two steps. Participants imagined the situation and verbalized all their thoughts. Any unadaptive thoughts were labeled as such by the experimenters, who discussed their self-defeating aspect. If adaptive ideas emerged, the differences between adaptive and unadaptive thoughts were discussed. During the three following treatments, the procedures were done for each of the four fearful steps as derived from performance on the Behavioral Avoidance Test.

Thought Stopping. People imagined the first situation and thought aloud. When unadaptive thoughts began, the experimenter shouted "Stop." This was repeated until the word *stop* consistently interrupted unadaptive responses. Then participants thought to themselves while imagining the fearful situation. They signaled when an unadaptive thought started, and the experimenter yelled "Stop." The next step was similar except that they themselves shouted "Stop" forcefully at the start of an unadaptive thought. Finally, the forceful "Stop" was said silently to themselves.

Covert Assertion. After labeling unadaptive thoughts, participants rated their anxiety on a scale from 1 to 10 and suggested assertive statements. When the experimenter signaled, participants imagined the situation, thought out loud, and convincingly said the assertive comment. The signal was given quietly at the beginning of any unadaptive statement. Then participants followed the same procedure without the signal by recognizing the unadaptive ideas themselves. Finally, the participants repeated the procedure but made the comments to themselves (covertly).

Thought Stopping and Covert Assertion. The thought-stopping procedure was presented as described above. Participants rated their anxiety (1 to 10) aroused by the imagined situation. Then they suggested a believable, assertive statement to make themselves less fearful. This statement was said aloud and convincingly after the last step of the thought-stopping procedure. They said the statement to themselves and repeated the process until their anxiety was 3 or less on the 10-point scale. Finally, they made the statements to themselves in a convincing manner.

Control Group. This was a "superficial insight" control

treatment. Participants were told that the therapy was meant to help them understand their fear and anxiety. They were asked about the cause and effects of their fear, and they were asked to describe other fears and to discuss their childhood and family. The experimenters were reflective but added minimal information.

All three tests of fear of snakes showed that the three treatments were more effective than the control treatment. However, all three treatments were equally effective. It is possible that convincingly saying "Stop" counteracts anxiety the way a covert assertive statement does. Further, adaptive thoughts may be indirectly increased by thought stopping, since more neutral or adaptive thoughts naturally occur. In this study, after the experimenter said "Stop," almost all the participants in the thought-stopping group made spontaneous positive comments. Covert assertion alone may be seen as a form of thought stopping, since unadaptive thoughts are interrupted.

COMMENTARY: The combined treatment was developed by D. C. Rimm ("Thought Stopping and Covert Assertion in the Treatment of Phobias," *Journal of Consulting and Clinical Psychology,* 1973, *41,* 466-467) and described in detail in D. C. Rimm and J. C. Masters, *Behavior Therapy Techniques and Empirical Findings* (New York: Academic Press, 1974). In the present study, the authors speculate about several possible experimental factors that could account for the lack of expected superiority of the combined treatment. One helpful notion is that learning to view some thoughts as maladaptive is therapeutic and may in itself lead to a diminishing of such thoughts. This is certainly in line with cognitively oriented therapies that teach the irrationality and destructiveness of some types of thoughts. Another useful piece of information is that there is no generalization from successfully treating a specific fear to lessening other fears. Therefore, different fears must be focused on, using some potentially successful method. Most useful is the simple finding that all methods were successful. Since thought stopping and covert assertion are both simple, brief methods, it is incumbent on therapists to add these tools to their repertoire in treating fearful, obsessive, or depressed people.

SOURCE: Arrick, M. C., Voss, J., and Rimm, D. C. "The Relative Efficacy of Thought-Stopping and Covert Assertion." *Behaviour Research and Therapy,* 1981, *19,* 17-24.

Performance-Based Treatments for Acrophobia

AUTHORS: Paul Bourque and Robert Ladouceur

PRECIS: Participant modeling (with or without therapist physical contact), modeling plus exposure, and therapist-controlled real-life exposure for fifty adults with fear of heights

INTRODUCTION: Past studies on differential effectiveness of various methods are reviewed and found to be ambiguous. This study contrasted five conditions that are often part of performance-based treatments. Performance accomplishments are the most influential source of information in the individual's expectation of successfully performing a behavior. Selected for study were fifty adults who could not go farther than the third landing of a specially constructed fire escape with six landings. These people (average age twenty-nine years and average length of fears twenty years) avoided any high places, such as balconies, ladders, fire escapes, bridges, and observation towers. Outcome measures included tests for height avoidance and fear arousal accompanying avoidance response (heart rate), as well as several specially adapted self-report measures, self-efficacy expectations, generalization tests (climbing heights), and total therapy time.

METHOD: All participants were told the rationale of treatment (all done individually).

   1. *Participant modeling.* The therapist modeled all behaviors to be performed on each landing. Behaviors included climbing the steps, walking on the landing, going near the edge, and

looking down at a large painted letter while holding onto the
rail and then without holding on. The clients performed the behavior just modeled and were helped by the therapist, if necessary. This help included making the steps more gradual, providing physical contact (typically, holding the person's arm), and
praising appropriate attempts. If the person still could not do
the task, the therapist modeled the behavior again or made the
task more gradual. The support was withdrawn as soon as possible. Usually, after doing a task twice the therapist gradually
ceased physical contact. The amount of time spent looking
down was gradually extended, and finally the participants
walked alone to the edge and looked down. The procedure was
carried out for each landing until the person could relatively
easily look down from the sixth landing.

2. *Participant modeling without therapist contact.* The
procedure was identical to participant modeling, but no physical contact took place. The therapist walked next to the person.

3. *Modeling plus response rehearsal.* After modeling a behavior, the therapist returned to his position approximately five
feet from the person, who then performed the task. No performance aids were given other than verbal guidance and praise.
Tasks were practiced until they could be easily performed.

4. *Therapist-controlled exposure.* After the rationale was
explained, the tasks were performed while the therapist
watched from ground level. No modeling took place, but verbal
guidance and praise were used.

5. *Client-controlled exposure.* After hearing the rationale,
participants did the tasks described on their own with no therapist present. The person checked into the therapist's office before and after each session. Reported progress was praised by
the therapist.

Each treatment was equally effective in reducing fear of
heights. Various speculations are offered, such as differing experimental conditions, to explain the lack of differences between treatments. With acrophobia, therapist proximity or
physical contact does not enhance treatment effectiveness. As
in past findings, the crucial element in reducing anxiety is repeated exposure to the cause of the fear. Also as in past studies,

gradual real-life exposure is an effective procedure. Strikingly, the self-controlled exposure treatment with minimal verbal persuasion was as effective as the therapist-controlled procedure. Therefore, verbal persuasion is not a necessary component of effective treatment for acrophobia.

COMMENTARY: This study is presented as a source for specific alternative methods for fears. Gradual, repeated exposure is applicable to other phobias. The equal effectiveness of each treatment condition might serve as a source of encouragement for a therapist to try any one that is most compatible with or convenient for that particular client and situation. Therapists who use an office-based verbal approach to phobias should heed one of Bourque and Ladouceur's conclusions. Some form of extinction permits change to occur when there is repeated exposure to fear without negative reinforcement. This means that an efficient means of fear reduction requires actual exposure, with or without the therapist's presence. There is a growing trend for therapists to give clients some form of "homework assignment" requiring exposure to the feared situation. This study supports this procedure, since therapist presence and verbal persuasion were not necessary for change. For clients who appear to require encouragement and physical contact, this study supports the effectiveness of those strategies.

SOURCE: Bourque, P., and Ladouceur, R. "An Investigation of Various Performance-Based Treatments with Acrophobics." *Behaviour Research and Therapy,* 1980, *18,* 161-170.

Physical Activity and Positive Images
to Reduce Test Anxiety

AUTHOR: Richard Driscoll

PRECIS: Short-term running in place while imagining pleasurable situations was as effective as lengthy taped desensitization for eighty college students

INTRODUCTION: Anxiety has been effectively reduced by various methods using clients' imagination of anxiety-producing situations under different conditions. When counterconditioning anxiety, positive feelings (such as confidence, security, achievement, enjoyment, and calmness) are critical. Positive feelings at the end of a scary event condition a positive association to that event. If a person sees continuing danger after an event, lingering apprehension results. Rather than muscle relaxation, positive images (promoting positive feelings) have been successfully used to promote relaxation and calm feelings. Strenuous physical activity also lowers anxiety, and running has been used to treat agoraphobia. Exertion is an active and assertive act that consumes tension and physiological arousal and is incompatible with anxiety. Sufficient exertion partly inhibits further arousal of anxiety. Moreover, physical activity is associated with recreational enjoyment, and enjoyment should reduce anxiety.

METHOD: Participants were college students who were severely anxious about test taking. Anxiety was measured by a composite scale including apprehension, debilitation, and physiological aspects. These items were rated on a scale, as were questions related to enjoyment of physical activity. Several weeks after treatment, midterms were given, and participants rated their anxiety immediately afterward. Treatment consisted of one thirty-minute session and a ten-minute session from two to nine days later.

Participants rated the following scenes from most to least anxiety-arousing: hearing a test announced in class, studying the

night before, walking into class and waiting, having the test
, passed out and seeing difficult items, doing the easier items,
doing the difficult items, getting a test back, and other relevant
situations. Participants completed details as relevant for them
(history exam, multiple-choice exam, and so on). Scenes were
presented from least to most anxiety-provoking. Three scenes
were presented twice for twenty-five seconds during each session. There was a twenty-second interval between presentations, in which participants were told to let their minds go
blank (except the "positive image" group, who were presented
with a positive scene). After the two presentations, participants
rated how realistic and anxious their experiences were. There
was a *control group,* who completed questionnaires with no
treatment. A *minimal treatment* group was also used to control
for the possible effects of excessive tension. These subjects were
told they would rehearse the scenes in a relaxed and supportive
setting. Twice, they practiced tensing and relaxing their shoul-
der muscles. When the scenes were described, they were told to
relax their shoulders.

Physical Exertion. Participants were shown how to run in
place by lifting their knees but not kicking their heels back.
They ran in place until each reported being tired. At that point,
the scenes were individually presented. Throughout presentation of the scene, the participant continued running.

Positive Images. Participants had been asked to describe
enjoyable, relaxing, secure, confident situations. These scenes
typically concerned physical recreation or free time with friends.
During the twenty-second interval after a presentation, a positive scene was described.

Exertion and Positive Images. Participants ran in place
and heard the positive scenes after the anxiety-provoking scenes
were presented.

Taped Desensitization. In a group, participants heard four
forty-five-minute tapes, two in each of the two sessions. Sessions began with relaxation instructions to tense, release, and relax all muscles. For four, six, and eight seconds, each of fourteen
test-related scenes was presented, followed by twenty-, twenty-,
and sixty- to one-hundred-twenty-second relaxation periods.

This desensitization method was a standard, thorough one and was of much longer duration than the above treatment methods.

Detailed results are reported supporting the anxiety-deconditioning effects of physical exertion and positive images. The minimal treatment did reduce anxiety somewhat, probably due to rehearsal under supportive circumstances and attention-placebo effects. Exertion only and positive images only reduced anxiety more than minimal treatment and much more than for the control group. The exertion and positive images group showed the most anxiety reduction, comparable to that produced by the much longer standard desensitization procedure.

COMMENTARY: Although more research is clearly called for, Driscoll points out the relative efficiency of very brief "exertion therapy." Physical exertion may well be of use in treating phobias and depression, in which patients can be taught to exercise to counteract fearful or depressing thoughts. We would speculate that running outside (rather than running in place) or other forms of exercise may be more enjoyable and effective in deconditioning anxiety, fears, or depression. Also noteworthy is that grade-point averages directly correlated with degree of anxiety reduction. Reducing test anxiety leads to better grades, and we speculate that reducing fears of other types with physical exertion may lead to more efficiency on the job. The success of the exercise program during work hours used in China has been widely discussed in the news media. Driscoll comments that the exertion-only method reduced anxiety but decreased later physical enjoyment of exercise. Positive images after the anxiety scenes prevent this negative conditioning to physical activity. Of great interest is Driscoll's pilot study suggesting that self-administration of exertion therapy is feasible and efficient. Therefore, therapists may employ this method in the office and have clients use exertion at appropriate times on their own. Physical activity is therefore not only good for your health, but it may well be a useful therapeutic method for specific problems.

SOURCE: Driscoll, R. "Anxiety Reduction Using Physical Exertion and Positive Images." *Psychological Record,* 1976, *26,* 87-94.

Primal Therapy and Desensitization

AUTHOR: Baruch Elitzur

PRECIS: Two-session crisis intervention for a severe phobia

INTRODUCTION: The most effective, brief approach is necessary for dealing with a severe phobic attack. Successful approaches described in the literature may be combined. Two very different methods are primal therapy and desensitization. Primal therapy encourages experiencing and openly expressing feelings, including crying and reliving strong feelings. Rather than the therapist's interpreting these events, patients make the connection between the phobia and past experience. Successful sessions are indicated by the most open experience and expression of painful feelings. Behavioral therapists induce bodily and mental relaxation. While the patient relaxes, the therapist describes more and more fearful situations. This desensitization is most effective when the patient is extremely relaxed.

METHOD: A thirty-two-year-old mother of two children wanted an immediate appointment because of extreme anxiety. She had just discovered lice in her twelve-year-old daughter's hair and became very anxious, cried hysterically, and could not touch her daughter's hair. She trembled frequently and was not able to eat or sleep. Owing to financial difficulties, she requested treatment in only one or two therapy sessions. The therapist decided to conduct one primal and then one desensitization session. Primal therapy was selected because one session often leads to meaningful insight (which she desired) and behavioral changes. She had read about (and had a friend who had experienced) primal therapy. Primal was used first because some people become frightened by early memories and feelings. The information revealed could then be used to construct a hierarchy of fears to be desensitized. Desensitization, which has been very successful with phobias, usually leads to feelings of relaxation and self-control. Therefore, each experience contributed to overcoming her fear, and the second session served as support for any overwhelming feelings induced by the first session.

In a soundproof room, the client lay on a carpet for the entire forty-five-minute first session. After describing her anxiety, she was told to close her eyes and imagine seeing her daughter's lice-filled hair. She became very anxious, cried, screamed, and begged the lice not to touch her. Very quickly, she began talking about her painful childhood fear of roaches and not being loved by her parents. She was encouraged to explore and express all her feelings, and she soon acted as if her parents, daughter, and husband were in the room. In a very emotional way she spoke of her mother's being dirty and not loving her. She expressed a very strong fear of being eaten by the roaches and not being protected by her unloving father. Her daughter's lice meant that she was dirty like her mother. She expressed feeling like a phony pretending to be strong, but really being weak and dirty. She desperately needed to be loved in spite of her perceived weaknesses. Near the end of the session, she was asked to sit and relate her experiences. She was told to wait a few hours and then write about the session. She was to try to understand the relation between her present fear and her past fear of roaches and feeling unloved.

During the next session, on the following day, she described her reactions. Although she cried for several hours, she had felt relieved. She said that she understood her general fear of bugs and lice and her ambivalent feelings about her husband and parents. Her fear lessened, and she did not panic when she saw a spider at home. Since her fear of roaches was so intense, this became the focus for desensitization. After fifteen minutes of effective relaxation, she was told to imagine being in a pleasant, safe place where roaches could not get near her. Initially, she could not think of a place, but then she described being inside a beautiful, safe volcano with trees and animals and no roaches. While relaxed, she was told to imagine seeing a few roaches at a far distance. Gradually, she was able to imagine the roaches coming toward her, but she became very anxious when they came close. She was told to try different ways of not feeling anxious. Imagining different people and then God helping her did not work. Imagining glass walls around her was successful, and she was soon able to calmly see different insects crawling on the glass. Finally, she could calmly imagine an ant crawling on her hand and then said that she imagined wearing the protective glass like a skin. She was instructed to practice relaxing every day and to call if she became anxious. Her fears of insects dramatically decreased, and she took care of her daughter's hair.

COMMENTARY: Elitzur cautions that one primal session might be harmful and some people may not be able to relax in one session. He believes that the patient learned the connection between her phobia and past experiences and learned to relax and not overreact. Strikingly, her insight that she was not as strong and clean as she pretended to be is very similar to insights gained by patients in a wide variety of psychotherapy approaches. This article may serve as a valuable model to show that effective treatment may be very brief. Many psychotherapists have stated that one or two sessions can only result in a superficial "flight into health," with no real lasting effect. This article is in the growing tradition that combined methods may be truly effective and brief. Repeatedly, we have seen people respond very quickly when they both gain some insight into a problem and learn some method of coping with their fear, anxiety, or depression.

SOURCE: Elitzur, B. "The Use of Primal and Desensitization Approaches in Crisis Intervention of Phobia: A Case Study." *Psychotherapy: Theory, Research, and Practice*, 1978, *15*, 35-38.

Paradoxical Intention for Phobias

AUTHOR: Hans O. Gerz

PRECIS: Diminishing anticipatory anxiety for twenty-nine phobic patients

INTRODUCTION: Anticipatory anxiety is characteristic of phobic neuroses. There are fears of passing out, blushing, riding in vehicles, bridges, heights, and heart attacks. Fear of an event and attempts to avoid it make the occurrence of a symptom more likely. For example, a person fears blushing, tries not to, and then blushes. Frankl's idea was to have people try to produce the fearful event (such as blushing). When the person is unable to bring on the symptom, his attitude changes. In "paradoxical intention," people try to achieve what they were previously afraid of (and to ironically and paradoxically like it). They are able to laugh at their symptoms, thus interrupting the vicious cycle. Wishing for a fear is voluntary, whereas the phobic process is involuntary. One of the basic principles of logotherapy is becoming responsible, and this method focuses on the person's responsibility and avoids dependency on the doctor. The person replaces a fear with a wish and detaches from the symptom with a humorous attitude. People cannot voluntarily produce an involuntary response, and the repeated use of paradoxical intention reconditions neurotic reflexive patterns. Additionally, the patient is positively influenced by the therapist's complete lack of anxiety about the symptom.

METHOD: Of twenty-nine phobic patients seen, twenty-two recovered, five were considerably improved, one relapsed, was treated, and recovered, and two were failures. The method is illustrated by the case of a twenty-nine-year-old mother of three children with multiple phobias. She was afraid of heights, being alone, vomiting, subways, supermarkets, crowds, driving alone, and screaming or swearing in church. Hospitalization, psychotherapy, and electroconvulsive therapy had been unsuccessful. Paradoxical intention was explained to her and discussed in detail. She was told to wish for whatever she was afraid of, and she was to take 15 mg of Valium daily. When dining with her husband and friends, she should vomit into their faces and make the worst possible mess. When driving to various places, she was to become as panicky as possible. She soon was able to drive all over by herself. Examples of her proud accomplishments were riding a bus and subway and going to the top of the Empire State Building. Her husband described her as being a different person and even enjoying sex.

Paradoxical intention is a supplement to dynamic therapy, not a replacement. A combination of paradoxical intention, logotherapeutic dereflection, and reconditioning therapy is used. The patients' symptoms are understood in the context of their unique life histories, conflicts, and meanings of their existence. Antianxiety and antidepressant drugs are often very useful. It is crucial that the therapist fully understand the paradoxical technique and believe in it. Many psychoanalysts expect paradoxical intention to work immediately. Success or failure depends on the patience and persistence of the therapist, especially since long-standing symptoms become separate and autonomous entities.

COMMENTARY: Paradoxical intention has been successfully used in treating phobias and obsessive-compulsive disorders. Gerz reports six successful outcomes with obsessive-compulsive patients, whom he helped to "defocus" (become nonchalant and uncaring about their symptoms). Diagnosis is important: Gerz states that paradoxical intention may cause overt psychotic behavior in pseudoneurotic schizophrenia. Most important is his comment that paradoxical intention is always combined with other methods, such as logotherapeutic dereflection and reconditioning therapy and is part of existential psychotherapy. Clearly, then, paradoxical intention is described as a tool to be used in eliminating or reducing symptoms as part of a therapeutic process. This idea neatly fits into the eclectic approach advocated in this book. A phobic person may be taught social skills, assertiveness, awareness and expression of feelings, and so on while using paradoxical intention to cope with anticipatory fear. Gerz's suggestion for the phobic woman to try to vomit in people's faces is strikingly similar to "flooding" techniques developed more recently. Patients are instructed to imagine their worst possible fears (such as vomiting, falling from high places, being bitten by hundreds of snakes), which leads to a dramatic reduction or elimination of their phobias. The therapist is thus intervening in the vicious cycle of repetitive fearful experiences.

SOURCE: Gerz, H. O. "Experience with the Logotherapeutic Technique of Paradoxical Intention in the Treatment of Phobic and Obsessive-Compulsive Patients." *American Journal of Psychiatry*, 1966, *123*, 548-553.

Cognitive Therapy for Fear of Flying

AUTHORS: Michel Girodo and Julius Roehl

PRECIS: Cognitive preparation and coping self-talk for fifty-six female college students

INTRODUCTION: Cognitive and behavioral methods have been used for stress inoculation training. People have learned to cope with the stress of pain, surgery, test anxiety, and anger by making positive coping statements to themselves. These statements relate to preparing for and handling stress, coping with overwhelming feelings, and self-reinforcement for coping. This is a type of beneficial worrying, in which anticipatory problem solving and cognitive rehearsal are used. Thinking about coping with stressful situations causes a moderate degree of arousal, which emotionally inoculates the person against future stress.

METHOD: Four groups of fourteen flight-apprehensive female

college students (average age twenty-one years) participated. Training took place on a Saturday and was followed by a Sunday flight. Self-reports of anxiety were made when the engine was turned on, after takeoff, at three consecutive ten-minute intervals, and after landing. The Self-Report Anxiety Inventory was used to assess anxiety at those times and after the staged "missed landing." (A missed landing was arranged whereby at 100 feet a warning horn sounded in the cockpit, and the plane climbed rapidly to 2,000 feet. The captain apologized, saying that an unauthorized plane was on the runway.) Most instructions for the groups were tape-recorded. Another feature of this study was the effect of being able to see the pilot and copilot in the cockpit. Therefore, experimental conditions were arranged regarding "door open" and "door closed" flights. Pre- and posttesting was accomplished with the Flight Apprehension Inventory and posttesting with a Treatment Effectiveness Questionnaire concerning use of self-statements. The plane used was a twin-engine short-takeoff-and-landing aircraft.

Self-Talk Training. The method used is described in D. Meichenbaum, "Self-Instructional Methods," in F. H. Kanfer and A. P. Goldstein (Eds.), *Helping People Change* (New York: Pergamon, 1975). Training took place in one two-and-a-half-hour session. The experimenter discussed positive self-statements as a means of coping with stress. All participants shared situations that made them anxious and their thoughts at those times. The rationale of stress inoculation training and a list of positive self-statements were played on a tape recorder. For the physical aspect of anxiety, a slow, deep breath was advised. Positive coping self-talk was described as the means for dealing with the mental aspect of anxiety. The tape presents a person who is anxious and makes negative self-statements while taking an examination. Positive coping self-statements should be used at this point. Meichenbaum's list of coping self-statements was then distributed. Participants were asked to imagine a stressful situation and then prepare and memorize their own list of coping self-statements. After a ten-minute learning period, their recall was tested. The tape continued about a person who was afraid of horses. Participants were told to vividly imagine a person making positive self-statements as the horse was approached, touched, mounted, ridden, and dismounted. Each participant then shared self-statements about flying and prepared and rehearsed a list to be used during the next day's flight.

Preparatory Information Training. Similarly to the start of self-talk training, participants were asked to discuss past anxiety-producing experiences. Acquiring prior information about stressful events was presented as a method for coping with stress, and test anxiety was given as an example. A tape recording presented the rationale for this method (see I. L. Janis, *Stress and Frustration,* New York: Harcourt Brace Jovanovich, 1971) and a detailed description of the next day's flight. Details included transportation to the airport, preflight procedures, description of the airplane, and takeoff and landing procedures. At appropriate points, twelve color slides showed the airport, plane, and views that would be seen during the flight. The pilot's extensive training, maturity, and twenty years of experience were described; pilots were depicted as "danger control authorities."

Combined Training. Preparatory information and self-talk training methods were both used.

Pseudotreatment Control. As in the other methods, participants shared their feelings and thoughts about stressful situations. Three twenty-minute films were then shown about the history of Canadian aviation. Participants were asked to share what they liked least and most about each film.

Strikingly, flying with the cockpit door open (rather than closed) led to more anxiety. With the door open, the self-talk-trained individuals coped better with the stress of the missed landing than did the information or control participants. Interestingly, the self-talk group did not cope as well with the missed landing as the other groups did when flying with the cockpit door closed. In fact, all treatment groups increased in anxiety during this period. Evidently, the ability to process information (see what is happening) is more important than any coping strategy. During the normal flight, the different treatments were equally effective.

A four-and-a-half-month follow-up study showed that

stress inoculation training (self-talk and combined) led to significant reduction in flight apprehension (compared with information and control groups) whether flying with the cockpit door open or closed. With the door open, the self-talk, combined, and information groups had significantly less flight apprehension, whereas the control group did not. With the door closed, the self-talk and combined groups had significantly less apprehension, but the information and control groups did not.

COMMENTARY: The main point of the study seems clear. Stress inoculation training (as reported in other studies) does reduce fearfulness of specific situations. Other findings are less clear. Girodo and Roehl speculate that self-talk may interfere with other coping mechanisms that require information processing and evaluation. This is their reasoning with regard to the relatively poor coping ability of the door-closed self-talk group when dealing with the missed landing. That group's "self-preoccupation" may have interfered with dealing with the relevant issues of this new situation. This type of interaction can serve as a warning to the reader that treatment of fears may not be simple. Just teaching positive self-talk may be effective with some people in some situations. Combining self-talk with training in alternative problem solving or psychotherapy may be a solution.

SOURCE: Girodo, M., and Roehl, J. "Cognitive Preparation and Coping Self-Talk: Anxiety Management During the Stress of Flying." *Journal of Consulting and Clinical Psychology,* 1978, *46,* 978-989.

Behavioral Techniques for Reducing
Fear of the Dark

AUTHOR: David A. Kipper

PRECIS: Treating nyctophobia by gradual exposure, relaxation, attention shifting, and self-practice

INTRODUCTION: Nyctophobia is fear (and uncontrollable anxiety) when experiencing or thinking about darkness and night. Victims avoid darkness and remain indoors at night. Although little is reported in the literature, some conclusions appear warranted. Fear of darkness is most intense in childhood, peaking at age four. One successful study enabled children to tolerate darkness by practicing saying sentences to themselves that stressed active control and competence. This fear is more frequent in adults than many think. In one study of adult psychiatric inpatients, nyctophobia was among the more frequent fears.

METHOD: Systematic desensitization has been very successful with phobias. Rather than imagining scenes, desensitization in real-life situations has been recommended when (1) clients cannot imagine scenes vividly or see an image for at least thirty seconds, (2) fears are not visual (sounds), (3) real-life situations are easily available, or (4) gradual exposure is possible so clients are not overly stressed at first. A crucial aspect in treating phobias is the successful confrontation of the fearful situation without the anticipated terrible consequences. Although gradual steps and relaxation are not necessary, they are useful in reducing anxiety.

Three weekly sessions were held during daytime to prepare for the desensitization. (1) A history was obtained and the treatment goal set. (2) The procedure was described and questions (what to expect, how long it takes, and how effective it is) answered. Progressive muscular relaxation was taught, and the client was told to listen to a tape and practice daily for one week. (3) A brief relaxation method was taught, and the client

was to practice focusing on breathing and telling himself to remain calm daily. Desensitization sessions were one hour each,
started just before sunset at home or in the office, and continued outside when it became dark. Streets were selected for
varying degrees of darkness, density of people and traffic, and
specific fearful stimuli. Sessions took place about three times a
week for a total of fourteen *in vivo* sessions, plus two half-hour
follow-up sessions.

The therapist accompanied the client for a ten-yard walk,
preceded and followed by relaxation. Several walks were taken
until the client experienced no anxiety. Then the client walked
ten yards toward (then away from) the therapist until no anxiety was present. Distances were gradually increased by ten yards
each time. It took four sessions to reach 200 yards. During this
period the client could always see the therapist, and practice
alone was not permitted. The procedure continued in the same
manner with the therapist concealing himself. The client to be
described was able to walk 100 yards without being able to see
the therapist, but he was still anxious (sweaty palms). Although
he was able to walk, his emotions were inappropriate, since he
was thinking about how he felt about darkness. Therefore, he
was taught to shift his attention from darkness to other topics
(counting open or closed windows or remembering items on display in windows). Anxiety was eliminated, and walking in the
dark became interesting for him. At this point "self-practice"
began, in which the client arrived at the session by bus after
sunset. Three sessions consisted of assignments such as riding a
bus for a few blocks and visiting places such as stores and movie
theaters.

CASE STUDY: A twenty-one-year-old single man became fearful of the dark because of a traumatic experience in the Israeli
army. He was cooperative, intelligent, and sensitive and had no
history of phobic reactions. Traditional psychotherapy had no
effect on his phobia. He could leave home after dark only in his
car, and he always managed to return home before sunset. Being
in the dark inside or outside or thinking about the dark caused
intense anxiety (excessive sweating, gasping, trembling, and diz-

ziness). Even with lights on, he could not fall asleep at night and began sleeping during the day. When he fell asleep by taking pills, he had terrible nightmares. He justified not sleeping at night as a way of avoiding nightmares and saw his outdoor fears as irrational. Any object in the dark scared him, and a group of trees was especially frightening.

The treatment described above completely eliminated his fear of darkness. All normal evening activities were pursued. Because of circumstances, treatment of the inability to sleep at night was not possible. A six-month follow-up found him totally free of any fear of darkness.

COMMENTARY: This article demonstrates the applicability of usual real-life desensitization procedures to fear of darkness. Kipper also describes a successful outcome with a thirteen-year-old girl whose inability to fall asleep was treated with a simple desensitization procedure. She closed her bedroom door slightly more each night and practiced progressive muscular relaxation. Within three weeks she was able to fall asleep. Again, we see a combination of methods being used. The "attention shifting" component is in line with the many reports coming from different theoretical systems in which positive thoughts are substituted for negative or fearful ideas.

SOURCE: Kipper, D. A. "In Vivo Desensitization of Nyctophobia: Two Case Reports." *Psychotherapy: Theory, Research, and Practice,* 1980, *17,* 24-29.

Implosive Therapy with Hypnosis for Cancer Phobia

AUTHOR: John M. O'Donnell

PRECIS: Three sixty-minute sessions in which an adult female is hypnotized to enhance vivid imagination of intense anxiety-arousing images of tumors

INTRODUCTION: Breast cancer and mastectomies have received much publicity, with emphasis on early detection and treatment. An increased fear of having cancer has been reported by many physicians. People with fears and/or hypochondriasis do not accept evidence or logic that they do not have any disease. Convinced that they have a medical problem, they do not seek psychotherapy. Additionally, hypochondriasis has been resistant to treatment. Implosive therapy was developed for treating phobias. Clients are instructed to imagine the most anxiety-producing situations possible. Images must be perceived vividly. Exposure to fears without negative consequences weakens the fear reaction. Hypnotic induction is used to heighten suggestibility, focus attention, and maximize bodily awareness.

METHOD: A twenty-nine-year-old married woman had relatives and a friend who died of cancer. Her childhood was unhappy, and she had several rejecting stepfathers. There was evidence that positive attention was received when she was physically sick. During the year before treatment, she had seen ten different physicians for forty-five visits and was hospitalized twice. At her own expense, she had undergone a brain scan, two barium swallows, and two dozen x rays. She was almost constantly preoccupied with having cancer and realized her irrational fear. Self-examination for tumors was so frequent that her body was visibly bruised. Since her current symptoms were being reinforced by attention from physicians and her husband, verbal therapy was ruled out. Behavioral approaches were described, and she chose implosive therapy because it might be quickly effective. If this did not work, desensitization would be used.

Within one week, three one-hour sessions were held with no imagery homework assigned. The first session consisted of practicing imagery for ten minutes and then twenty minutes of hypnotic induction focusing on relaxation and bodily awareness (body areas of most concern). For the remaining thirty minutes, implosive imagery was presented by the therapist. The client imagined tumors developing on parts of her body that she was most worried about. Every growth was described as appearing, smelling, feeling, and tasting horrible. Her body was vividly described as deteriorating into a gigantic tumor, which disgusted all her relatives and friends. They were described as uncaring and rejecting of her throughout her long, horrible, extremely painful death. After death, she was to spend eternity as a disgusting, writhing, rotten mass.

This procedure was repeated twice at two-day intervals. Hypnotic induction was very successful, and the client was extremely anxious throughout the sessions. Anxiety peaked after about twenty minutes and then diminished somewhat. Each session concluded with five minutes of debriefing, in which she described feeling exhausted with little anxiety. After the second and third sessions, she laughed about her ridiculous symptoms.

She completed a 5-point fear rating scale every half hour during five weeks spread over a ten-month period. Baseline, post-treatment, and follow-up data are presented. A clear diminishing of self-reported fear occurred. During the year after treatment, she saw only one physician, for her regular annual physical examination.

COMMENTARY: O'Donnell cautions that improper use of implosive therapy might increase sensitivity to fears and that length of exposure time to imagery is a crucial factor. Guidelines for proper exposure time are not presented. It is apparent that, as in all methods, therapists must base treatment decisions on their knowledge of the particular patient and be especially sensitive to patient reactions to treatment. A very useful approach is to describe alternative treatments, giving clients a choice based on information and likely outcome. O'Donnell does discuss the lack of clarity about the rapid effectiveness of combining implosive therapy with hypnosis. Possible explanations concern the role of covert conditioning, self-instruction, paradoxical intention, and expectancy factors. However, we agree with his conclusion that this combined approach may be applicable to other neurotic symptoms that do not respond to treatment. There is a growing need for brief treatments, especially in areas where longer-term treatment is unavailable or too costly. Less sophisticated clients with specific fears may be maximally responsive to this approach.

SOURCE: O'Donnell, J. M. "Implosive Therapy with Hypnosis in the Treatment of Cancer Phobia: A Case Report." *Psychotherapy: Theory, Research, and Practice,* 1978, *15,* 8-12.

Behavior Therapy Compared with Group Psychotherapy for Fear of Flying

AUTHORS: Leslie Solyom, Richard Shugar, Shirley Bryntwick, and Carol Solyom

PRECIS: Aversion relief, systematic desensitization, habituation, or group psychotherapy for forty patients

INTRODUCTION: In one study, fear of flying was intense in 10 percent of the population and mild in 20 percent. Systematic desensitization (with or without drugs) has been relatively effective in overcoming air travel phobia, while conventional psychotherapy has not. The present study used people with an overwhelming fear of flying and an avoidance or inability to fly without extreme anxiety. Pre- and posttreatment testing consisted of the IPAT Anxiety Scale, Fear Survey Schedule, Maudsley Personality Inventory, psychiatric interview, and a fear of flying questionnaire.

METHOD: The behavioral therapies took place in a room with sixteen standard airplane seats, motion picture facilities, and finger electric shock equipment. Clients (five in each treatment group) sat in the front row facing the screen, and the therapist was behind a one-way mirror. The film shown was fifteen minutes long and showed airplanes taking off and landing, passengers' activities during flight, and airport scenes.

Systematic Desensitization. Hourly sessions took place twice a week for four weeks. Clients were taught relaxation and an anxiety hierarchy was presented during the first four sessions. For the next four sessions the flight film was shown while the clients relaxed.

Aversion Relief. Each participant wrote three to five descriptions of any past flying experiences. These were written in the first person, present tense, and focused on anxiety-producing events (sound of the engine, bumpy ride, and so on). Any bodily reactions, thoughts, and behavior accompanying anxiety were also described. Audiotapes of these descriptions were made by the participants and played for them during eight thirty-minute sessions. Just before the anxiety response, a twenty-second silence was followed by a mild electrical shock to a finger. When a button was pressed, the shock ended and the tape continued. Therefore, the relief of the shock ending occurred while the anxious situation was being described. An example follows. "When I am"—twenty seconds, shock, button pressed (relief), "fastened to the seat"—twenty seconds, shock, button pressed, "I feel trapped"—twenty seconds, shock, button pressed, "my heart is racing."

The flight film was shown during the next eight sessions, and relief similarly occurred during fearful experiences. Electrical shock after every pause was gradually reduced to only 20 percent of the pauses. An example follows. A flight attendant walks down the aisle—twenty seconds, shock, button pressed, "Fasten your seat belts"—twenty seconds, shock, button pressed, "Bumpy weather ahead."

Habituation. This method was the same as aversion relief, but shock was not administered. However, the audiotape and the film were interrupted at the same twenty-second intervals.

Group Psychotherapy. Discussions included descriptions of participants' phobias, rationalizations, other neurotic problems, and so on. Five weekly two-hour sessions were held. Then an experienced pilot met the participants at the airport and discussed air travel safety, pilot training, and many other issues. The same pilot took the group and the therapist for a fifteen-minute flight one week later.

The three behavior therapies were equally and significantly effective in diminishing fear of air travel. Group psychotherapy was relatively ineffective immediately after treatment but had improved to the same level of success as the behavior therapies at a follow-up after approximately one year. With more severe phobias, systematic desensitization and aversion relief were equivalent in a past study. However, habituation has been ineffective with phobias (especially agoraphobia). Perhaps the relatively low initial anxiety level of the habituation group led to the equivalent results. In conclusion, repeated controllable exposure to the sights and sounds of flying in a safe environment reduces the fear of flying. The ability to stop the experience is an important ingredient.

COMMENTARY: The three behavioral methods equally reduced fear of flying, tending to confirm recent beliefs that fear extinguishes when the person is repeatedly exposed to the fearful situation while feeling safe. Strikingly, group psychotherapy was effective only several months after the experience. This supports many psychodynamic therapists who believe that dealing with past trauma and resolving sources of anxiety lead to improvement in the long run. We must point out that this group psychotherapy did include one real-life flying experience. Once again we see the probable desirability of combining methods. Behavioral techniques can lead to immediate improvement, and verbal psychotherapy may contribute to more self-confidence and improved general functioning. This combination may be particularly appropriate with fearful persons with extensive flying experience, since this group benefited less from treatment. The effectiveness of all the methods is a clear indicator that air travel phobia (and other phobias) can be reduced or eliminated with relatively brief methods. There is no reason (given client motivation) for any long-term treatment not reducing a phobia.

One probable reason for existing ineffectiveness is the tendency of some therapists to talk to clients and not insist on gradual, controlled exposure to the fear.

SOURCE: Solyom, L., Shugar, R., Bryntwick, S., and Solyom, C. "Treatment of Fear of Flying." *American Journal of Psychiatry,* 1973, *130,* 423-427.

Guided Imagining for Fears

AUTHOR: Milton Wolpin

PRECIS: Improving symptoms by brief therapy focused on visualization of wished-for behavior

INTRODUCTION: Guided imagining has been successfully used with all kinds of people with fears of being alone, snakes, public speaking, and other things. At least some improvement has been seen with all clients in under twelve sessions. There have been no instances of problems worsening. In desensitization methods, anxiety is kept low, and clients gradually imagine (while relaxed) more and more fearful situations until they visualize what they would like to be able to deal with. Implosive therapy maximizes anxiety and uses imagined scenes that are much more anxiety-provoking than would actually occur.

METHOD: In contrast to desensitization or implosive therapy, the present method does not use any procedure to inhibit any response. No attempt is made to influence people's reactions, and they are allowed to respond in any way to imagined scenes. If a person cries, the scene continues to be described during the crying. The scene is not presented in separate pieces, nor are things described beyond what someone wants to face. Each description is the entire behavior that the person is desirous of

doing. Many details are described, and there is a warm-up period. This first part consists of non-anxiety-producing activities
that would be likely to occur before the fearful event.

A detailed example is presented of an imagined scene regarding fear of snakes. The person closes his eyes. The therapist describes the scene in great detail, from sitting down to getting up, leaving the building, walking outside, going into a building, and opening the door to a room with a snake. The person is
to imagine opening the cage, removing the snake, holding it,
watching it crawl and stick out its tongue, putting it back, and
leaving the building. Throughout, phrases such as "imagine
yourself," "picture yourself," "visualize yourself," "imagine
that," and "notice how" are used. There are no guidelines for
how people are to feel. They are to imagine the actual behavior
that they would like to be able to perform. Each act is broken
down into the actual movements. After each imagined scene,
questions are posed to clients concerning how they visualized
the scene and what their feelings were. Rather than what was
described, they are asked to say what they saw and how they
felt. When scenes are not imagined as presented, it is often because clients are uncomfortable about some activity. The therapist insists that the person imagine exactly what he had previously stated. Thus, this is a type of operant reinforcement of
the desired behavior. Often, people give more details that enable
the therapist to make scenes more realistic, which facilitates
generalization to real life.

The therapist uses questions designed to assess the moments of greatest anxiety. These behaviors are usually the most
difficult to perform, and the next scenes emphasize those behaviors. In the previous example of a snake phobia, it is typical
that picking up the snake is the most difficult to imagine. That
behavior is described in the most vivid, detailed way possible,
and other parts of the scene are eliminated or deemphasized.
When clients cry or express any type of discomfort, they are
told to continue and experience whatever they feel. They are
not made to face anything beyond what they had stated, but
they are not allowed to stop imagining because they are uncomfortable. Anxiety often decreases after a few repeated scenes,

showing a type of adaptation. Therapist reinforcement and self-reinforcement are probably operative.

COMMENTARY: Wolpin says that doing something in imagination increases the probability of actually doing that behavior. He discusses catharsis and improved self-image as possible causal factors of doing feared behavior. Regardless of cause, we see this simple procedure as extremely useful both for pinpointing moments of greatest anxiety and as a direct treatment tool. As in any method, therapist sensitivity and manner of presentation are important. A client may be told about the past effectiveness of this technique. Then the therapist clearly describes many realistic details of the situation in which the fear is faced and handled. Feelings that emerge are matter-of-factly accepted and discussed. Therefore, this type of brief therapy may be the treatment of choice for specific fears. In the near future we may be able to predict which type of fearful client would respond better to methods such as guided imagining, desensitization, or implosive therapy. Until then, therapists may select a method that they believe in and/or that is compatible with their therapeutic style.

SOURCE. Wolpin, M. "Guided Imagining to Reduce Avoidance Behavior." *Psychotherapy: Theory, Research, and Practice,* 1969, *6,* 122-124.

Additional Readings

Biran, M., and Wilson, G. T. "Treatment of Phobic Disorders Using Cognitive and Exposure Methods: A Self-Efficacy Analysis." *Journal of Consulting and Clinical Psychology,* 1981, *49,* 886-899.

   Guided exposure requires people to attempt increasingly difficult encounters with feared situations. Therapists help give homework assignments when necessary and support, encourage, and verbally reinforce self-directed performance and self-mastery. Cognitive restructuring consists of relabeling, discussing irrational beliefs, rational restructuring, and self-instructional training. When encountering feared situations, clients prepare, confront, cope, and reinforce themselves. Modifying self-talk at home was accomplished by recording the description of the situation, initial anxiety level, irrational thoughts, rational thoughts, and subsequent anxiety level. Participants were men and women (average age forty years and average duration of phobias twenty years), of whom fifteen had fear of heights, five feared elevators, and two were afraid of darkness. Treatment was five individual fifty-minute sessions over a two- to three-week period. As predicted, the performance-based technique (exposure) had significantly better results than the purely cognitive procedure. The durable behavioral changes were obtained in five or fewer sessions. For those who did not respond to cognitive treatment, exposure later was highly effective. Compared with cognitive treatment, exposure reduced performance fear and physiological reactivity and enabled clients to engage in activities that they could not previously perform. Cognitive therapy may be successful for more cognitively based disorders, such as test anxiety. However, it is not the treatment of choice for phobias, in which behavior has a major role and physiological arousal is prominent.

Denholtz, M. S., Hall, L. A., and Mann, E. "Automated Treatment for Flight Phobia: A 3½ Year Follow-Up." *American Journal of Psychiatry,* 1978, *135,* 1340-1343.

Scenes were taken from TV commercials that were pleasurable or induced anxiety in flight phobics. Twenty-seven paired scenes (anxiety/pleasurable) from low to high anxiety arousal were shown to fifty-one flight-phobic adults by housewives or college students. The instruction tape induced relaxation, and participants were told to push a button to indicate the presence or absence of anxiety after viewing each pair. The tape induced relaxation between scenes. When anxiety was indicated, the scene pair was repeated until no anxiety was reported. The film was completed in two to ten half-hour sessions. This method combines desensitization, modeling, and positive reinforcement in a totally automated program administered by nonprofessionals. About 78 percent of the participants became able to fly and also showed significantly less anxiety on personality tests. Improvement was maintained at follow-up. A modified treatment was developed with home practice of taped relaxation and four viewings of the film. This resulted in a success rate of 83 percent among 28 persons. Participants in both studies reported feeling more relaxed in general and able to reduce tension by relaxing in stressful situations. This supports the coping interpretation of fear reduction in that clients develop coping skills in dealing with a variety of stressful situations.

Fensterheim, H., and Baer, J. *Stop Running Scared! Fear Control Training: The New Way to Conquer Fears, Phobias and Anxieties.* New York: Dell, 1977.

Intense, irrational fear is described as a habit that can be controlled or eliminated. Fear Control Training is a step-by-step plan for overcoming fears of heights, crowds, closed spaces, animals, thunderstorms, and so on. A separate chapter provides a proven plan for overcoming fear of flying. Methods include progressive relaxation, thought stoppage, thought switching, success rehearsal, and systematic desensitization (in reality and in fantasy). This book is specifically written for the public and includes many illustrative cases.

Hall, R. A., and Dietz, A. J. "Systematic Organismic Desensitization." *Psychotherapy: Theory, Research, and Practice,* 1975, *12,* 388-390.

A twenty-year-old male college student had fears of heights, driving, and sitting in classrooms. Desensitization consisted of an abbreviated form of deep muscle relaxation and creating three fear hierarchies. Questioning revealed that in class he tended to look at the ceiling and the floor and made many head movements. This indicated possible involvement of the vestibular canals of the inner ear. It was hypothesized that a common element in all three hierarchies was not an external environmental situation but an organismic variable, such as an inner-ear infection that occasionally caused a gag reflex. During the third session, the client surprisingly said yes to the inquiry about a possible inner-ear infection. At first he was unwilling to work on desensitizing the fear of choking, but he later agreed, and a fear hierarchy was constructed. The bottom items of the three fears were desensitized. After six sessions, he was encouraged to expose himself to feared situations. To his surprise, his anxiety was gone. A three-year follow-up revealed no fears. Careful analysis may reveal transsituational organismic elements (rather than focusing on external situations). Desensitization of this common denominator is an efficient treatment approach.

Kipper, D. A. "Behavior Therapy for Fears Brought On by War Experiences." *Journal of Consulting and Clinical Psychology,* 1977, *45,* 216-221.

War-induced fears, compared with peacetime phobias, produced many daily anxiety attacks, extreme restlessness, and extreme withdrawal. Fear of noises, especially sudden ones, is typical. Also frequent are fears of the sight of airplanes, tanks, ambulances, blood, physical injuries, open or closed places, and darkness. Self-administered *in vivo* desensitization consisted in the patient's learning and practicing to relax himself through recorded instructions. A fear hierarchy was constructed by the therapist and patient. The patient relaxes and exposes himself to the feared situation for five, fifteen, and thirty seconds, repeating the process until no anxiety is felt. Two successful cases are described (fear of bandages and fear of noises). *In vivo* desensitization in dyads resembled the above procedure except that the patient was treated by a fellow patient. Two persons suffering from different kinds of phobias were assigned to treat each other. Successful treatment is described for a claustrophobic and a social phobic. These treatments can now be added to the therapies used to treat war neuroses—narcosynthesis with sodium pentathol, brief or group psychotherapy, convulsive shock therapy, general convalescent care, and occupational therapy. Dyadic desensitization adds the factor of patients' competing with each other to get well sooner. At times it induces restlessness and should not be used with patients in generally poor psychological condition. Both forms of desensitization alleviate pressure on a wartime psychologist and permit the carrying of an increased caseload.

Linden, W. "Exposure Treatments for Focal Phobias." *Archives of General Psychiatry,* 1981, *38,* 769-775.

Focal phobias include phobic-anxiety reactions to clearly limited stimuli (such as small animals) and agoraphobia (fear of leaving home). Approaches such as systematic desensitization, implosive therapy, flooding, and cognitive restructuring are reviewed and distinguished by whether the patient comes in direct contact with the fear-producing situation. Psychological treatment resulted in maintenance of improvement for the majority of phobic patients (the lowest rate reported—58 percent). Exposure treatments resulted in higher improvement rates (75 to 100 percent). Complete remission of symptoms is rare, but treated patients show diminished phobias and minimal work and social disruption. Prognosis is not predicted by social anxiety, depression, severity, or type of phobia. *In vivo* exposure is currently the behavioral treatment of choice for focal phobias. The following conclusions are drawn. (1) The critical duration of exposure is thirty to sixty minutes of continuous, uninterrupted exposure. A minimum of sixty minutes of exposure is recommended. (2) Physiological measurement should occur to ensure a decrease in sympathetic arousal before the exposure session is terminated. (3) Different *in vivo* exposures have been equally efffective. Therefore, economical approaches such as flooding in groups and self-control procedures may be used. (4) Contingent reinforcement appears to increase treatment effectiveness. (5) An anxiety-reducing drug is especially useful when panic attacks are present.

Mavissakalian, M., and Barlow, D. H. (Eds.). *Phobia: Psychological and Pharmacological Treatment.* New York: Guilford Publications, 1981.

This book presents a variety of assessment and treatment procedures for phobias and anxiety. Various perspectives are discussed, including many behavioral and psychoanalytic methods. Practicing clinicians are helped to develop therapy programs for specific phobias and agoraphobia. Pharmacological and psychological approaches are presented in an integrated manner. Arguments for or against each treatment are clearly presented.

Muller, B., and Armstrong, H. E. "A Further Note on the 'Running Treatment' for Anxiety." *Psychotherapy: Theory, Research, and Practice,* 1975, *12,* 385-387.

Running treatment, developed by Irwin, was successfully used with eight agoraphobics. The present case involved a forty-two-year-old woman with a twenty-two-year history of elevator phobia. She was afraid of being trapped and unable to get free. The first session involved jogging with the therapist to a department store. She was fatigued, was out of breath, and had a rapid heartbeat and a weak feeling in her legs. Although these reactions were similar to her fear reactions, she felt unexpectedly calm and rode the elevators up and down for one floor. She would not go for a second ride, as she became aware of her fear. After jogging again, she repeated the ride. During the second session, she jogged and rode to the twenty-eighth floor and continued to practice without the therapist present. Knowledge of elevators was taught by an elevator supervisor. She learned the mechanics and safety devices of elevators and was shown how to escape in case of an emergency. A four-month follow-up revealed regular use of elevators and minimal experience of fear. Relaxation methods for desensitization are time-consuming and difficult. Jogging produces bodily phenomena autonomically identical to fear. This reality is perceived as normal (fatigue), not as abnormal fear. The person alters his or her interpretation of autonomic arousal without controlling or altering the arousal.

Pearlman, T. "Behavioral Desensitization of Phobic Anxiety Using Thiopental Sodium." *American Journal of Psychiatry,* 1980, *137,* 1580-1582.

A random sample of twenty-five treated patients were evaluated. They were adults with a variety of phobias, including fear of open or confined spaces, traffic, thunder, dentists, exams, cancer, and animals. Most of the patients were taking antianxiety drugs (mainly benzodiazepines). Treatment was given biweekly for two weeks and then weekly for four weeks. Solid foods were not eaten for three hours before treatment, and patients remained in the waiting room after each session until all dizziness passed. While the patient reclined, 50 mg of thiopental sodium in a 2½ percent aqueous solution was injected intravenously in a single dose. A twilight state existed for four to six minutes, and the patient was relaxed but alert. With eyes closed, patients vividly imagined previous attacks of phobic anxiety. They then imagined an attack beginning but with themselves able to diminish or eliminate the attack by being relaxed. After the six minutes of drug-induced relaxation, they spent ten to twelve minutes associating anxiety-producing stimuli with the relaxation response. They were encouraged to reduce intake of tranquilizers. At least twice daily, they practiced muscle relaxation while imagining the phobic situation. At a twenty-four-week follow-up, fourteen patients were symptom-free and fifteen were tranquilizer-free. The therapy is particularly useful in treating phobias in communities with a shortage of psychiatrists.

Shapiro, D. H., and Gilber, D. "Meditation and Psychotherapeutic Effects: Self-Regulation Strategy and Altered State of Consciousness." *Archives of General Psychiatry,* 1978, *35,* 294-302.

This general review article discusses thirteen studies in which phobias and other stresses are reduced by meditation. Successful outcomes are reported for fear of enclosed places, exams, elevators, being alone, and heart attacks. Four studies combined meditation and other methods, with meditation used first, second, or simultaneously. The first study using a control group reported consistent and greater reduction of anxiety for the meditation group. Different forms of meditation have been used. A popular one is Zen breath meditation. Meditators are instructed to ignore any perceptual changes or hallucinations, let them go, and continue to focus on breathing. Meditation has been viewed as an altered state of consciousness; people describe feeling a "unity," "union," "oneness with all things," "enhanced sense of reality," and an "alteration of time and space." There is general agreement that meditation produces a state of relaxation (effortless breathing). Consistently reported are reduced heart rate, decreased oxygen consumption, decreased blood pressure, and increased skin resistance and alpha activity. Some believe that meditation reduces phobias because it is a type of global desensitization. As meditators relax and learn to witness random thoughts, there is a reciprocal inhibition of anxiety-producing thoughts.

Stamm, J. L. "An Illuminating Hour—Fear of Sore Throats and Its Relationship to Bisexuality." *Psychiatry Digest,* June 1964, pp. 23-32.

A forty-two-year-old woman was terrified of developing a sore throat. Psychoanalysis revealed an overwhelming guilt complex toward her mother, a need for punishment, and a masochistic identification with her mother. Another crucial area was her long-standing conflict about her identity, especially her femininity. She never accepted her role as a woman, had an unconscious violent competition with men, and had rape fantasies linked with an early childhood wish to be raped and impregnated by her father. When she developed a sore throat, she had to think about the word *pregnancy* and shake her breasts. The glands in her neck were swollen and felt like two large testicles. She also feared having bugs in her throat. A significant memory was having received injections to bring on normal menstruation in order that she would become a woman and be able to become pregnant. The injection was linked with the penis and being impregnated by the doctor. A significant interpretation was her concern about oral impregnation (sucking on a penis) and a fantasy of having a penis hidden inside her. The suffering surrounding a sore throat partly gratified her insatiable oral yearnings, her masochistic fixation, and her need for punishment. The sore throat also condensed wishes to be both a man and a woman. Coitus, oral impregnation, and incorporation of male genitalia are symbolized.

Toomim, M. K., and Toomim, H. "GSR Biofeedback in Psychotherapy: Some Clinical Observations." *Psychotherapy: Theory, Research, and Practice,* 1975, *12,* 33-38.

GSR feedback is seen as an integral part of a dynamic psychotherapy process. The therapy used was eclectic, with an emphasis on emotional flooding. Peaks or paradoxical GSR reactivity were emphasized in order to intensify a client's experience and facilitate emotional release. The instrument used quantifies skin conductance in micromhos and has a psychotherapy scale that amplifies rate of change of conductance. Electrodes and cream were applied to the palm of the dominant hand. The client and the therapist could hear the feedback tone (signaling intensity and length of time for conductance to decrease). An example is given in which a client's habit of touching his bicep caused a large increase in GSR conductance. Questioning revealed that he sat at the dining room table with his father at his left and always felt uncomfortable about people sitting to his left. People can be classified as GSR overreactors, underreactors and variable reactors, and illustrative cases are presented. One case involved a woman who awoke in panic very early every morning. A flat GSR was related to a guilty childhood fantasy. The GSR feedback tone is a guide to therapist and client about the possible value of the content being discussed. Immediate awareness of the body/mind relationship is possible. The feedback technique allows direct training of dysfunctional sympathetic nervous system reactivity patterns and identifies some of the attitudes that maintain a stress response.

3

Generalized
Anxiety
Disorder

According to DSM-III (p. 233), the following are diagnostic criteria for generalized anxiety disorder.

A. Generalized, persistent anxiety is manifested by symptoms from three of the following four categories:

   (1) *motor tension:* shakiness, jitteriness, jumpiness, trembling, tension, muscle aches, fatigability, inability to relax, eyelid twitch, furrowed brow, strained face, fidgeting, restlessness, easy startle

   (2) *autonomic hyperactivity:* sweating, heart pounding or racing, cold, clammy hands, dry mouth, dizziness, lightheadedness, paresthesias

201

(tingling in hands or feet), upset stomach, hot or cold spells, frequent urination, diarrhea, discomfort in the pit of the stomach, lump in the throat, flushing, pallor, high resting pulse and respiration rate

(3) *apprehensive expectation:* anxiety, worry, fear, rumination, and anticipation of misfortune to self or others

(4) *vigilance and scanning:* hyperattentiveness resulting in distractibility, difficulty in concentrating, insomnia, feeling "on edge," irritability, impatience

B. The anxious mood has been continuous for at least one month.

C. Not due to another mental disorder, such as a Depressive Disorder or Schizophrenia.

D. At least 18 years of age.

According to DSM-III, mild depressive symptoms are common, as is abuse of alcohol, barbiturates, or antianxiety medications. Impairment in social or occupational functioning is usually no more than mild.

Although in DSM-III no incidence figures are given for generalized anxiety disorder, at least one group (M. Raskin, G. Johnson, and J. W. Rondestvedt, "Chronic Anxiety Treated by Feedback-Induced Muscle Relaxation," *Archives of General Psychiatry,* 1973, *28,* 263-267) stated that 5 percent of the U.S. population has been estimated to suffer from "chronic anxiety." In another summary article (N. Hare and D. J. Levis, "Pervasive ('Free-Floating') Anxiety: A Search for a Cause and Treatment Approach," in S. M. Turner, K. S. Calhoun, and H. E. Adams (Eds.), *Handbook of Clinical Behavior Therapy,* New York: Wiley, 1981), the authors estimate that pervasive or chronic anxiety is one of the most common problems encountered by practitioners in the mental health fields. The same authors point out that years ago one therapist (J. R. Cautela, "A Behavior Therapy Approach to Pervasive Anxiety," *Behaviour Research and Therapy,* 1966, *4,* 99-109) wrote that for pervasive anxiety no general treatment has been devised, and very little has been accomplished since that time. On the brighter side, the reader will note in the following digests and additional readings that although no one general treatment has been devised, there is an array of successful treatments.

In what follows the reader will find reports of the lowering of anxiety through psychoanalytic treatment, exposure both in real life and in imagination to threatening events, relaxation alone and as part of various desensitization procedures, self-monitoring or focusing on various aspects of one's anxiety, skills for coping with anxiety, exercise, rest, diversion, trying out a new role in life, stopping self-defeating statements, altering perceptions, exaggerating one's symptoms, and drugs. Further still, various combinations of these measures have been used with skill. One article sounds a helpful warning beneath all the therapies: be sure that a person's anxiety is not being caused by some physical ailment.

Cognitive Self-Control Methods

AUTHOR: John Barrow

PRECIS: Teaching people to detect their anxiety early and to apply a series of cognitive strategies

INTRODUCTION: Two fairly recent trends in therapy are noteworthy. The first is an increased interest in how people think, beyond how people behave, which is the emphasis of the behaviorists. The second is an emphasis on increasing people's capacity for self-control. Cognitive therapy strategies are ideally suited for self-management, unlike behavior therapy methods, which are often therapist-controlled. Cognitive methods, too, are inexpensive, requiring no costly or unwieldy equipment. People such as university students are especially receptive to these possibilities. They pride themselves on their abilities to think, and they value self-control.

The proliferation of cognitive methods provides a wide range of possibilities to people who wish to learn to allay anxiety by controlling themselves. Therapists may be especially helpful in teaching people to size up how their anxieties originate and then teaching them how to control them.

TREATMENT: Therapists using self-control cognitive therapy can offer the following services.

Assessment. Two basic things must be uncovered: the situations that make the person anxious and the extent to which the person's thoughts contribute to the anxiety. For the first of these, a distinction must be made. If the person's anxiety boils down to one or two discrete phobias, desensitization (described elsewhere in this section) may be appropriate. If, however, the anxiety is generalized across an array of situations, self-control may work. To get at the extent to which thoughts promote anxiety, various measures such as interview, self-report questionnaires, and self-monitoring can be used. If worrisome ruminating seems to predominate, then cognitive methods are in order. If emotional responses seem to dominate, relaxation may suffice.

Early Detection Training. Therapists must help clients to focus on what happens at the time they feel anxious. Clients then see what cues they must look for and then apply anxiety-reducing strategies. The therapist assigns this kind of careful focusing as homework. Besides helping to tell clients that they must apply new strategies, this focusing often causes clients to associate the anxious cues with taking action.

Analyzing Self-Talk. The next step is to get clients to see what goes through their minds in anxious moments. Various analyses are useful here. Some clients are helped by looking at anxiety-producing experiences they have had, discovering that the situation did not produce the anxiety but rather an intervening self-statement did, and then looking for what the self-statement was. These often take the form of self-defeating statements, which fall into two categories: worrying about performing adequately and preoccupation with gaining approval of others. Still other clients are helped by seeing that they become anxious when they focus on themselves rather than the task at hand. Clients find it useful to monitor these experiences, writing down the situations, their feelings, and what they said to themselves.

Redirecting Self-Talk. The goal of self-control cognitive therapy is to get clients to catch themselves becoming anxious and then change anxiety-producing self-statements to counteractive statements. Following the analysis of self-talk described above, two approaches seem to be helpful to clients: the first is to challenge the accuracy of the self-defeating statement, the second is to change the focus from oneself to the task at hand. Different clients respond to different measures.

Self-defeating statements can be challenged in a variety of ways. One way is for the client to check himself on whether he is exaggerating the actual importance a situation has to him. For example, one may say, "Is it really so crucial that he have a good opinion of me?" Self-challenge of such perceptions as needing approval from everyone or wanting things to be perfect is often helpful. Therapist and client must find an approach to self-challenge that fits the client. In addition, the therapist can teach methods of thought stopping.

The second variety of redirecting an anxious client is to discuss ways he can take his attention off himself and onto what he is supposed to be doing in any given situation. Sometimes self-instructions are useful, such as "Be a good listener," telling oneself to listen to and remember people's names, for example. This second set of techniques is actually guiding clients to do something positive, rather than to avoid doing something negative, as in the first variety described above.

Transfer of Training. Obviously, clients are being trained to change the way they think, and this is easier said than done. Therefore, some intermediate steps can be suggested. Clients can be asked to imagine using new strategies in old situations, to try out strategies in their lives that have been discussed in therapy, to experiment with ways of changing their destructive self-talk, to find ways to cue themselves to change their self-talk in a productive way, and to write down what they tried.

The therapist will find it helpful to keep up an ongoing assessment of a client's current concerns, to be selective and flexible in suggesting anxiety-reducing strategies, and to take into consideration what the client wants from therapy and what his unique problem-solving style is.

COMMENTARY: These well-thought-out steps for treating anxiety might be applicable to numerous disorders, particularly phobias and obsessive-compulsive problems. The therapist diagnoses carefully to see whether the anxiety is actually phobic (apply desensitization), based on emotions (teach relaxation), or based on thoughts (use cognitive methods). He then helps anxious clients to focus on their feelings, look at what is going on when anxiety arises, and examine what is going through their minds; to aid this, he suggests self-monitoring. He then teaches coping strategies, in particular constructive self-statements or focusing on the task at hand rather than on themselves. And last, he teaches how they can generalize from what they have learned. This emphasis on generalizing is seldom stressed enough. The author suggests that the therapist constantly look at how the therapy is going and be flexible in changing therapeutic measures. In addition to this extraordinary set of principles,

Barrow reminds therapists not only to remember what the client wants from therapy but to appraise how the client characteristically solves problems and make the most of it. The overall focus on self-control here is admirable.

In teaching coping strategies, Barrow emphasizes the focusing away from oneself to the job at hand and stresses the traditional constructive self-statements. The reader might want to add still other measures from this section or even the entire book—for example, meditation, physical exercise.

SOURCE: Barrow, J. "Cognitive Self-Control Strategies with the Anxious Student." *Psychotherapy: Theory, Research, and Practice,* 1979, *16,* 152-157.

A Comparison of Ways of Teaching Progressive Relaxation

AUTHORS: Irving Beiman, Eileen Israel, and Stephen A. Johnson

PRECIS: Live presentation of progressive relaxation training shown to be more effective for reduction of physiological arousal than taped presentation, self-relaxation, or biofeedback for anxious adults

INTRODUCTION: Progressive relaxation is widely used as a method for treating anxiety. The question remains, how can it be taught most effectively and economically? Taped training would be, for example, more economical than training provided in person by a therapist. Biofeedback is expensive in terms of equipment, but if it could be demonstrated to be most effective, the results might be worth the cost. Self-relaxation would certainly be a treatment of choice because of its economy. This study was undertaken to determine the relative efficacy of these four methods in reducing physiological arousal and subjective tension.

METHOD: Nineteen men and twenty-one women were chosen from a group that had answered a newspaper ad requesting tense people who would participate in a psychological study to alleviate tension. Their ages ranged from twenty to fifty-four, and they were chosen because they were not acutely disturbed, were not taking drugs or in therapy, had no training in any of the treatments used, and reported that tension was a serious problem. Each subject was randomly assigned to one of four training conditions: live progressive relaxation, taped progressive relaxation, self-relaxation, or biofeedback. The therapist scheduled six sessions, three or four days apart. To control for physiological reactions, each woman received her first session at least one and not more than two weeks after the onset of her current menstrual cycle. During all sessions, physiological measures (heart rate, respiration, muscle tension, and galvanic skin response) were taken on all subjects. Verbal reports of experienced anxiety were taken during the first and last sessions. Sessions generally lasted about thirty minutes.

Subjects receiving relaxation training were instructed either by a live presentation by the therapist or by tape-recorded instructions. Subjects receiving self-control training were told that they had potential to develop control over tension by regular practice of relaxation. They were then instructed to relax but not to go to sleep. Biofeedback training involved pairing forehead muscle relaxation with a tone; the goal was to maintain a state of relaxation so that the tone could remain on continuously for fifteen seconds.

The effects of the training were assessed during the sixth session. Subjects were asked to relax as much as possible, using the skills they had developed during the previous five sessions. This assessment period lasted ten minutes, after which subjects were given self-report questionnaires to measure anxiety levels.

The results indicated that, during training, live relaxation training was superior to taped relaxation training in reducing physiological arousal. Self-relaxation training and biofeedback were equal to each other in reducing physiological and subjective arousal, with one exception: self-relaxation training was more effective in reducing heart rate. The authors suggest that biofeedback procedures involving complex and expensive equipment may be less effective than simple self-relaxation instructions in inducing in-session relaxation for chronically anxious clients. After training, live relaxation was superior to the other procedures for reducing physiological arousal and appears to be the treatment of choice when client control over bodily signs of anxiety is a major goal of therapy.

COMMENTARY: This is an article about the refinements of teaching relaxation: which method is most economical and effective? A costly method—live presentation by the therapist—is the method of choice found here. The relative effectiveness of self-relaxation should not be overlooked, as this suggests that if a live presentation is not possible, self-relaxation might be satisfactory. However, the important thing may be that, for maximum effectiveness, progressive relaxation should be supported generously with other therapeutic measures included in this section.

SOURCE: Beiman, I., Israel, E., and Johnson, S. A. "During Training and Posttraining Effects of Live and Taped Extended Progressive Relaxation, Self-Relaxation, and Electromyogram Biofeedback." *Journal of Consulting and Clinical Psychology,* 1978, *46,* 314-321.

Ruling Out Organic Disorder

AUTHOR: James T. Dietch

PRECIS: The importance of discovering physical causes of anxiety to avoid misdiagnosis

INTRODUCTION: In a large study of people admitted to a psychiatric clinic, the researcher found that 8 percent had an undiagnosed organic disorder that explained their psychological symptoms. In addition, 22 percent had an undiagnosed organic disorder that markedly contributed to their psychological symptoms. For example, one study of hyperthyroid people showed that their MMPI profiles were typically "neurotic," revealing anxiety, depression, physical discomfort, and loss of psychological control. However, after treatment for hyperthyroidism, their psychological profiles were "normal."

The neglect of this crucial subject is seen in the fact that, insofar as anxiety is concerned, extensive coverage of physical causes of anxiety is conspicuously absent from major psychiatric and medical textbooks. In the current article, the focus is on organic disorders that produce a combination of symptoms easily seen as anxiety, either panic or chronic.

METHOD: For some people a short stay in the hospital may be necessary to do tests and observe symptoms, especially if the anxiety attack is acute. For acute onset, the staff should obtain vital signs, particularly cardiac rhythm, an electrocardiogram (ECG), arterial blood gases, blood glucose, serum calcium, and a urine specimen for metanephrine assay.

What follows is an overview of the major physical disorders that can produce anxiety symptoms, from mild apprehension to obvious panic.

Cardiopulmonary Disorders. Whereas many of these difficulties can produce one acute anxiety attack, specific ones more characteristically bring about recurrent attacks or chronic symptoms. The symptoms of *angina pectoris* are chest pain or discomfort, often with palpitations and difficulty in breathing.

This is often difficult to diagnose with only a history, an ECG, and a stress test. Coronary arteriography and a positive response to nitroglycerin are sometimes helpful, but certainty of diagnosis is difficult. *Cardiac arrhythmia* may show palpitations, chest discomfort, difficulty in breathing, dizziness, and fainting. The diagnosis can be established if there is aberrant cardiac rhythm during a symptomatic attack, but arrhythmia may also be secondary to hyperthyroidism, pheochromocyctoma, and other conditions. Arrhythmia can also be brought about by caffeine, nicotine, various medications, and emotional stress. A Halter monitor, recording the person's electrocardiographic rhythm over twenty-four hours, is useful in diagnosis. *Mitral valve prolapse* (MVP) is common in women and is seen in acute and chronic anxiety and agoraphobia. Echocardiography and auscultation are helpful in diagnosis. *Hyperkinetic heart syndrome* symptoms may be acute or chronic; the patient complains of palpitations or increased cardiac awareness. Diagnostic signs are a systolic murmur and evidence of left ventricular hypertrophy. *Recurrent pulmonary emboli* may be seen in acute anxiety with marked hyperventilation and difficulty in breathing. A good diagnostic test is the ventilation-perfusion lung scan, but pulmonary angiography may be necessary.

Endocrine Disorders. Chronic rather than acute anxiety may be seen in *hyperthyroidism,* which also may be present in symptoms such as nervousness, palpitations, increased perspiration, heat intolerance, and diarrhea. The examiner should look for rapid pulse, tremor, weight loss despite increased appetite, and hot, moist skin. Symptoms of Graves's disease should be looked for, as this is the most common cause of hyperthyroidism. Diagnosis can be made with the use of thyroxine (T4), tri-iodothyronine resin uptake (RT3 U), and T3 radioimmunoassay (T3 RIA) serum tests. *Pheochromocytoma* is rare; the symptoms are often headache, flushing, and hypertension. Although the plasma catecholamine assay is the best diagnostic test, it is seldom available. However, decent aids in diagnosis are urine assays for free catecholamines, metanephrine, and vanillylmandelic acid. *Hypoglycemia* shows itself in acute anxiety with sweating, hunger, tremor, headache, and fatigue as common symptoms. The disorder is confirmed through a blood glucose sample obtained during an episode. Examination should be made for one of the three categories of causes of hypoglycemia —drug induction, insulinoma, and reactive hypoglycemia. *Hypoparathyroidism* can be shown in a wide range of symptoms of intellectual impairment, neurosis, or psychosis, but anxiety is a fairly common feature. Diagnostic signs are muscular cramps, parasthesias in the hands and feet and around the mouth, carpopedal spasm, history of thyroidectomy, abnormally low parathyroid hormone level, and hypocalcemia and hyperphosphatiemia in the presence of normal kidney function. *Cushing's syndrome* is seen in anxiety, depression, or psychosis. Diagnosis is aided by the overnight 1-mg dexamethasone suppression test.

Neurologic Disorders. A wide group of symptoms, particularly fear and bodily changes, are common to *partial complex seizures* (temporal-lobe seizures). The most efficient diagnostic procedure is a continuous telemetry-monitored EEG with simultaneous video recording; but what may be substituted is an EEG with nasopharyngeal lead recordings, a sleep record, and an attempt to activate a seizure through hyperventilation.

Toxic/Metabolic Disorders. Anxiety can be produced by *medications* of a wide variety (for example, diet and cold pills) and other *substances* (for example, caffeine, cocaine). Anxiety can also be produced by withdrawal from opiates, barbiturates and other sedative-hypnotics, nicotine, neuroleptics, and tricyclic antidepressants, but the symptoms here are self-limiting. A history taken with a cooperative patient will help in diagnosis.

Other Disorders. Many organic conditions produce anxiety, but these conditions are ordinarily related to specific disorders. Prominent among these are Wilson's disease, acute intermittent porphyria, systemic lupus erythematosus, chronic pulmonary disease, aortic arch syndrome, intracranial tumors, menopause, neuroleptic-induced akathisia, and tyramine-induced crises occurring in people taking a monoamine oxidase inhibitor (MAOI).

Beyond the scope of this paper is a discussion of the diagnosis of individual symptoms of anxiety syndromes. For example, episodic fainting can be seen in at least thirty disorders.

Therapists should be especially sensitive to history and

physical symptoms, even if a person comes referred as having a psychological problem.

COMMENTARY: This summary article introduces an important topic in therapy that, as the author points out, is often neglected. Both medical and nonmedical therapists may wish to be knowledgeable enough on this topic to know when they should refer a person for medical diagnostic work-up. Following the author's lead here, it seems obvious that considerable time and money spent in therapy might be saved with those people whose anxiety (or other psychological symptoms) has a physical cause and can be altered medically.

SOURCE: Dietch, J. T. "Diagnosis of Organic Anxiety Disorders." *Psychosomatics,* 1981, *22,* 661-669.

Meditation and Flooding plus Relaxation

AUTHOR: Michel Girodo

PRECIS: Of nine anxious people, five respond to meditation and four to relaxation and fantasy flooding

INTRODUCTION: Active muscle relaxation may be seen as inhibiting anxiety. Meditation has been shown to produce relaxation. In particular, a specific form of meditation, Transcendental Meditation (TM), has been shown to markedly reduce cardiac output, heart rate, respiration, excessive perspiration, and the symptoms of claustrophobia. The current study was undertaken to test the effect of TM with a group of people suffering anxiety and the effect of the widely used technique of flooding on those people for whom TM is not successful.

TREATMENT: The therapy group consisted of seven men and two women, aged eighteen to forty-two, suffering anxiety from five to seventy-one months. These people were given an anxiety self-report questionnaire to act as a baseline for changes in anxiety. Treatment began a week following the second testing.

Each person was taught a meditation method similar to TM. He was told that consistent practice of this meditation would produce calm, relaxation, peacefulness, and tranquility. All nine persons were given the same word to focus on, *rama*. They were to sit in a quiet room with eyes closed and attend passively to the word, expending no effort to concentrate on it. If their minds wandered, they were not to attend but quietly return to the sound of *rama*. Once they developed the technique through demonstration and practice, they were instructed to do it twice a day, morning and afternoon, for twenty-minute periods. At intervals of seven to fourteen days, they had a session with the instructor during which they reported on how they were meditating and how they felt during and after the exercise. They were again given the original anxiety questionnaire and then encouraged to continue the meditation regimen.

After an average of eight sessions, five of the people showed marked decline in anxiety and four showed no real difference.

The latter four were given individual sessions during which the therapist first taught them relaxation techniques to replace the meditation. Then, while relaxed, they were to imagine the worst thing that could happen to them. The anxiety-ridden scenes were repeated until the people could imagine them without feeling anxious. After about thirty minutes of this flooding, they reported feeling less anxious, emotionally drained, and exhausted. Sessions were held every seven to ten days and lasted about seventy-five minutes; patients filled out the anxiety questionnaire before each session.

Treatment for the nine persons lasted six to eight months. Six months after the treatment, all subjects filled out the anxiety questionnaire and returned it by mail.

The meditation group's marked decrease in anxiety after the first eight weeks stabilized through follow-up. The flooding group showed a decrease in anxiety shortly after flooding began, and this dropped steadily to approximately the same low level as for the meditation group; follow-up revealed stability at this level.

The remaining question was, What explains why one group responded to meditation and the other group to fantasy flooding? Two differences between the groups emerged. First, the average length of anxiety for the meditation group was much shorter than for the flooding group. Second, although the two groups showed no significant difference in severity of either emotional or bodily symptoms, the meditation group showed significantly more severe cognitive symptoms than the flooding group. The interpretation of these findings is that meditation may help reduce anxiety in people who are still trying to overcome it. The possibility exists that not only the flooding but the relaxation as well may have helped decrease anxiety in the second group.

COMMENTARY: Although the sample for this study is small, the results are provocative. The vogue for meditation seems to have diminished, but therapists might keep it in mind as adjunctive treatment for people with anxiety. This study helps eradicate what seemed to be a dominant impression during the heyday of meditation: that meditation might be a panacea for all anxious people, if not for a wide variety of problems. Instead, it might be very helpful for a select group of people, and more studies might suggest just which group this is. For example, research has shown that some people experience anxiety in terms of worry, rumination, and other cognitive activities; others, by contrast, experience their anxiety mostly through bodily means. The possibility exists, then, that meditation might be more effective for those whose anxiety is mainly cognitive, with flooding techniques being the treatment of choice for those with mainly bodily symptoms.

Although meditation practices such as TM may still seem strange to some Westerners, therapists might keep in mind that noncultish meditation groups exist, as do highly intelligible books on the subject.

Barrow (1979), whose therapy procedures are digested in this section, suggests that if ruminating is predominant, then cognitive therapy is needed, while if emotional responses are more troublesome, relaxation may do the trick. What suggests itself is that, for more cognitive people, cognitive therapy might be used along with meditation. With more emotional people, relaxation might be joined with flooding; perhaps the maximally effective method employing both would be anxiety management training (see Suinn, 1976, under Additional Readings in this section).

SOURCE: Girodo, M. "Yoga Meditation and Flooding in the Treatment of Anxiety Neurosis." *Journal of Behaviour and Experimental Psychiatry*, 1974, *5*, 157-160.

Modified Progressive Relaxation

AUTHORS: Scott B. Hamilton and Philip H. Bornstein

PRECIS: Teaching a client to be aware of and then relax bodily tensions

INTRODUCTION: Clients trained in progressive relaxation techniques typically practice coping maneuvers while imagining specific anxiety-provoking scenes in the treatment setting. However, for clients suffering from pervasive anxiety, such a focus on specific imaginal content may minimize treatment generalization. This problem can be handled by focusing treatment efforts on bodily cues associated with anxiety, separate from their situational context.

CASE STUDY: A twenty-five-year-old man was referred for treatment of pervasive anxiety occurring in many situations. After the initial interview, the client developed a list of a wide range of anxiety-producing situations, arranged in order of increasing anxiety. Scenes from this hierarchy were presented, on a random basis, as the client verbalized his emotional state and labeled the amount of anxiety experienced for each scene on a scale of nine levels of subjectively experienced anxiety, or "subjective units of disturbance." Levels 1 to 3 were defined as representing low anxiety, 4-6 moderate anxiety, and 7-9 high anxiety. With practice, the client was able to report reliably the level of anxiety he experienced in different anxiety-producing situations. Throughout the treatment period, the client recorded the dates, the situations, and the subjective units of disturbance he experienced outside the treatment setting.

After a ten-day baseline period, three sessions of conventional progressive relaxation training were conducted. "Modified induced anxiety" sessions then followed: The client was told to relax completely and turn his attention inward. The therapist suggested that the client "feel a small feeling start to grow," and he encouraged the client to be aware of bodily aspects of anxiety, such as indications of muscular tension, increased swallowing, and breathing irregularities. When a predetermined anxiety level was reached (that is, 3, 6, or 9 subjective units of disturbance), the client was instructed to begin relaxing in the face of these bodily experienced anxiety cues. Five repetitions of the induced-anxiety/relaxation technique were completed during each session. The modified induced-anxiety training covered three sessions, with a higher level of anxiety induced at each subsequent session.

The client continued to monitor and report his subjective experienced anxiety during a twenty-four-day follow-up period. The treatment appeared to be effective in that the client's reported anxiety levels were dramatically reduced during the follow-up period. While low levels of anxiety responded to conventional progressive relaxation training, bodily cues associated with moderate and high anxiety levels appeared to respond only to the modified induced-anxiety technique described here.

COMMENTARY: The findings here suggest that when therapists use some form of desensitization with relaxation for moderate- to high-anxiety people, the modified induced-anxiety procedure described is worth considering. The results obtained here in only six sessions are impressive, but we should not overlook that self-monitoring in the form of the man's recording dates, situations, and subjective disturbance went on for ten days prior to treatment and all during treatment as well. As we point out elsewhere in this book, it may be that the value of clients' becoming acutely aware of their disturbances, as in various kinds of self-monitoring, may have been underplayed by therapists, even those who use it extensively.

Note that these impressive results are recorded here with only one client. It may be, as we point out repeatedly, that for other clients a totally different therapy or an array of procedures may be necessary.

SOURCE: Hamilton, S. B., and Bornstein, P. H. "Modified Induced Anxiety: A Generalized Anxiety Reduction Procedure." *Journal of Consulting and Clinical Psychology*, 1977, *45*, 1200-1201.

Anxiety Management Training,
Applied Relaxation Training, and
Simple Relaxation Training Compared

AUTHORS: Donald F. Hutchings, Douglas R. Denney, JoAnn Basgall, and B. Kent Houston

PRECIS: Teaching relaxation, stressing self-control, and showing anxious college students how to relate the two

INTRODUCTION: Numerous behavior therapy methods have existed for the treatment of phobias but not for chronic, generalized anxiety. The reason may have been that phobias are more related to specific situations, which lend themselves to behavior therapy. Generalized anxiety is, of course, vaguer and not limited to specific situations. Unlike behavior therapy, cognitive therapy transcends specific situations and is geared toward more generalized problems. The increased interest in cognitive therapy and the relatively stable professional interest in behavior therapy has resulted in a joining of forces—cognitive behavior therapy. What appears promising in the treatment of anxiety is two methods emanating from this new combination of therapies —applied relaxation training and anxiety management training, both of which are applicable to general problems rather than specific problems.

Applied relaxation training emphasizes self-control over anxiety through learning relaxation and then applying this coping skill to real-life situations. This training has been effective with such specific anxieties as test anxiety and speech anxiety, but it has not been applied to general anxiety.

Anxiety management training includes applied relaxation training with the addition of structured rehearsal of relaxation skills within therapy sessions, involving attention to specific cues that signal anxiety arousal in individual patients. This training has been shown to relieve chronic anxiety.

The question for therapists is how these two therapies compare in effectiveness in the removal of chronic, general anxiety. If applied relaxation training is just as effective as the more complex system, then it may be the treatment of choice.

METHOD: Sixty-three college students screened for the presence of chronic, general anxiety were divided into various groups, in which different combinations of techniques were administered in order to carefully evaluate the two systems under consideration. Each group had five to seven members and met once a week for six weeks. Sessions lasted one and a quarter hours.

Other than the control group, which was given no therapy at all, and the placebo group, the three other groups were given therapy as described below.

Applied relaxation training began with the therapist's explaining the self-control rationale. Patients were then given audiotaped instructions in progressive relaxation. For homework they were to practice twice a day what they had learned about relaxation and record the progress they were making. In the ensuing five sessions, patients discussed the effectiveness of the homework and then did ten minutes of relaxation practice.

Anxiety management training followed exactly the same procedure with the addition of structured rehearsal, which involved patients' visualizing past situations that provoked severe anxiety. They were told to focus on all aspects of their anxiety in order to rearouse the feeling. When they aroused the anxiety, they were instructed to focus on the situation associated with the anxiety and then switch off the scene and practice relaxation to remove the anxiety. At the end of the third session, the therapist taught the group relaxation-based coping skills and how to apply them in real-life situations when they felt tense. In the last three sessions, the therapist devoted time for discussion and more coaching in applications of the coping skills they had learned. (See the Additional Reading by R. M. Suinn for further discussion of anxiety management training.)

Relaxation only was given with the same audiotaped relaxation instructions plus the same homework assignments given the two groups described above. However, the therapist made no mention of their applying self-control to allay anxiety nor instructions about applying relaxation in anxiety-arousing situations. He simply gave the group a "passive" rationale that, through practicing relaxation, their anxiety would gradually be supplanted by relaxation.

Anxiety management training, involving structured rehearsal, showed superior effectiveness for treating chronic, generalized anxiety over the other therapies, as demonstrated through the patients' self-reports and their use of learned coping strategies in anxiety-provoking situations. Applied relaxation therapy involving relaxation and the self-control rationale plus homework and explicit instructions about how to use relaxation in real-life situations was moderately effective. Relaxation along with nonspecific treatment did not fare well, having little impact on general anxiety. The addition of structured rehearsal to relaxation therapy, then, was shown to be a crucial addition. It seems likely that rehearsal makes people aware of the physical signs of anxiety more quickly. In addition, practicing in the safety of therapy sessions may make people better prepared to use coping skills and more confident that they can handle their anxiety themselves.

COMMENTARY: What was shown here was that adding structured rehearsal to applied relaxation is superior to applied relaxation for the relief of anxiety. That is, the treatment of choice is to teach people not only how to relax but how to focus on their anxiety and cope with it. The emphasis in both systems is on self-control, but anxiety management teaches coping skills to add to a person's self-control abilities. In addition, people learn to clearly face their anxieties, which must produce additional self-confidence. This study shows that although more time is needed for anxiety management training than for applied relaxation, the expenditure is worth it. Anxiety management training is undoubtedly also applicable to phobias.

SOURCE: Hutchings, D. F., Denney, D. R., Basgall, J., and Houston, B. K. "Anxiety Management and Applied Relaxation in Reducing General Anxiety." *Behaviour Research and Therapy,* 1980, *18,* 181-190.

A Review of Physical Activity and Other Methods for Reducing Anxiety

AUTHOR: William P. Morgan

PRECIS: Combinations of mild and strenuous physical exercise, systematic desensitization, fantasy, meditation, and rest compared

INTRODUCTION: An idea widely accepted at present is that daily exercise is good for both the mind and body, particularly that it reduces tension. The possibility exists, however, that tension is reduced during the vigorous phase of a person's daily exercise routine, only to rise again gradually until the next day's vigorous exercise. What people are after, of course, is not a temporary tension or anxiety reducer but something more lasting. This is nowhere more relevant than for the estimated 10 million Americans suffering anxiety neurosis whose condition originates in unrelieved stress. If it could be shown that physical exercise of one level or another has a more than temporary effect on stress, this would be of great potential value. A review of research on exercise and its relation to anxiety points to some answers.

METHOD: The various methods tried for stress reduction are these:

Mild Exercise. In a study of bowling, an overwhelming percentage of a large sample of bowlers reported feeling less tense after bowling. A study of walking, however, did not show an exercise effect on anxiety. Various studies have failed to find an effect of light exercise on state anxiety (as opposed to trait anxiety). One explanation of the bowling study is that its diversional nature accounts for the report of decreased tension.

Vigorous Exercise. Numerous studies suggest that, after strenuous activity, anxiety decreases not only in normal people but in clinically anxious people as well. Unexplained sex differences (decrease in anxiety for men, no decrease for women) were revealed in some studies.

Exercise, Systematic Desensitization, and Fantasy Combined. Exercise alone and pleasant fantasies alone both lowered anxiety, but the combination of the two (along with systematic desensitization) lowered anxiety even more.

Strenuous Exercise, Meditation, and Rest Compared. In a study of people not displaying clinical anxiety, both strenuous exercise alone and meditation alone were followed by a significant decrease in anxiety. The unexpected finding was that in this same study the control group showed a decrease in state anxiety after a mere quiet rest. The finding may not, however, be generalizable to a clinical population.

The question remains, What causes lowered anxiety? Unquestionably, exercise brings about physiological changes not evident in relaxation training, biofeedback, and so on. It may be that the effect of strenuous exercise on brain biochemistry is causal in improving feelings.

Studies suggest that not only exercise but meditation and biofeedback and, most surprising of all, rest have all shown high *quantities* of reduced anxiety. The question remains whether the *quality* is similar. Certainly what must now be considered is that diversion itself may account for some of the effects of lowered anxiety reported in studies of various forms of exercise.

COMMENTARY: What seems obvious from this open, un-biased, and careful review of the literature on the effects of physical exercise on mental states, particularly anxiety and de-pression, is that few if any conclusions can be safely made. As the author points out, some studies do support the relation be-tween exercise and absence of discomforting mental states, but what causes what is not clear. One may surmise that what will be found is that certain kinds of activities, such as strenuous exercise, mild exercise, meditation, and biofeedback, are helpful to certain kinds of people. As is shown in other digests in this section, therapists may do best to diagnose patients' problems carefully and then devise highly individualized programs involv-ing an array of therapeutic measures. Therapists should not overlook the almost sure value of supplementing their therapy with programs of exercise for their clients. The apparent value of simple diversion of many different kinds—simply getting out and doing something, almost anything, different—has long been known. Although it is almost a cliché, we probably should not forget it.

SOURCE: Morgan, W. P. "Anxiety Reduction Following Acute Physical Activity." *Psychiatric Annals,* 1979, *9,* 24-45.

Personal Constructs Therapy

AUTHOR: Linda L. Viney

PRECIS: Altering labels and hypotheses in viewing the world relieves anxiety in a twenty-four-year-old woman

INTRODUCTION: People's lives are controlled by the constructs (or labels) they have for anticipating their experiences. (Kelly's thesis is that constructs enable us to predict and control experience.) People come to therapy because their constructs are inadequate and they want to broaden their understanding of their experience (be better able to predict and control their lives). The therapist's goal is to help clients make better choices. This can be done by using therapy like a laboratory where hypotheses can be made, experiments designed for clients to try, and results evaluated. The therapist does this in various ways: helps to put new labels on old experiences, helps the client to rid himself of ineffective constructs, increases the client's choices and experiences, helps design new experiments for the client, and gives feedback about the way the client sees life. Therapist and client work together as coresearchers, the therapist providing another view of life but restricting his attention only to the client's choices. To fulfill this role, the therapist must be active, assertive, creative, and flexible, have above-average verbal skill, and have the ability to focus primarily on the client's meaning rather than his own.

CASE STUDY: Susan, a twenty-four-year-old, unmarried secretary working toward a degree at an Australian university, applied to the university counseling center for help with her anxiety. According to personal constructs theory, her anxiety suggested that she was unable to make sense of her experience, that her experiences were beyond her ability to give them constructs or meaning. (To Kelly, anxiety occurs when a person does not have a construct for an event or an experience.) She feared close personal relationships because she believed they would require her to change. Aware of this, the woman therapist proposed three to four exploratory sessions, after which they decided to continue their weekly sessions as coresearchers working with the personal constructs approach, which Susan comprehended. The therapist presented the Repertory Grid Technique, in which the client compares three people in her life, finding some quality two of them have and the third lacks, gives this quality a label or name (construct), and then gives the opposite label (such as the construct "friendly" and its opposite, "unfriendly"). This is repeated with a cast of nine or more people in the client's life. Particularly troublesome to Susan were her construct sets of "strong/more dependent" and "independent/dependent," constructs that confused her and fed her anxiety. The therapist shared her own perceptions of Susan's labels and thus helped Susan clarify them. After four more sessions Susan began to trust the therapist, but for fourteen sessions she would begin by proposing to quit therapy, only to follow this by wanting to extend her therapy hour. The therapist showed her the pattern, and Susan began to develop a new set of constructs for this experience with her therapist and with others as well.

The therapist initiated field experiments, one of which was fixed-role therapy, in which a new role is set up for the client to try out as an experiment and see how applying new constructs to oneself works out. The therapist designed a fixed role for Susan, employing Susan's own preferred constructs. Part of the written description was "[She] is a *friendly* young woman who is *open and frank* with the people she meets. She enjoys *giving* to these people and the feelings of *companionship* she has with them. She sees herself as *united* with her fellows, as *part of the world* with them." Only after six more sessions did Susan decide to try out the role, and when she did, things went very well. She learned that if she saw herself differently, others reacted to her differently. In therapy Susan began to look for more ways to check out her changing way of viewing the world; for example, she began to read psychology, she brought in dreams with her interpretations. She was not only picking up and trying out new constructs but shedding old, restricting ones.

At the twenty-third session, she said she wanted to quit therapy, and the therapist suggested that Susan fill out another Repertory Grid to test out Susan's decision. This revealed that her constructs were now clearer and that she was able to apply to herself the more positive pole of her bipolar descriptions. She had more confidence, saw herself more as she would like to be, and idealized the therapist less. After twenty-five sessions, she left therapy. On six-month follow-up, Susan reported that she was still living at home but experienced it as less troublesome and that she was getting along very well with a man with whom she was going to travel after her graduation.

COMMENTARY: The reader will recognize this therapy as one of the cognitive therapies, under which would also be classified Beck's and Ellis's systems (see Index). The difference between Kelly's system and the other two is perhaps more apparent than real. The emphasis on constructs (or labels) in Kelly's system helps clients focus on their *predictions* about life and ways to *control* what happens, a focus not unlike those of Beck and Ellis. One difference here is in the therapeutic use of the client's labels, which the reader may want to consider carefully.

The therapy might have progressed more quickly and have affected the client more broadly if the therapist had used additional therapeutic techniques—for example, assertion training and other cognitive measures such as a look at the sentences the client said to herself. Note that twenty-five sessions were used here, and compare this with the fewer sessions required in other therapies discussed in this section, particularly diversified programs. The Kelly system, however, should be considered for therapists and clients who find it compatible. It can obviously be used for many different disorders. It is highly unlikely that the drama of fixed-role therapy would fit everyone. Note the extensive talents required of the therapist.

SOURCE: Viney, L. L. "Experimenting with Experience: A Psychotherapeutic Case Study." *Psychotherapy: Theory, Research, and Practice,* 1981, *18,* 271-278.

Cognitive Behavior Modification

AUTHORS: Raie Woodward and R. B. Jones

PRECIS: Combined cognitive restructuring and modified systematic desensitization for blue-collar people with long-standing anxiety shown to be more effective than either of the two therapies alone

INTRODUCTION: Generalized anxiety is notoriously hard to treat in some people, and many questions remain about which treatments are effective with which people. For example, the intellectual challenging of irrational beliefs used in Albert Ellis's rational-emotive therapy has been said to be too difficult for some clinical patients. A less intellectual revision in which negative self-statements are changed into more productive self-statements has been tried with a clinical population and found wanting. However, the general idea is too challenging to drop, and therefore revisions and additions should be tried. In this study, cognitive restructuring (briefly described above) was combined with a variation of systematic desensitization to see how the combination might affect a clinical population.

METHOD: To test the individual therapies and the combination of therapies, a study was done with sixteen females and eleven males, from a predominantly blue-collar area, on the waiting list of a hospital where they sought treatment. All suffered from general anxiety, defined as neurotic anxiety without any specific phobia and diagnosed by a professional worker. The average age was forty years and average duration of symptoms thirty months.

The patients were divided into four groups, each of which was placed under a different regimen: seven were given cognitive restructuring, seven modified systematic desensitization, six cognitive behavior modification (a combination of the first two therapies), and seven no treatment.

People in the three treatment groups came for eight

group sessions, one per week, each lasting about one hour and a quarter, led by the same therapist. The therapist treated the groups as follows (using D. Meichenbaum, "Therapist Manual for Cognitive Behavior Modification," unpublished manuscript, University of Waterloo, Ontario, Canada).

Cognitive Restructuring. Therapist and patient worked at getting a grip on the presenting problem and developing a therapy plan from the patient's self-defeating statements and his irrational beliefs. The therapist explained the general nature of these statements and beliefs and how they produce anxiety. He then taught the patient to focus on the self-statements and finally to modify the statements and develop more adaptive ones.

The patients were also taught to handle anxiety-provoking situations by going through four stages in dealing with stress: preparing, confronting, coping, and reinforcing. At each session patients practiced imagining anxiety-producing situations and then coping with them, using the four stages.

Modified Systematic Desensitization. The therapist used tapes to instruct this group in progressive relaxation (see Index for other references), and the members practiced from tapes at home. Each person set up a hierarchy of anxiety-provoking situations. During sessions three to eight, members first had a twenty-five-minute relaxation exercise and for the rest of the session practiced modified systematic desensitization: they imagined an anxiety-producing situation from their hierarchy and then imagined themselves coping through relaxation.

Cognitive Behavior Modification. The therapist combined the two therapies described above, first teaching cognitive restructuring and in the third session adding all the steps of modified systematic desensitization, as an alternative way of dealing with anxiety.

No-Treatment Control. These seven persons came for an initial interview and did not return until two months later for retesting.

Cognitive behavior modification, the combination of teaching people to change the sentences they say to themselves and teaching people to imagine coping with anxiety by relaxation, had more effect on the group on which it was used than the single therapies had on their respective groups. Cognitive restructuring alone did not reduce anxiety. There is the suggestion that cognitive restructuring adds something to imaginal relaxation coping exercises but is not powerful enough to work alone, at least with these particular people (blue-collar, highly anxious people).

Two additional findings are noteworthy. Those who think most about their problems tended to report the most anxiety, but cognitive restructuring did not show a marked effect on time spent thinking about problems. The second finding was that the greater the frequency and the more severe the anxiety symptoms, the more positive effect of treatment.

COMMENTARY: The first of the above two additional findings invites comment. A reader particularly interested in cognitive therapy should note the implication that cognitive restructuring is questioned by the researcher as a treatment to be used alone for people who ruminate excessively about their problems. This is a reminder of our frequently made point that the therapy chosen for a particular person should fit that person.

What is notable about this study is the effort to adapt a therapy obviously favored by the authors to a group of people often overlooked by therapy theorists. Clients with the YAVIS (Young, Attractive, Verbal, Intelligent, and Successful) syndrome are often favored over other groups, and when we find that methods found suitable with this group are unsuitable for another group, such as blue-collar workers, we are stuck. In this section the reader will find an array of treatments, many of which are potentially useful for various groups.

SOURCE: Woodward, R., and Jones, R. B. "Cognitive Restructuring Treatment: A Controlled Trial with Anxious Patients." *Behaviour Research and Therapy*, 1980, *18*, 401-407.

Two Approaches to Systematic
Desensitization Compared

AUTHOR: Robert Zemore

PRECIS: A standard systematic desensitization procedure and a modified procedure equally effective for treated and additional anxieties

INTRODUCTION: Joseph Wolpe's standard systematic desensitization procedure (to be described) has been shown effectively to decrease specific anxieties. Obviously, what would be desirable is a method that would generalize across a broader array of situations. Marvin Goldfried has modified the standard procedure (also to be described here) and demonstrated its effectiveness in a case of generalized anxiety. This demonstration, however, does not prove that his method is superior to Wolpe's standard procedure. If Goldfried's procedure could be shown to be clearly superior to Wolpe's in reducing anxiety in both treated and untreated situations, then Goldfried's method would be a treatment of choice for anxiety. A study was undertaken to compare the two procedures.

TREATMENTS: Twenty men and twenty women undergraduate students reporting a high degree of anxiety in both public speaking and test taking were selected for treatment.

All subjects were told that the treatment had been found to decrease anxiety in specific situations but that the present study was undertaken to see whether anxieties other than those directly treated might also decrease. They were then told they must give a speech before treatment and one after treatment to determine the effect of the treatment. In both instances, the same assessment procedures were used. Before giving the first speech, the client was given a self-report questionnaire concerning performance anxiety. During the speech, observers rated the client on performance anxiety. After the speech, the client rated himself on both degree of anxiety and confidence while speaking.

To measure test anxiety before and after treatment, all clients filled out at home a self-report scale rating their anxiety in specific test-taking situations.

Five groups were organized, each with two men and two women randomly selected: a no-treatment control group, a standard desensitization group and a modified desensitization group for test anxiety, and the same two treatment groups for public speaking anxiety.

All treatment was given by a male graduate clinical psychology student in eight forty-five-minute group sessions over a four-week period. The two basic treatments were as follows.

Standard Systematic Desensitization. The therapist began with the four persons working on public speaking anxiety by giving the group a rationale for the procedures to be used. He then taught them progressive relaxation (see Index). Using a list of twelve public speaking situations, the clients as a group placed them in a hierarchy of least to most anxiety-producing. The therapist explained to the group about forming mental images of situations. The group relaxed according to progressive relaxation training and imagined the anxiety-producing situations one at a time, beginning with the least anxiety-producing. Each item was presented at least twice. If, on the second time around, any member signaled anxiety, the item was repeated until everyone could picture the situation without feeling anxiety. The procedure with the group working on test anxiety was the same except that the group worked on a hierarchy of test-taking situations rather than public speaking items.

Modified Systematic Desensitization. The basic difference here was in the rationale of the treatment, which was explained to the group: relaxation is used to actively cope with anxiety as it arises. The treatment was to teach people how to relax as tensions begin to build. The group was to practice relaxation in specific situations. The therapist focused on relaxation training, helping people to sensitize themselves to rising tension and to relax as soon as tensions arose. In imagining anxiety-producing scenes from the hierarchies devised by the group, they were not to stop the image when they experienced anxiety, as in the standard procedure, but to try to relax. The same twelve-item lists were used as in the standard procedure, and all items were presented twice. However, each situation was presented either for sixty seconds or for a twenty-second anxiety-free period. On the second time around, items were presented until all members were free of tensions while imagining the scene. Again, of course, the public speaking items were used for one group, test-anxiety situations for the other.

The control group went through the assessments but was given no treatment.

The major result of the study was that both standard and modified systematic desensitization procedures produced significant reductions in both treated and untreated anxieties. That is, people treated for public speaking anxiety with either procedure diminished in test anxiety also, and vice versa.

COMMENTARY: The authors point out that the two sets of anxiety-provoking situations treated here are both anxieties about being evaluated, and a study of markedly different anxieties should be done. Although the application to generalized anxiety could only cautiously be made from this study, the more general approach of the modified procedure would seem to be promising. In fact, as noted in the introduction, its effectiveness with generalized anxiety has been demonstrated. The fact that the results generalized to untreated anxieties should be noted.

The reader may ask whether the study suggests any reason for not using the more global modified procedure. None is shown here. In fact, although Wolpe had suggested that continuing to imagine fearsome situations in the presence of felt anxiety encourages phobic reactions, this was not shown. The fact would seem to be, as suggested in the self-control therapies digested here, that, given effective skills, people are capable of handling many difficult problems. In effect, the standard procedure here is a therapist-oriented desensitization method for the eradication of specific anxieties, while the modified procedure is more of a skills training, self-control method to be used for anxiety whenever it appears.

Again, one wonders how much more effective both procedures might have been if the clients had been given other treatments, such as psychotherapy or cognitive therapy, in conjunction with systematic desensitization.

SOURCE: Zemore, R. "Systematic Desensitization as a Method of Teaching a General Anxiety-Reducing Skill." *Journal of Consulting and Clinical Psychology*, 1975, *43*, 157-161.

Additional Readings

Benson, H., Beary, J. F., and Carol, M. P. "The Relaxation Response." *Psychiatry*, 1974, *37*, 37-46.

Nonpharmacological, self-induced, altered states of consciousness have received attention, partly because of their allegedly helping people to reduce tension and anxiety. Evidence exists to support the idea that there is a central nervous system reaction, called the "relaxation response," that is associated with these altered states of consciousness. The relaxation response includes physiological changes (for example, reduced heart rate and oxygen consumption) opposite to the "flight or fight" response, often associated with stress and tension. A therapeutic technique for highly anxious people would be to teach relaxation-response techniques, which can then be used to reduce anxiety in stressful situations.

To elicit the relaxation response, four elements are required: (1) *mental device*—focusing on a word, sound, or object in order to shut out the external world; (2) *passive attitude*—disregarding distracting thoughts and redirecting attention to the sound or word; (3) *decreased muscle tone*—getting into a comfortable position with minimal muscular effort; and (4) *quiet environment*—sitting in a quiet place, often with the eyes closed.

The authors discuss techniques, many of them within Western or Eastern religious contexts, that have existed for centuries which facilitate the relaxation response. A summary table is presented comparing current techniques that bring about physiological changes associated with this response: Transcendental Meditation, autogenic training, hypnosis, Zen, yoga, progressive relaxation, sentic cycles (self-induced emotional experiences), and cotention (focus on a single object in the environment).

No adverse side effects have been reported for people who practice the relaxation response for limited amounts of time, such as two twenty-minute periods daily. Some people who practice it for longer periods have experienced a general withdrawal from life and symptoms ranging from insomnia to hallucinations. It is difficult to interpret this finding because of the possibility that some of the people who engage in intensive, extended meditation techniques may have had preexisting psychological problems.

Fay, A. *Making Things Better by Making Them Worse.* New York: Hawthorn Books, 1978.

The author gives a popular presentation of paradoxical intention—the exaggerating of symptoms to rid oneself of them—as used by therapists and as used by patients on themselves. It is applied to anxiety, fears and phobias, depression, self-downing, perfectionism, and other problems. Illustrations are given from therapy sessions and from people using paradoxical therapy on themselves.

The book may be useful to therapists wishing to explain the use of this method to patients or to patients as adjunctive reading for self-help.

Girodo, M., and Stein, S. J. "Self-Talk and the Work of Worrying in Confronting a Stressor." *Cognitive Therapy and Research,* 1978, *2,* 305-307.

What people do while waiting for a potentially anxiety-producing situation can affect their feelings when they are actually in the situation. Thus, constructive worrying may inoculate people against anxiety in a situation when they are actually in it. In anticipating painful situations, people can do anticipatory problem solving and mentally rehearse coping methods for dealing with the anticipated stress. To test this idea, various treatments were given to people before seeing an industrial-accident film. Forty women college students were randomly put into one of four treatments: (1) Information, in which the therapist described in detail the film the women were about to see, (2) Arousal Self-Talk, in which the women were given the above information plus "stress inoculation training" and taught to give sixteen coping self-statements that focused on internal events, (3) Film Self-Talk, in which the women were told about the film and then taught to give sixteen denial and intellectualization statements, and (4) Control, in which the women were told nothing at all. Measures of anxiety, heart rate, and thought content were used. The general results were that the second group of women, who were told what they would see and in addition were given stress inoculation training, worried more and were more apprehensive than the other women while waiting to view the film; they were less worried and apprehensive while seeing the film. This suggests that, in preparing for stress, people are better off when they plan a coping strategy and actually rehearse it. However, they must expect to feel anxiety during the preparation period. Thus, constructive worrying, though a bit painful, may significantly decrease the pain that might otherwise be felt in actual anxiety-provoking situations.

Greenblatt, D. J., and Shader, R. I. *Benzodiazepines in Clinical Practice*. New York: Raven Press, 1974.

    The benzodiazepines, safer than the barbiturates, are probably the drugs of choice for anxiety. They are also the most popular of the antianxiety drugs. They are, in general, very safe. Side effects, other than drowsiness, are minimal.

    Physical addiction is believed to be produced only after long use of very high dosages. Therapists, however, should take care with addiction-prone patients. After withdrawal, various situations have been reported: depression, agitation, hallucinations, delirium tremens, and one death. Therapists should expect that hostility and aggression masked by anxiety symptoms can be revealed when the drugs lessen the anxiety. An extensive review of studies suggests that antianxiety drugs are better used during acute periods rather than continuously.

    The major benzodiazepines are diazepam (Valium), chlordiazepoxide (Librium), flurazepam (Dalmane), oxazepam (Serax), and clorazepate (Tranxene).

Hare, N., and Levis, D. J. "Pervasive ('Free-Floating') Anxiety: A Search for a Cause and Treatment Approach." In S. M. Turner, K. S. Calhoun, and H. E. Adams (Eds.), *Handbook of Clinical Behavior Therapy*. New York: Wiley, 1981.

The authors give an overview of theories and therapies for generalized anxiety. The therapies include drug therapies, psychoanalysis, behavior therapies, modified systematic desensitization, chemical counterconditioning facilitators (specifically carbon dioxide and LSD-25), relaxation, packages of coping strategies, and a few miscellaneous therapies. Very little systematic research, however, has been done on the subject. Little more can currently be said than that to date no overall method for overcoming pervasive anxiety has been proved unequivocally successful. Antianxiety drugs are the most popular today, and of these, the benzodiazepines are used most. Five main benzodiazepines are used: Librium, Valium, Serax, Tranxene, and Dalmane.

The authors end with a rationale and brief therapeutic description of implosive therapy, their choice of treatment. (See Levis, 1980, in Additional Readings.)

There is an extensive bibliography of original sources.

Kutash, I. L., Schlesinger, L. B., and Associates. *Handbook on Stress and Anxiety: Contemporary Knowledge, Theory, and Treatment*. San Francisco: Jossey-Bass, 1980.

This is a comprehensive book of readings concerning research, theories, and treatments of stress and anxiety. The positions covered are psychoanalytic, learning and behavioral, developmental, sociological, ethological, physiological, and neurobiological. Therapists will be particularly interested in the section on treatment, covering assessment measures, psychoanalysis, behavior therapy, biofeedback, drugs, and education.

Levis, D. J. "Implementing the Technique of Implosive Therapy." In E. B. Foa and A. Goldstein (Eds.), *Handbook of Behavioral Interventions*. New York: Wiley, 1980.

Therapy is based on a theory of how pervasive anxiety originates: a person responds anxiously to certain internal or external cues; the person then focuses on the physiological reactions of anxiety rather than on the cues; and finally the anxious person uses the anxiety as an excuse to get away from the original cues. Thus, the implosive therapy attempts to extinguish a person's anxiety by searching out the cues and then getting the person to face them either actually or in imagination and experiencing the accompanying emotion until the cues no longer provoke anxiety. Specific techniques for accomplishing this are explained.

Meichenbaum, D., and Turk, D. "The Cognitive-Behavioral Management of Anxiety, Anger, and Pain." In P. O. Davidson (Ed.), *The Behavioral Management of Anxiety, Depression, and Pain.* New York: Brunner/Mazel, 1976.

The authors describe a self-management procedure for anxiety, involving three steps. First, the therapist explains the nature of stress and then gives some means of coping, such as ways to get out of situations or sentences to say to oneself to counteract anxiety. The second step is for the anxious person to practice what he has learned, particularly the use of positive self-statements and disuse of anxiety-provoking self-statements. In the third step, the person's success is tested with laboratory procedures designed to arouse anxiety, such as films.

This cognitive therapy employing some behavioral ideas would appear to hold promise; the reader might especially note the feedback provided in the last step of the procedure.

(See also Novaco, 1977, under "Antisocial Personality Disorder.")

Raskin, M., Johnson, G., and Rondestvedt, J. W. "Chronic Anxiety Treated by Feedback-Induced Muscle Relaxation." *Archives of General Psychiatry,* 1973, *28,* 263-267.

Although an estimated 5 percent of the United States population suffers from chronic anxiety, effective therapies for large numbers of people are nonexistent. Symptomatic change is effected by insight therapies and behavior therapies in roughly half the people treated. Studies of minor tranquilizers, the most popular current treatment, present confusing results, and questions arise about side effects. Given the current interest in muscle relaxation and biofeedback, the present study was undertaken to investigate the effect of relaxation on chronic anxiety and its accompanying distresses, insomnia and tension headaches.

Six men and four women, average age twenty-seven years, suffering anxiety despite two years of individual psychotherapy and drugs, were selected for feedback treatment. Five rejected antianxiety drugs, while the other five were on moderate dosages during the study. They were taught relaxation with a muscle feedback instrument (equipment and procedures described fully in T. Budzynski, J. Stoyva, and C. Adler, "Feedback-Induced Muscle Relaxation: Application to Tension Headaches," *Journal of Behavioral Therapy and Experimental Psychiatry*, 1970, *1*, 205-211). When they could remain deeply relaxed for twenty-five minutes, they were given intermittent sessions without feedback and also told to practice relaxation at home. When they could stay relaxed for twenty-five minutes with or without feedback, they were put on an eight-week schedule of two half-hour relaxation periods at home daily, keeping charts of their progress, and laboratory checking twice a week. Various measures—self-report, self-administered anxiety questionnaires, therapist observation—were used to appraise the effects of treatment.

The therapy had unimpressive effects on general anxiety: one person improved markedly, three improved moderately, six showed no change. Effects on sleep and headache, however, were somewhat more impressive. Five of the six persons with sleep difficulties found they could go to sleep right away by relaxing, something they had not been able to do during the eight weeks prior to therapy. However, four of the five woke up intermittently during the night or very early in the morning; and although they could get back to sleep by relaxing, the sleep was not as restful as sedative sleep. The four patients with headaches found considerable reduction in frequency and intensity of headaches and could also abort beginning headaches and reduce the pain of established headaches. This treatment does not appear to be an effective method to alleviate chronic anxiety when used alone but may hold promise as an adjunctive therapy.

Rubin, M. "Verbally Suggested Responses for Reciprocal Inhibition of Anxiety." *Journal of Behavior Therapy and Experimental Psychiatry,* 1972, *3,* 273-277.

The anxious, fearful person is hypnotized and given a fearful situation in which the therapist suggests that the patient attend to an element in the situation that is pleasurable rather than anxiety-producing. For example, for someone who is fearful of showers, the therapist may suggest that the shower water is like raindrops, which the person likes. Successful therapy reports of complex anxiety problems are described. The author suggests that implosion (see Levis, 1980, Additional Readings, this section) or flooding is really a part of the therapy, but it is not yet clear how important it is to the success of the method.

Suinn, R. M. "Anxiety Management Training to Control General Anxiety." In J. Krumboltz and C. Thoresen (Eds.), *Counseling Methods.* New York: Holt, Rinehart and Winston, 1976.

Anxiety management training (AMT) was developed to deal with aspects of anxiety not handled by systematic desensitization (which depends on the client's ability to identify specific cues that trigger anxiety) or implosion and flooding techniques (which often leave the client feeling emotionally drained from anxiety arousal). AMT does not require cue specificity and permits the client to learn anxiety-reduction techniques so that sessions end in a state of calm rather than arousal. This approach involves relaxation training, imagery to initiate anxiety arousal, attention to bodily cues of anxiety, training in switching from arousal imagery to relaxation imagery, and experience in anxiety arousal followed by self-induction of anxiety control. The training generally requires five to six sessions. The following case study illustrates these principles.

A successful, thirty-seven-year-old married woman with three children came to therapy because of generalized emotionality that often swept her out of control. She had a history of overreacting to situations and was concerned about her lack of control in important decisions. She began to spend whole mornings feeling anxious and on edge before dealing with an important issue. She would deal with her anxiety by compulsively revealing her feelings and worries to her friends, who began to tire of her self-centered revelations. Treatment began with a brief version of deep muscle relaxation. Though initially reporting that she felt too "hyper" to relax, she began to feel her body relax as she concentrated on specific muscle groups. The therapist encouraged her to report how she was feeling during the relaxation procedure, which lasted about thirty minutes. The next step was a shift to relaxation imagery; she chose "sitting in front of her easel in her studio with the morning sunlight coming through the window" as a calming image. Two more sessions were completed with emphasis on controlled relaxation. She found additional calming scenes to imagine. By the fourth session, she was able to sit in a reclining chair, close her eyes, and achieve relaxation within one minute with only the therapist's instructions of "get comfortable, close your eyes, and signal me when you're deeply relaxed." At this point, AMT was introduced: she was instructed to imagine a scene that triggered anxiety; when she reported feeling anxious, the therapist immediately told her to turn off the scene and focus on deepening the relaxation of specific muscle groups, such as the right hand and fingers. During the rest of the session, the same procedure was repeated, with anxiety arousal followed by verbal instructions to return to a state of relaxation.

By the fifth session, she was taught to initiate a moderate level of anxiety by herself and notice which body cues were associated with anxiety (for example, increased heart rate, tense neck). After each anxiety arousal, relaxation was induced through the therapist's verbal instructions. After a number of these sequences, the therapist asked her to complete the sequence by herself. "Switch on the anxiety scene, pay attention to how you feel anxious, then switch off the scene and do whatever seems to be the best method for bringing back the relaxation." She reported that she had no difficulty with this task.

During the sixth session, the same procedure was followed, but the client was told to use scenes that triggered higher levels of anxiety than before. Gradually more responsibility was placed on her for completing the entire arousal/relaxation sequence. The client began to improve after the fifth session: she began to stop her compulsive talking when anxious and started to prepare for stressful events by practicing relaxation ahead of time. By the twelfth session (this client was seen for more than six sessions because of her volatile emotionality), she was less out of control emotionally. The number of tension-arousing situations in her life was reduced, and she began to think of herself as more in control of herself. Follow-up two years later revealed that she was in control of her emotionality, although there were a few situations that triggered anxiety from time to time.

Wolpe, J., and Lazarus, A. A. *Behavior Therapy Techniques: A Guide to the Treatment of Neuroses.* New York: Pergamon Press, 1966.

The technique of systematic desensitization, the major focus of this book, involves three steps: (1) training in deep muscle relaxation, (2) construction of anxiety hierarchies, and (3) pairing relaxation with the anxiety-producing stimuli from the hierarchies. Relaxation training generally takes about six sessions of twenty minutes each, with the client asked to practice at home for two fifteen-minute periods each day. After the rationale of the approach is explained to the client, relaxation training proceeds in the following sequence: arms and hands (first session); forehead and eyebrows (second session); teeth, lips, and tongue (third session); neck and shoulders (fourth session); back and shoulders (fifth session). The general procedure is to make the client aware of the particular part of the body being worked on by contrasting and tensing the muscles, followed by relaxing and letting go. (Verbatim instructions are listed in the appendix of the book.)

The second step is to construct an anxiety hierarchy (or more than one hierarchy if necessary), a graded list of situations or specific stimuli that arouse different levels of anxiety in the client. This is the most difficult procedure in the desensitization technique and requires painstaking arranging and grading of the items by the therapist and client. If the relevant sources of anxiety are not correctly identified, the procedure will not be successful. The therapist looks for common themes in the anxiety-arousing situations (for example, fear of rejection, fear of specific objects). Although themes are often obvious, the therapist must guard against being misled. For example, fear and avoidance of social situations may turn out to be based on fear of criticism or rejection. (Examples of hierarchies from actual case studies are presented.)

The third step of the desensitization procedure involves presenting items from the anxiety hierarchy to the client while he is in a state of relaxation. The goal is to train the client to respond with relaxation rather than anxiety to the items. With the client sitting or lying comfortably with eyes closed, the therapist encourages a state of deep relaxation by directing the client to become progressively more relaxed, to let go, to become calm, and so on. (For clients who cannot relax, in spite of the training, hypnosis or drugs are occasionally used.) The therapist first presents a neutral situation, for which the client is not expected to have an anxiety response, and then presents the lowest anxiety item from the hierarchy. The client lifts a finger if anxiety is experienced and does nothing if he remains calm and relaxed. If the client signals anxiety, the item is presented until no anxiety is signaled. Three or four presentations of an item are usual, although ten or more may be necessary. If no anxiety is signaled, the therapist goes on to the next item. Presentation of hierarchy scenes usually takes fifteen to twenty minutes.

The authors suggest how to handle three common difficulties therapists may encounter when using this technique: clients' inability to relax, the construction of misleading or irrelevant hierarchies, and the inability of some clients to imagine themselves in the anxiety-generating situations that are the cause of their difficulties.

In addition to this detailed discussion of desensitization, the book also contains chapters on other behavior therapy techniques such as assertion training, thought stopping, exaggerated-role training, flooding, and "emotive imagery."

Wolpe, J., Brady, J. P., Serber, M., Agras, W. S., and Liberman,
R. P. "The Current Status of Systematic Desensitization."
American Journal of Psychiatry, 1973, *130,* 961-965.

The authors review the method of systematic desensitization, its indications and contraindications, its effective elements, and its success in various cases. Among the procedures
that have been found helpful in inducing a state of relaxation
are hypnosis, inhalation of carbon dioxide, injection of sodium
methohexitol (Brevitol), and the use of a metronome (sixty
beats per minute) that is paced with instructions to "relax" and
"let go."

Systematic desensitization works well with clients who
have fears or anxieties that are localized on objects or situations
external to the client and unrelated to interpersonal issues. Clients must be capable of some degree of vivid imagery and
should display relatively good personal and social functioning.

Clients who have multiple fears and many problems and
deficits are not good candidates for systematic desensitization.
Similarly, clients who have had psychotic episodes or are diagnosed as schizoid may be poor at vivid imagery and hence may
not fare well. Success is also less likely with clients who have ill-
defined fears, whose fears shift from day to day to different
objects or situations, or who feel tense, uncomfortable, or un-
natural when in a state of relaxation. Clients who have specific
interpersonal anxieties are probably better treated by assertion
training or social skills training. Systematic desensitization is
not recommended for clients who are achieving secondary gains
from their anxiety, such as attention and support from family
or friends.

4

Obsessive-
Compulsive
Disorder

According to DSM-III (p. 235), the diagnostic criteria for obsessive-compulsive disorder are as follows.

A. Either obsessions or compulsions:
Obsessions: recurrent, persistent ideas, thoughts, images, or impulses that are ego-dystonic—that is, they are not experienced as voluntarily produced but rather as thoughts that invade consciousness and are experienced as senseless or repugnant. Attempts are made to ignore or suppress them.
Compulsions: repetitive and seemingly purposeful behaviors that are performed according to certain rules or in a stereotyped fashion. The behavior is not an end in itself but is designed to produce or

prevent some future event or situation. However, either the activity is not connected in a realistic way with what it is designed to produce or prevent, or it is clearly excessive. The act is performed with a sense of subjective compulsion coupled with a desire to resist the compulsion (at least initially). The individual generally recognizes the senselessness of the behavior (this may not be true for young children) and does not derive pleasure from carrying out the activity, although it provides a release of tension.

B. The obsessions or compulsions are a significant source of distress to the individual or interfere with social or role functioning.

C. Not due to another mental disorder, such as Tourette's Disorder, Schizophrenia, Major Depression, or Organic Mental Disorder

In addition, according to DSM-III, anxiety and depression are common, as well as avoidance of situations at the heart of the existing obsessions (such as dirt or contamination). Symptoms are chronic and may begin in childhood but are more common in adolescence or early adulthood. Predisposing factors are unknown. Symptoms may be incapacitating, as will be seen in some of the digests that follow. The disorder is seen equally in men and women. Complications include major depression and abuse of alcohol and antianxiety medications.

Disagreement exists concerning the incidence of this disorder. In DSM-III the statement is made that the disorder is apparently rare. At the other extreme, obsessive-compulsive disorders have been estimated to be widely present in the general population and particularly in the clinical populations (L. Salzman and F. H. Thaler, "Obsessive-Compulsive Disorders: A Review of the Literature," *American Journal of Psychiatry*, 1981, *138,* 286-296, p. 296). One difficulty may be that the various symptoms blanketed by the term *obsessive-compulsive disorder* are fairly varied, and this fact is sometimes hidden. For example, one sees articles under the title of the general disorder when the articles are primarily about ritualistic behavior, which indeed may be rare enough that it is seldom seen in private practice. Yet, obsessions of various kinds and intensities may be seen more commonly. Thus, estimates of incidence may depend mainly on who is looking at what.

There are attempts to classify the various symptoms under the umbrella term. DSM-III clearly distinguishes between compulsions and obsessions. Further distinctions seem worthwhile. One estimate is that a large proportion of patients diagnosed as obsessive-compulsive are ritualizers, either washers or checkers. A minor proportion of ritualizers can be classified either as repeaters or as having symptoms of avoidance, completeness, and slowness (R. S. Stern and J. P. Cobb, "Phenomenology of Obsessive-Compulsive Neurosis," *British Journal of Psychiatry*, 1978, *132*, 233-239). In obsessions at least five symptoms are commonly seen: fear of causing harm to oneself or others, fear of loss of control, pervasive doubts, sexual fears, and religious fears (E. B. Foa and G. S. Steketee, "Obsessive-Compulsives: Conceptual Issues and Treatment Interventions," in *Progress in Behavior Modification,* Vol. 8, New York: Academic Press, 1979, p. 6).

What is needed in this book is a classification system that is helpful in guiding therapists. A particularly useful one for therapists, reflecting current thinking and not at odds with DSM-III, was devised by E. B. Foa and A. Tillmans "The Treatment of Obsessive-Compulsive Neurosis," in A. Goldstein and E. B. Foa (Eds.), *Handbook of Behavioral Interventions* (New York: Wiley, 1979). DSM-III reflects the conventional approach: obsessions are thoughts, compulsions are acts. We generally speak of obsessive thoughts and compulsive acts. Foa and Tillmans shift the emphasis to the discomfort involved. Acts, thoughts, or images that bring about anxiety are obsessions, and whichever of these reduce anxiety are compulsions. This would classify some thoughts as compulsions, particularly rituals, such as covert counting to ward off catastrophe (we do not believe that acts would ever be thought of as obsessions). We end up with observable rituals, cognitive compulsions, and obsessions. Foa and Steketee (1979) suggest that nervous habits (for example, nailbiting), addictive behaviors (for example, alcohol and drug addictions, gambling, overeating), and deviant acts (for example, exhibitionism) should not be classified under obsessive-compulsive disorders. None of the above suggestions are in any fundamental discord with the DSM-III definitions given above.

The importance of classification for our purposes lies in the implications for therapy. Foa and Steketee (1979) make the generalization that compulsions, whether thought or action, should be blocked, while obsessions should be treated by prolonged exposure. A therapist who does not follow this principle could classify a ritualistic thought as an obsession rather than a compulsion and treat it with exposure, only to find that the symptoms get worse.

Other established authors in this field have made equally strong statements: "Faced with the task of decreasing ritual behavior in a group of encrusted obsessive-compulsive individuals, . . . do not concern yourself with insight, existential encounters, or empathy. And do not waste time with systematic desensitization, thought stopping, progressive relaxation, or aversion relief. So administer a series of performance-based methods such as *in vivo* flooding, response prevention, and participant modeling" (S. Rachman and R. Hodgson, *Obsessions and Compulsions,* Englewood Cliffs, N.J.: Prentice-Hall, 1979). This statement, of course, refers to ritual alone; the previous statement above refers to the broader categories of obsessions and compulsions. The reader can see that researchers feel safe with at least some generalizations in a field where only a few years ago the statement was made, "The prognosis of obsessive-compulsive neurosis . . . is probably worse than that of any other neurotic disorder" (Solyom and others, 1972, p. 291; digested in this section). What follows in this section is a wide range of therapies: behavioral, cognitive, psychodynamic, drug, and psychosurgery. These treatments are intended for various specific disorders—compulsive rituals, covert compulsions, and obsessions. For the sake of clarity, we have stated in the titles what particular disorder a therapy is intended for.

The reader should be aware that in this section we are not dealing with the symptoms described under compulsive personality disorder, although we estimate that these symptoms not only are fairly frequently seen in people coming for therapy but are difficult for therapists to handle. DSM-III states that the disorder is apparently common, particularly in men. Included in compulsive personality disorder are perfectionism, indecisiveness, stinginess (both emotional and material), all work and little play, concern with rules and the like, formality, conventionality, and insistence that others do things one's way. We suspect that readers would look hungrily for hints on how to help with such problems. Surprisingly, we found a dearth of therapy literature for the disorder as described. We therefore had to eliminate this category. We hope that readers searching for therapy ideas to help people with the symptoms of compulsive personality disorder will find some helpful ideas in the therapy literature given in this section.

The therapies for obsessions should be useful with clients experiencing obsessive thoughts of a less dramatic quality than those cited here—for example, obsessions with power or sex. Similarly, therapies for compulsions given here should be helpful with compulsive behavior of various kinds, such as unusual and time-consuming neatness and cleanliness.

Behavior Therapy for Morbid Preoccupations and Compulsive Avoidance

AUTHORS: Gary M. Farkas and Steven Beck

PRECIS: Response prevention and various forms of exposure to reduce the obsessions and avoidance behavior of two men

INTRODUCTION: Exposure and response prevention have been enthusiastically reported as effective treatments for washing and checking compulsions. However, various reports of exceptions slightly dampen the enthusiasm. For example, people who are severely depressed and/or perceive that their obsessive fears are realistic may not respond to exposure and response prevention. In this instance, the therapist must do something about the depression. Thus, differentiating between symptoms and trying to find therapies appropriate to specific groups of symptoms would seem to be in order.

The two following cases show the efficacy of specific forms of response prevention and exposure for a specific combination of obsessive-compulsive difficulties—morbid ruminations and compulsive avoidance behavior.

CASE STUDY ONE: A twenty-three-year-old male college graduate and art student referred himself to the clinic because of fears of hurting someone and of being mentally ill, fears that had begun two years before. His art work was suffering; he drank excessively to lower anxiety; and he avoided people for fear of going crazy while with them or harming them. He never acted on these thoughts but felt they were irrational, and he felt guilty. He had begun to read the Bible and books on rational thinking, and he avoided other books, television, or movies for fear of being confronted with people who had killed someone or gone crazy. He also avoided handling knives or sharp instruments in the company of his parents, with whom he lived, especially his mother, whom he feared he might hurt.

The therapist saw him for ten sessions. Initially, the therapist exposed him to a set of knives, asking him to hold them until he felt minimal anxiety. The young man was instructed to handle knives at home in the presence of his mother and was given various homework assignments. He was to stop reading anxiety-allaying books, including the Bible, and instead read a textbook on abnormal psychology, read newspaper clippings and novels about murders, and go to violent movies. He was to read the daily paper and watch evening TV news.

His morbid ruminations steadily decreased, but during the end of therapy, when sessions were only once a month, he again became bothered by thoughts of harming people and going crazy. With no prompting, however, he resumed his handling of knives and doing prescribed reading, both of which he found lowered his anxiety. On follow-up at two months he reported no morbid thinking and an ability to use the coping strategies he had been taught. He was enjoying his art work, dating, interacting with his mother comfortably, and not drinking alcohol. He even showed lowering of the depression present at intake. He said that he had faith in the exposure procedure and this encouraged him to follow therapy procedures.

CASE STUDY TWO: A fifty-eight-year-old white married male civil servant with three children referred himself to the clinic because of fears of harming others and becoming mentally ill, both of forty years' standing. He avoided potentially harmful instruments, standing behind people, and TV programs and newspaper stories involving violence or insanity. He had never acted on his morbid thoughts, considered them alien to himself, and prayed to get rid of them.

The therapist saw him for eight sessions. The man was first shown a group of potentially harmful instruments—for example, knives, hammer—which he was asked first to hold and then to bring nearer and nearer to the therapist. He reported that although he felt acutely anxious doing this, the therapist's trust in him led him to believe that he would never use these instruments toward violent ends. He also saw that his anxiety with instruments was capable of being diminished.

The therapist also took him through one of the hospital's

adult wards and assigned homework, which the therapist monitored during therapy sessions. For one hour a day, the patient
was to read about violence in newspapers and magazines, view
violent TV programs, handle scissors while talking to people,
carry a pocket knife and hold it while near people, and display
a gift of knives in his kitchen. If a morbid thought arose, he was
to expand it to a longer, more gruesome story to the point of
his becoming bored with it. He also had to go to movies about
mental hospitals and horrible acts by normal people who had
gone mad.

At the same time he was told not to leave anything he
feared nor engage in anything that distracted him from his fears,
including prayer for the purpose of relieving his morbid ruminations.

By the end of therapy and on follow-up the client showed
dramatic and rapid cessation of both morbid ruminations and
avoidance behavior relating to fears. He stated that his trust in
the therapist was crucial and that his belief that exposure would
end in reduction of anxiety helped him to follow treatment procedures faithfully.

COMMENTARY: These procedures might be used by only a
limited number of therapists because of the apparent risks. The
therapist would have to have utter faith in the procedure and no
fear that during therapy the patient would act on his destructive, even murderous impulses. Since past behavior is the best
predictor of future behavior, this therapy should probably not
be used with impulsive clients who have done highly destructive
things in the past. The therapist must be careful that the client
trusts him and believes the therapy will work. In addition, the
therapist must be willing to spend considerable time with a client, accompany the client far afield of the therapy office, and
model fairly bizarre behavior (for example, touching garbage
cans and then rubbing his own face).

SOURCE: Farkas, G. M., and Beck, S. "Exposure and Response
Prevention of Morbid Ruminations and Compulsive Avoidance." *Behaviour Research and Therapy,* 1981, *19,* 257-261.

Exposure Treatments for Rituals

AUTHORS: Edna B. Foa, Gail Steketee, Ralph M. Turner, and Stephen C. Fischer

PRECIS: Along with response prevention, imagined exposure combined with real-life exposure found more effective on long-term follow-up than real-life exposure alone among a group of fifteen people

INTRODUCTION: Checking rituals seem to develop in people who believe that checking will aid in staving off potential catastrophes. Translating this idea for therapeutic maneuvers could plausibly entail one or more of at least three currently popular measures: preventing the person from performing the rituals; exposing him to actual feared items in the environment; and requiring him to flood his imagination with his feared catastrophes. Repeated demonstrations of the merits of the first (response prevention) might cause a therapist to choose this as a must. Tests of the relative merits of the latter two—*in vivo* exposure and imaginal exposure—have not uncovered any differences. However, it stands to reason that if in ritualistic behavior the person believes the ritual will forestall the catastrophe, then real-life exposure would appear to require backing up by imagined catastrophes for best results. A study of therapeutic effectiveness was developed to investigate this idea.

TREATMENT: Eight males and seven females with mean age of thirty-seven years and absence of psychosis were chosen for the study on the basis of their engaging in checking rituals and fearing disastrous consequences if they failed to carry out the rituals. This was their major distress, and its severity caused great disruption to their daily lives. All had received more than ten sessions of psychotherapy with no reported diminishing of symptoms. No one had any therapy for three weeks prior to the beginning of this study.

All subjects were required to engage in response prevention. Otherwise, the fifteen people were divided into two groups:

The first group received imaginal exposure combined with real-life exposure, while the second group engaged only in real-life exposure. Everyone came for four ninety-minute sessions held over a period of two weeks for interviews from which their therapy programs were devised: designating supervisors for response prevention and designating which rituals were to be prevented, developing scenes for imaginal exposure, and preparing situations for *in vivo* exposure.

People in the combined treatment group came for ten daily sessions, excluding weekends, in which they spent one and a half hours flooding their imagination with their feared catastrophes and thirty minutes in real-life exposure. People in the second group came for ten daily sessions of real-life exposure only.

Descriptions of the treatments are as follows:

Response Prevention. Although normal checking was allowed, no rituals were permitted. Prevention was under the supervision of supervisors at home or in the hospital, depending on where the patient lived. The supervisor stayed with the person when an urge to check was hard to resist. Supervisors never used physical force to prevent a ritual, but they reported all violations to the therapist.

Exposure in Imagination. From the initial interviews, the therapist devised three to four scenes, varying in their anxiety-provoking potential. The person lay on a recliner with his eyes closed and tried to imagine the prescribed scene as vividly as possible. When the person's anxiety lowered, the therapist prescribed a more anxiety-provoking scene.

Exposure in vivo. The person was progressively exposed to real-life situations that evoked progressively higher anxiety and the urge to check repeatedly. Each day a new situation was added to the previous ones; during the second week, sessions six to ten, all situations were presented in every session. Patients' homework was to practice the exposures for two hours between sessions every day, including weekends.

After two weeks of therapy, everyone was allowed to check a predetermined list of objects every day, and patients were urged to expose themselves to situations that had previously evoked checking urges. About half of the total group came for additional sessions to discuss other problems, and the therapist offered social skills training, marital therapy, and so on.

Assessment of results was done by an independent assessor after treatment was over and again at a follow-up session from three months to two and a half years later. At the end of treatment, all patients improved, and no differences were seen in amount of improvement between the two groups. However, the people receiving no imaginal exposure showed more relapse than people receiving combined treatment. The obvious conclusion is that treatment including imaginal exposure brought about more stable gains than real-life exposure alone. The suggestion here is that although a person exposing himself to feared objects that elicit compulsions would appear also to be accustoming himself to accompanying feared disasters, additional direct confrontation of the feared disasters in imagination may bring more lasting results.

COMMENTARY: This therapy is, of course, incredibly intense and requires a great deal of time and energy from both patient and therapist. Although this kind of expenditure would be difficult for therapists in private practice and patients on an outpatient basis, it might be modified for outpatients through intensive weekends or six to seven nights per week. Another difficult aspect is the use of supervisors for response prevention; ex-patients might conceivably be used instead. The therapy here has direct relevance to phobias, since in most therapies for phobias, *in vivo* exposure is used alone. The contribution of this study is that adding imaginal exposure stabilizes improvement.

SOURCE: Foa, E. B., Steketee, G., Turner, R. M., and Fischer, S. C. "Effects of Imaginal Exposure to Feared Disasters in Obsessive-Compulsive Checkers." *Behaviour Research and Therapy*, 1980, *18*, 449-455.

Covert Modeling for Compulsions

AUTHORS: William M. Hay, Linda R. Hay, and Rosemary O. Nelson

PRECIS: A twenty-seven-year-old obsessive-compulsive woman practices imagining herself as coping, removes her compulsions, and generalizes her coping abilities to another major area

INTRODUCTION: Whereas in overt modeling the therapist shows the patient examples of behavior contrary to the patient's symptomatic behavior, in covert modeling the patient himself imagines adaptive behavior to replace maladaptive behavior. Covert modeling has been found to be therapeutic in various situations. Demonstrations of its efficacy for a wide array of disorders would be important because of the inherent advantages of the method: no elaborate therapeutic aids are needed; it may be used where live or filmed models cannot be used; the person himself is responsible for the outcome; and the learning of the procedure might allow the person to use it in areas other than that for which it was originally learned.

The method was used successfully with problems not previously attempted: a woman with obsessive-compulsive problems and a man with a serious drinking problem. Therapy with the obsessive-compulsive problem is reported below.

CASE STUDY: A twenty-seven-year-old woman, separated from her husband and caring for two children, was admitted to a state hospital because of obsessive-compulsive difficulties of six years' standing, anxiety, and depression. For four years prior to entering the hospital she had had outpatient treatment, including psychotherapy, drugs, and electroconvulsive shock, to no avail.

Her obsessive-compulsive behaviors included a preoccupation with cleanliness and checking compulsions (turning light switches off and closing doors). While in the hospital, she stopped her cleanliness obsession but developed a preoccupation with the number 3; for example, she would throw away the third item in a box, refuse to carry three things, and so on. She stated that if she failed to do these things correctly, something terrible would happen to her.

Since her obsessive thoughts were almost ceaseless, the therapist decided to focus on her compulsive behaviors, among which three were chosen: checking that room lights were off and that her door was closed and her behaviors relating to the number 3. She was asked to record the daily frequency of these behaviors, which she continued to do throughout treatment.

After the first week, covert modeling was taught to her, but she was to apply it to only one behavior at a time. The procedure in all instances was similar. In each session, the therapist gave eight scenes and responses from which the woman practiced, in imagination, that she was coping with the specific compulsion. She was required to signal when the scene was clear and to stay with it until she had coped. Each scene was gone over twice during the session.

Two weeks were devoted to each of the following target behaviors separately: the first two weeks to checking light switches, the next two weeks to checking door closing, and the final two weeks to her obsession with the number 3. The treatment lasted six weeks; twice-weekly sessions were forty-five minutes long, and she practiced daily with the aid of tapes prepared by the therapist.

At the end of six weeks, the frequency of all three behaviors had decreased substantially, and she reported that her urges had decreased. She also felt that she now had skills to handle them when they did arise. In the seventh week she was discharged from the hospital. At three- and six-month follow-ups she reported that her compulsiveness had ceased, and this was corroborated in a telephone contact with her mother. She also said that she had adapted covert modeling to her cleanliness obsession, and this had abated. However, she was still depressed at times, a condition that she felt resulted from her not being able to find a job.

The procedure has been used successfully by others with some alterations: imagining a coping model rather than a mastery model, a similar rather than a dissimilar model, a reinforced rather than a nonreinforced model, a multiple rather than a single model. Whether the model is oneself or someone else seems to be irrelevant.

COMMENTARY: This is a remarkable case study on a number of accounts. First, the time with the therapist was brief, particularly considering the severity, longevity, and resistance to treatment of the problem. One could speculate that the infrequency of contacts with the therapist may have itself been therapeutic in that this focused responsibility for cure on the patient herself. The therapy is, of course, similar to other self-control therapies described in this book. Noteworthy is that after leaving the hospital she spontaneously generalized the techniques she had learned to other behaviors, thus again taking responsibility for herself. Second, surprisingly, the therapy here for ritualistic behavior was successful without the inclusion of response prevention, one of the few currently accepted basic therapies for ritualizing. The therapy might have gone more quickly with the addition of response prevention. Third, the currently acceptable procedures include exposure (or flooding), while the technique here involves the addition of the person's coping in fantasy with the stress herself. This provocative technique might be tried more often, not only with ritualistic behavior and other compulsions but with totally different disorders, such as depression and anxiety.

Note the use of self-monitoring here, a procedure often included in the treatment of depression but perhaps not frequently enough with compulsions. This self-awareness technique might also be tried with many kinds of disorders. (See Paquin, 1979, digested in this section.)

In addition, there might have been occupational counseling while the woman was in the hospital to forestall the later depression.

SOURCE: Hay, W.M., Hay, L.R., and Nelson, R.O. "The Adaptation of Covert Modeling Procedures to the Treatment of Chronic Alcoholism and Obsessive-Compulsive Behavior: Two Case Reports." *Behavior Therapy*, 1977, *8*, 70-76.

Cognitive Behavioral Therapy for
Obsessive-Compulsive Neurosis

AUTHORS: Miles E. McFall and Janet P. Wollersheim

PRECIS: Many current therapeutic approaches to alter an obsessive-compulsive person's unrealistic ideas about the world and his own self-worth

INTRODUCTION: Obsessions and compulsions arise initially from ideas a person has about himself; he must be perfect to be worthwhile and avoid criticism; he should be punished for being anything but perfect; his having certain thoughts or feelings can lead to catastrophe; and he can prevent catastrophe by obsessive thoughts and/or compulsive acts. Therapy, therefore, should be directed toward the person's becoming more realistic in his appraisal both of threat and of his ability to handle it with means other than obsessions and compulsions. Basically, therapy should alter the person's unrealistic beliefs, especially those relating to his self-worth. A composite of many existing therapeutic measures may be used to accomplish these ends.

TREATMENT: Therapy covers seven basic goals, which can be accomplished with specific therapeutic measures currently in use, as follows:

Help the person be more accepting of both his negative and positive features. There are various ways to do this: (1) Verbally reassure the person with statements such as "Heavens! Having sexual and hostile feelings and thoughts is not bad but simply evidence that you are a thinking, feeling person and part of the human race. What counts is what you do with these feelings and thoughts. When you learn not to upset yourself so much for having them, you'll realize that, indeed, you do have control over them and won't act them out." (2) Give the person support and information, such as assuring him that most people have sexual and hostile thoughts. (3) Help him discriminate between having a thought or feeling and acting on it. (4) Help him see that he has the ability to control acting out his thoughts. (5)

Help him recognize that although undesirable consequences can result from some actions, they are not necessarily catastrophic. (6) Aid him in seeing that acting on one's feelings does not make one a less worthwhile person.

Be warm, accepting, and nonjudgmental. Provide a relationship with the person in which he can accept parts of himself that he usually denies. The therapist should even be willing to express his own feelings and make appropriate disclosures.

Help the person recognize his feelings both in and outside therapy. One way to do this is to get the person to label his feelings twenty to forty times a day in different situations. He may also be encouraged to label these feelings as pleasant or unpleasant but not to dwell on or analyze them.

Encourage him to gradually make some behavior changes. The therapist can use various current methods in doing this: response prevention, flooding, positive reinforcement, and thought stopping (described in various digests in this and other sections). These may be started in the therapist's office, and then the patient can do them on his own.

Help him see himself as a more capable person in dealing with his environment, despite his symptoms. Together, the therapist and client write a character sketch of the client as he is now; this should be in the third person, using a fictitious name for the person, and written as if by a caring, knowledgeable, sympathetic friend. This sketch should be discussed so the client gets some perspective on the sources of his difficulties. Then prepare a second sketch, this time of the person as a nonsymptomatic, well-functioning, but not perfect person. Lastly, get the client to try to live this new role, without committing himself to any permanent behavior changes. He should be asked to do this gradually, beginning with one day a week.

Focus on the unrealistic assumptions behind the person's distress. Begin with asking him to fantasize his catastrophic fears and/or think unacceptable thoughts in an exaggerated way during therapy (see Index for implosion, flooding, imaginal exposure, paradoxical intention), then help him to identify the unreasonable assumptions behind his discomfort. Emphasize that all of us live in an uncertain world and that he is in control to the extent that he can choose not to carry out rituals intended to control events. Along with this, the therapist should help the person to alter his perfectionistic strivings. Finally, provide the person with practical skills designed to help him cope with troublesome thoughts and behaviors.

An alternative device is the following: The patient defines a problem and then goes through a situation in imagination, giving a full account of his thoughts and feelings. Therapist and patient discuss the underlying unrealistic assumptions. The therapist then imagines the scene but gives a more reasonable way to deal with the situation.

COMMENTARY: This extraordinary array of therapies illustrates our emphasis on combining approaches. The approach here is not one of just getting rid of symptoms but a holistic approach. The therapy of Carl Rogers is seen in the warm, accepting, nonjudgmental, and even self-exposing stance for the therapist. There is also the focus on feelings through the therapist's requesting the client to label his feelings. The behavioral approach is represented by response prevention, positive reinforcement, and so on. The cognitive approach, particularly the approach of Albert Ellis, is seen in the therapist's attack on the client's assumptions about himself and the world. Even the therapy of George Kelly (see Index), not a popular therapy, is seen in the therapist's asking the client to write a character sketch of himself as he is and as he would like to be and to try out a new role. Added to all these, the authors suggest the reassurance of simple information, such as that most people have sexual and hostile thoughts.

SOURCE: McFall, M. E., and Wollersheim, J. P. "Obsessive-Compulsive Neurosis: A Cognitive-Behavioral Formulation and Approach to Treatment." *Cognitive Therapy and Research*, 1979, *3*, 333-348.

Induced Anxiety to Uncover
Basic Conflicts

AUTHOR: J. Robert Noonan

PRECIS: Fostering deep feelings and related associations to produce quick revelation of unexpressed conflicts for the removal of compulsions and obsessions

INTRODUCTION: Neither dynamic psychotherapy nor behavior therapy has produced convincing and consistent relief from obsessions and compulsions. Insight, or dynamic, therapy is long and often unsuccessful, even perhaps strengthening the obsessions or compulsions in some people. Behavior therapy, though reportedly successful in some instances, has not been proved to be thoroughly satisfactory. Since both approaches have merit, a reasonable alternative might be a therapy including elements of both systems. Thus, the conflict presumably underlying the obsessive-compulsive symptoms might be uncovered and emotionally responded to in a relatively short time with the direct and active posture of behavior therapists. This approach has been called "induced anxiety."

TREATMENT: The goal of therapy is to uncover basic conflicts quickly and have the person respond strongly to them. This is done by suggesting to the patient that he is beginning to have deep feelings, urging him to display his feelings, and asking for associations to the feelings. Specifically, the therapeutic steps are as follows:

1. The therapist helps the person to relax deeply.
2. He suggests to the client that a feeling is growing within and that the client should let it grow.
3. When the client shows signs of growing feelings—for example, twitching, quick breathing—the therapist urges him on until the feelings become powerful.
4. The therapist then asks the client to reveal his associations to his feelings.

5. The therapist continues to urge the client to let his feelings express themselves until the patient "abreacts," or dramatically relives conflictual life experiences.

6. The therapist then induces relaxation and desensitizes the patient to the associations producing the anxious feelings.

7. The therapist and patient review what has happened by interpreting the experience, attempting to explain it, and giving it some structure.

CASE STUDY: A thirty-five-year-old, unmarried graduate student came to therapy complaining of his engaging in meaningless rituals, feeling extremely inadequate, and strongly fearing authority. He had several times gone through incapacitating periods of handwashing and going to confession several times a day following obsessive self-examination. Although these obsessions and compulsions had not become entrenched, the man was rigid and moralistic; for example, he rejected any relationship with a woman that went beyond the platonic. He had taken an academic course with the therapist and had previously asked to come for therapy with him. There were seven sessions of varying lengths, as follows:

First Session, 80 Minutes. Therapist and patient discussed the man's presenting symptoms; the therapist briefly tested him, diagnosing the difficulty as an obsessive-compulsive reaction with extreme feelings of inadequacy.

Second Session, 40 Minutes. The therapist explained induced anxiety as a technique and informed the patient of the brief but intense nature of the therapy, and they discussed whatever fears the man had about therapy. The therapist tried to begin the therapy, but the patient intellectualized and kept revelations on a very superficial basis, avoiding any show of feeling. The therapist expressed disappointment and disapproval.

Third Session, 1 Hour. The therapist induced relaxation in the patient, instructed the patient to look inward, and suggested that the patient had a feeling growing in him. The patient began to show signs of anxiety—restlessness, sweating, and quick breathing. The therapist encouraged him with "That's it," "Just let it go," and so on, and the patient's emotional expressions became even stronger. Asked to associate, the patient talked about his family interactions, especially his mother's dominating behavior and martyrdom, adding with not much feeling that he felt guilty about his anger toward his mother and certain ways he had treated his sister. Before the session ended, the therapist relaxed him and desensitized him toward his associations.

Fourth Session, 75 Minutes. Exposed to the therapist's previous introductions, the patient expressed much more intense feelings and centered his associations on his mother's behavior. He suddenly said that his scrupulous behavior was a "screwy" way to deal with his hatred of his mother and wondered why he had not admitted his feelings in the first place. After awhile, he said he smelled "bathroom odors" and added that this happened to him occasionally, especially when he became close to people. The therapist again relaxed and desensitized him.

Fifth Session, 65 Minutes. The usual procedure was followed, and the patient showed strong emotion. He related an experience when he was three and a half years old in which he had defecated on the floor at home and his mother had rubbed his face in the feces. She followed this with tears and accused him of making her induce this punishment. On recounting this, the patient gasped, choked, pounded, thrashed about, and rubbed his face, apparently "abreacting," or fully reliving the incident. He finally settled down, looking exhausted but satisfied, and asked to leave.

Sixth Session, 35 Minutes. Although the therapist believed that no further abreaction was necessary, he nonetheless followed the induced anxiety procedure. The patient, however, displayed no discomfort, saying only that he felt good.

Seventh Session, 40 Minutes. The therapist and patient went over what had happened, and the therapist answered questions and attempted to prepare the patient for the future. This ended the therapy.

No formal follow-up was undertaken, but in casual meetings with the therapist, the patient seemed more confident, calm, and happy. In addition, the patient wrote a letter to the therapist twenty months after therapy terminated, saying that he was doing well socially and vocationally, had improved his relations with women, and had no anxiety about authority.

COMMENTARY: A Freudian analyst might see this therapy as a working through of one early recollection and associated feelings, although an analyst would not be as directive as the therapist was in this case. The patient gets onto something emotionally laden, the therapist asks him to free-associate, and the patient free-associates and then abreacts. Relaxation and desensitization are clearly a part of this therapy, as is shown in the steps, but their value are not illustrated in the case study. The patient left the dramatic abreaction session without being relaxed and desensitized by the therapist. It is possible that the therapist's clearly running the session allowed the young man to say what he really wanted to say, since he was, in a sense, not responsible. The therapist not only expressed his approval but urged the man to express his feelings, as is done in many kinds of therapy. Implied here is imaginal exposure, commonly used with obsessive-compulsive disorders, but the therapist does not guide it. This therapy might be used with anyone suffering a discrete set of traumatic events. In fact, it is not dissimilar from flooding therapies for people depressed by recent losses, such as death of a spouse. The brevity of the therapy in the case study seems to reflect the discreteness of the man's problems. Even with problems of a wider scope, however, the therapy might be used to bring out intense feelings.

SOURCE: Noonan, J. R. "An Obsessive-Compulsive Reaction Treated by Induced Anxiety." *American Journal of Psychotherapy*, 1971, *25*, 293-299.

Daily Monitoring to Eliminate
a Compulsion

AUTHOR: Michael J. Paquin

PRECIS: Daily recordkeeping of a face-picking compulsion by a twenty-year-old woman to remove the compulsion

INTRODUCTION: An old concern among therapists is the extent to which therapeutic interventions might interfere with patient responsibility, autonomy, and self-control. During the administering of most behavior therapies, therapists require patients to observe and keep records of the behavior about which they came to therapy. What has been found is that the feedback the patient gets by monitoring is sometimes therapeutic in itself. Monitoring oneself is a solitary activity for which a patient can be nothing but totally responsible and autonomous. If, as has been found, recordkeeping alone is therapeutic, then it would be not only economical but maintaining of the patient's complete autonomy. If it turned out not to be therapeutic, it would still provide the behavioral information needed to administer various behavioral techniques.

CASE STUDY: A twenty-year-old, bright, single second-year medical student suffered a compulsion of five years' standing to pick her face to such a degree that serious infection was risked. She did this two or three times a day for a total of about twenty minutes. Intensity was correlated with anxiety-provoking events, such as exams. She was referred by the student counseling service for behavior therapy when tranquilizers, counseling, and hypnotherapy failed, although several other problems had been taken care of.

She came for behavior therapy sessions for twenty-five weeks, during which time she was also taking tranquilizers for anxiety and antibiotics for facial problems, both of which she gave up after therapy was over.

For the first two weeks, therapist and patient discussed her problems, gathered data, and established rapport. In the third week the therapist explained the treatment rationale: compulsions are learned behaviors, and in order to treat them, the therapist needs detailed records of the compulsive behavior. The young woman agreed to a behavioral contract involving her keeping careful, daily records, with the end goal of eradicating the compulsion.

By the eleventh week of recordkeeping, her face-picking had drastically reduced. She later confided that by this time she was feeling considerable control over her compulsion.

In the twelfth week, as the therapist had planned, he introduced the therapeutic technique of covert sensitization, involving the patient's imagining engaging in compulsive behavior followed by imagined punishment—for example, nausea. She continued for five weeks, during which time her face-picking increased. She later explained that the procedure divested her of the rewards she felt in controlling the compulsion herself. She also began to associate even recordkeeping with the unpleasantness. The covert sensitization procedure was stopped, but recordkeeping was retained until contacts stopped at the end of twenty-five weeks total. By this time the frequency of face-picking had diminished 93 percent and duration 99 percent. The young woman reported feeling more confident, more relaxed in interpersonal situations, less anxious academically, and pleased with her visible facial improvement.

Follow-up sessions were held thirty-seven and fifty-two weeks after treatment, at which time she reported only minor incidents of face-picking. A roommate chosen as independent observer corroborated the accounts.

COMMENTARY: The possible therapeutic effectiveness of simply becoming aware of what one is doing is beautifully illustrated here. One must, however, question how many people with compulsions would find total relief by monitoring alone. Considering lack of further evidence, one can do no more than guess that, for most people with compulsions, monitoring must be accompanied by other procedures. This is not to say that with some people the procedure alone might not do the trick, particularly if the therapist preceded the introducing of it with the statement that it had been found on occasion as sufficient in itself to cure a compulsion. Considering its great economy, it is certainly worth a try.

Another interesting point is illustrated here: A client's marked distaste for a particular therapeutic procedure can be generalized to a dislike for other, previously neutrally or positively regarded and helpful procedures. Therapists might wish to be sensitive to their clients' feelings about procedures despite their own enthusiasms.

SOURCE: Paquin, M. J. "The Treatment of Obsessive Compulsions by Information Feedback: A New Application of a Standard Behavioral Procedure." *Psychotherapy: Theory, Research, and Practice,* 1979, *16,* 292-296.

A Therapy for Rituals Is Rejected by Patients and They Recover

AUTHORS: A. D. Rabavilas, J. C. Boulougouris, and C. Stefanis

PRECIS: Compulsive checking diminished in four patients when therapy instructions to overcheck were totally disobeyed

INTRODUCTION: If a person behaves in a certain way in order to stave off a dire condition and believes his behavior accomplishes its end, the person is apt to exaggerate the behavior in a compulsive way. For example, if a person feels compelled to check a water tap more than once and the unpleasant condition does not appear, the overchecking is reinforced and a compulsion is established. In addition, a given number of repetitions becomes established as a safety signal that things will be all right. Presumably, repetitions beyond the safety point would have no reinforcing power.

TREATMENT: Three males and one female with an average age of thirty-five years had engaged in compulsive behavior for an average duration of over ten years. With one form or another of therapy, most of their compulsions had diminished, but checking remained strong enough that they were afraid their compulsions would reappear.

In individual treatment sessions, the therapist told the client that when he felt compelled to check more than once, he should continue checking far beyond the point at which he felt he was safe, even up to fifty checkings. The therapist further instructed him to follow the prescription with all checking compulsions except one, which they would use as a base point when therapy was over. For six months, the client was to follow the rules but never without cause. That is, he was to exaggerate only when a checking compulsion (either behavioral or thought) arose; the therapist encouraged him to give in to checking compulsions in order to practice the method. The therapist even modeled the method to make it perfectly clear.

In addition, someone living with the person was enlisted as an observer but with no power to control the person.

The therapist saw clients four times—before the treatment began, then at intervals of one week, one month, and six months, at which points the clients and observers gave ratings of symptoms.

According to client and observer ratings, *all* checking behaviors markedly diminished but did not disappear. Improvement began the first week after the instructions were given and held to six months follow-up. There were, however, no changes in general anxiety level or any other residual compulsions.

The surprise of the study was that none of the clients followed the therapist's instructions. They lost interest in checking, stating that following the prescription served no purpose.

The speculation is that the compulsive checking became meaningless because the patients equated it with the meaningless checking prescribed by the therapist. Therefore, neither was worth doing.

COMMENTARY: The outcome of this study, surprising to its authors, contributes a potentially valuable twist to the methods of flooding (in its repetitiveness) and paradoxical intention (in its seeming nonsensical quality)—both covered elsewhere in this book. In these two methods the emphasis is on the catastrophe the person is trying to avoid, not on the compulsive ritual that is designed to prevent the catastrophe. The twist in the present study is that the client is to exaggerate the symptom, not the catastrophe. Ritualizers are presumably in conflict about their rituals: they do not want to engage in them, and yet they must do so to avoid dire happenings. Thus, what may be important here is that people are forced to do what they know seems to be ridiculous. The method might be used with phobics (for example, suggesting that an agoraphobic person should not even get anywhere near the doorway that leads outside) and obsessive people ("think of it at least 150 times a day").

SOURCE: Rabavilas, A. D., Boulougouris, J. C., and Stefanis, C. "Compulsive Checking Diminished when Over-Checking Instructions Were Disobeyed." *Journal of Behavior Therapy and Experimental Psychiatry*, 1977, *8*, 111-112.

Behavior Therapy With and Without Antidepressant Drugs for Rituals

AUTHORS: S. Rachman, J. Cobb, S. Grey, B. McDonald, D. Mawson, G. Sartory, and R. Stern

PRECIS: Removing compulsive rituals in forty adults with exposure, modeling, pacing, and response prevention and decreasing accompanying depression and anxiety with clomipramine

INTRODUCTION: For some people with compulsive rituals, exposure to feared situations, with or without modeling of fearlessness by the therapist, has been found to be effective. Despite treatment, however, other people have made little or no stable progress. The presence of severe depression, which sometimes accompanies compulsions, appeared to retard progress. Since clomipramine has been found effective with depression, it would make sense to try supplementing behavior therapy with a drug of this kind to remove the depression. A study was undertaken to compare behavior therapy, specifically exposure, plus clomipramine with exposure plus placebo. In addition, relaxation training was used for comparison because of its presumed effectiveness, even though it has been shown to be less effective than exposure with and without modeling.

TREATMENT: Forty adults (eleven men and twenty-nine women), age range eighteen to fifty-nine, with handicapping compulsive rituals of at least one year's duration but no psychosis, were selected for a controlled study of the relative therapeutic values of combinations of behavior therapy, relaxation training, clomipramine, and placebo. They were randomly assigned to four groups: behavior therapy plus clomipramine, behavior therapy plus placebo, relaxation training plus clomipramine, and relaxation training plus placebo. For four weeks all forty were outpatients; twenty were given clomipramine and twenty were placed on placebo. At the end of four weeks, the twenty persons on clomipramine were getting an average dosage of 164 mg, with average blood plasma levels of the drug reaching 157 mg/100 ml.

At this point all forty were admitted to the hospital as inpatients, continued with clomipramine or placebo, and treated with either exposure plus modeling or relaxation training. (After thirty-six weeks the clomipramine was gradually lowered until the fortieth week, when it was stopped altogether.)

Behavior therapy sessions were forty-five minutes long and given every weekday. First the therapist told the patients that their discomfort would eventually disappear if they faced their fears and stopped ritualizing. The therapist selected the major theme of a patient's obsession and modeled the activity the person avoided, but he did not ritualize. He thus demonstrated his lack of concern for the negative consequences. For example, a person with a handwashing compulsion was taken to the hospital garbage can, where the therapist touched the can and then rubbed his hands over his face and hair; the therapist then suggested the patient imitate. After exposure exercises, patients were told not to engage in rituals for a specific period of time. They were told to do the exposure exercises during the day and to keep records of their performance of the tasks. Hospital staff offered encouragement. Released for weekends at home, they were to continue exposure and response prevention. Relatives at the patients' homes were instructed to help patients in exposure and response prevention.

Behavior therapy, as expected, lessened the compulsive rituals; clomipramine lessened the rituals and also anxiety and depression. The suggestion was that the antidepressant drug affected the rituals only secondarily. That is, the drug affected the depression, which presumably helps to maintain the compulsions. The possibility of a direct effect of clomipramine on rituals is not well founded. The suggestion for therapists is that people suffering not only compulsive rituals but depression as well should be given both behavior therapy and clomipramine.

COMMENTARY: Numerous observations may be made about this provocative study. First, the possibility exists that antidepressant drugs other than clomipramine might be just as effective; side effects are probably the primary consideration for whatever drug is administered. These therapies demonstrated effectiveness with compulsive rituals, but generalizing the results to other compulsions or to obsessions (in the sense of unwanted, intrusive thoughts) is not warranted. Therapists might consider replacing drugs with current psychological treatments of depression and anxiety, notably behavioral techniques other than those used here—cognitive therapies, various forms of psychotherapies, and others.

A major unanswered question in this report is which of the behavioral techniques accomplished the lowering of ritualistic behavior. Foa and others (1980), digested in this section, found good results with both checking and washing rituals without either modeling or pacing. If these difficult and time-consuming procedures could be eliminated, therapy might go easier and faster. In addition, Foa and others suggest that lessening of washing rituals must have imaginal exposure in order to prevent slipping back. The present authors mention washing rituals as examples of the problems of their clients but do not say whether all their clients suffered the same kind of ritualizing behavior. The authors suggest that different rituals might require different treatments.

SOURCE: Rachman, S., Cobb, J., Grey, S., McDonald, B., Mawson, D., Sartory, G., and Stern, R. "The Behavioural Treatment of Obsessive-Compulsive Disorders, With and Without Clomipramine." *Behaviour Research and Therapy,* 1979, *17,* 467-478.

Tailor-Made Therapy for Obsessions and Compulsions

AUTHORS: Luis O. de Seixas Queiraz, Maria A. Motta, Maria B. B. Pinho Madi, Dirceu L. Sossai, and John J. Boren

PRECIS: Looking for what initiates and maintains each patient's worrisome behavior and devising a package of techniques and steps to improve overall functioning and reduce obsessions and compulsions

INTRODUCTION: Although only a small percentage of psychiatric patients are diagnosed as obsessive-compulsive neurotics, obsessive thoughts and compulsive behaviors are much more common in people with all kinds of additional problems. Still, no one therapy has been established, although some techniques for specific problems seem to be effective. All in all, as it stands today, obsessive-compulsive problems are difficult to treat.

One approach to these difficulties is to examine carefully

the various conditions that instigate and maintain each troublesome behavior and design techniques to counteract these conditions. The approach is strictly individual. Since no single treatment exists for any large group, the therapist must design a
unique set of therapies and a step-by-step procedure.

There appears to be some substance to the criticism of
behavior therapy that if a particular behavior is eradicated without getting at its source, symptom substitution may occur, and
therefore a therapist must direct great attention to what maintains the painful thoughts and behavior. Some of the treatment
may be indirect (for example, working with the patient's relatives, priest, and so on), and some may be a frontal attack on a
specific behavior of the patient. In any case, many if not most
of these patients have not only personal behavior inadequacies
but interfering life conditions involving other people. Therapy,
therefore, is not apt to be limited to office visits alone.

TREATMENT: The therapist does the following: (1) carefully
specify the obsessions and compulsions, (2) determine how the
behaviors are maintained by any measures at the therapist's dis-
posal—for example, seeing people in the patient's environment,
observing the person in his home, (3) develop behavioral alternatives, (4) search out important rewards for the person, (5) devise a hierarchy of behaviors that are apt to bring reward to the
person, (6) try to cut down conditions that keep the obsessions
and compulsions going, (7) work with people in the person's environment who can reinforce him, (8) teach him assertive behavior, and (9) work to cut down the person's fear responses.

The steps are best illustrated by a case study.

CASE STUDY: A fifty-four-year-old, married man with five
sons was brought to the clinic after being discharged from a psychiatric hospital as a "schizophrenic-paranoid type with obsessive manifestations." He had been unemployed for five years
prior; his work experience was a series of failures. His wife and
sons increasingly took away responsibilities from him and then
criticized him for his lack of initiative. His upbringing had been
strict, punitive, and rigorously religious.

The treatment followed the steps prescribed in the procedure:

Description of Obsessive-Compulsive Behavior. He had numerous painful obsessions concerning sins against God, the Virgin Mary, and various saints, sexual thoughts about other people, his becoming a devil, and so on. These arose when he was at church, in the presence of other people, and in other situations. He spent much of his time isolating himself and praying for forgiveness.

Maintenance of Obsessive-Compulsive Behavior. He consulted his priest two to three times a day, confessing his sins, gaining absolution because he had sinned. His wife had taken on all family responsibility; he was, however, criticized for his immaturity and could do nothing right.

Alternative Behavior. The therapist and client established ways to increase logical thoughts, such as meeting with people and describing them accurately, helping at home to get some reward and avoid punishment, working at a paying job outside the home, engaging in constructive activities when obsessive thoughts arose.

Important Reinforcers. What was valuable to him was working in a paying job, being useful to his wife and sons, having the priest's and therapist's support, being successful even in small things, being thought of as a good Christian, and getting positive attention from his family.

Hierarchy of Behavior to Get Positive Reinforcement. Part of the extended sequence (from easiest to hardest) the therapist outlined for training the patient was: helping at home, interacting with people outside the home, more complex responsibilities (such as taking care of the home budget), and appropriate work behavior. When appropriate, the therapist accompanied the man and even modeled coping behavior, stopping as soon as the man became competent.

Source Maintaining Obsessive-Compulsive Behavior. In order to alter the reinforcements for the obsessive-compulsive behavior, the therapist did such things as asking the priest to say there was no need for confession since the man had not sinned, asking the wife to share the responsibility of the home by allowing her husband to do even the simplest things, and asking the family not to criticize the man.

Social Agencies to Reinforce Alternative Behavior. The therapist counseled the priest to reinforce adequate behavior by saying such things as "That's just what a good Christian should do!" The sales supervisor on the job the man obtained was asked to emphasize the man's accomplishments.

Assertive Training in the Clinic. The man was taught, and he rehearsed, more assertive job and family behavior.

Reduction of Fear Responses. Since his fears were largely focused on religious images, systematic desensitization and *in vivo* desensitization were used.

At the time of this report, therapy had lasted fifteen months. The therapist began with fear reduction, and the fear of being at church subsided, but obsessive ruminations went on. Family counseling was dropped because it seemed ineffective. However, work behavior became more and more successful, and the man began to spend more time outside the home. His obsession with confession reduced dramatically. Obsessions decreased to one a day, distress was extremely low, and the feeling of disablement disappeared totally. His depressions disappeared and he gained weight. He no longer discussed any obsessions at home.

The man continued therapy, discussing religious and sexual issues, but he stated, "I feel like a new man," "I feel good," "God is with me."

COMMENTARY: These authors admirably illustrate the efficacy of flexibility on the part of therapists, a broad array of therapeutic measures, and fitting the therapy to the client's problems. There is an implicit reminder here for a therapist to look into all areas of a client's life. Note that although the person had been diagnosed as a schizophrenic-paranoid type, the therapist made excellent progress with the holistic approach. The therapist's flexibility is shown in his dropping an approach, in this case family counseling, when it did not seem to be getting anywhere.

Following the broad-spectrum approach described here

might be difficult for some therapists for two reasons: (1) The therapist is expected to be unusually directive of the client's life, a position that might not be to some therapists' liking. Some therapists might, for example, have difficulty telling a priest what he should say to the patient about certain religious matters. (2) Along with this, the therapist is expected to be somewhat peripatetic. He goes to the client's home, accompanies him on the street, goes to the man's church, and so on. It may be that the only choice with some people as incapacitated as this man is aggressive, flexible, directive, multifaceted, holistic, and involving as many important people in the client's life as possible. This article is another model encompassing many approaches that might be used for numerous disorders.

SOURCE: Queiraz, L. O., Motta, M. A., Madi, M. B., Sossai, D. L., and Boren, J. J. "A Functional Analysis of Obsessive-Compulsive Problems with Related Therapeutic Procedures." *Behaviour Research and Therapy*, 1981, *19*, 377-388.

Paradoxical Intention for Obsessions

AUTHORS: L. Solyom, J. Garza-Perez, B. L. Ledwidge, and C. Solyom

PRECIS: Extreme exaggeration of obsessions in order to get rid of them

INTRODUCTION: By 1972, only 46 percent of published cases of treatment of obsessive-compulsive disorder were rated improved. Many behavior therapies exist for the disorder, but a satisfactory theory to explain it is missing. A promising treatment is suggested by one central aspect of the disorder: Paradoxical thinking runs through all the symptoms. That is, the person is driven to think or act in a manner contrary to his own judgment or wishes. For example, he is sexually obsessed with someone he dislikes, or he is compelled to act in a way he feels is absurd. Various therapies have picked up on this fact and employed paradoxical intention: the therapist urges the person *not* to avoid what he fears, pushes him to will the unwanted thought, suggests he deliberately repeat the troublesome symptom. Paradoxical intention was used as treatment for one obsessive thought in patients in the following study.

TREATMENT: Four men and six women, with an age range of twenty-two to thirty-seven years, ill from four to twenty-five years, were selected for treatment. All patients had previously received psychotherapy and drug therapy; four had been given electroshock treatment. Seven of the ten had been hospitalized.

Patients were given various psychological tests and answered a questionnaire measuring on a 0 to 4 scale four kinds of symptoms: obsessive thoughts, rituals, compulsions other than rituals, and temptation to do something horrible. Patients were required to choose two of equal strength from their list, eliminating any involving aggressive, murderous intent.

The group was then instructed in the paradoxical intention method. Each was told that instead of trying to push away the unwanted thought, he should dwell on it deliberately, elaborate and exaggerate it, and convince himself of its validity. For example, a person with the obsession that he was going insane was to tell himself, "It is true, I am going insane, slowly but surely.... I will be admitted to a mental hospital, put into a straitjacket, and will remain there neglected by everybody until I die." Patients were to use paradoxical intention as often as a thought disturbed them. The therapist explained in a simple way to each person, "The nature of obsessions is such that instead of the intended thought, image, or intention, a contrary thought, image, or intention comes automatically to the mind. The more one tries to avoid thinking obsessively, the more one fails. In order to reverse this process, one must deliberately think obsessively."

Patients were seen individually for one-hour periods over six weeks. All continued the medication (trifluoperazine, diazepam, and so on) they were previously on. Other aspects of their mental condition were not discussed.

Treatment was restricted to a single target symptom. A 50 percent improvement rate was obtained. The treatment either alone or in combination would seem to hold promise for some people; the fact that it is relatively fast is particularly attractive.

COMMENTARY: In the therapeutic technique of paradoxical intention, the client is pushed to intend exactly what he fears. The phobic person puts himself deliberately into the situation in which he feels most anxiety; the obsessive-compulsive person deliberately tries to think about that which threatens him. With compulsions the person must do the very things that his compulsion avoids. For example, a compulsively clean woman is urged to touch dirt repeatedly. A twist in Frankl's original paradoxical intention method is that the therapist proceeds with as much humor as possible, which helps the person put himself at a distance. (See V. Frankl, *The Doctor and the Soul,* New York: Knopf, 1965.) Frankl also had patients at specific times of the day do or think what they were avoiding, thus eventually giving them the feeling of self-control *not* to have the symptom. (See V. Frankl, "Paradoxical Intention: A Logotherapeutic Technique," *American Journal of Psychotherapy,* 1960, *14,* 520-534.) In the present study, neither humor nor the specific time element was reported. These might have added to the power of the method, although trying to be humorous may not be something the therapists wanted to do.

The 50 percent improvement rate given here is extraordinary, considering the degree of illness of the clients. This therapy might be tried first with obsessive clients in the interest of saving time, and if it does not work, try something else. A slight dampener to this statement is that the authors were dealing with only one symptom. If each symptom required six weeks, treatment might be considerably more extensive. However, it is well worth the try to see whether the treatment seems to fit the style of a particular patient. Note that the therapy is given for obsessive thoughts and not compulsive acts or thoughts. The repeated statement by Foa and colleagues (see digests, this section) that obsessions are best treated by exposure is borne out here. (Rituals, it is suggested, are best handled with response prevention.) Particularly important here is the fact that the rationale was explained to the clients, a practice that is increasing among therapists.

We may speculate that the method could be used profitably as an adjunct to other treatments, as hinted by the authors. It seems unlikely, however, that it could be used effectively unless the therapist thoroughly agreed with its premises and could use it with skill, as it might otherwise seem foolish to patients and cut away at a therapist's credibility.

See Rabavilas and others (1977), digested in this section, for an account of a group of clients who refused to cooperate with a similar therapy for compulsions and improved.

SOURCE: Solyom, L., Garza-Perez, J., Ledwidge, B. L., and Solyom, C. "Paradoxical Intention in the Treatment of Obsessive Thoughts: A Pilot Study." *Comprehensive Psychiatry*, 1972, *13*, 291-297.

Response Prevention and Withholding Positive Reinforcement to Decrease Rituals

AUTHOR: Frank J. Vingoe

PRECIS: Decreasing checking rituals in an adult male by rewarding him for decreasing rituals and increasing acceptable behavior

INTRODUCTION: Response prevention in conjunction with other treatments is widely considered effective in facilitating change in obsessive-compulsive disorders. In addition, the suggestion has been made that two other techniques might be useful in treating obsessional ruminations: withholding of positive reinforcement and making comfort and reassurance dependent on acceptable, nonpathological behavior. Since hospital treatment alone often ends in relapse, an alternative would be concurrent home and hospital treatment. A combination of all these measures was undertaken with a seriously incapacitated adult male.

CASE STUDY: A married mechanical engineer who had had unsuccessful psychiatric treatment for his frequent and extreme ritualistic behavior, starting at age ten, was placed in the hospital to consider psychosurgery. He thought of his compulsive checking "like an evil force" inside him and looked on psychosurgery favorably.

His rituals over the years covered a wide range. During school he checked his work excessively. In his twenties he began checking and counting his washing, bathing, and toilet behavior. Six years before admission to the hospital his hour-long toilet ritual, including counting and wiping, had resulted in hemorrhoids and anal bleeding. He checked the furniture and carpet for burns, checked his clothing during dressing and undressing, checked electrical plugs, taping wires and unnecessarily rewiring electrical equipment, and stopped his car to check the rear and underneath to be sure his wife or son had not been caught by the rear bumper. In addition, he harbored a fear of something entering his body through his ears, anus, and so on. He saw all his rituals as helping him avoid hurt to himself and others. He had steadily increased his ritualizing, becoming highly agitated and tense.

Since behavior therapy had never been tried with him, the hospital staff raised it as worth trying and investigated whether it could be carried out efficiently by the staff, who would have fairly heavy responsibilities placed on them. The staff promised cooperation, and his wife agreed to monitor and record his behavior when the time came for his release from the hospital.

The treatment involved focus on the helpers' withholding specific things the client had become accustomed to and was dependent on until he decreased his rituals to a specified level. Staff members were to compliment him on any successes. Both his ritualistic behavior and any acceptable, nonpathological behavior were to be monitored and recorded when he went home on weekends.

The man himself was tested and interviewed to discover the things that had positive meaning to him; these were cigar smoking, drinking coffee, going to the local pub for a drink, and going home on weekends. To obtain these he was expected to reduce his rituals 30 percent (from the baseline previously established) during the first week in the hospital and his first weekend at home. In addition, in order to do things he liked, he was expected to increase the time he spent in nonpathological behavior, such as walking, going to the theater, gardening, and going to the cricket club. The surprising thing was that he never failed to earn his reinforcements. In fact, by the end of the first week he had reduced his ritualizing 50 percent instead of the hoped-for 30 percent.

By the end of the third week his checking behavior had stopped, and his dressing, washing, and toilet behaviors were normal; there was no regression of these results during his weekend at home, where he also showed an increase in social and leisure activities. His progress was so great that he was sent home for a week, after which he returned to the hospital and was then discharged. Shortly after this he returned to work full-time. His wife and he returned for follow-up three months and six months later; improvement had been maintained, and he had steadily increased his social activities.

The patient himself attributed the success to receiving reinforcement for his changes, although his own and his wife's motivation and cooperation were significant contributions.

As hoped for, concurrent hospital and home treatment prevented relapse.

COMMENTARY: This is a remarkable history, considering the seriousness and extreme chronicity of the illness and the brevity of treatment. Home treatment by family members is often used, but it may be that the high motivation and hard work of both husband and wife should not be overlooked as possibly crucial to rapid and lasting success.

One is tempted to remark that addition of other techniques, such as cognitive behavior therapy or psychotherapy, might have added to success, but the progress could hardly be improved on. The simplicity of treatment (though not easy to carry out, in this instance) may be just the thing for some patients, perhaps particularly for unsophisticated people for whom more elaborate and possibly seemingly mysterious treatments might be perceived as something beyond the grasp of patient and family. Self-therapies probably need to be carefully suited to the patient, and perhaps particularly to the family, for maximum effectiveness.

SOURCE: Vingoe, F. J. "The Treatment of a Chronic Obsessive Condition via Reinforcement Contingent upon Success in Response Prevention." *Behaviour Research and Therapy,* 1980, *18,* 212-217.

Additional Readings

Ananth, J., Solyom, L., Bryntwick, S., and Krishnappa, V. "Chlorimipramine Therapy for Obsessive-Compulsive Neurosis." *American Journal of Psychiatry,* 1979, *136,* 700-701.

Beneficial effects for obsessive-compulsive neurosis have been reported for tricyclics such as imipramine, amitryptyline, desipramine, and doxapine. This study investigates the effectiveness of chlorimipramine. Eighteen men and women, aged twenty-three to sixty-four, with treatment-resistant obsessional neurosis of two or more years' duration were selected for outpatient or inpatient treatment. Administration of the drug was on a fixed, changing-dosage schedule: 100 mg/day for the first week, 150 mg/day for the second, 225 mg/day for the third, and 300 mg/day for the fourth. Dosage for four people was altered because of side effects, and three people did not go beyond 150 mg/day because of improvement. The number of obsessive symptoms as well as the severity substantially decreased for the group as a whole. Obsessional severity decreased significantly by the end of the first week, whereas depressive symptoms decreased only at the end of the second week. This suggests that the overall improvement was related to effects of the drug on the obsessions directly rather than primarily on anxiety or depression and only secondarily on the obsessions.

Daniels, L. K. "An Extension of Thought Stopping in the Treatment of Obsessional Thinking." *Behavior Therapy*, 1976, *7*, 131.

For people who want to stop obsessive thoughts, acute anxiety attacks, or depressive thinking, the author has found a successful sequence of activities taking three one-hour sessions. First, the therapist teaches deep muscle relaxation. Thought stopping is taught by asking clients to imagine a threatening scene and then stopping it. Patients are told next to count backward from 10 to 1. They then learn to control their relaxation on cue and finally reward themselves by imagining the most pleasurable scene they can think of. The author characterizes the sequence as "Yell 'Stop,' inhale, exhale, say 'Relax,' and shift to a pleasant scene." The important aspects of the treatment are the client's feeling of self-control and the rapid success when he uses the techniques successfully.

Foa, E. B., and Steketee, G. S. "Obsessive-Compulsives: Conceptual Issues and Treatment Interventions." *Progress in Behavior Modification*, 1979, *8*, 1-53.

This review of behavioral treatments (with short sections on drugs and surgery) is thorough and informative. The authors give an informed analysis of the symptoms, course, acquisition, and maintenance of obsessions and compulsions. In the bulk of the review, they analyze systematic desensitization, implosive therapy, paradoxical intention, exposure, response prevention, and the use of multiple techniques. The behavioral therapy model for treatment is two-pronged: suppress the compulsive/ritualistic behavior and eliminate the anxiety arising when the person is faced with anxiety-provoking stimuli. Anxiety that accompanies the fear of catastrophe is reduced with the combination of imaginal and *in vivo* exposure. Definitive conclusions about treatment are hard to come by. Currently, therapists are able to do more about behavior than about thoughts. Specifically, behavior therapy, drugs, and psychosurgery all appear to diminish observable rituals more than covert rituals and obsessions. Unfortunately, even when treatment of rituals, compulsions, or obsessions is successful, often what is still left is a generally obsessive person. These people still cannot make decisions easily, nor can they categorize events so that they can discriminate between events more efficiently. Making up for these two deficits is very difficult. It is possible that the person is afraid of the criticism that may come if he makes the wrong decision. If this is the situation, then therapy should be focused on reducing the sensitivity to making errors.

The authors review studies of drug and surgical treatments. Unfortunately, as they point out, their conclusions were necessarily based on uncontrolled studies: drugs seem to affect either the depression or anxiety accompanying the obsession or compulsion, rather than the primary symptoms themselves. Leucotomy, the major surgical treatment for this disorder, brings improvement but is so drastic that it should be used only when other treatments fail.

Foa, E. B., Steketee, G., Grayson, J. B., and Doppelt, H. G. "Treatment of Obsessive-Compulsives: When Do We Fail?" In E. B. Foa and P. M. G. Emmelkamp (Eds.), *Failures in Behavior Therapy*. New York: Wiley, 1982.

Seventy-five percent of people treated for obsessive-compulsive disorders benefit from the treatment. There is strong evidence that this disorder is best treated with both exposure and response prevention. The question is, What accounts for failures? The authors present a rich summary of answers to this question. The answers fall into four categories: some people refuse treatment, some drop out, some are not given proper treatment, and some relapse after having initially improved.

About 25 percent of those offered treatment refuse it.

Dropouts can be accounted for in various ways: some feel too much family pressure whereas they lack interest in treatment, some fear the discomfort of treatment, some do not expect treatment to work, some believe that exposure treatment will bring about the catastrophe they fear, and some simply cannot devote the extraordinary amount of time treatment requires (two hours daily, four hours of homework daily, for three to four weeks).

What about the effects of therapists? It appears that the behavior of the therapist is important in the initial factfinding stages of therapy but less so as the rigors of behavior therapy are established. Therapists should be respectful, understanding, interested, encouraging, challenging, and explicit. The authors carefully delineate in detail the efficacies for different kinds of patients using imaginal exposure only, *in vivo* exposure only, response prevention only, *in vivo* exposure plus response prevention, and the combination of imaginal and *in vivo* exposure plus response prevention. Findings are that patients fare better with multiple techniques. Compulsive washers treated with response prevention only eliminate the compulsion; their anxiety is not affected. *In vivo* exposure, in contrast, reduces their anxiety but not their compulsion. Exposure plus response prevention affects both anxiety and ritualistic behavior. With checking rituals, imaginal exposure appears to help prevent relapse.

Some basic problems with patients are that some lack faith, some do not comply with treatment prescriptions, some are not sufficiently committed. Severe depression appears to be a bad sign both for improvement and for relapse. The same is not true for high anxiety, which does not spell failure. People with low depression and low anxiety fare well. The younger the person at onset of symptoms, the more success is predicted for treatment, but neither long duration nor severity of symptoms predicts failure. Arousal is important to the success of exposure: those who avoid exposure must be activated, and overreactors to the exposure must have arousal decreased. Relaxation procedures and clomipramine should be available to help overreactors.

Marks, I. M. "Review of Behavioral Psychotherapy, I: Obsessive-Compulsive Disorders." *American Journal of Psychiatry*, 1981, *138*, 584-592.

This thorough and explicit article giving rules for handling rituals and obsessions should be very helpful to anyone treating these difficult problems. The current practices of exposure and response prevention were seen years ago in Janet's observation that people living under strong discipline, as in institutions like the army and convents, recover from their ritualizing. Reports of success with *in vivo* exposure for ritualizers come from the United States, Britain, Greece, and Australia. Treatment should not be given immediately. Procedures should be explained clearly. The patient's commitment to therapy should be unequivocal; a written contract is sometimes helpful. People close to the client should be used as cotherapists, and their duties should be explained openly in front of the client. To increase the client's motivation, the therapist and others close to the client should be willing to model behavior. A sense of humor in the patient is helpful to get him through the difficult treatment. Homework is essential and must be done; failure to do it is a bad prognostic sign. Improvement in the first few sessions is a good prognostic sign. Improvement usually lasts for years, although booster sessions are occasionally needed for some people. With some people who are also depressive, the depression remains despite diminishing of rituals through exposure and response prevention. Tricyclic drugs, especially clomipramine, can be used successfully with these people, but depression returns when the medication is stopped.

Treatments for obsessive thoughts are much less reliable than for rituals. The article is rich with suggestions and with helpful theoretical speculations about causes for obsessions and compulsions that relate to therapeutic issues.

Rachman, S. "Primary Obsessional Slowness." *Behaviour Research and Therapy*, 1974, *121*, 9-18.

Extreme and incapacitating slowness has been assumed to be simply a by-product of compulsive disorders, in particular checking. This is undoubtedly accurate in many instances, but there also seems to be a kind of slowness that is a primary dysfunction of its own, affecting most if not all of a person's life. The slowness often occurs with no accompanying checking or other ritualistic behavior, although checking and slowness are, of course, often related.

Ten people fitting this description were selected for treatment; the slowness in each person was severe and incapacitating and was not secondary to rituals such as checking. In each case the disorder was present in early adulthood and became chronic, ending as incapacitating; all ten people were socially isolated.

For therapy, flooding was of little use, modeling was of some use, but the effective techniques were prompting, shaping, and pacing. The therapist instructs the person on how to be quicker and may or may not model quicker accomplishment of a task; then he *prompts* the person while he is carrying out the task being treated. The therapist next helps *shape* a behavior by pushing for improvements and discouraging slowness. External *pacing* can first be done by the therapist or someone in the person's home until the person himself is ready to monitor his own performance. For most of the ten people, the therapy produced speedier performance with little or no disturbance. On occasion, external prompting led to slower performance and some distress. It appears that people who are under stress or are emotionally disturbed respond neither well nor easily to treatment. Home supervision, particularly for external prompting, should be arranged if at all possible. It seems possible that gains may succumb to stress or emotional disturbance.

The author gives a brief case history to illustrate the therapy in one instance of helping a man reduce the forty-five minutes it took him to brush his teeth before going to bed.

See also I. Bennun, "Obsessional Slowness: A Replication and Extension," *Behaviour Research and Therapy,* 1980, *18,* 595-598.

Rachman, S. "The Modification of Obsessions: A New Formulation." *Behaviour Research and Therapy,* 1976, *14,* 437-443.

Neither thought stopping nor paradoxical intention has

proved itself effective enough in the treatment of obsessive-compulsive disorders. For at least one group of people generally diagnosed under these disorders, those whose obsessive ruminations lead to a necessity to put things right, a new method called the "satiation method," a kind of detoxification, was devised. The therapist tells patients that unwanted thoughts are common but when they are accompanied by depression or agitation, they are hard to get rid of. He adds that patients will be asked to deliberately form these thoughts and hold them. They are then told that they must not neutralize the thoughts by any rituals, either external or internal, and that both the exposure and the response prevention may be painful. He places great stress on self-management, both in monitoring their thoughts and behaviors and in practicing at home. The whole procedure is presented as a skill that they can carry with them when treatment is over.

Three successful case histories are given, involving a checking ritual, a touching ritual, and a visual ritual. In every case, ruminations and rituals are reported to have been reduced significantly.

Salzman, L., and Thaler, F. H. "Obsessive-Compulsive Disorders: A Review of the Literature." *American Journal of Psychiatry,* 1981, *138,* 286-296.

This comprehensive coverage of the theory and therapy for obsessive-compulsive disorders from 1953 to 1978 should be very helpful to therapists.

Although systematic desensitization has been shown to be effective with phobias, it has not generally been useful in the obsessive-compulsive disorders. The authors use the term *systematic desensitization* to include not only Wolpe's classic method (see Index) but exposure (flooding).

About 75 percent of patients exhibiting *ritualizing* behavior showed improvement with modeling, flooding, and response prevention; but only nine patients in the entire literature of the period covered were totally free from ritualizing compulsions when treatment was over. At least one author has found that when obsessional thoughts lead to putting-right compulsions, an effective method is to expose the patient to the disturbing thought for a given period and then instruct him not to carry out his ritual. This is probably more effective than thought stopping or the exposure alone (see Rachman, 1976). Aversive therapy (using electrical shock, inducing nausea or vomiting, and so on) has been effective with compulsive gamblers.

For *obsessions,* paradoxical intention has been claimed by its originator to cure 46 percent of people with obsessions, but the bulk of other authors believe that it could be adjunctive to dynamic therapy but not supplant it. Thought stopping for obsessions has not been shown to be more effective than exposure in fantasy.

In general, behavior therapy seems to be much more promising for compulsive behavior than for obsessional thoughts.

Antianxiety drugs are apparently useful in reducing the anxiety often accompanying these disorders; antidepressants reduce the depression. However, results are not conclusive.

Bilateral prefontal lobotomy (leucotomy) and variations of this procedure are sometimes done when all else fails. Results are not conclusive, but while most people with obsessions and accompanying anxiety were not cured, their symptoms went from severe to moderate.

The obsessive-compulsive disorders have also been treated occasionally with carbon dioxide, electroconvulsive therapy, and hypnosis, all with good results reported.

The authors' summary is depressing: the few innovative therapies do not hold promise, behavior therapy shows no lasting solutions, and the physical therapies are worth less than their high cost.

For another summary and very different conclusions, see Foa and Steketee (1979), in Additional Readings, this section.

Sifneos, P. "Psychoanalytically Oriented Short-Term Dynamic or Anxiety-Producing Psychotherapy for Mild Obsessional Neuroses." *Psychiatric Quarterly,* 1966, *26,* 352-361.

Obsessional patients must be carefully selected for short-term psychoanalytically oriented therapy. They should be fairly well adjusted, anxious, motivated to change, capable of interacting with the therapist, and of above-average intellect. In addition, there should be in their history at least one close relationship, and their obsessive symptoms should have had an acute onset. Helpful therapeutic measures include working for and using early positive transference, focusing on unresolved conflicts, carefully avoiding the transference neurosis, and limiting the duration of therapy. Reported results are limited: patients' feelings about their symptoms were altered more than the symptoms themselves. However, patients seemed happier.

Turner, S. M., Hersen, M., Bellack, A. S., Anrasik, F., and Capparel, H. V. "Behavioral and Pharmacological Treatment of Obsessive-Compulsive Disorders." *Journal of Nervous and Mental Disease,* 1980, *168,* 651-657.

Varying reports exist about the relative values of behavioral techniques, particularly response prevention, and drugs, particularly clomipramine. Four people with extreme obsessive-compulsive problems were given treatments expected to remove obsessions and compulsions and alleviate depression.

(1) A forty-three-year-old with a long history of hand-washing, checking, excessive orderliness, rages, and high alcohol consumption was treated with imipramine and response prevention. Overall, the clinical improvement was small; some reduction in rituals came when response prevention was given with imipramine. (2) A twenty-five-year-old mother, hospitalized repeatedly and given ECT, among other treatments, to no avail, suffered handwashing and other cleaning rituals for seven years. Imipramine dosage of 250 mg daily seemed to directly reduce her rituals. It may be that the effect on the rituals was secondary to the reduction in anxiety and depression. Her other extreme problems, centering on interpersonal problems, were unaffected. (3) An eighteen-year-old boy with a ten-year history of handwashing and checking rituals, ruminations about heterosexual relations, and urges to rape was treated first with imipramine, which not only seemed to aggravate his symptoms but produced auditory hallucinations. Response prevention was tried to no avail. The authors note that this was the only person of the four who, besides his behavior rituals, had cognitive rit-

uals and ruminations as well. (4) The only outpatient was a thirty-year-old man with an extensive history of checking and washing rituals as well as social and occupational problems. Covert sensitization was added on the eighty-fourth day to doxepin. Covert sensitization was somewhat effective, but the doxepin added little or nothing.

It seems clear that no one strategy is effective for all people with obsessive-compulsive disorders. Tricyclic antidepressant drugs are effective with some problems, and the same can be said of behavioral techniques. The fact seems to be that obsessive-compulsive disorder is not a uniform syndrome and that different treatments will have to be used for specific patterns. In addition, other problems, such as marital or social problems, often accompany the primary symptoms and must be dealt with if treatment is to be complete. It may be that if these accompanying problems are solved, alleviation of the primary symptoms may be more lasting.

Part Three

Personality
Disorders

According to DSM-III, people have a personality disorder when their long-standing characteristic behaviors and traits are so inflexible or maladaptive that they lead to serious difficulties in social or occupational functioning and/or to subjective distress. Although they may regard many of their traits as undesirable, these people often find they cannot change them even with great effort. They commonly complain of depression or anxiety but are rarely hospitalized (with the exception of antisocial, borderline, and schizotypal people).

DSM-III groups eleven personality disorders into three clusters. The first cluster includes disorders that involve odd or eccentric behavior: paranoid, schizoid, and schizotypal disorders. The second cluster involves dramatic, emotional, or er-

293

ratic behavior: histrionic, narcissistic, antisocial, and borderline disorders. The third cluster includes disorders with a strong element of fear or anxiety: avoidant, dependent, compulsive, and passive-aggressive disorders.

This classification system may have some implications for treatment, with the "eccentric" group exposed to group therapy, the "emotional" group to drug treatment, and the "fearful" group to supportive therapy (J. R. Lion, "A Comparison Between DSM-III and DSM-II Personality Disorders," in J. R. Lion (Ed.), *Personality Disorders: Diagnosis and Management* (2nd ed.), Baltimore: Williams & Wilkins, 1981). However, there is disagreement regarding the placing of personality disorders into the three clusters. For example, Millon believes that any number of dimensions could have been used to group the eleven personality disorders in DSM-III (T. Millon, *Disorders of Personality: DSM-III: Axis II,* New York: Wiley, 1981); he questions the value of the three clusters and suggests listing the disorders either alphabetically or in order of severity. Because not all therapists would necessarily agree with any given criteria of severity, we decided to follow Millon's first suggestion and list the personality disorders in alphabetical order.

Personality disorders are relatively common, though the use of any particular diagnosis depends in part on various factors. First, the incidence of personality disorders varies, according to the population studied, from 5 percent of psychiatric admissions nationally in both public and private mental hospitals (M. Kramer, unpublished statistical data, 1973, cited by Lion, 1981) and 11 percent in a private psychiatric hospital in the northeast (Lion, 1981) to as high as 63 percent in military settings (R. E. Strange, "Personality Disorders in the Military Service," in J. R. Lion (Ed.), *Personality Disorders: Diagnosis and Management* (2nd ed.), Baltimore: Williams & Wilkins, 1981). Second, certain disorders are more commonly found in some groups than in others. For example, the antisocial personality is a frequent diagnosis in prisons, while the compulsive, borderline, and histrionic disorders are more often diagnosed by therapists engaging in long-term therapy in private practice (Lion, 1981). Men are diagnosed as having an antisocial disorder more frequently than women, who are more often diagnosed as histrionic (M. W. Penna, "Classification of Personality Disorders," in *Personality Disorders,* 1981). Third, the therapist's theoretical orientation may affect the diagnosis, with psychodynamic therapists more likely to diagnose a client as having a personality disorder than behavior therapists. Fourth, diagnostic decisions are affected by the availability of specific behavioral guidelines and diagnostic categories. The increased specificity of DSM-III over previous systems may lead to therapists' making finer discriminations and using new diagnostic categories. A comparison of DSM-III with DSM-II reveals changes that will affect future diagnostic decisions: asthenic and inadequate personality disorders were dropped altogether, explosive personality disorder was included under disorders of impulse control (not a personality disorder), obsessive-compulsive personality disorder was changed to compulsive personality disorder, hysterical personality disorder was changed to histrionic personality disorder, and five new personality disorders were introduced: narcissistic, dependent, avoidant, borderline, and schizotypal.

Clinicians apparently find it easier to agree on the diagnosis of certain personality disorders than others; they have a high level of agreement for schizoid, histrionic, and antisocial disorders and find it more difficult to agree on other categories (Penna, 1981). This lack of agreement may be partly due to the differences in diagnostic criteria for the different personality disorders provided by DSM-III. For example, a detailed behavioral profile is provided for the antisocial disorder, while the narcissistic disorder is less specific and requires more judgment by the therapist. The result is that some disorders can be diagnosed with more certainty than others (Penna, 1981). For clients who have characteristics of several personality disorders, a multiple diagnosis is suggested in DSM-III. (For detailed descriptions of the clinical pictures presented by people with multiple diagnoses, see Millon, 1981.)

Four personality disorders were omitted because of the lack of references in the literature: passive-aggressive, compulsive, schizotypal, and avoidant disorders. The passive/aggressive disorder, though frequently diagnosed, has been the focus of very little therapy literature (Penna, 1981). Methods applicable to this disorder may perhaps be found under antisocial and dependent disorders. The compulsive, schizotypal, and avoidant disorders are new categories in DSM-III. Therapies possibly applicable to some of the problems related to these disorders may be found in the sections on obsessive-compulsive disorder, schizoid personality disorder, and social phobia (or avoidant personality disorder).

As we said above, psychodynamic therapists are more likely to diagnose a client as having a personality disorder than behavior therapists. However, using DSM-III descriptions, J. H. Stephens and S. L. Parks ("Behavior Therapy of Personality Disorders," in *Personality Disorders,* 1981) listed ten maladaptive behaviors or characteristics shared by two or more of the eleven diagnostic categories: social withdrawal, lack of emotionality, attention seeking, low self-esteem, trouble being alone, manipulativeness, suicidal tendencies, indecisiveness, excitability, and aggression or impulsivity. Behavioral treatment focuses on the modification of these specific behaviors. A number of behavioral techniques have been used for behaviors associated with personality disorders: token economy, contingency management (which requires the performance of a specific behavior in order to obtain an agreed-on reward), systematic desensitization, and assertiveness training (Stephens and Parks, 1981). Readers will find descriptions of these behavioral techniques and maladaptive behaviors throughout the digests that follow. The range of therapies available seems to depend in part on the type of personality disorder. For example, we found a wide range of behavior therapy techniques described for antisocial and dependent disorders and few for borderline disorder, which is represented primarily by psychodynamic approaches.

Therapists treating clients with personality disorders may also find that they often must deal with two other common problems associated with personality disorders—anxiety and depression. Techniques for dealing with these problems are found in the appropriate sections elsewhere in this book.

5

Antisocial Personality Disorder

According to DSM-III (pp. 320-321), the following are diagnostic criteria for this disorder.

    A. Current age at least 18.
    B. Onset before age 15 as indicated by a history of three or more of the following before that age:
        (1) truancy (positive if it amounted to at least five days per year for at least two years, not including the last year of school)
        (2) expulsion or suspension from school for misbehavior
        (3) delinquency (arrested or referred to juvenile court because of behavior)
        (4) running away from home overnight at least

twice while living in parental or parental-surrogate home

(5) persistent lying

(6) repeated sexual intercourse in a casual relationship

(7) repeated drunkenness or substance abuse

(8) thefts

(9) vandalism

(10) school grades markedly below expectations in relation to estimated or known IQ (may have resulted in repeating a year)

(11) chronic violations of rules at home and/or at school (other than truancy)

(12) initiation of fights

C. At least four of the following manifestations of the disorder since age 18:

(1) inability to sustain consistent work behavior, as indicated by any of the following: (a) too frequent job changes (e.g., three or more jobs in five years not accounted for by nature of job or economic or seasonal fluctuation), (b) significant unemployment (e.g., six months or more in five years when expected to work), (c) serious absenteeism from work (e.g., average three days or more of lateness or absence per month), (d) walking off several jobs without other jobs in sight (Note: similar behavior in an academic setting during the last few years of school may substitute for this criterion in individuals who by reason of their age or circumstances have not had an opportunity to demonstrate occupational adjustment)

(2) lack of ability to function as a responsible parent as evidenced by one or more of the following: (a) child's malnutrition, (b) child's illness resulting from lack of minimal hygiene standards, (c) failure to obtain medical care for a seriously ill child, (d) child's dependence on neighbors or nonresident relatives for food or shelter, (e) failure to arrange for a caretaker for a child under six when parent is away from home, (f) repeated squandering, on personal items, of money required for household necessities

(3) failure to accept social norms with respect to lawful behavior, as indicated by any of the following: repeated thefts, illegal occupation (pimping, prostitution, fencing, selling drugs), multiple arrests, a felony conviction

(4) inability to maintain enduring attachment to a sexual partner as indicated by two or more divorces and/or separations (whether legally married or not), desertion of spouse, promiscuity (ten or more sexual partners within one year)

(5) irritability and aggressiveness as indicated by repeated physical fights or assault (not required by one's job or to defend someone or oneself), including spouse or child beating

(6) failure to honor financial obligations, as indicated by repeated defaulting on debts, failure to provide child support, failure to support other dependents on a regular basis

(7) failure to plan ahead, or impulsivity, as indicated by traveling from place to place without a prearranged job or clear goal for the period of travel or clear idea about when the travel would terminate, or lack of a fixed address for a month or more

(8) disregard for the truth as indicated by repeated lying, use of aliases, "conning" others for personal profit

(9) recklessness, as indicated by driving while intoxicated or recurrent speeding

D. A pattern of continuous antisocial behavior in which the rights of others are violated, with no intervening period of at least five years without antisocial behavior between age 15 and the present time (except when the individual was bedridden or confined in a hospital or penal institution).

E. Antisocial behavior is not due to either Severe Mental Retardation, Schizophrenia or manic episodes. This disorder is more common in men than in women.

Millon (*Disorders of Personality*, 1981) has suggested that the DSM-III criteria focus too much on the "criminal personality" and not enough on those who have similar characteristics but who have avoided criminal involvement.

The therapeutic approaches digested here range from the treatment of specific antisocial behaviors to general guidelines for dealing with clients who present the complete picture of this disorder.

Modeled Assertion for Controlling Rages

AUTHORS: David W. Foy, Richard M. Eisler, and Susan Pinkston

PRECIS: A man's explosive rages controlled by being told what to watch for in the behavior of a videotaped assertive model

INTRODUCTION: Inappropriate explosive outbursts occur because the individual lacks appropriate behavioral alternatives. The purpose of this treatment is to teach the person to respond assertively instead of aggressively in problem situations.

A fifty-six-year-old carpenter was hospitalized after an explosive outburst with his foreman at work. He showed signs of acute anxiety—trembling and nausea—and said that he was so angry that he felt the only solution was to kill the foreman or himself. His second wife had left him after many marital difficulties accompanied by his periodic beatings of her. The client's chronic pattern was to attack people verbally or physically when he could no longer control his anger over what he considered unreasonable demands. He had no physical or neurological abnormalities.

METHOD: The client's work-related interpersonal problems were assessed and treated in four stages over eighteen sessions: (1) baseline; (2) modeling alone; (3) modeling plus focused instructions; and (4) follow-up.

Baseline (Three Sessions). Seven scenes were constructed that depicted work-related difficulties. Three of the scenes involved the client's specific problems; four revolved around more general situations that typically require assertive responses, such as "You want to ask the boss for a raise" or "You are blamed for making a mistake that is not your fault." The therapist described each scene and then role-played the foreman or supervisor. The client's responses were videotaped for later scoring. The client responded to all seven scenes in each session.

On the basis of an analysis of the client's videotaped baseline responses, the therapist selected target behaviors for modification. Behaviors to be decreased were hostile comments, irrelevant comments, and compliance with unreasonable demands. Behaviors to be increased were requests for the other person to change his behavior.

Modeling Alone (Three Sessions). A videotape was constructed in which the therapist modeled assertive, socially appropriate responses for each of the seven scenes presented during the baseline period. The therapist clearly demonstrated the target behaviors—that is, increased requests for the person to change—and decreased hostile, irrelevant, or compliant comments. The client was told to pay attention to the model's behavior in each scene and then to practice responses to the same situation before going on to the next scene. As before, the client responded to all seven scenes in each session.

Modeling plus Instructions (Twelve Sessions). The same procedure continued, but the therapist added specific instructions. During the first three sessions, the client was asked to notice how the model responded without making hostile comments. During the next three, he was told to focus on the model's refusals to give in to unreasonable demands. The next three sessions were focused on how the model stayed on the main topic without making irrelevant comments. During the last session, the client was asked to notice how the model asked the other person in the scene to change his behavior.

Follow-up. The same seven situations were presented, but without modeling or instructions. The client's responses were videotaped, as they had been during the training. The initial session of the follow-up was on the day after the last training session. The patient was immediately discharged. Four follow-up sessions were obtained during outpatient visits over a period of six months.

A comparison of the client's responses throughout the four stages revealed a decrease in problem behaviors and an increase in desired behaviors. The adding of specific instructions to the client on what to look for facilitated and maintained the changes in the target behaviors.

According to the client, his relationship with his supervisors improved. He had reduced his verbal abusiveness and increased his appropriate requests; his foreman had improved his working conditions. He also reported an improved relationship with his son and no recurrence of the acute anxiety he had displayed on admission to the hospital.

COMMENTARY: This case study suggests that clients may change their behaviors more quickly if they are not only exposed to a model but also told exactly what to look for. It also calls attention to the possibility that clients may often need to be in a crisis situation before they are sufficiently motivated to change. The therapist used both specific and general situations for training; this tactic was successful in that the treatment effects transferred not only to specific work-related situations but to another situation as well (relationship with client's son). The follow-up, which included both client self-reports and video-taped behavior, demonstrated the relatively long-term effects of the intervention.

SOURCE: Foy, D. W., Eisler, R. M., and Pinkston, S. "Modeled Assertion in a Case of Explosive Rages." *Journal of Behaviour Therapy and Experimental Psychiatry,* 1975, 6, 135-137.

The Dynamic Treatment of Acting Out and Impulsivity

AUTHOR: John Frosch

PRECIS: Supportive therapy for the more primitive impulse disorders and exploratory and interpretive therapy for acting-out disorders

INTRODUCTION: The term *antisocial behavior* is often used to describe both acting out and disorders of impulse control, disorders that differ in many ways. The need to distinguish between these two forms of antisocial behavior is illustrated by the following example. Two adolescent delinquents are chronically truant. The first typically gets sidetracked on the way to school and decides, on the spur of the moment, to go to a movie or take a walk on a nice day. The second loiters around school in such an obvious way that he is apprehended by the authorities. In the first case, the problem is inability to control an impulse, and the behavior appears to serve as a release for built-up tension. In the second, the problem is one of acting out, and the behavior appears to be a substitute action in the service of other needs—in this instance, perhaps the need for punishment.

An "impulse" is the unpremeditated welling up of a drive toward some activity that has the qualities of hastiness, impetuosity, suddenness, and at times violence. Impulse-ridden people cannot postpone reactions; they are body people, who communicate and relieve their tension through action instead of thought. Their life-style is characterized by restlessness and a constant need to be on the go. Their occasional explosive behavior may be followed by self-reproach and depression. Although their behavior may be labeled as psychopathic, it is not, since true psychopathic individuals by definition do not experience the guilt that characterizes impulse-ridden individuals.

Acting out is defined as inappropriate activity, or activity that should not appear in the form or at the time it does. It occurs when impulses, wishes, and fantasies are frustrated and cannot work their way through the usual channels. Since acting-out behavior is a means of resolving problems, it tends to be repetitive.

TREATMENT: The therapist's first step is to evaluate the client's level of psychological development. The higher the level of development, the more likely the person will act out rather than be impulsive. This is determined partly by the therapist's observing the extent to which the person is capable of organized fantasies, planning, and evaluation. At a lower level of development, the person jumps directly from a tension state to its immediate satisfaction, as seen in children. By contrast, acting out involves a greater ability to delay gratification through the use of cognitive activities that involve several steps between the impulse and the following action.

The two types of disorders require different treatment approaches.

Supportive Therapy for Impulse Disorders. The impulse-ridden person has a defect in ego structure, as well as possibly a constitutional weakness, resulting in an inability to delay gratification. Because such individuals have a biologically or psychologically damaged control apparatus, the therapist must utilize and strengthen whatever resources the client has. The first goal is the establishment of a therapeutic alliance between therapist and client. The therapist can then begin to offer corrective feedback about the client's behavior, particularly for situations that endanger the client or others. In imposing limitations, the therapist must be tolerant when the client is unable to observe such limitations, especially at the onset of treatment. Since such clients often live from crisis to crisis, the therapist must be available by telephone at all times, even during vacations.

Drugs may be prescribed as a means of aiding clients to control their impulses. Dilantin has been used successfully with some clients with abnormal EEG patterns. Librium must be used with caution. Although it has relieved clients' anxiety, in some cases it has also resulted in the release of impulsive behaviors, such as overexcitability, overtalkativeness, and poor judgment in relation to others.

Exploratory Therapy for Acting-Out Disorders. The acting-out person's behavior reflects defense rather than defect and serves as a substitute action for distorted or hidden needs. The therapist seeks to find the defensive meaning of the acting-out episodes by examining the client's life history and pattern of past behavior. Treatment revolves around exploration, clarification, confrontation, and interpretation. Recurrent themes from the client's life may emerge: fears of abandonment, of being lonely and unloved, of not being able to recapture an early state of overgratification, and so on. If the therapist proceeds too quickly, he may unwittingly reproduce an earlier symbiotic relationship from the client's past; the client may be overwhelmed and respond by increasing acting-out and impulsive behaviors. If the extent of the client's impulsivity appears confined to issues raised in therapy, further exploration and interpretation are required. If, however, the impulsivity permeates the client's life, then the therapist must back off and return to the supportive approaches suitable for impulse-ridden people.

Differences between these two disorders have been emphasized. In actual clinical practice, however, therapists often see a blending of the two—an underlying impulsivity combined with episodes of acting out. The best therapeutic tactic is to begin the early stage of treatment with the supportive approach, gradually phasing into the exploratory, interpretive approach.

COMMENTARY: The major point of this article is that in order to successfully treat antisocial clients in dynamic therapy, therapists must determine the extent to which a client's antisocial behaviors represent a release of built-up tension and/or are substitute actions satisfying other needs. Insight-oriented therapy may not work with impulsive clients until they can begin to gain a sense of control, through supportive therapy and/or drug treatment. (See the Additional Reading by Allen and others in this section.) These clients may also benefit from other approaches, such as cognitive therapy to reduce impulsivity (see the digest by Templeman and Wollersheim) and behavior modification techniques for acting out.

SOURCE: Frosch, J. "The Relation Between Acting Out and Disorders of Impulse Control." *Psychiatry*, 1977, *40*, 295-314.

Altering Antisocial Behavior
Through Treating Depression

AUTHOR: John R. Lion

PRECIS: Teaching clients to use fantasy, confront, understand, and handle their depression resulting from daily frustrations rather than act out aggressively

INTRODUCTION: Explosive and antisocial clients characteristically are unable to handle depression resulting from frustration; they react to any kind of frustration with rage and violence. These clients are often described as unmanageable and resistant to therapeutic intervention. Treatment of these clients on an outpatient basis is possible, however, as long as the therapist focuses on understanding the clients' underlying depression. One of the main tasks of therapy is to get the client to recognize some of these feelings and to briefly reflect on them, with the result that less impulsive, aggressive activity is apt to occur. Many antisocial clients, unable to tolerate depression, will not remain in treatment. The therapist must warn the clients that feelings of despondency may be stirred up but that ultimately they will feel better if painful things can be brought out into the open and discussed. A helpful analogy one can tell a client is that lancing an abscess hurts but drains the pus.

TREATMENT: There are a number of techniques for discussing depression with an antisocial client:

Focus on Day-to-Day Life. The therapist should focus on the client's daily activities rather than on his past. By focusing on daily frustrations and the accompanying depression, the client has tangible goals to deal with. Common sources of frustration are job difficulties, marital arguments, and trouble with in-laws. Only when these basic daily frustrations are dealt with can the therapist begin to explore the client's past.

Fantasizing. Many antisocial clients find it difficult to fantasize, to think about the possible consequences of their behavior, or to indulge in daydreams related to their feelings. The therapist deals with this difficulty by encouraging the client to elaborate on the possible consequences of his actions, to discuss possible solutions to his problems, and to talk about his feelings and fantasies concerning a particular behavior.

For example, a man who told the therapist he wanted to kill his wife was made to dwell on the fantasies about the actual murder and its ultimate result—jail. Similarly, a client who habitually drove recklessly when drunk was made to fantasize in great detail about a possible accident, the revocation of his license, and being in jail. The fantasies of being in jail are especially important in order to emphasize to the client the consequences of his behavior. These fantasies stir up many depressed feelings and make the client face his own weaknesses and limitations. A violent client is violent only to the extent that he cannot come to grips with his own feelings of weakness and helplessness and cannot tolerate the depression associated with these feelings.

Relationship with the Therapist. Most antisocial clients do not understand psychotherapy and have never talked seriously to another person about their feelings. They often see the therapist as similar to an authority of the law. In general, they see the world as a hostile place that requires an aggressive, self-protective stance. The therapist points out how restricted the client's views of people are and how unsatisfactory and depressing this must be for him. The therapist says he does not expect the client to trust him; in fact, the therapist himself mistrusts certain clients because he fears they will leave therapy or not pay him. The therapist tells the client that this is sad; he says that it would be nice if things were otherwise and they could trust each other and that perhaps they can someday. He suggests that they at least try to work on it.

Changing Clients' Perception of Depression. Antisocial clients, in their impulsive search for momentary pleasure and relief from tension, often believe that feelings of depression are abnormal. The therapist points out that life is often depressing and that most people have problems, some of which are insoluble. This does not mean that enjoyment and pleasure cannot be found, but that troubles are extremely common and the client is not alone when he feels frustrated about the world.

Clients' Ability to Tolerate Depression. While antisocial and impulsive clients need to confront and understand their depression, the therapist must continually monitor their ability to tolerate it. He must be supportive, empathic, firm, and available in times of crisis, such as incidents involving aggressive acting out or suicide threats resulting from unmanageable levels of depression.

Two other aspects of treatment have emerged as a result of working with explosive and antisocial clients in an outpatient setting. First, simply offering clients a place to come to when they feel impulses getting out of control is often a helpful therapeutic tactic. Second, group therapy, which emphasizes verbal alternatives to aggressive behavior, may aid clients in curtailing their violent and impulsive tendencies.

COMMENTARY: This approach reflects the belief that acting-out behaviors in general are adaptive attempts to cope with disturbing feelings. The assumption is that if these underlying feelings are dealt with, the problem behaviors will decrease. One might wish to deal with the problem behaviors more directly by adding individual and group behavior modification techniques. The approach described here may be particularly useful at the onset of therapy, other methods being used once the initial relationship with the therapist has been established. There are similarities between this method and rational-emotive therapy, since both attempt to correct the client's misbeliefs.

SOURCE: Lion, J. R. "The Role of Depression in the Treatment of Aggressive Personality Disorders." *American Journal of Psychiatry*, 1972, *129*, 123-125.

Stress Inoculation for Anger
and Violence

AUTHOR: Raymond W. Novaco

PRECIS: Using cognitive preparation, skill acquisition, behavioral rehearsal, and application practice with a thirty-one-year-old male

INTRODUCTION: Anger is seen here as an emotional response to provocation that is determined by three aspects: cognitive, bodily-physiological, and behavioral. At the cognitive level, anger is caused by a person's appraisals, attributions, expectations, and self-statements that occur in a provocative situation. At the bodily-physiological level, anger is often primed and aroused by tension, feelings of agitation, and ill humor. At the behavioral level, a person may withdraw, which leaves the source of anger unchanged, or may act in an antagonistic manner, which may make the situation worse. Although anger may be adaptive at times, chronic anger or proneness to anger provocation can become a serious problem. A cognitive behavior therapy approach called "stress inoculation" has been used successfully with clients having serious problems with anger control. The therapy consists in developing a client's cognitive, emotional, and behavioral coping skills; the client then practices these skills with exposure to regulated doses of stressors that arouse but do not overwhelm the client's defenses.

TREATMENT: The stress inoculation approach involves three basic steps: (1) cognitive preparation, (2) skill acquisition and rehearsal, and (3) application practice.

Cognitive Preparation. Clients are given an instructional manual that describes the nature and functions of anger, when anger becomes a problem, and how anger can be regulated. During this phase, the therapist and client focus on (1) identifying the persons and situations that trigger anger, (2) aiding recognition of the difference between anger and aggression, (3) understanding the cognitive, emotional, and behavioral causes of anger, with emphasis on anger-arousing self-statements, (4) discriminating justified from unjustified anger, (5) recognizing signs of arousal and tension early in an anger-arousing situation, and (6) introducing anger management strategies.

Skill Acquisition. This stage involves the client's familiarization with cognitive, emotional, and behavioral coping strategies, the therapist's modeling of appropriate techniques, and the client's rehearsal of these techniques. *Cognitive strategies* include teaching the client how to alternatively view provoking situations by changing personal viewpoints (constructs) and by modifying the exaggerated importance often attached to events. The client's irrational beliefs are examined and modified, and the development of empathic ability is encouraged. Two major cognitive devices for regulating anger are taught: to view the anger-arousing situation from a task orientation (that is, to focus on the desired outcome and to design behavior to produce that outcome) and to use coping self-statements (that is, statements that aid the client in controlling his behavior). *Emotional strategies* include the learning of relaxation skills through systematic desensitization (see Index), mental relaxation, and deep-breathing exercises. A sense of humor is encouraged, and the therapist emphasizes not taking oneself and one's predicaments too seriously. *Behavioral strategies* include teaching the client to communicate his angry feelings rather than to let them accumulate, to behave more assertively, and to follow a task-oriented, problem-solving strategy. Poor behavioral adjustment is linked to an inability to provide problem-solving responses that are effective in achieving one's goals. The client is instructed to manage his anger by focusing on issues and objectives. (The reader is referred to the article on problem-solving therapy by D'Zurilla and Goldfried in the section on dependent personality.)

Application Practice. Regulation of anger depends on the client's ability to manage a provocative situation; in this treatment stage, the client is given a chance to demonstrate his proficiency. He is exposed to manageable levels of anger stimuli by means of imagined and role-playing situations. The context of these situations is constructed from a hierarchy of anger situations that the client is likely to encounter in real life. Therapist and client progressively work on each hierarchy scene, first in imagination, then in role playing. By rehearsing these skills with the therapist, the client improves his ability to manage his anger.

CASE STUDY: An inpatient in a psychiatric ward of a general hospital was a thirty-eight-year-old male, married, father of six, diagnosed as depressive neurosis. Anger was overcontrolled at work and then he would "explode." At home and church, he resorted to verbal and physical outbursts to control the behavior of his children. After three weeks in the hospital, the therapist (author) was brought in for the treatment of anger problems. Treatment included three sessions a week for three and one-half weeks during hospitalization and biweekly follow-up sessions for two months. The client realized that he was reacting "out of proportion" but felt helpless to do anything about it. He was instructed to keep an "anger diary," and incidents from the diary were discussed during sessions. Treatment involved modeling, rehearsal, and practice of coping procedures. Improvement was judged by behavior ratings in the hospital setting and self-ratings at the hospital, on weekend home visits, and after discharge. All measures showed improvement. Also lowered was his impulsive aggression as a punitive response to his children's disruptive behavior. Nothing is noted about alteration of his depression.

COMMENTARY: This cognitive therapy or teaching procedure would seem particularly well suited for clients who are highly motivated to control angry outbursts and who receive little or no gain from outbursts. The author blends the use of and acknowledges his debt to Kelly's personal constructs therapy, Ellis's rational-emotive therapy, Jacobsen's relaxation therapy, and Lazarus's assertion training. The author notes that the procedure described here is a refinement of that described in an earlier work, *Anger Control: The Development and Evaluation of an Experimental Treatment* (Lexington, Mass.: Lexington Books, 1975). The inclusion of *depression* in the title of the current article may mislead readers interested in therapies for depression rather than anger, although Novaco has a few theoretical remarks about the relation between depression and anger.

SOURCE: Novaco, R. W. "Stress Inoculation: A Cognitive Therapy for Anger and Its Application to a Case of Depression." *Journal of Consulting and Clinical Psychology,* 1977, *45,* 600-608.

===

Humor to Inhibit Anger

AUTHOR: Ronald E. Smith

PRECIS: Inserting humorous content into a hierarchy of anger-producing situations to reduce uncontrollable anger

INTRODUCTION: This treatment approach is based on the assumption that humor can have anger-reducing properties. The patient was a twenty-two-year-old female who referred herself for treatment because of her reported lack of ability to control extreme anger responses with her husband and her three-year-old son, who constantly misbehaved. The patient reported that when she became angry at her husband and child, she would often scream at the top of her voice, jump up and down, smash things, and physically attack them. Acquaintances and relatives referred to her "violent temper," which had been present since childhood. The patient had been contemplating suicide because "my temper makes everyone, including me, miserable."

TREATMENT: Initially, standard systematic desensitization procedures were followed: the patient was trained in deep muscular relaxation, and two ten-item hierarchies of anger-inducing scenes were constructed, one involving her husband and another

her child. In each session, a deep state of relaxation was induced, and the patient was instructed to imagine the anger-arousing scenes and to signal the therapist if a scene resulted in anger arousal.

After seven sessions, little progress had been made: the state of deep relaxation was not able to inhibit the strength and explosive quality of the patient's anger responses to most of the scenes. The lack of success with relaxation led to a search for another potential anger-reducing response. Previous researchers had suggested that humor can have anger-reducing qualities; the therapist inserted as much slapstick humor into the items in the hierarchies as possible. For example, an item involving her son's misbehaving while the patient is driving was presented as follows:

> As you're driving to the supermarket, little Pascal the Rascal begins to get restless. Suddenly he drops from his position on the ceiling and trampolines off the rear seat onto the rear view mirror. From this precarious position, he amuses himself by flashing obscene hand gestures at shocked pedestrians. As you begin to turn into the supermarket parking lot, Pascal alights from his perch and lands with both feet on the accelerator. As the car careens through the parking lot, you hear Pascal observe: "Hmmm, . . . 25 to 80 in 2 sec . . . not bad." But right now your main concern is the two elderly and matronly women that you're bearing down upon. . . . One . . . utters a string of profanities, throws her coupons into the air, and lays a strip of Neolite as she sprints out of the way and does a swan dive into a nearby open manhole. . . .

As in the relaxation sessions, the patient was asked to signal the therapist if a scene evoked anger. The therapist then would emphasize some humorous aspect of the situation being described.

The use of humor appeared to be highly effective: During the first humor session, all the scenes in both hierarchies could be presented without the patient's expressing anger. During the next eight sessions, she generally reacted to the scenes with laughter and amusement and seldom reported anger. She reported reductions in the frequency and intensity of her anger responses with her husband and son. After three sessions, relatives reported a marked improvement in her "temper." She became capable of instituting a behavior modification program for her son, whose constant misbehaviors decreased. She was able to remain calm in situations that had previously infuriated her. She also reported that her depressive episodes and suicidal thoughts had ceased.

Posttreatment measures, obtained one month after the humor sessions, indicated a large and generalized decrease in emotional arousal to the anger-producing situations. There was also a reduction in anger to imagined situations that had not been explicitly dealt with in treatment.

COMMENTARY: This study illustrates that humor may be more effective than deep relaxation in inhibiting intense and explosive anger in some clients. The author also points out that the humorous content was successful partly because it not only prevented anger from being aroused but also allowed the patient to view the anger-arousing situations from a new perspective. The success of this approach would depend on the therapist's ability to construct material that is perceived as funny by the patient.

This approach resembles implosive therapy but focuses on the humorous content instead of the fearful content. The use of humor has not been often reported in the therapy literature (but see the digest by Fay in the section on paranoid personality disorder). Injection of humorous content into hierarchies may well be applicable for other situations involving intense fears, phobias, and social anxiety.

SOURCE: Smith, R. E. "The Use of Humor in the Counterconditioning of Anger Responses: A Case Study." *Behavior Therapy*, 1973, *4*, 576-580.

Cognitive Behavioral Therapy
for Antisocial Clients

AUTHORS: Terrel L. Templeman and Janet P. Wollersheim

PRECIS: Motivating clients by appealing to their self-interest and helping them to change through fixed-role therapy, practice in problem solving, and self-instruction training

INTRODUCTION: Treatment approaches for antisocial clients that have focused on forming a close positive relationship with the client or on instilling some sense of morality have been unsuccessful. Instead, a cognitive behavior modification approach appears to be more effective. It relies neither on a warm relationship nor on appeals to conscience, but reflects the assumption that therapy will be more effective if it operates within the psychopathic client's own viewpoint. This approach does not rely on external controls but is designed to teach the client self-control.

The first goal of treatment is to motivate the client to change. This is particularly difficult, since the psychopathic client has usually been coerced into treatment and does not see any need to change. He is not moved by appeals to the public good or by comments about the harm he has caused others. He seems to have no desire for love or approval from others. However, he does appear to be motivated by things that he believes will advance his own best interests—possessions, money, or recognition.

TREATMENT: The therapist begins by aligning himself with the client's best interests but makes it clear he does not condone antisocial behavior. The therapist assumes that the client's goals are similar to most people's; it is only the methods the psychopathic person uses that are antisocial and self-defeating. The therapist's position has two advantages: (1) it prevents power struggles in which the therapist wastes time in defending society and moral values, and (2) it places the client in a powerful bind: he cannot resist the therapist without resisting his own interests.

When the client perceives the therapist to be in tune with his own interests, he is more likely to be open to the therapist's influence. At this point the therapist suggests that the client's ways of thinking and behaving have not really been in his own best interests but have actually been self-defeating. The client is shown how his actions have really prevented him from achieving his goals. The therapist suggests that a better way to achieve his goals is to abide by rules and cooperate with others. This approach reflects the assumption that psychopathic clients will be motivated to change when they realize that they have not really been acting in their best interests. This assumption may not be true for many psychopathic clients, who will continue to be suspicious of the therapist and resistant to change. This problem can be handled in two ways: fixed-role therapy and training in problem solving.

Fixed-Role Therapy. Clients are asked to try out different roles in various situations just to see whether some of them might work better than their previous behaviors. The therapist and client put together one or more role sketches that include prosocial behaviors the client would not normally use. The client immerses himself in the role, role-plays it a few times for the therapist, and then tries it out in real life for a week or two, carefully noting the reactions of others to his new behaviors. The real-life monitoring of others' responses is important, since any positive feedback the client gets will be more effective in maintaining changes in his behavior than simple praise from the therapist.

Training in Problem Solving. The psychopathic client is taught how to solve problems following the approach suggested by D'Zurilla and Goldfried (described in the section on dependent personality). The client is trained to think about life difficulties as problems to be solved, to state the problems clearly and specifically, to systematically examine alternative solutions, and to verify the effectiveness of the chosen solution. This approach works well with psychopathic clients, who are already familiar with a problem-oriented approach to life; that is, they see life as a series of obstacles between their goals and themselves. They are poor problem solvers, however, since they are often getting into trouble. The client is asked to weigh the costs and benefits of each alternative behavior available in each problem situation. Behaviors with the most positive and least negative outcomes are chosen.

A second major problem with psychopathic clients is their impulsiveness and inability to delay gratification. Hence, treatment procedures should be highly structured: feedback must be immediate and continuous, reinforcement contingencies must be clearly spelled out, and the tendency toward self-distracting thoughts that stem from impulsiveness must be decreased through self-instruction training.

Self-Instruction Training. A lack of verbal control may contribute to psychopathic impulsiveness. Self-instruction training involves six steps: (1) the client defines a problem situation, often involving impulsiveness; (2) the therapist models the desired behavior by role-playing the situation as the client, talking aloud and weighing the costs and benefits of alternative actions; (3) the client role-plays the situation and he and the therapist discuss the costs and benefits of each alternative; (4) the client role-plays the situation alone, talking aloud to himself; (5) the client rehearses the situation alone, this time thinking to himself; and (6) the client is assigned to run through the procedure in real life during the week. After coping with each situation in real life, the client should reinforce himself, either with self-praise or with some tangible reward. The general goal of this training is to teach the psychopathic client to think in concrete and constructive ways that result in self-control rather than impulsiveness.

CASE STUDY: After six months of therapy, a bright, young, male psychopathic prisoner was getting nowhere. The therapist and client finally decided that the client's major goal was to get out of prison and stay out. Alternatives for attaining this goal were discussed. Breaking out of prison was rejected as a method because it did not offer long-term freedom. Working in the prison to earn a school furlough was a possibility, but it involved problems: the client often defied prison rules, which led to disciplinary action that placed his furlough in jeopardy. The therapist asked the client to write down the costs and benefits of every single decision he made during the week. The therapist helped the client practice this during therapy sessions. Being aggressive and hostile toward the guards resulted in some potential benefits: feelings of superiority and a higher status among the inmates. The potential costs included reduced chances of a furlough, a closer monitoring of his behavior in the future, possible disciplinary action, and increased likelihood of further encounters with the guards. The therapist challenged poor decisions by saying, "Is this getting you nearer your goal of freedom?" The client was instructed to ask himself the same question. After several weeks, the client remarked, "You know, I've decided it's more important for me to get out of here than to get even with the guards." He is now attending a university on a school furlough.

COMMENTARY: The innovative feature of this approach is that the therapist appeals to the antisocial client's self-interest as a means of getting him to alter his behavior. It also includes suggestions about how to deal with two characteristics commonly associated with antisocial clients: resistance to therapy and impulsiveness. The approach is geared for "unsuccessful" psychopathic clients whose antisocial behavior has led them into serious societal difficulties and who are difficult to treat.

It would seem obvious that the techniques described—focus on the client's self-interests, fixed-role therapy, problem solving, and self-instruction training—offer a strategy for a wide range of problems.

SOURCE: Templeman, T. L., and Wollersheim, J. P. "A Cognitive-Behavioral Approach to the Treatment of Psychopathy." *Psychotherapy: Theory, Research, and Practice,* 1979, *16,* 132-139.

Psychodynamic Treatment of
Antisocial Individuals

AUTHOR: George E. Vaillant

PRECIS: Using the underlying anxiety and concern for others in inpatient treatment of chronic antisocial individuals

INTRODUCTION: According to textbook conceptions, socio-pathic clients have three major characteristics: they do not ex-perience anxiety, they lack motivation for change, and they are unable to experience depression. In the eyes of many therapists, they appear incorrigible, inhuman, unfeeling, unable to learn from experience, and frightening. They rarely remain in out-patient treatment. However, in situations where control is estab-lished and flight from therapy is not possible, such as prison set-tings, a different picture emerges: their "psychopathic" charac-teristics become understandable as defensive strategies used to cope with problems, especially those involving people. The in-accuracy of the textbook picture of sociopaths was revealed in the therapy of three narcotics addicts with extensive criminal records. All were hospitalized against their will and showed an absence of anxiety, an absence of the motivation to change, and an absence of overt depression. A number of common themes emerged from their lives. All had lacked a loving, sustained rela-tionship with the same-sex parent. All were afraid of intimacy and assuming responsibility for it. They could not believe that others could tolerate their anxiety. They feared responsibility for achieving success through open competition. They could not identify with authority or accept its criticism.

As therapy progressed, it became clear that many of their seemingly mindless antisocial behaviors could be seen as defen-sive mechanisms against overwhelming anxiety, depression, and fear of open competition. These sociopathic people were no longer perceived as being born that way or as incapable of change.

Sociopathic individuals tend to use defenses that are rela-tively primitive: avoiding unpleasantness through fantasy, pro-jection, turning against themselves, excessive concern with physical health, and antisocial acting out. The result is that these individuals are delinquent, prejudiced, passive-aggressive, and hypochondriacal—characteristics that elicit little sympathy from others, including therapists. The therapist dealing with a sociopathic person must not condemn these behaviors, but must try to understand their defensive function.

TREATMENT: Conventional psychiatric management is not the answer to effective treatment of sociopathic individuals, as the following suggestions show:

1. Before treatment can begin, the therapist must find a way to stop the patient's self-destructive behavior through parole, commitment to a prison hospital, or the strong influence of a therapeutic-community group. Sociopathic individuals are too immature for the therapist to suggest that a certain behavior is self-destructive and then to stand by when they do it. The therapist's passivity in such instances is interpreted as lack of concern. Moreover, the therapist himself is often frightened by the client's acting out.

2. Control also helps the sociopathic client deal with his fear of intimacy. The therapist must stop the client's running from the pain of honest human encounter and from tenderness. The challenge is to separate control from punishment and to separate help and confrontation from social isolation. Possible choices include sustained employment enforced through parole, halfway house residence enforced by probation, or methadone clinics in the case of drug addicts. Jail or psychiatric hospitalization should be avoided if possible. Sociopathic clients should work for liberty rather than pay for past mistakes.

3. Too much intervention or protection from harm can be as bad as too little. The sociopathic client should be allowed to experience his anxiety. Often the therapist's wish to control the sociopath's anxiety through drugs or solitary confinement really springs from his own anxiety. Instead, the therapist should show the client that one can be anxious and still in control. These clients have often been taught that anxiety is too dreadful to bear and too awful to confess; the therapist can counter-

act this message by expressing his own anxiety to the client and by bearing the client's anxiety with him and not trying to alleviate it.

4. The therapist can place little trust in childhood histories as initially given, since these clients tend to repress parental neglect.

5. The therapist must accurately assess each of the sociopathic client's defenses. He must try to help the client develop a substitute for each defense. For example, addicts give up their addiction little by little; their abstinence is achieved by a process similar to mourning. Many criminals have replaced acting out with behaviors that have a prosocial focus. The therapist may also attempt to deal with immature defenses through confrontation with the client.

6. One-to-one therapeutic relationships are rarely effective in changing sociopathic clients. What is needed is something that operates around the clock—the church, self-help residential treatment, or addicting drugs. The ways out of sociopathy are usually independent of intensive psychotherapy and often involve peer relationships. Of possible use are self-help groups like Alcoholics Anonymous, altruistic but revolutionary groups like the Black Panthers, or marriage to someone as needy as the client himself. A real job outside prison offers more than vocational counseling. A therapeutic community at the maximum security ward of the Utah State Hospital, where inmates hold the keys both to the outside and to the seclusion rooms, offers more than programs that try to change sociopaths into patients.

Sociopathic individuals know they have harmed others; they can identify only with people who feel as guilty as they do. Only acceptance by "recovered" peers can restore their defective self-esteem. They need more loving than one person can provide; this need can be satisfied only by a group to which they can belong with pride.

COMMENTARY: According to Vaillant and others, true antisocial clients—as distinguished from clients who display antisocial behaviors but who do not satisfy the DSM-III criteria for anti-social personality disorder—can benefit from therapy only if powerful external control is present (as in a prison or hospital) that prevents a flight from therapy. Although the clients can learn to explore and accept their own anxiety through therapy, the author points out that one-to-one therapy is unlikely to change them unless combined with some kind of round-the-clock support, such as the church, self-help groups, or marriage. Consequently, therapists should be well informed about facilities available in the community and should have a wide range of contacts that may be of help to antisocial clients.

SOURCE: Vaillant, G. E. "Sociopathy as a Human Process." *Archives of General Psychiatry*, 1975, *32*, 178-183.

Additional Readings

Allen, H. E., Dinitz, S., Foster, T. W., Goldman, H., and Lindner, L. A. "Sociopathy: An Experiment in Internal Environmental Control." *American Behavioral Scientist*, 1976, *20*, 215-226.

Forty-one prisoners participated in an experimental six-month drug treatment program at a medium security prison, the Chillicothe Correctional Institute in Ohio. Nine prisoners were diagnosed as sociopathic: they had no fewer than four previous arrests, had spent at least 30 percent of their lives in prison, and were considered sociopathic on psychometric tests. The possibility exists that certain types of sociopathic individuals have a nervous system dysfunction that results in a chronic state of underarousal, whch in turn leads to their seeking high levels of external stimulation to make up for this deficit. Administration of arousal-inducing drugs may calm these persons down so they can become more receptive to other forms of therapy. After initial testing, some of the forty-one prisoners were given placebo medication for one month, imipramine hydrochoride (pamoate) for three months, then placebo again for two months. A subgroup received only placebo during this period. Of particular interest was the group of nine sociopathic prisoners, who, in general, were positively affected by the treatment: they had improved, as reflected in behavioral ratings and cooperation. More important, they reported themselves to be more energetic, less anxious, sleeping and eating better, less impulsive, less irritable, and, most of all, having an increased sense of well-being. This experimental study suggests that this approach offers possibilities for the treatment of nonincarcerated, chronic sociopathic individuals.

Boren, J. J., and Colman, A. D. "Some Experiments on Reinforcement Principles with a Psychiatric Ward for Delinquent Soldiers." *Journal of Applied Behavior Analysis*, 1970, *3*, 29-37.

A group of soldiers diagnosed as having character and behavior disorders participated in five experiments designed to increase appropriate behaviors. Within the context of the psychiatric ward token economy, the staff followed principles of positive reinforcement, differential reinforcement, and reinforcement schedules. Target behaviors that were increased included participating in a half-mile run, attending an early morning meeting, delivering a verbal report, and talking about personal problems. Punishment, in which points were taken away for nonattendance at a meeting, was ineffective and resulted in breaking of rules and fighting. Exposure to a model (a psychiatrist ward officer) was also ineffective, perhaps because of the patients' past difficulties with authority figures.

Hamberger, K., and Lohr, J. M. "Rational Restructuring for Anger Control: A Quasi-Experimental Case Study." *Cognitive Therapy and Research*, 1980, *4*, 99-101.

A twenty-seven-year-old student was referred to a psychological clinic because of a history of marital difficulties involving verbal and physical aggression toward his wife. Rational-emotive therapy consisted of thirteen weekly sessions of fifty minutes each. The student initially completed an irrational beliefs questionnaire, receiving high scores on High Self-Expectations, Blame Proneness, Frustration Reactivity, and Anxious Overconcern. After three sessions of supportive therapy, the therapist began to teach the student to challenge irrational self-statements and to replace them with rational self-statements. The student kept informed records of emotional distress in real-life situations. The therapist listened to therapy tapes and recorded the frequency of statements that represented Blame Proneness, Emotional Irresponsibility, and Frustration Reactivity, as well as independent self-statements. The rational restructuring procedures were effective in modifying the student's irrational beliefs and emotional distress.

Harbin, H. T. "Family Therapy with Personality Disorders." In J. R. Lion (Ed.), *Personality Disorders: Diagnosis and Management.* Baltimore: Williams & Wilkins, 1981.

Family therapy can be an effective approach for the treatment of antisocial clients, though the therapist may need pressure to get the client and his family to cooperate. Since antisocial clients often bolt when therapy becomes difficult, outpatient treatment may not be successful. In a hospital or prison setting the patient may be forced into treatment. Unless the family is involved in treatment, however, the client is likely to return to his old pattern of behavior upon discharge. The importance of the family's setting limits for the client is stressed. The author describes the case of a hospitalized nineteen-year-old white male, in which the major focus was the modification of the parents' attitudes. The therapist pointed out the necessity of setting limits, of changing his long-standing pattern of rule breaking, and of standing up to him. Upon his discharge, weekly family sessions were held for four months. At that time, therapy was discontinued with the client, who had learned to control his antisocial tendencies and had a stable job. The therapist continued to see the parents for a time in order to work out problems in their own relationship.

Kellner, R. "Drug Treatment in Personality Disorders." In W. H. Reid (Ed.), *The Treatment of Antisocial Syndromes.* New York: Van Nostrand Reinhold, 1981.

Relatively few controlled studies have been done with personality-disordered clients, mainly because of the lack of precision in diagnostic classification. The studies to date with antisocial clients suggest that drugs may reduce symptoms of mood swings and aggressive behavior.

Minor tranquilizers, such as chlordiazepoxide (CDP) and diazepam, may reduce anxiety, irritability, and verbal hostility; however, the findings are inconsistent and complex. Oxazepam may reduce hostility more than other benzodiazepines. Studies of neuroleptics have been disappointing, with little conclusive evidence. Anticonvulsants, perhaps in larger doses than usually prescribed, may reduce uncontrollable impulsivity or explosive behavior in some clients. Stimulants (methylphenidate) may be effective for antisocial adults who have a history of minimal brain damage in childhood. Lithium has been found to reduce impulsiveness, anger, and aggression. (See the Additional Readings by Tupin in this section).

Leaff, L. A. "Psychodynamic Aspects of Personality Disorders." In J. R. Lion (Ed.), *Personality Disorders: Diagnosis and Management* (2nd ed.). Baltimore: Williams & Wilkins, 1981.

The relatively few cases in which therapy with antisocial clients has been successful occur either in hospital settings for long periods of time or in long-term outpatient therapy. Therapists must be able to cope with the client's enormous demands and aggressive impulses. Manipulative techniques are to be avoided at all costs—the therapist must provide an atmosphere of trustworthiness, reliability, integrity, and availability. Firm, clear limits must be set. At the onset of therapy, clients should determine the degree of intimacy and set their own pace, though regular appointments are essential. Clients often have strong feelings of hostility toward authority figures. A useful approach has been to place them in positions of authority and responsibility, either in the hospital setting or in their real lives. In this way, they can begin to identify with a stable authority figure and begin to control or modify their primitive impulses.

Lion, J. R. "Countertransference and Other Psychotherapy Issues." In W. H. Reid (Ed.), *The Treatment of Antisocial Syndromes.* New York: Van Nostrand Reinhold, 1981.

The author discusses techniques for individual dynamic therapy with antisocial clients. He suggests that therapists must be aware of their own countertransference reactions in such cases and may need careful supervision. The therapist should make no attempt to remain neutral, but should try to consistently confront the client, though keeping in mind the client's vulnerability. The therapist should focus on and encourage the client's fantasies and emotional reactions (for example, depression). (See the digest of Lion, 1972, for more details.) The therapist must watch closely his own responses to the client, who has difficulty dealing with fantasy and emotions and depends on the therapist for guidance.

Outpatient treatment of antisocial clients often follows a somewhat predictable course: an initial "honeymoon" phase in which the client has unrealistically high expectations of the therapist, followed by a "testing" period in which the client tests the therapist's knowledge and limits. The client may be guarded and suspicious during the first year or two of therapy, and a sense of trust between client and therapist is slow to develop.

Therapists often become depressed because of their inability to cope with the client's need to exploit, act out, manipulate, and avoid intimacy or trust with the therapist. When therapy has gone well and clients have dropped their facade to reveal an inner core of emptiness and despair, therapists must use their own resources to help the client learn about meaningful skills and emotional outlets, such as hobbies, sports, and social attachments.

Successful treatment is seen in the fragile and tender moment when the therapist and client can discuss together an acknowledgment of life's limitations and complex problems and a genuine sense of intimacy develops.

Matthews, W. M., and Reid, W. H. "A Wilderness Experience Treatment Program for Offenders." In W. H. Reid (Ed.), *The Treatment of Antisocial Syndromes.* New York: Van Nostrand Reinhold, 1981.

There are some fifty Wilderness Experience Programs in the United States today serving juvenile and adult offenders.

These programs have been studied and evaluated, and the results have been strongly favorable. Potential participants are screened for the program; if they are chosen, the program is usually included as part of an overall treatment plan, with the hope that it will be a powerful experience or turning point on which to base the remainder of the individualized treatment program. The program is sometimes used for already incarcerated clients as part of their process of qualifying for parole and/or reentry into the community.

The program includes three phases. The training phase, from three to five days, begins with basic instruction in the use of camping gear, hiking, physical fitness, first aid, and so on. The staff continuously focuses on the need for individual and group responsibility and the recognition of the immediate and powerful consequences of one's actions or inactions in the wilderness. The second phase, expedition, lasts eight to ten days and involves concrete group objectives such as the climbing of a mountain or navigating through a desert environment. The staff fosters increased group responsibility for decisions in stressful problem-solving situations. More and more, participants are placed on their own and must deal with any mistakes they make. The final expedition is a kind of final examination in which individual abilities and strengths must be coordinated with those of others and the group in a stressful, physically rugged, unyielding situation. After the final expedition, the individuals and the group as a whole meet with the staff to discuss their reactions and their applications to real life.

On the basis of personality tests, interviews, and recidivism rates, it appears that the program has succeeded with many people in giving them an increased sense of personal mastery, responsibility, and trust in themselves and others. In this treatment approach, the concept of mastery is a primary focus. The simplicity and concreteness of the Wilderness Experience appear to be important to its success. Though not a panacea, the program promotes insight that can evolve into emotional control and interpersonal experience that can result in improved behavior control, improved problem solving, and increased ability to plan one's actions.

Rimm, D. C., De Groot, J. C., Boord, P., Heiman, J., and Dillow, P. V. "Systematic Desensitization of an Anger Response." *Behaviour Research and Therapy*, 1971, *9*, 273-280.

Male college students who experienced inappropriate anger while driving were treated with systematic desensitization (see Index). In the first session, each student constructed a hierarchy of increasing anger. At the next session, the students began with deep muscle relaxation followed by the actual desensitization procedure. The relaxation and desensitization continued until they had covered the entire hierarchy. The treatment resulted in significant reduction of subjective feelings of anger, though no attempt was made to observe real-life situations.

Thorne, F. C. "The Etiology of Sociopathic Reactions." *American Journal of Psychotherapy*, 1959, *13*, 319-330.

The author describes the typical pattern of development of sociopathic life-styles by presenting a hypothetical case study. He also presents a list of requirements for successful therapy with antisocial clients, based on long-term therapy with seven clients. The clients all came from wealthy families who could assume the high costs of therapy over a period of years. Sociopathic clients are considered untreatable unless the family has large financial resources. In several cases, the cost of therapy was $15,000 a year for as long as ten years in order to bring about a successful outcome. Among the author's suggestions are the need for the therapist to completely control the client's finances so that the client receives no money unless he attends therapy sessions regularly, no "bail-outs," firm limits and controls, making sure that the client faces the consequences of his actions, communicating with the client in his own language or jargon, a search for a leverage point (usually money), unceasing pressure for the client to see himself more realistically, removal of rewards for antisocial behavior, and, perhaps most of all, patience.

Tupin, J. P. "Treatment of Impulsive Aggression." In W. H. Reid (Ed.), *The Treatment of Antisocial Syndromes*. New York: Van Nostrand Reinhold, 1981.

The management of violent behavior in psychiatric patients can be divided into two phases: initial emergency control and long-term treatment. In the initial emergency situations, the goal is to sedate the patient to the point of safe control rather than to use a drug as a specific treatment for aggression. The choice of medication (antidepressants, stimulants, benzodiazepines, lithium, anticonvulsants, and so on) will depend on its effectiveness, safety, and low potential for interacting with any other drugs the patient has been taking. Long-term treatment involves accurate psychological and neurological assessment, along with identification of cultural, social, and physiological or genetic factors that may contribute to potential for violence.

A number of studies have strongly suggested, but not proved, that lithium is effective in preventing recurrent, impulsive, violent behavior. People who appear to be good candidates for lithium therapy have (1) a tendency to respond violently to minimal provocation, (2) no capacity to think about or weigh the circumstances that provoke violence, and (3) a lowered capacity to regulate anger and the attacking behavior once control is lost. Lithium should be prescribed as in manic-depressive disorders. Patients are started on 600 to 1800 mg daily and carefully monitored for side effects. Therapists should consult recent literature for prescribing and monitoring guidelines. Since individuals with impulsive violence have been found to have an unusually high incidence of peptic ulcers, therapists should stop lithium in the case of reported gastrointestinal distress.

Lithium is not helpful in the emergency control of severely agitated patients. Personality characteristics such as nonviolent antisocial behavior and acting out are not changed by lithium and may continue to be a serious problem. Most lithium research with antisocial clients has used prison populations; studies with outpatients have not yet been done.

Tyce, F. A. "PORT of Olmstead County, Minnesota." *Community Psychiatry*, 1971, *22*, 74.

The Probational Offenders Rehabilitation and Teaching Program (PORT) is a program with a board of directors composed of court judges, an attorney, a local banker, a psychiatrist, the PORT director, one client, and one client aide. Residents of the program, referred by court, range from thirteen to thirty-two years of age and have offenses including running away from home, arson, and burglary. After a probationary two-week period, in which the client is screened, he is assigned to a resident-volunteer (in most cases a college student volunteer, who acts as a model of appropriate behavior). Besides working or going to school, the client meets with a group of other clients three times weekly. Extra meetings are scheduled if a crisis arises. The directors believe that group process and the pressure it exerts on the residents are the major core of the program. Clients and staff together decide how much freedom each client should have. Probation officers aid clients in managing such activities as buying a car or renting an apartment. A psychotherapist is available at all times. Clients pay for all or part of room and board at the residence.

Results have been encouraging: of ten clients discharged in one year, six were considered successfully rehabilitated, and three of the remaining four, though again institutionalized, were to be readmitted to the program at a later date. (See L. Fink, M. Denley, and J. P. Morgan, "Psychiatry's New Role in Correction," *American Journal of Psychiatry*, 1969, *126*, 542, for a description of another therapeutic community at Clinton Prison, Dannemora, New York.)

6

Borderline
Personality
Disorder

According to DSM-III (p. 322), the following are characteristic of the individual's current and long-term functioning, are not limited to episodes of illness, and cause either significant impairment in social or occupational functioning or subjective distress.

A. At least five of the following are required:
   (1) impulsivity or unpredictability in at least two areas that are potentially self-damaging, e.g., spending, sex, gambling, substance use, shoplifting, overeating, physically self-damaging acts
   (2) a pattern of unstable and intense interpersonal relationships, e.g., marked shifts of attitude, idealization, devaluation, manipulation (consistently using others for one's own ends)

333

(3) inappropriate, intense anger or lack of control of anger, e.g., frequent displays of temper, constant anger

(4) identity disturbance manifested by uncertainty about several issues relating to identity, such as self-image, gender identity, long-term goals or career choice, friendship patterns, values, and loyalties, e.g., "Who am I?", "I feel like I am my sister when I am good"

(5) affective instability: marked shifts from normal mood to depression, irritability, or anxiety, usually lasting a few hours and only rarely more than a few days, with a return to normal mood

(6) intolerance of being alone, e.g., frantic efforts to avoid being alone, [being] depressed when alone

(7) physically self-damaging acts, e.g., suicidal gestures, self-mutilation, recurrent accidents or physical fights

(8) chronic feelings of emptiness or boredom

B. If under 18, does not meet the criteria for Identity Disorder.

Individuals with this diagnosis often show signs of other disorders, such as Schizotypal, Histrionic, Narcissistic, and Antisocial Disorders. They often function poorly socially and/or occupationally.

This disorder is common and is more likely to be found in women than in men.

The essential feature of this disorder is instability in a number of areas, including interpersonal behavior, mood, and self-image. Millon (*Disorders of Personality,* New York: Wiley, 1981) refers to this disorder as "the unstable pattern." However, others think of this condition in terms of a particular form of weakened personality organization rather than as a personality disorder. A number of theorists (for example, O. Kernberg, *Internal World and External Reality,* New York: Jason Aronson, 1980; T. Millon, *Modern Psychopathology: A Biosocial Approach to Maladaptive Learning and Functioning,* Philadelphia: Saunders, 1969) do not use the term to refer to a specific diagnostic type; rather, they suggest that it should be used as a supplementary diagnosis that communicates how severely impaired a person is in terms of ego functioning and interpersonal relationships.

The term *borderline* has been criticized because it means a level of severity and is not a descriptive term (Millon, 1981, p. 332). The word suggests that we are dealing with a disorder that borders on something, but it is not clear what that "something" is. However, the DSM-III clinical description is actually much clearer than that and suggests that a more suitable and communicative name could have been found. Millon (*Disorders of Personality*, 1981) believes that any of the following would have been preferable: *cycloid, unstable, ambivalent, erratic, impulsive,* or *quixotic personality disorder.*

Because of the lack of clarity of this term, readers will find a wide range of characteristics and problems in clients who have been diagnosed as having this disorder.

Psychoanalysis

AUTHOR: L. Bryce Boyer

PRECIS: A seven-and-a-half-year treatment of a woman involving dream interpretation, analysis of transference, and the therapist's use of his own emotional responses

INTRODUCTION: Successful treatment of borderline personality disorders often results partly from the therapist's ability to use his emotional responses in his interpretations and to discover connections between the client's problems and early experiences through empathic, accurate, and timely confrontations and interpretations. Most important, the therapist must understand and interpret the client's transference: an unfolding relationship with the therapist in which the client works through problems and patterns with significant people from the past. In addition, the following principles must be followed: (1) initially the therapist should discuss a client's negative reactions to him in here-and-now terms without attempting to relate them to the past; (2) he should point out the client's defensive strategies when they occur; (3) limits must be set to curtail any acting out of the transference; (4) the client's positive responses toward the therapist are encouraged, though the client's tendency to see the therapist as all good or all bad must be pointed out; (5) the client's distortions about the therapist's interventions and about real-life events should be clarified; and (6) the client's initial bizarre and psychoticlike fantasies about the therapist must be worked through in order to reach a point where the client can relive actual childhood experiences.

The therapist takes notes during each session. In addition to recording the client's behavior and fantasies in detail, the therapist also records his own emotional reactions and fantasies, which may remain private or may be communicated to the client. This notetaking does not appear to interfere with the session and seems to communicate to the client that his comments are important.

CASE STUDY: Mrs. X was fifty-three years old when she entered treatment. She was white, twice divorced, with three institutionalized children. She was living alone, friendless, and had an undemanding job as a file clerk. She had been a chronic alcoholic for twenty years, had been hospitalized repeatedly with the diagnosis of schizophrenia, had engaged in casual sex with many men whom she picked up in bars, had lived in a faith-healing colony for one year, and had received many kinds of therapy, none of which had worked. She entered treatment because she wanted to deal with her problems, which she believed were based on unconscious conflicts. In addition, a recent therapist had told her that her interactions with her psychotic son were making him worse, and she wanted to stop contributing to his illness.

Mrs. X was seen three times weekly in psychoanalytic couch sessions for five years, then twice weekly for two years, making a total of over 800 sessions in seven and a half years. Only the highlights of the case study, involving over 2,000 pages of notes, are presented here.

The general goal of treatment was to uncover the client's unconscious and unresolved conflicts by looking into her past. Only after years of therapy did the significant events become evident: confusion about sexuality as a result of early sexual experiences involving her parents, intense sibling rivalry, and the loss of a beloved grandfather whose death the client could not accept.

Life History. The client's mother was self-centered, unapproachable, and hypochondriacal. The father, an outcast at home, was chronically alcoholic, with the result that the family, including the client and three sisters, lived largely on the generosity of relatives. At the onset of therapy, the client idealized her mother and hated her father.

When the client was three years old, she had taken an ocean voyage and had seen something in a stateroom that had frightened her. She believed that the outcome of her treatment hinged on the recall of that memory and on the therapist's ability to accept whatever she had to say without disgust, anger, or anxiety. In her second year of school she also remembered a vague sexual experience with a family chauffeur who wore black gloves. The only consistently dependable person in her childhood was her maternal grandfather, who died when she was seven.

Mrs. X's first marriage ended in divorce after she bore three children: two defective daughters and an autistic son who was institutionalized until early adolescence. The marriage was characterized by long periods of living apart and sexual promiscuity. The client believed her defective children were in some way associated with her actions with the chauffeur. She began to drink in secret.

For the next twelve years she was occupied with sexual encounters in which she was abused and which she could not remember afterward. She trained as a practical nurse and worked in psychiatric hospitals, where she had difficulty keeping a job because of her drinking. In one hospital she met a patient with whom she lived and whom she later married. She reported enjoying sex, which often included their lying in their excreta or her eating her menstrual blood, but she did not have an orgasm. The husband divorced her after nine years for reasons the client did not understand, since she was supporting him at the time.

TREATMENT: The therapist began by giving the client an orientation on the practical aspects of treatment involving scheduling, payment of bills, and so on. When the client asked what to expect about the therapist's behavior, he replied that he would keep the scheduled sessions and would be on time; he did not give advice unless deemed necessary; he saw his role as seeking to understand as much as he could about the client and would tell her what he had learned when he considered her ready, and he expected to be wrong at times; the final validation would depend on the client's own responses and memories.

The first year of therapy revolved around the vicissitudes of the client's relationship with the therapist. She often came to sessions drunk or hung over and engaged in vulgar language and obscene or threatening behaviors, which she did not recall later. She appeared to be testing the therapist's level of tolerance for what she believed was anxiety-producing and disgusting. Dream analysis revealed that she saw the therapist as two people: as loving, good, and helpful and as totally hateful, bad, and a sadistic voyeur who is sexually aroused by spying on his patients. When the therapist pointed out to her that she had described herself, she agreed. The therapist suggested that the recurrent themes of mutilation, murder, and desertion in her dreams revealed repressed anger toward her father and authority figures in general. More events were recalled, involving specific sexual acts with the chauffeur and having seen her father masturbate.

Two especially noteworthy events occurred during the first year: a suicide attempt and the therapist's insight about his own emotional reactions.

The unexpected suicide attempt occurred during the therapist's first six-week absence. Subsequent discussion revealed that the client had hoped that her death would lead to the therapist's professional destruction. When the client came for her session after being released from the hospital, the first thing she said was that she was looking for a white elephant. The search for a white elephant was related to her grandfather, who had promised her a white elephant before he died. She believed that if she found a white elephant, she would also find her grandfather, and once again she would have a dependable, loving relationship with a person who did not misuse her. The therapist stated his belief that the death of her grandfather had caused her to lose her capacity to learn and to use fantasy in an adaptive way.

The client told of her bringing home men and engaging in sexual acts in front of her son, who was home visiting. The therapist reacted to these stories with irritation and sleepiness. Through analysis of his own dreams he realized that he had identified with the son and was expressing anger toward the client by withdrawing. By understanding his own emotional reactions, the therapist was able to be more objective. He told the client that she apparently wanted to provoke him into abusing her. She responded by recalling dreams in which she was forced to watch women raped. Three years later, it became clear that she had experienced terror and feelings of dissolution when she watched her parents' sexual activities.

Mrs. X found separations from the therapist difficult to tolerate. During the second Christmas separation she went on a binge of promiscuity, interpreted as the result of anger toward the therapist, whom she saw as deserting her like a parent. The following summer she was first jailed, then hospitalized after a prolonged drunken spree. She said she had wanted to humiliate the therapist by destroying herself. She believed that she had protected herself by getting hospitalized, which she felt was an adaptive move.

Therapy continued, with gradual improvement in her behavior. By the third Christmas, Mrs. X did not act out and could spend time with her mother and sisters with less uneasiness. The therapist continued to focus on and clarify the recurrent themes of early sexual trauma and confusion, sibling rivalry, and the related intense therapeutic relationship.

By the fifth year, Mrs. X was functioning well in school and at work but continued her idealization of the therapist, who suggested a trial separation for six months. After her return, she worked through feelings of intense jealousy toward her mother and sisters. She eventually revealed a fantasy in which she saw fragmented geometric hand/arm symbols. This fantasy aided her in remembering the experience that had frightened her on board the ship: she had observed her father having intercourse with a nursemaid. He had seen her watching. In a final dream, she was being decapitated as huge waves were swallowing her up. While describing this dream, she said she might vomit and would thus ejaculate with her whole body. She said she feared that the therapist would cut off her head because of her desire to render him powerless by making her treatment a failure. These ideas were interpreted as representing an early wish to demasculinize her father as her mother had done. She had identified herself with her father's phallus, with the related fantasy that she could supplant her father's sexual role with her mother. She and her mother could thus live together in an idyllic union. However, fusion with her mother would be dangerous because it would mean the loss of personality identity.

During the final six months of treatment, Mrs. X did well. She could control her jealousy of coworkers and mother and sisters, and she became more relaxed with the therapist. At the last interview she said she felt separate from the therapist and a real person. At the end of treatment she still could not maintain a lasting relationship with a man, had not truly mourned for her grandfather, and had not worked through her idealization of the therapist. However, she was capable of warm, responsible, calm relationships with her family, drank socially, had been promoted at work, and was proud of herself and happy. A year later, she returned for a follow-up interview. She was beginning to date eligible men, no longer idealized the therapist, and appeared to have satisfactorily mourned her grandfather.

The therapist's planned absences were an important part of treatment, which raised issues of being deserted. The various ways the client responded to these absences were helpful not only as a focus during therapy but also as a measure of the client's improvement over time.

COMMENTARY: This case study is a good example of the psychoanalytic treatment of a seriously disturbed borderline client. The term *borderline* is a confusing one and has often meant different things to different therapists. In this case, the author points out that the client might have been diagnosed as a severe histrionic personality with schizoid, depressive, and impulsive trends. According to DSM-III criteria, however, the client is borderline, as shown by her long-standing life pattern of impulsivity, unstable and intense interpersonal relationships, inappropriate and intense anger, identity disturbance (wanting to be fused with her mother), emotional instability, and physically self-damaging acts. A unique feature of this approach is the use of the therapist's absences as part of the treatment rather than its interruption. We may speculate on how this client would have responded to behavior modification techniques.

SOURCE: Boyer, L. B. "Working with a Borderline Patient." *Psychoanalytic Quarterly*, 1977, *46*, 386-424.

Relaxation Technique as an Adjunct to Psychodynamic Treatment

AUTHOR: Kalman Glantz

PRECIS: Reducing a borderline client's anxiety through deep and rhythmic breathing

INTRODUCTION: Borderline clients typically display three characteristics that serve as diagnostic criteria and are the focus of treatment. The first, dissociated ego states, is an unusual alternation of mood, personality, and attitudes, often involving complete reversals in the way clients feel about themselves, others, and the world. These switches occur periodically and without warning. As a result, these clients have no stable concept of themselves or their environment. For example, clients frequently switch for no apparent reason from affection to hostility, with no middle ground. Therapists dealing with such clients may be hurt and confused by these unpredictable shifts. The second, lack of an observing ego, is the clients' lack of ability to see themselves from a stable vantage point. Since they cannot see themselves oscillate from one mood to another, they cannot stop themselves. Their memory is also affected, so that when they are angry, they have no memory for pleasant events; when affectionate, they have no memory for their feelings of anger. The third, intolerance of ambiguity, is reflected in their inability to tolerate normal levels of uncertainty. Everything must be cut and dried, or one way or another. Situations or relationships involving some uncertainty result in such intolerable levels of anxiety that borderline clients will flee.

The traditional psychoanalytic method of free association has not been successful with borderline clients. More active methods have been suggested in which the client must be made to face and deal with these alternating states. However, this active approach often causes the client to be so anxious that hospitalization is required. The following procedure describes a technique for helping borderline clients reduce their anxiety through relaxation.

CASE STUDY: Over a period of eight months, a male client displayed the alternating states described above: he was either in a state of total anger or in one of total happiness. For example, in therapy his memory depended on whatever state he was in. If angry, he had no memory for positive events, and if the therapist pursued this issue, the client became verbally abusive. His daily life reflected a similar pattern of rapid switches from one state to another. He crossed over whenever he had to make an important decision or deal with an interpersonal difficulty. However, he "spaced out" whenever he switched states; that is, his mind wandered and he felt cut off from the surroundings and people, though he had no memory of anything else. These spacing-out periods appeared to be related to anxiety. The therapist tried to prevent such occurrences by teaching the client to relax when he felt an attack coming on.

The Relaxation Technique. Relaxation is often threatening to borderline clients, partly because of their fear of facing themselves and their lack of trust in the therapist. The technique was introduced gradually and only after the therapist and client had developed a state of trust.

The therapist casually asked the client to "relax a little" by taking several deep breaths. He then asked the client to inhale and exhale "a bit more deeply" whenever he felt anxious. After six weeks, the client spontaneously closed his eyes and breathed more deeply and rhythmically whenever the therapist told him to relax. After a few more sessions, the therapist referred to this procedure as "the relaxation exercise," thus acknowledging that it was a specific therapeutic technique.

The therapist suggested relaxation only when the therapist was trying to bridge the gap between the conflicting states or when they occurred naturally during the session. This timing is an important factor in the success of this approach. After the relaxation, if the client brought up material that aroused great anxiety, the therapist would suggest relaxation again. Indicators of anxiety were facial expressions, body language, and speeded-up talking.

First Relaxation. The technique was introduced when the client said, in response to a question, that he was "going to space out." After relaxing, the client said he had experienced great fear. This established the link between anxiety and the transition between the two states.

Second Relaxation. The client began the session by complaining of feeling tired, depressed, and resentful. The therapist asked him whether he ever remembered feeling differently, and he said no. He responded with hostility to additional questions, and relaxation was then introduced. After a few moments, he suddenly described his "perfect" relationship with his mother and became excited and giggly. After more relaxation, the therapist asked him whether his mother had ever tricked or betrayed him. He responded angrily and then was instructed to relax. Continued use of confrontation followed by relaxation led to the client's revealing that he had seen the bad actions of his mother as belonging not to her but to the devil. He also said he had felt as a child that the devil was somewhere in him and that he was now trying to expiate the sins of his family.

Third Relaxation. The relaxation procedure was continued. The client began to realize that he had two selves, thus demonstrating the beginning of an "observing ego," or stable point from which he could gain perspective and some control over his changing states. The client began to realize he needed therapy, showed signs of positive transference, and began to have a better memory for what happened from session to session. It became clear that the period between states was not really blank but full of highly condensed events of which the client was unaware. By slowing down the sequence through relaxation, the client could begin to be aware of some of these events. He began to speak of feeling anxious but not spaced out.

Fourth Relaxation. This session resulted in the client's realizations of his wish not to be like his father and his increased ability to act on these realizations outside therapy.

Fifth Relaxation. Here he revealed his fear of changing, which he viewed as betrayal. He began to see that he had the right to experience changes of mood and feelings; he could see himself as a whole being. He began to be able to tell others how he was really feeling. He found that people actually were willing to support and help him.

Sixth Relaxation. In this important session, the therapist and client discovered what caused the alternation between states. When describing his relationship with a woman, he spoke of sometimes feeling dominant and at other times passive. The therapist asked him to relax and to imagine passive and dominant states simultaneously. He said, "It's my mother. Both are my mother." He revealed strong ambivalence toward her, both needing and resenting her. His relationships reflected a pattern with women in which he was first passive and then angry at himself for being passive. His anger would drive them away, with the result that he was sad and angry because he was alone.

Eventually, through further therapy, the client began to understand and modify his behavior with others. During therapy, his alternations of mood decreased, greater continuity between sessions was achieved, angry outbursts disappeared, he became more cooperative and calm, and difficult material from earlier years could be discussed without uncontrollable levels of anxiety.

COMMENTARY: This article describes an unusual approach combining the use of a relaxation technique as an adjunct to psychodynamic treatment. By learning to relax through deep and rhythmic breathing, a borderline client was able not only to discover previously unrecognized anxiety but to reduce anxiety to the point that difficult material could be discussed in therapy.

As the author points out, these exercises must be used with caution in order to avoid frightening the client away. Relaxation must not be attempted until the therapist has the client's trust. Relaxation can be unpleasant if thoughts that arise during relaxation are disturbing. Timing of the relaxation is important; it should be introduced only when the repetitive alternations between states have been observed over time. Relaxation must occur when the client is in the zone of fear that lies between the two states, not during the states themselves. When dealing with a relaxed and apparently cooperative client, therapists are cautioned against making suggestions or pushing the client toward some goal. It is important that the client's attention be directed inward and allowed to find whatever is there. Any attempt to direct or make suggestions to the client while in a state of relaxation may cause the client to feel manipulated and lead to resistance to the further use of this approach.

This method, utilizing deep breathing, suggests that other approaches using similar techniques (for example, meditation) might offer promise for use with borderline clients. In addition, since many clients experience anxiety when discussing painful material, the technique described here might be applicable to a wide range of problems.

SOURCE: Glantz, K. "The Use of a Relaxation Exercise in the Treatment of Borderline Personality Organization." *Psychotherapy: Theory, Research, and Practice,* 1981, *18,* 379-385.

Different Treatments for Subtypes of Borderline Personality Disorder

AUTHORS: John C. Lyskowski and Ming T. Tsuang

PRECIS: Pharmacological treatment or psychosocial therapy for two adults both diagnosed as borderline personalities

INTRODUCTION: The borderline personality disorder, as defined in DSM-III, includes a varied group of clients who share certain signs and symptoms but who require different treatments. A review of the clinical literature suggests that some borderline clients have an illness related to schizophrenia, while others have a disorder more related to affective illness and general personality disorders. Specific criteria for subdividing borderline clients into different categories for purposes of treatment may eventually be established. In the meantime, therapists must individualize treatment approaches for each client and not be misled by the "personality" label.

The following case studies illustrate different intervention strategies for two adults, both meeting the DSM-III criteria for borderline personality disorder.

CASE ONE: A twenty-one-year-old man was referred by his father because of unpredictable temper and lack of family interaction. He had led a normal life until age seventeen, when he began to withdraw socially for no known reason. Subsequently, he deteriorated: multiple job failures, brief and poor performance in college, and return home, where he displayed unusual and impulsive behaviors. He shoplifted items he did not need, walked into strangers' homes, had outbursts of temper, and cut his wrists. He had received antipsychotic medication, which was discontinued because of side effects. He did not drink alcohol or take drugs.

On admission, Mr. A displayed flat emotional reactions, answered questions vaguely, and said he had feelings of chronic emptiness. He was socially withdrawn and often lost control of his anger; there was no evidence of thought disorder. Mr. A refused antidepressant medication and was therefore started on trifluoperazine in dosages that were gradually increased; there were no side effects. After two weeks, he was brighter, more spontaneous, more social, and able to control his temper. He was discharged and maintained on the same dosage. Follow-up indicated that he had continued improvement but was still without a job.

Mr. A met the DSM-III criteria for borderline personality disorder; he would not be diagnosed as schizophrenic or schizotypal according to DSM-III criteria. However, the sudden onset of symptoms at age seventeen, the gradual deterioration, the withdrawal and inappropriate behaviors suggest that he had a schizophrenialike disorder. Therefore, drug therapy was the treatment of choice.

CASE TWO: Ms. B, aged thirty-six, was referred by her psychiatrist because of chronic depression from age twelve. She had been hospitalized a number of times after age eighteen. She did not respond to antidepressant, antipsychotic, or antianxiety drugs, which she had used in several suicide attempts. Ms. B. had quit school in the tenth grade and had been married and divorced twice. She had four children by four different men. For a period of years she had been exclusively homosexual, but she was currently involved in only heterosexual relationships. She had been alcoholic and was a member of Alcoholics Anonymous. At the time of admission she was under medication (doxepin and lorazepam). She was mildly depressed and had crying spells, little sexual interest, and vague thoughts of death. Her energy, sleep, and ability to concentrate were normal. She experienced mood swings, with frequent depressive episodes and irritability, followed by cheerfulness. She said her biggest problem was lack of a constant male companion.

Treatment included individual and group therapy, relaxation training, and discontinuance of medication. She was discharged to the care of her psychiatrist, and arrangements were made for her to see a social worker.

Ms. B met the DSM-III criteria for borderline personality but not those for depressive disorder. Because her problems began at an early age and persisted, she represents an example of a combined affective and general personality disorder. Therefore, psychotherapy seemed to be the treatment of choice, instead of drug therapy.

COMMENTARY: This article emphasizes a general problem that therapists encounter when dealing with personality disorders—namely, that clients who meet the DSM-III criteria for a certain personality disorder may have widely divergent life-patterns and may require different treatment approaches. Therapists should accept the diagnostic label with caution; they should examine carefully the client's long-standing personality patterns, age of onset of symptoms, clinical features, and response to medication and nonpharmacological approaches in order to individualize the treatment for each client.

SOURCE: Lyskowski, J. C., and Tsuang, M. T. "Precautions in Treating DSM-III Borderline Personality Disorder." *American Journal of Psychiatry*, 1980, *137,* 110-111.

Psychoanalytic Treatment

AUTHOR: James F. Masterson

PRECIS: A twenty-year-old man's relationship with the therapist used as a means of analyzing his unresolved difficulty with
"separation/individuation" from the past

INTRODUCTION: A crucial step in an individual's development is his or her ability to deal with both the need to be loved
and accepted by the parents and the need to be independent
and separate from them. If mutual trust exists between mother
and child, the mother can encourage the child's efforts toward
separation/individuation; the result is that the child has the capacity to tolerate anxiety and frustration and to see the world
in realistic terms.

Borderline clients have failed to resolve the issue of sepa-
ration/individuation; they do not basically trust others, have a
limited capacity to tolerate anxiety and frustration, and may be
insensitive to the differences between past and present, reality
and fantasy, and mature and infantile aspects of their life. Their
limited emotional capacities make it difficult for them to form
a relationship with the therapist, a crucial precondition for psychoanalytic treatment.

The typical mother of the future borderline client, who
herself would be considered borderline, rewards the child for infantile clinging and dependency and withdraws her affection
whenever the child tries to become independent. As a result, the
child perceives that his mother is all good—warm, approving,
and affectionate—or all bad—attacking, critical, and angry. When
the mother is approving, the child feels good, taken care of, and
happy; when she is angry, the child feels chronic anger, frustration, and underlying abandonment depression. Eventually the
child introjects these interactions with the mother as part of his
or her own personality. The child's self is either all good, passive, and compliant or bad, helpless, guilty, and empty. This
split view of himself or herself is projected onto other people,
including the therapist. Borderline clients do not relate to the

therapist as a real, whole person who has both positive and negative characteristics, but rather as an incomplete person who is completely good or bad.

The borderline client is also dominated by the pleasure principle—the desire to seek pleasure and avoid pain. Through interaction with the mother, the child has learned that clinging leads to pleasure and separation leads to pain, with the result that a vicious cycle is created that prevents the child from gradually moving toward the reality principle—the desire to deal with the world in terms of what is real, even if it is disagreeable.

In therapy, the client alternately projects onto the therapist these split selves. When the client perceives the therapist to be "bad," therapy is perceived as leading to feelings of abandonment and is seen as worthless. These painful feelings in turn lead the client to perceive the therapist as "good," with the result that the client feels good but also may behave in an infantile, clinging, self-destructive way. The therapist's initial goal is to make the client aware of the ultimate destructiveness of the dependent, clinging behavior. When the client begins to become more independent and separate, however, the negative aspects return. The client, afraid of being abandoned, is thus pushed back toward being dependent again. The client is motivated primarily by the desire to relieve separation anxiety and depression resulting from abandonment. The therapist's goal is to get the client to turn to the therapy for this relief rather than habitually falling back into dependent, regressive behaviors.

The therapist gradually builds up the therapeutic alliance with the client by confronting the destructive aspects of the relationship: the client's tendency to see the therapist in distorted terms as either all good and rewarding or all bad and punishing. Only when the client can relate to the therapist as a whole person is it possible for him or her to give up the infantile search for security and begin to work together with the therapist for insight and progressive understanding. Thus, the major therapeutic goal with a borderline client is the building up of an alliance with the therapist.

CASE STUDY: Mr. A, a twenty-year-old student, had dropped

out of college because he was severely depressed and could not work. He reported feeling unable to perform, study, or even think. His mother had verbally and physically attacked him throughout childhood; his father did not come to his aid but had demanded that the boy submit to the mother's attacks in order to get his approval. The client's split view included a negative aspect in which he saw his mother as attacking and his father as withdrawing, had feelings of abandonment depression, and saw himself as inadequate and no good. The positive aspect included seeing the father as a rewarder of passivity and seeing himself as an obedient child. This split self-concept was revealed in Mr. A's massive passivity at the beginning of therapy. He expected the therapist to take over, direct him, and give advice. When the therapist did not do that but instead confronted him with his passivity, he became angry and accused the therapist of not helping him. This anger represented the activation of the negative aspects of himself and the therapist. Mr. A revealed his anger by being late, by blocking, by silences, by missing sessions, and by accusing the therapist of not being interested in him, being rigid, monotonous, and bored, and caring only about money. The client was critical of the therapy framework—the specified hours, the time limits, the fees, and so on. He refused to answer the therapist's questions about why these details upset him so much. He appeared to be acting out with the therapist his early deep disappointment and rage at his father for failing to support him. His anger was so intense that there was no chance for a relationship with the therapist to develop. At the same time, as a result of his "splitting" defenses, he continued to idealize and praise his father, in spite of evidence of the father's lack of interest in the client. Nothing the therapist did was considered any good; the father, who had done nothing, was perceived as perfect.

Mr. A had difficulty distinguishing between his feelings from the past and his feelings about the therapist. He felt that the therapist owed him advice. It was too early in treatment to challenge this transference acting-out beyond holding firm against his anger; instead, the therapist disagreed with the client as strongly as necessary and stressed the idea that it was neces-

sary at least to discuss the various issues from different points
of view. After ten months of therapy, three times weekly, a
therapeutic alliance had begun to develop. The therapist had refused to reinforce the client's wishes to be taken care of and did
not reject him because of his anger. The therapist had focused
quietly but firmly on the limitations of reality.

Mr. A acted out less during therapy, his symptoms diminished, and he returned to college. However, his progress activated his fears of abandonment and rejection. He suddenly re-
gressed and resumed his dependent stance with the therapist:
"Your behavior is just like my father's, you sit back passively,
you don't stimulate discussion, . . . I need more anticipation,
more activity on your part." When the therapist questioned
these feelings and why they had come about at this point, Mr. A
became argumentative and threatened to see another therapist.
The therapist responded by saying that he was entitled to see
another therapist but he would have to work out these same
feelings with him.

At this point the therapist offered an interpretation:
These feelings had nothing to do with the therapist but were
more related to the fact that the client was making progress in
treatment. What he was feeling was that he was being abandoned just as he had been when, as a child, he had attempted to
express himself with his father. He saw the therapist as an exact
replica of his father and was trying to replay his relationship
with the father in order to avoid the pain of facing the feelings
he had about his father. Mr. A agreed and then discussed at
length his lifelong search for a father, which had prevented him
from "doing his own thing." For the first time, he linked his
need for his father to his need to express himself. This led to resistance about facing feelings of hopelessness about his father.
Only after more confrontations and acting out with the therapist was the client able to face his memories of his father's neglect and his mother's attacks.

By the end of the twentieth month of therapy, Mr. A was
attending college full-time and living alone. This further progress triggered feelings of hopelessness. He had a dream in which
he saw the therapist replacing him with another patient because

he was making too much noise. The client woke up feeling that the therapist had betrayed his trust and that his case was hopeless. The therapist pointed out that the purpose of Mr. A's fantasy, which he acted out with the therapist, was to gain the father he felt he never had and to avoid feelings of hopelessness regarding his relationship with his father. These acting-out behaviors occurred every time he made progress in therapy. Mr. A said that he had felt a responsibility to his father not to be angry, not to cause a commotion. When the therapist asked what had happened to the anger, Mr. A. said he put it on himself. Otherwise, it was like "hitting my father in the face." The therapist pointed out that he was destroying himself in order to deal with his anger at his father.

At the end of therapy, which had lasted approximately three years and eight months, Mr. A had worked through his feelings of hopelessness about his father and had faced his underlying rage at his mother. He graduated with honors and continued on to graduate school.

COMMENTARY: Readers may want to note that the client's presenting symptoms of depression and inability to work were not the focus of therapy. Instead, the therapist emphasized the transference relationship as a means of uncovering a more basic, underlying problem—in this case, an inability to deal with the separation/individuation issue. The assumption was that when this issue was resolved, other symptoms, presumably including the depression, would decrease. (See the report of Jacobsen, 1975, in Additional Readings, Chapter One, for a description of a psychoanalytic approach.) One wonders what would have happened if the client had been treated with other approaches toward depression, which may or may not have reduced the period of time spent in therapy.

The author apparently used the client's intrapsychic dynamics (for example, tendency to "split," to be governed by the pleasure and pain principle, and to have difficulty with separation/individuation) as the basis of his diagnosis. Not enough information was provided to determine the extent to which the client would display five or more of the criterion symptoms listed for the DSM-III description of this disorder. Regardless of the agreement on diagnostic classification, however, this case study presents a model for dealing with transference, which is a major focus of psychoanalytic therapy and represents an approach used for a wide range of problems.

SOURCE: Masterson, J. F. "The Borderline Adult: Therapeutic Alliance and Transference." *American Journal of Psychiatry,* 1978, *135,* 437-441.

Short-Term Psychoanalytic Therapy

AUTHOR: Robert Mendelsohn

PRECIS: Focusing on only one or two major conflicts and actively directing the client toward material related to these areas in the therapist/client relationship

INTRODUCTION: Recent interest in borderline personality disorders has led to modifications in psychoanalytic technique, including emphasis on an active, confronting stance by the therapist. Standard psychoanalytic technique allows the treatment session to develop out of the transference, daily events and memories, and changing moods of the client. Traditional therapists tend to be neutral and to respond equally to whatever the client says with "evenly suspended attention." By contrast, the approach described here includes a more directive, active role for the therapist. Short-term therapists, compared with traditional, long-term therapists, use active attention in setting treatment goals, in evaluating the client's psychological state and readiness for intervention, and in narrowing the focus of both therapist and client. A second active technique, called "focusing," is defined as the active pursuit of selected material within therapy. The therapist focuses on one or two of the client's major conflicts and actively directs the client toward discussion of material related to them. He also may selectively ignore or direct the client away from material he considers not helpful in working through these conflicts.

A prominent characteristic of borderline clients is the constant state of change, flux, and disturbances in their interpersonal relationships. These difficulties are reflected in the therapist/client relationship, which is often confusing, intense, and chaotic. Although these clients often function at a superficially adjusted level in real life, their therapy behavior is often erratic and fragmented. Borderline clients often are in conflict about separation from versus primitive union with the therapist and have difficulty dealing with sexual and aggressive feelings and fantasies. The strong emotional responses of client and therapist to each other (the transference/countertransference relationships) must be faced and systematically analyzed. If the therapist is not careful, therapist and client can become pathologically merged into mutual role playing that results in an avoidance of crucial issues involving their relationship. These issues are best handled by a therapist who avoids the traditional neutral stance and who is instead active, focused, and confronting.

The following case study provides an example of the use of active attention and focusing on the transference/countertransference in the treatment of a borderline client.

CASE STUDY: A twenty-six-year-old, white, married man had been involved in petty embezzlements and insurance frauds. His father, who had a background of similar unlawful activities, had brutalized him; his mother was overprotective and intrusive. Initially, the client idealized the therapist and made rapid, early gains (for example, getting a job, becoming less promiscuous, and marrying). Therapy revealed that the client had a desire for primitive merging with a good and all-powerful parent who would take care of him as he had never been taken care of before. The major transference/countertransference issue was the belief, shared by both therapist and client, that therapy would be "all good and providing." After a while, however, the client began to resist paying his fee. His fantasy was that the good and kind therapist (or parent) would take care of him and provide him with unlimited love, which included treating him without a fee. At the same time, the client believed that the therapist did not really love him and that the client would have to "embezzle" and force love out of the therapist just as he had tried to embezzle money out of others. The therapist's belief (reflecting his own countertransference response to the client) was that therapy was powerful enough to "cure" the client and that the client needed kindness and no confrontation. Thus, the therapist fell into the trap of agreeing with the client's perception and permitted the fee to go unpaid for a time. It was as if both therapist and client shared the same perception of the hopelessness of the treatment.

These transference and countertransference issues were explored, and the therapist "actively attended" to the central focus of the client's and his own associations. This active stance led to the discovery that the client's associations were filled with fantasies of unlimited power and love. He both idealized the therapist as a powerful provider and was contemptuous of him because of the therapist's weakness and passivity. The therapist's perceptions agreed with the client's. The therapist's active position brought all this material into the open. Battles over the fee began, the client could discuss his desire to "embezzle" the therapist, and the client appeared to be a more integrated person.

CONTRAINDICATIONS FOR AN ACTIVE APPROACH: This active approach should be used with the following points kept in mind.

First, if the therapist is too active, the client may respond with passivity, allowing the therapist to take over entirely. In its extreme form, this active stance might foster further primitive merging with the therapist in some borderline clients.

Second, a too-active approach might lead to further denial and resistance by some clients.

Third, therapists who have a strong need for power and control over a client should avoid this approach. If the client discovers he is being manipulated, his anger and disappointment at the therapist may be turned against himself, resulting in increased self-destructiveness. Even more commonly, the split-off anger and contempt are directed at another person in the client's life, such as a spouse, while the client continues to idealize the therapist. Long, unsuccessful treatment may follow, with the client seeing his spouse as "all bad" and the therapist as "all good."

Finally, this approach is not recommended for therapists who have difficulty dealing with hostility and aggression that may arise from an active approach. If the therapist is uncomfortable with aggression, he may lead the client to suppress his aggressive feelings or to act out aggression that cannot be faced by either the client or therapist during treatment sessions.

COMMENTARY: The author presents a discussion of the difficult treatment issues associated with borderline clients. He suggests a modification of traditional psychoanalytic approaches by describing a relatively short-term psychodynamic therapy involving an active approach. By actively and clearly directing therapy sessions to a systematic analysis of the therapist/client relationship, many hidden issues can surface and subsequently be worked through. The transference/countertransference issues are especially important with borderline clients, whose major symptoms are often revealed in the way they relate to therapists. However, many of the therapist and client reactions described here are not limited to borderline clients. The article offers helpful guidelines to issues that may arise in various kinds of therapy with clients who present a wide range of problems. A helpful feature of this article is the author's discussion of contraindications for the use of this approach.

SOURCE: Mendelsohn, R. " 'Active Attention' and 'Focusing' on the Transference/Countertransference in the Psychotherapy of the Borderline Patient." *Psychotherapy: Theory, Research, and Practice,* 1981, *18,* 386-393.

Drug Treatment for Emotionally Unstable Clients

AUTHORS: Arthur Rifkin, Frederic Quitkin, Carlos Carrillo, Arnold G. Blumberg, and Donald F. Klein

PRECIS: Using lithium to control the mood swings of twenty-one inpatients

INTRODUCTION: The diagnosis of "emotionally unstable character disorder" (EUCD) is applied to clients with long-standing maladaptive behavior patterns, such as poor work history, manipulativeness, truancy, impulsivity, unstable interpersonal relationships, and, most important, unpredictable depressive and elated mood swings. This diagnosis is more likely to be used for, though not limited to, adolescent girls. Although these clients might be labeled histrionic, their emotionality has a different quality: histrionic clients use their emotionality as a manipulative strategy and return to normal when their demands are met; by contrast, EUCD clients are often unable to account for their depression, which seems unrelated to external events. During their hypermanic periods, they are giddy, silly, overtalkative, and angry if frustrated. Afterward they report that they felt "driven" and that their experience was unpleasant in spite of the laughter and good mood. This study describes the use of lithium carbonate to control the unpredictable mood swings in a group of hospitalized EUCD patients.

METHOD: On the basis of daily interviews over a five-day period, twenty-one patients (age and sex unspecified) in a private psychiatric hospital were diagnosed as EUCD. All had been drug-free for at least three weeks prior to the study and received no medication except lithium during treatment.

The study consisted of a six-week lithium period and a six-week placebo period. Patients were randomly assigned to either the lithium period first or the placebo period first. In clients on lithium, blood levels were monitored to assure appropriate drug levels. Neither the patients nor the staff knew when they were taking lithium or placebo. Ward nurses rated each patient daily for the usual side effects of lithium, which were minimal. Thus, the evaluators were not able to detect when the patient was taking lithium by the presence of side effects.

During the last week of each six-week period, the patient was interviewed daily for five days. The patients' behavior was rated independently by two evaluators, who then reached a consensus for each patient through discussion. The rating scale consisted of six items: mood, communicativeness, aggression, sociability, activity, and grooming. Each item was scaled from +6 to −6, and each point was defined in behavioral terms.

At the end of each patient's twelve weeks, and before the staff or patient knew when the lithium had been administered, the evaluators chose the six-week period in which the patient did better. Of the twenty-one patients, fourteen were judged better with lithium and four better with placebo, and three showed no difference. There was less day-to-day variation in mood for the lithium-treated group. Whether the patient began with placebo or with lithium had no effect. The therapeutic implications of this study are that EUCD patients may need to have their mood disorder treated before they can respond to nonpharmacological treatment approaches.

CASE STUDY: A twenty-five-year-old female secretary had mood swings for at least ten years. During periods of depression, lasting from several hours to more than a day, she avoided friends, planned suicide, and stayed in her apartment. During manic episodes, lasting for one or two hours, she laughed inappropriately, talked too much, and was hyperactive. In addition, her seductive, manipulative, and theatrical behaviors had a histrionic quality.

During the week before the study she had violent mood swings from day to day. She received placebo for the first six weeks; no change was observed in her behavior. There was marked improvement after six weeks of lithium: she experienced reduced depression and had no manic episodes.

She was discharged after the study and discontinued lithium. Although she was on a vacation under pleasant circumstances, her mood swings returned. After returning to the city she could work only when her moods made it possible. Two months after discharge she resumed lithium treatment. Within three weeks her mood swings disappeared and she was not impaired by depression or mania, though problems related to her histrionic behaviors continued.

COMMENTARY: The EUCD diagnosis is not included in DSM-III. However, it appears that clients given that diagnosis would be considered to have a borderline personality disorder, according to DSM-III criteria. In some cases a mixed diagnosis, including histrionic and antisocial characteristics, might be appropriate.

It would be important to rule out other possible causes of mood swings, such as organic conditions (see the Additional Reading on organic personality disorders by Blumer). As the authors point out, lithium is not necessarily the only intervention technique but can be used to control clients' moods so that they can then respond to other psychotherapeutic approaches. In the case study, the client displayed both depressive and histrionic symptoms. Lithium reduced the depressive symptoms but did not affect the histrionic behaviors, which would presumably be treated by some of the approaches described in the section on histrionic personality disorders.

SOURCE: Rifkin, A., Quitkin, F., Carrillo, C., Blumberg, A. G., and Klein, D. F. "Lithium Carbonate in Emotionally Unstable Character Disorders." *Archives of General Psychiatry,* 1972, *27,* 519-523.

Difficulties in Psychodynamic Therapy with Borderline Clients

AUTHOR: Edward R. Shapiro

PRECIS: Therapists must deal with their own emotional reactions to borderline clients, clients' defensive strategies, and clients' reactions to the therapist

INTRODUCTION: Borderline clients typically have difficulties with other people, especially in terms of their sense of aloneness and their tendency to see interpersonal difficulties as coming from outside themselves. These often emerge in the unstructured, intense, and intimate relationship with the therapist. By expecting these difficulties, therapists can be more effective with the client and better able to handle their own reactions.

CLIENTS' CHARACTERISTIC REACTIONS TO THE THERAPIST: In intensive therapy, borderline clients often display dramatic shifts in perception, thinking, and feeling about themselves and the therapist, usually without awareness of the contradictions. In therapy they are emotionally rigid, have little tolerance for guilt, anxiety, or depression, have difficulty in identifying bodily sensations and emotions, and cannot tolerate frustration or control their impulses. They often see the therapist not as a person but as an object, which they use as an infant uses a favorite blanket to protect himself against the dangers of the outside world. They find difficulty in asking the therapist for help, since that would imply that the therapist is a separate, real person who might refuse the request. Unable to cope with the anxiety-arousing and angry fantasies that a refusal would bring, the client either angrily demands a response or ignores the therapist in the session while gaining a sense of comfort from the therapist's presence. Borderline clients' responses are often polarized: they alternate between magical and completely negative expectations from therapy. They are in conflict, since they fear both being dependent and being intimate. They attempt to solve this conflict by maintaining the "proper" distance from the therapist, neither too close nor too distant.

CHARACTERISTIC DEFENSES USED IN RELATIONSHIPS WITH THE THERAPIST: Borderline clients tend to use two defensive strategies, which the psychoanalytic theorist Otto Kernberg calls "splitting" and "projective identification."

In splitting, clients have difficulty bringing together and integrating loving and hating aspects of both their self-image and their images of other people. They seem unable to sustain a sense of caring for the person who frustrates them. When the therapeutic relationship is gratifying, the client has positive fantasies; when it leads to frustration, only negative thoughts are generated, and the client seems to lose all memory for the positive aspects. Thus, the client alternately views the therapist as all-powerful and completely worthless. The client does not experience concern or affection for the therapist but shifts suddenly from total dependence to total devaluation.

The second major defensive strategy involves "projective identification": here clients reject certain aspects of themselves involving impulses, negative self-image, and guilt and project them onto another person. They identify with this person because they see him or her as like themselves. They are selectively inattentive to real aspects of the other that contradict or invalidate the contents of their projection. Although they may consciously see the other person as unlike themselves because the person has characteristics that they have rejected, unconsciously they attempt to develop, and involve the person in, a relationship in which those same characteristics are encouraged. Habitual use of this strategy may result in the client's being extremely dependent, lonely, fearful of parting, and fearful of the loss of the ability to love. Borderline clients are often sensitive to other people's unconscious impulses and psychic sore points. This sensitivity can be used manipulatively. For example, they may be aware of a therapist's unrecognized anger or frustration; they will then provoke a response that justifies their distrust in the therapist, with the result that they may reject all the therapist has to offer.

CHARACTERISTIC THERAPIST REACTIONS TO BORDERLINE CLIENTS: Therapists must be prepared for frustrations related to their need to be helpful to the client, who withdraws, devaluates the therapist, and often seems to have no memory for positive therapy experiences. When analyzing their own reactions, therapists often discover their feelings of anger, desire to punish the client in some way, and resulting guilt. These feelings, if perceived by the client, validate the client's projection and make therapy more difficult.

Therapists must withstand these onslaughts from the client without withdrawing or retaliating. They should try to create a "holding environment": (1) reflect, understand, and give feedback to the client's responses; (2) maintain contact, concern, and emotional availability; (3) set limits to help the client manage overwhelming levels of internal and external stimulation; and (4) in general, develop a more accurate, empathic understanding of the client's responses, including the ambivalence toward the therapist.

COMMENTARY: The reader should be aware of the underlying assumptions in this article and in psychoanalytic treatment in general: that therapy takes a long time, that clients' difficulties originated in early experiences that must be uncovered, and that a major focus of therapy is the relationship with the therapist. Therapists need not necessarily accept these assumptions, however, in order to find these suggestions helpful for a variety of therapeutic approaches. Regardless of the specific strategy, therapy always involves some kind of interaction between therapist and client, and therapists may be more effective if they are sensitized to the issues discussed in the article.

Obviously, therapists of different theoretical orientations would proceed in a very different manner. For example, cognitive and behavior therapists might focus on modification of the client's specific current difficulties and beliefs, with no attempt to effect a global change. Unfortunately, the clinical literature contains virtually no reports of such treatments, since the diagnosis of borderline personality disorder has been limited primarily to clients being treated by psychoanalytic therapists.

SOURCE: Shapiro, E. R. "The Psychodynamics and Developmental Psychology of the Borderline Patient: A Review of the Literature." *American Journal of Psychiatry,* 1978, *135,* 1305-1315.

Additional Readings

Adler, G. "The Borderline-Narcissistic Personality Disorder Continuum." *American Journal of Psychiatry,* 1981, *138,* 46-50.

    Borderline and narcissistic clients are viewed as having similarities in their developmental patterns, so that as borderline clients improve in therapy, they begin to display characteristics of narcissistic clients. In dealing with these clients, therapists should be aware of the extent to which clients have (1) a stable sense of self, (2) interpersonal relationships in which other people are not used in order to supply the client's own missing functions, and (3) a capacity to be alone without being overwhelmed by feelings of emptiness, hopelessness, and despair. Borderline and narcissistic clients are at the opposite ends of the continuum, and these differences emerge in the relationship with the therapist. In these three areas, borderline clients are deficient, while narcissistic clients function relatively well. The therapist's goal is to help the borderline client to work through problems in these areas.

    A case study of a female graduate student's four-year treatment is presented. The woman sought treatment because of difficulties in completing her doctoral dissertation and inability to maintain sustained relationships with men. Over the four years, she was able to resolve issues of borderline aloneness. She had a greater cohesiveness of self and had relatively stable relationships with others. She was also able to accept the ambivalence she felt toward the therapist and others, and in therapy she focused on issues of her vulnerable self-worth. The therapist felt that the client had progressed in therapy from the borderline end of the continuum to the narcissistic personality end.

Blumer, D. "Organic Personality Disorders." In J. R. Lion (Ed.), *Personality Disorders: Diagnosis and Management.* (2nd ed.) Baltimore: Williams & Wilkins, 1981.

The possibility of some type of organic brain syndrome must be considered in marked personality change that involves one or more of the following: emotional lability, impulsiveness, marked apathy and indifference, and suspiciousness and paranoid thoughts. If the brain disorder is relatively widespread, the symptoms may involve either an exaggeration of personality characteristics, so that the person becomes a caricature of his former self, or a reversal to the opposite (for example, a quiet, considerate woman becomes aggressive and inconsiderate).

If the brain disorder is relatively localized, more specific personality characteristics emerge, especially in frontal-lobe and temporal-lobe lesions. Frontal-lobe lesions are associated with urinary incontinence along with total lack of concern for the accident, though no intellectual impairment occurs. Two types of personality changes occur: (1) apathy and indifference in which clients lose all initiative and seem to function like automatons and/or (2) puerility and euphoria, involving lack of restraint, promiscuity, irritability, coarseness, hyperactivity, and/or paranoid-grandiose thinking. Apathy may be mistaken for depression, but clients with a frontal-lobe lesion show empty indifference, while depressed clients generally show preoccupation with the depressing thoughts. Puerile-euphoric clients may resemble manic or hypomanic patients, though their affect may be more shallow. If their antisocial acts are in marked contrast to their previous personality, organic lesions should be suspected. Both incontinence and seizures are definite signs of an organic lesion.

Temporal-lobe lesions are associated with the "epileptic personality," a complex set of personality and behavioral changes that often follow temporal-lobe seizures. Among these changes are a deepening of emotional responses, involving a damming up and discharge of anger and rage or an intensification of ethical-religious feelings. These clients may consider the right and wrong of every issue, may give speeches or write down thoughts reflecting their ethical concerns, and are completely humorless. Lack of response to these issues may trigger angry outbursts. Paranoid and schizophrenialike symptoms may occur. The diagnosis of temporal-lobe lesions is made through the study of EEG patterns and the therapist's observations that clients display a pattern of brief episodic events followed by a confused, amnesic state.

Friedman, H. J. "Psychotherapy of Borderline Patients: The Influence of Theory on Technique." *American Journal of Psychiatry,* 1975, *132,* 1048-1052.

The author questions the validity of the British object-relations viewpoint regarding the origin of borderline personality disorders. He believes that the resulting therapy techniques can be destructive to borderline clients. The author calls attention to three assumptions that must be questioned: (1) borderline clients are especially sensitive to abandonment, with the result that the therapist is often indulgent; (2) long-term hospitalization is more effective than short-term outpatient treatment; and (3) destructive outbursts should not be kept at a minimum, for they often lead to therapeutic gains. Suggestions are made for an alternative approach, "active psychotherapy," based on the importance of setting limits in therapy, establishment of positive rapport, and recognition of the client's specific ego defects. Short-term hospitalization or outpatient treatment is often effective when this approach is used.

Gallahorn, G. E. "Borderline Personality Disorders." In J. R. Lion (Ed.), *Personality Disorders: Diagnosis and Management.* (2nd ed.) Baltimore: Williams & Wilkins, 1981.

The following are important issues in the therapy of borderline clients: emphasis on change, supportive therapy in times of crisis, limit setting, transference and countertransference, group therapy, and the question of short-term or long-term hospitalization. Of particular interest are the author's warnings about the use of medication for these clients. They do not usually respond well to tranquilizers when their lives are relatively untroubled; they often complain of distortions of body image and feelings of depersonalization when taking those drugs. During transient psychotic episodes, however, tranquilizers may be effective in reducing anxiety and relieving psychotic symptoms. Although borderline clients complain of depression, there is no study showing that the tricyclic antidepressants have been effective with this group. Amphetamines and minor tranquilizers should never be used, because of borderline clients' potential for drug addiction.

Gunderson, J. G., and Kolb, J. E. "Discriminating Features of Borderline Patients." *American Journal of Psychiatry,* 1978, *135,* 792-796.

Borderline clients can be distinguished from other diagnostic categories (schizophrenic, neurotic depressed, and a mixed group) on the basis of seven criteria: low achievement, impulsivity (often related to alcohol or drug use), manipulative suicidal gestures, intense emotional reactions (especially anger) and the relative absence of feelings of satisfaction, mild psychotic symptoms, compulsive socialization and intolerance of being alone, and disturbed close relationships. (The authors point out that no attempt was made to use these criteria to distinguish borderline clients from other personality-disordered groups.) By using these criteria, therapists can more quickly diagnose clients and thus anticipate certain clinical problems. Among these are the inadvisability of unmodified psychoanalytic treatment or antipsychotic drugs, the possibility of strong reactions and disagreements regarding treatment among the staff, and the tendency to overestimate or underestimate the client's potential level of functioning. The low level of borderline clients' social, work, and school achievements suggests that social learning programs (groups, rehabilitation, milieu therapy) may be effective intervention strategies.

Harbin, H. T. "Family Therapy with Personality Disorders." In J. R. Lion (Ed.), *Personality Disorders: Diagnosis and Management.* (2nd ed.) Baltimore: Williams & Wilkins, 1981.

Borderline clients often respond to family therapy, but the therapist may encounter many difficulties, especially because there are often two or three persons with the borderline diagnosis in one family. The author feels that family therapy with these clients presents more difficulties than with any other diagnostic group. Many borderline clients and their families appear to have insight into themselves, to be in control, and to want to change. This is only a facade, and if the therapist proceeds too quickly, the family may respond with destructive acting-out behaviors. These families are often explosive during treatment. Therapists must proceed slowly with a realization of the limits of both the client and the family. The author has found that the major theme in therapy revolves around extreme dependency or emotional involvement. A goal of therapy is to help these clients to differentiate themselves from other family members. Since these clients present a wide variety of symptoms (for example, paranoia, acting out, depression), no case example is presented.

McDaniel, E. "Personality Disorders in Private Practice." In J. R. Lion (Ed.), *Personality Disorders: Diagnosis and Management* (2nd ed.) Baltimore: Williams & Wilkins, 1981.

The author describes her approach to the therapy of borderline clients seen in private practice. These clients often have a history of marginal functioning, and they may remain in crisis situations on and off throughout the treatment. The crises do not usually arise from interpersonal problems but from more threatening events, such as an encounter with the police or an overdose of drugs. They resemble histrionic and narcissistic clients in that they use primitive and massive defenses. They are rarely psychotic, with delusions, hallucinations, or lack of contact with the outside world.

Therapy is usually long-term and is both supportive and insight-oriented. The therapist must be flexible: sessions may have to be scheduled at different times from week to week, intervention in the client's real-life situations may be necessary, and other modes of treatment (for example, group therapy) may be required. A case study is presented of a twenty-year-old male with a history of drug use, compulsive homosexual escapades, and difficulty with the law over a forged prescription. Treatment included assignment to a methadone clinic, group therapy, and individual therapy, which was often scheduled four to five times a week during crisis periods.

Nadelson, T. "Borderline Rage and the Therapist's Response."
American Journal of Psychiatry, 1977, *134,* 748-751.

Therapists face common countertransference problems when dealing with borderline clients in psychoanalytic therapy. Therapists must feel good about themselves and be able to separate themselves from the client. It is important to be aware of the client's negative self-feelings, which are projected onto the therapist, who may in turn take these feelings on. Thus, when a client accuses the therapist of being ineffective and lacking understanding, the therapist may agree with the client and think of himself or herself as ineffective and insensitive. Therapists may also unconsciously wish to rid themselves of a difficult client who pushes them toward uncomfortable self-analysis. Therapists must avoid reacting to the client with rage, apathy, or counterattack; instead, they must direct attention to their own emotional state so they can better understand the client's vulnerability.

7

Dependent
Personality
Disorder

According to DSM-III (pp. 325-326), the following are characteristic of the individual's current and long-term functioning,
are not limited to episodes of illness, and cause either significant
impairment in social or occupational functioning or subjective
distress.

      A. Passively allows others to assume responsibil-
ity for major areas of life because of inability to function independently (e.g., lets spouse decide what kind
of job he or she should have).

      B. Subordinates own needs to those of persons
on whom he or she depends in order to avoid any
possibility of having to rely on self, e.g., tolerates
abusive spouse.

  C. Lacks self-confidence, e.g., sees self as helpless, stupid.

  Individuals with this disorder often display symptoms of another personality disorder, such as histrionic, schizotypal, narcissistic, or avoidant personality disorder. They are often anxious and depressed, and they feel uncomfortable when alone for more than brief periods of time.

  Dependent personality disorder is apparently common and is diagnosed more frequently in women.

Problem Solving to Increase Independence

AUTHORS: Thomas J. D'Zurilla and Marvin R. Goldfried

PRECIS: Teaching a dependent woman to define her problem, find alternative solutions, make decisions, and verify the results for herself

INTRODUCTION: Our daily lives are filled with situational problems that we must solve in order to maintain an adequate level of effective functioning. Much of what is viewed as "abnormal" behavior or "emotional disturbance" may be seen as ineffective behavior and its consequences, in which the person cannot resolve certain situational problems in life. Attempts to do so have undesirable effects, such as anxiety, depression, and the creation of additional problems. Training a client to use a problem-solving approach is one of several possible behavior modification techniques for facilitating effective behavior.

The problem-solving approach involves five stages:

1. *General orientation, or "set."* The client is encouraged to develop a general orientation that includes the attitude to (a) accept the fact that problems are a normal part of life and that it is possible to cope with most of these situations effectively; (b) recognize problematic situations when they occur; and (c) inhibit the tendency either to respond on the first impulse or to do nothing.

2. *Problem definition and formulation.* The client is encouraged to describe the problem in a specific and comprehensive way; it is important to avoid vague or ambiguous terms and to consider all the facts and information available. Additional information seeking may be necessary.

3. *Generation of alternatives.* The major task is to generate as many solutions as possible in such a way as to maximize the likelihood that the most effective response will be among those generated. The "brainstorming" technique is recommended, with its four basic rules: (a) criticism is ruled out; (b) freewheeling is welcomed—the wilder the idea, the better; (c) quantity is wanted, reflecting the idea that the greater the num-

ber of ideas, the greater the probability of useful ideas; and (d) combination and improvement are desired—that is, clients should suggest how an idea can be improved or how two ideas can be joined into still another idea.

4. *Decision making.* The client tries to weigh and compare the various alternatives, considering the values of the various expected consequences as well as their estimated likelihood of occurrence. Eventually a judgment is made as to which alternative is best.

5. *Verification.* After the chosen course of action has been carried out, the client assesses the outcome so as to make self-correction possible. In other words, the client decides whether the action worked and then decides how to modify the behavior.

The most appropriate case for this technique is the dependent client who cannot cope with problematic situations on his or her own but who can perform quite effectively with a minimum of difficulty when the therapist outlines exactly what to do. This type of client has an adequate repertoire of general performance skills but a deficit in independent problem-solving ability. The major goal of treatment should be to teach new problem-solving skills, not to merely feed the client an unending series of solutions.

CASE STUDY: A homemaker, Sally, reported the following problematic situation: "I became upset and depressed last night because my husband was out working late and I was home alone." Sally was trained in a behavior modification program that provided the five stages described above.

1. *General orientation.* Sally's treatment began with an explanation and discussion of the rationale and course of treatment, including the changes that were expected to result from it. She was encouraged to recognize the occurrence of problematic situations and to avoid the tendency to react automatically without carefully thinking things through. She was instructed to observe her own behavior in real-life settings between sessions, to keep a daily record of problematic situations, and to be aware of emotional reactions (feelings of uncertainty, confusion, frustration, and so on).

2. *Problem definition and formulation.* Sally was told to state the problem in more detail, to describe the problem in more specific, concrete terms, to include both external events and thoughts and feelings, and to include related background information. This process resulted in the following description of the problem: "My husband and I have been married for three years and have a two-year-old child. During the past six months, my husband has had to work late in the evening, usually until about 10 P.M. He will continue to work these late hours for some time, as we need the money badly. However, I have been feeling increasingly lonely, anxious, and depressed in the evening after our child goes to bed and I am waiting for my husband to come home . . . ." She indicated also that she wanted to spend more time with people, was afraid that someone might try to break in when she was alone, and wanted more sex with her husband, who was often tired when he got home late.

Once the situation was described, Sally was taught how to formulate the problem by identifying her major goals, which were desire for social interaction on weeknights, desire for more sex during the week, and desire to feel safer in the evening.

Sometimes a goal stated initially by the client is not really the most basic one. This can often be determined by following a stated goal with a "why" question. For example, when Sally first stated that her goal was to get her husband to spend more time at home in the evenings, she responded to the why question with the three more basic goals stated above.

3. *Generation of alternatives.* Sally was taught to distinguish between a "strategy" and a "specific behavior." Following instruction in the four rules of brainstorming, she began generating strategy-level responses, keeping in mind her basic goals. Her list of strategies included taking steps "to get a girlfriend and relative to visit me occasionally on weeknights," "to get my husband to be more interested in sex during the week," "to have an affair with another man," and "to arrange safeguards against someone's breaking in." The therapist encouraged her to stay with the task of generating strategies by providing her with questions and possible examples.

4. *Decision making.* Sally began by roughly screening her list of strategies to eliminate the obviously inferior ones (those

that would likely lead to negative consequences). Then she considered the remaining strategies by asking, "If I were to carry out this particular course of action, what are the various possible consequences?" To facilitate this procedure, she explored possible consequences in four categories: personal, social, short-term, and long-term. Evaluation of the possible consequences of strategies was made easier by using three categories: "highly likely," "likely," and "unlikely." Similarly, assignment of values to the various possible consequences was made in terms of "positive," "negative," and "neutral." The information was recorded on a special checklist so she could more easily compare the various alternatives.

Once a set of strategies was selected, Sally returned to the generation of alternatives in order to produce specific behavioral alternatives for implementing her strategies, using the same procedures she had used in generating the strategies. For example, regarding "take steps to get a girlfriend or relative to visit me occasionally on weeknights," Sally came up with "Ask my mother to spend an evening with me at least one night a week," "Ask several neighbors if they would like to have a card game at my house one night each week," and "Inform my friend that I am beginning to conduct a sewing class one evening each week." Sally then chose the alternative that appeared to be the most effective.

5. *Verification.* There is a danger that this approach teaches the client little else but to become obsessive in his or her thinking. Consequently, the role of the therapist was to encourage the client to act on her decision and then to verify the extent to which her prediction of the outcome was accurate. Sally was trained to observe and record the consequences of her actions. Her decisions had required her to engage in a variety of different behaviors, including asking friends in for a card game once each week, enrolling in an evening adult education class, wearing sexy clothing when her husband came home, occasionally initiating sex early in the morning, and having special locks put on all outside doors. Sally reported "satisfactory" outcomes to her actions, and it appeared that her problem-solving approach had worked.

COMMENTARY: The authors point out that another type of client who might benefit from this technique is one who has good problem-solving skills but who fails to use them because of emotional inhibitions. Such clients might respond to a graded-task approach to problem-solving training. Clients who have a combination of difficulties, including an inability to carry out the selected course of action because of lack of assertiveness and related skills, would probably respond to problem-solving training only if it were used along with other techniques, such as behavior rehearsal (as described in the digest of MacDonald, 1975) or systematic desensitization. (The reader is referred to the article by Templeman and Wollersheim, in which this method is used with an antisocial client.)

SOURCE: D'Zurilla, T. J., and Goldfried, M. R. "Problem Solving and Behavior Modification." *Journal of Abnormal Psychology*, 1971, *78*, 107-126.

Short-Term Role Playing to Increase Assertive Behavior

AUTHORS: Richard M. Eisler, Peter M. Miller, Michel Hersen, and Harriet Alford

PRECIS: Two case studies using assertion practice in situations involving people in the client's life modeled by a therapist assistant

INTRODUCTION: Assertive training was designed as a treatment strategy for people who have difficulty expressing their true feelings in a variety of interpersonal situations. In the context of role-played personal encounters, training included instructions from the therapist, rehearsing the desired behavior, seeing assertive behavior modeled by the therapist, and performance feedback. The major purpose of this study was to discover to what extent the changes observed during training generalize to actual interpersonal situations.

Two married couples with passive-avoidant husbands were chosen to assess the effects of the husbands' assertive training on subsequent marital interaction. The couples were videotaped while discussing their marital difficulties. The husband's assertive deficits were identified through this initial videotape. He then received four forty-five-minute assertive training sessions. Within forty-eight hours after completion of the training, marital interaction was again videotaped to provide posttreatment assessment of the training effects.

In Case One the husband received assertive training with relatively unstructured scenes related to pretreatment interaction. In Case Two training involved structured scenes related to specific areas of the husband's marital conflicts.

CASE STUDY ONE: A forty-five-year-old high school teacher responded passively to his extremely critical wife. The twenty-four-minute videotape revealed that the husband expressed neither positive nor negative feelings about his wife's behavior, eye contact was limited, and his verbal responses to her were short. When he did give an opinion, he failed to elicit her viewpoint on the issue. Neither spouse smiled.

The following specific measures were obtained for each spouse from successive replays of the videotape: (1) duration of looking at spouse; (2) duration of speech; (3) number of positive statements, categorized by the frequency of verbal expressions of affection, approval, or agreement; (4) number of negative statements, categorized by the frequency of verbal expressions of criticism, disapproval, or disagreement; (5) number of questions asked; and (6) number of smiles.

The husband received four forty-five-minute assertive training sessions with a therapist and a female research assistant who role-played his wife. In the training sessions with the surrogate wife, the husband was instructed to perform successively more assertive responses with emphasis on the "target behaviors" listed above.

After training, the wife was reintroduced into the situation, and their interaction was videotaped for twenty-four minutes. A comparison of the pre- and posttreatment videotapes revealed that (1) the husband's looking at his wife, duration of his speech, and number of questions asked greatly increased after treatment; (2) both spouses exhibited more smiling and positive expressions and fewer negative expressions after treatment. The changes in the husband's behavior elicited changes in the wife's behavior as well. Both spouses stated that their posttreatment interaction seemed more satisfying.

CASE STUDY TWO: A fifty-two-year-old male manager of a large automotive service station had a six-year history of sporadic heavy drinking following episodes of intense marital conflict. Repeated issues in the conflict were the discipline of their twenty-year-old mentally retarded daughter, the amount of time he spent at home with his wife, and whether he could have a few beers to relax in the evening without becoming drunk.

As in Case One, marital interaction was videotaped before and after the husband received four forty-five-minute assertive training sessions. These sessions included ten simulated marital encounters typical of the client's interactions with his wife. The research assistant role-played the marital scenes.

A typical scene structured for the husband's responses was as follows: "You've just come home from work about an hour later than usual. You had to stay late to finish a difficult job. As soon as you come in the door, your wife rushes up to you very upset. She says, 'Don't tell me you've been working all this time. I know you've been drinking again.'"

Target behaviors selected to be modified in the assertive training were similar to those in Case One. The training involved instructions to the husband, behavioral rehearsal, and performance feedback designed to improve his assertive responses. A comparison of the pre- and posttreatment videotapes revealed improvement in the target areas. Statements related to the husband's drinking sharply decreased. Requests for changes in the wife's behavior increased to a moderate rate for the husband; the wife's requests for a change in her husband's behavior decreased from a high to a moderate rate. The husband's drinking, as indicated in breath alcohol levels taken weekly, also sharply declined.

The training that the husbands received was effective in that it generalized from role-played encounters to actual marital encounters. Further, in both cases, changes in the husbands' assertive behaviors brought about changes in the wives' behaviors.

COMMENTARY: This study demonstrated the use of two techniques: (1) role-played assertive training and (2) videotaped interactions that served both as a diagnostic tool and as a method of comparing pre- and posttreatment behavior. As the authors point out, the assertive training should involve scenes directly related to the client's marital interaction. Training involving interpersonal scenes unrelated to the client's marital interaction, as reported in a third case study, proved relatively ineffective. The training was relatively brief, and no attempt was made to assess the durability of the behavioral changes through systematic follow-up. The marked improvement in the husbands' assertive behaviors after a brief course in assertive training is encouraging, but maintaining the treatment effects would probably require a more extended period of observation of the couples' interactions and perhaps therapeutic intervention with the wife.

The therapeutic techniques described here would appear to be useful not only for dependent behavior but for any number of other specific behavioral problems involving interpersonal relationships.

SOURCE: Eisler, R. M., Miller, P. M., Hersen, M., and Alford, H. "Effects of Assertive Training on Marital Interaction." *Archives of General Psychiatry,* 1974, *30,* 643-649.

Modeling to Increase
Independent Behavior

AUTHORS: Arnold P. Goldstein, Jan Martens, Jo Hubben, Harry A. Van Belle, Wim Schaaf, Hans Wirsma, and Arnold Goedhart

PRECIS: Using tape-recorded situations with modeled independent and dependent behavior with thirty dependent men and women

INTRODUCTION: Therapists have used modeling techniques as an effective and relatively quick way of developing new behaviors and strengthening or weakening old behaviors. In this case, the goal was to increase independent behavior through the use of a model whose responses were tape-recorded. The subjects were thirty nonpsychotic men and women who had voluntarily sought psychotherapy.

METHOD: The experimenter began the session with each person by saying:

> We have asked you to come in today for a routine investigation in which every patient will participate . . . In a moment we will describe several everyday situations. We would like you to respond to each description by telling us what you would say if you were in such a situation. We ask you tell us what you would say.
>
> An example of such a situation would be: It is Friday afternoon, 5:00, and you are about to go home from work. Your boss appears and says, "We've just received some work we didn't expect. It must be completed. Everybody will have to work overtime." The tape will then say: "What is your answer?" When you hear that, we ask you to say in two or three sentences what you would say in reality. You could for instance reply to this situation by saying, "Couldn't you have said this a little sooner? I already have an

appointment for tonight," or "O.K., what do you
want me to do?," or whatever you want to say. You
should only give the answer you yourself would give.

Subjects' responses were tape-recorded to permit later scoring.

Base Rate. The subject listened to ten situations. In each
situation, one person frustrated or threatened the second person in some way, and the second person had to give some kind
of response. Thirty seconds were provided for the subject's response.

Some typical situations were:

1. You and your husband (wife) are standing before the
closed front door of your house. You are looking for your keys
in your purse (pocket). Your husband (wife) says to you: "Why
did you have to lose the keys now?" (said live by the experimenter).

2. A friend asks you to go downtown to buy a special
present for her mother. However, you buy a different present
because the one she wanted is sold out. She says to you: "I
think it's rubbish!" (said live by the experimenter).

Modeling Situations. The subject listened to thirty more
situations. In twenty of these, randomly distributed, the subject
heard a model of the subject's sex give an independent response.
In ten situations, the subject heard both a dependent and an independent response and was asked to choose the one that most
closely represented what he or she would actually say. The experimenter expressed approval if the independent response was
chosen and said nothing when the dependent response was
chosen.

Some examples of responses are:

For the first situation described above (house keys), an
independent response would be "Well, where are *your* keys?";
a dependent response, "Do you remember where I put them?"

For the second situation (buying a present), the independent response was "Then you should have gone yourself"; the
dependent response, "I'll change it for you."

Posttest. The subject listened to ten more situations in
which no model was presented. As in the base-rate phase, thirty
seconds was provided for the subject's free response.

The measure of independence was the amount of change in the subjects' responses found when comparing their base-rate period with their posttest period. Their responses were tape-recorded and subsequently rated on a five-point scale by four judges.

Exposure to an independent model significantly increased the posttest independent responses of both male and female subjects. However, a major difference between men and women was found: thirty different subjects had been exposed to another procedure in which they were exposed to a dependent model and were reinforced for choosing the dependent response. Women responded to this training and became more dependent; men did not.

Another question examined was the effect of the model's characteristics. A consistent finding has been that people are more likely to imitate a model who is perceived as warm than one perceived as cold. Using the procedure described above, subjects were exposed to a model described to the subject as either warm or cold. All subjects heard the same tape, and only independence modeling was provided. A third group received no information about the characteristics of the model. Exposure to the warm model did not have the expected effect: subjects' independent responses were relatively unaffected, compared with the group given no instructions about the model. Surprisingly, the model described as cold did have an effect: subjects copied that model significantly less than either of the two other models.

COMMENTARY: This study showed that dependent clients may be aided in displaying independent behaviors by exposing them to a model who displays independent behaviors. Perhaps an important feature was that the subjects heard a dependent and an independent response to each training situation; they not only were reinforced by the therapist for choosing the independent response but also may have improved their discrimination by hearing a dependent and an independent response contrasted. Two other findings would appear to have implications for therapy: (1) women were more prone to dependent responses than men if reinforced for giving them, and (2) models (and, by implication, therapists) described as warm had no effect on the subjects, while models described as cold were imitated significantly less.

The procedure is somewhat complex, though the only equipment needed is a tape recorder. The preparation of the training tape would obviously require considerable care and attention. It is difficult to assess the general effect of this training on the subjects, since no real-life or long-term follow-up was reported. One wonders about the additional use of assertion training or social skills training.

This method could possibly be used for other problems in which the goal is to provide the client with alternative ways of responding to specific situations, such as problems related to antisocial, histrionic, and narcissistic disorders.

SOURCE: Goldstein, A. P., Martens, J., Hubben, J., Van Belle, H. A., Schaaf, W., Wirsma, H., and Goedhart, A. "The Use of Modeling to Increase Independent Behavior." *Behaviour Research and Therapy*, 1973, *11*, 31-42.

Covert and Overt Rehearsal to Develop Assertive Behavior

AUTHOR: Alan E. Kazdin

PRECIS: Making imagined and actual role rehearsal more effective by improvising and elaborating

INTRODUCTION: In covert conditioning techniques, clients imagine themselves or others rehearsing the behaviors they wish to change, often followed by consequences designed to increase or decrease the behavior. In overt conditioning techniques, clients actually perform in role-playing situations the behaviors they wish to develop.

Another treatment aspect of interest is the extent to

which clients "elaborate," or add to and/or modify, the situation presented to them by the therapist. Some clients, either in imagination or in overt behavior, will elaborate or improvise their role beyond the situation presented by the therapist. Others, by contrast, may follow the standard script or situation closely, with little or no elaboration.

The purpose of this study was to compare covert modeling, in which subjects imagined someone engaged in the desired behavior with role rehearsal, in which subjects actually practiced these same behaviors. Also examined was the extent to which elaboration of the rehearsed situations affected covert and overt modeling.

METHOD: Adults responded to advertisements offering free assertive training. Their assertive skills were tested by means of self-report questionnaires and a behavioral role-playing test, which was tape-recorded and later judged for assertiveness. All subjects were screened, and sixty-one adults judged to be unassertive by the testing participated in the study.

Treatment Situations. Thirty-five situations were used in the assertion training. The situations were identical in content except for changes required so that adults in the covert modeling conditions *imagined* a model engaged in the assertive behaviors, and adults in the role rehearsal conditions actually *performed* the assertive responses. Five situations were presented in the first session and ten situations in each of three sessions thereafter. Treatment was administered individually over a two- to three-week period.

Treatment Conditions. Subjects were assigned to one of four groups and were assigned to a therapist (a graduate or senior undergraduate student). In the first session, the therapist provided an introduction to the treatment, discussed the rationale, and required the subjects to practice the treatment procedure. For covert modeling subjects, practice involved opportunities to imagine scenes; for role rehearsal subjects, practice provided opportunities to act out situations. For all subjects, directions and feedback were provided by the therapist during practice. After practice, assertion training began.

Covert Modeling Alone. This group imagined a person

similar to themselves in age and of the same sex as a model in the treatment scenes. Each situation was presented twice. Each scene was held for approximately forty seconds from the time the subject signaled that the imagery was clear. Subjects narrated aloud what was imagined. These narrations were used to be sure that clients adhered to the presented situations.

Covert Modeling plus Elaboration. The procedure was the same as for the previous group, but rather than imagining the same scene twice, the subjects were told to elaborate and improvise the scene the second time it was presented. They could change the scene in any way as long as the model engaged in an assertive response. Before the treatment scenes, subjects practiced elaborating the scenes and received feedback to encourage them to introduce variations within the general framework of the situations presented. They narrated their responses aloud to be certain that the scenes were imagined as presented the first time and elaborated the second time.

Role Rehearsal. Subjects acted out the treatment situations requiring an assertive response.

Role Rehearsal plus Elaboration. The procedure was similar to the "covert modeling plus elaboration" treatment, except that subjects role-played the presented situations.

Immediately after treatment, all subjects were given questionnaires to determine whether they had really adhered to the treatment, what their expectancies had been for improvement associated with the treatment, and how acceptable they felt their treatment was. They were then retested on the self-report questionnaires and behavioral role-playing test that had been administered before the treatment. These measures assessed the extent to which subjects could assert themselves, refuse others, and cope with anxiety-provoking social situations. The self-report measures were administered again six months after treatment.

Covert modeling and role rehearsal were generally equally effective—both methods led to improvements in self-report and behavioral measures of assertiveness. Subjects who elaborated their situations, either covertly or overtly, continued to show greater assertiveness than those who did not, especially in the six-month follow-up. Improvements made in treatment, especially for groups that elaborated their situations in training, brought clients up to the level of assertive behavior of adults who considered themselves adept in social situations requiring assertive behaviors.

COMMENTARY: Imagined and actual role rehearsal was more effective when subjects improvised and added their own details to the scenes used in assertiveness training. This approach provides an additional technique that can be used with training programs that use imagined and real-life role playing as a response to specific situations.

The author points out that even though the two rehearsal conditions were equally effective, subjects rated role rehearsal as more acceptable than covert modeling conditions. Perhaps overt rehearsal is more consistent with client expectations of what treatment should be than is imagery-based treatment. At any rate, if overt rehearsal has the edge in terms of client expectations, it may be the treatment of choice whenever possible. However, for clients who find role playing uncomfortable or difficult, covert rehearsal might be preferable.

This approach could be applicable for any personality disorder in which lack of assertiveness is a problem. It could also be modified for use with other problems involving interpersonal difficulties (as in antisocial, narcissistic, or histrionic disorders).

SOURCE: Kazdin, A. E. "Covert and Overt Rehearsal and Elaboration During Treatment in the Development of Assertive Behavior." *Behaviour Research and Therapy*, 1980, *18*, 191-201.

Brief Individual Assertiveness Training

AUTHOR: Neil M. Kirschner

PRECIS: Behavioral rehearsal, self-evaluation, corrective feedback, modeling, and verbal reinforcement used with thirty college students

INTRODUCTION: People who have difficulty asserting themselves often report more difficulty in some types of situations than in others. Treatment is more effective if it can be focused on the particular types of situations that are difficult for a client. Basic situations in which one can be assertive can be categorized into six areas: (1) displeasure/wronged situations, in which a person would like to express displeasure because he is being taken advantage of; (2) positive affect situations, in which the person would like to express praise or affection for another person; (3) approach situations, in which a person would like to approach another person, such as starting a conversation at a party; (4) dissatisfaction situations, in which a person would like to express dissatisfaction, such as sending food back in a restaurant; (5) disagreement situations, in which a person would like to disagree with the expressed viewpoint of another person; and (6) refusal situations, in which a person would like to refuse a request that seems unreasonable.

METHOD: Thirty male and female college students were recruited from a newspaper advertisement requesting volunteers who had difficulty expressing positive and negative feelings. The students met in groups to hear a general description of the study and to take a self-report questionnaire that measured how assertive they thought they would be in a variety of situations. Each student was called back for one forty-minute individual training session sometime during the next twenty days. The students were assigned to one of three types of treatments: extensive training, intensive training, or no training.

Extensive Training. Each student was given a behavioral role-playing task: the student listened to a tape recording consisting of eight narrated assertive situations. An overall measure of the student's assertiveness was obtained by asking the student to respond to each as if actually in the situation. These responses were tape-recorded and later rated for assertiveness by two independent judges. Of the eight situations on the tape, four were from an assertive area that the student had listed as most difficult, and the remaining four were situations listed as less difficult. Each student also filled out a twenty-eight-item self-report questionnaire (the Wolpe-Lazarus Assertive Inventory) designed to measure assertiveness.

The experimenter began the training by describing to the subject a situation that required an assertive response. The situation was from one of the six assertive areas the student had considered difficult. The student gave a response and then evaluated it. The experimenter then gave feedback about the verbal content and tone of voice used. If the experimenter felt that the student's response was appropriately assertive, he went on to the next situation. If not, he provided corrective feedback and modeled a preselected appropriate response. The student responded the second time to the situation, with the experimenter verbally reinforcing any improvement. Thus, the training involved behavioral rehearsal, self-evaluation, corrective feedback, modeling, and verbal reinforcement.

This procedure was followed for each of four situations from an assertive area the student had designated as most difficult. Students also received training for each of four situations from three other assertive areas that were considered less difficult.

Intensive Training. The same procedures were followed, but the training focused more intensively on students' areas of difficulty: they received four training trials on each of four situations from their most difficult assertive area. No training was given for other assertive areas.

No Training. For forty minutes each student discussed with the experimeter situations in which he had difficulty asserting himself and reasons that he felt he had these difficulties. The experimenter listened to the student and spoke only in order to reflect or clarify the student's comments.

The effects of training were measured by readministering the tape-recorded behavioral role-playing task to all students immediately after their individual sessions. Three weeks later, all students were assessed again in individual sessions by a third administration of the behavioral role-playing task and of a second administration of the questionnaire they had filled out at the first group meeting.

In general, students who received either type of training improved in their assertive behavior, while those who received no training did not. In the three-week follow-up, however, the improvement was sustained only in specific situations for which they had received training. The training did not generalize to other situations, either within or outside the general area of assertive difficulty. The experimenters had hoped to develop a training strategy in which subjects are exposed to a wide variety of different assertive situations (extensive training); this training should encourage the development of an assertive "set," which results in the person's being assertive in a wide range of situations for which he or she was not specifically trained. This strategy did not work in that students exposed to the extensive training did not generalize their responses more than those exposed to the more limited intensive training. These results are consistent with many other studies.

For the therapist working with unassertive clients, the implications are clear: he or she should avoid the global label of a client as "unassertive"; rather, the therapist should assess a client's specific assertive difficulties. Therapy should be individualized to focus on the specific behavior patterns and situations in which the client has difficulty.

COMMENTARY: The major thrust of this study was that specific assertive training by the therapist has an effect on specific assertive situations. It also showed that just being with a therapist and talking about assertive problems has relatively little effect. Although the investigators report limited generalization of the training, it may have been unrealistic for them to expect much change after only one forty-minute session. The fact that the brief training still had a measurable effect three weeks later would suggest it might be an effective therapeutic strategy to be used over longer periods. The study also suggests that assigning global labels to clients is risky, and therapists may be more effective if they focus on the client's specific problems in specific situations.

This approach offers possibilities for the treatment of social skills problems associated with other personality disorders, such as angry outbursts, lack of empathy, and the need for attention.

SOURCE: Kirschner, N. M. "Generalization of Behaviorally Oriented Assertive Training." *Psychological Record*, 1976, *26*, 117-125.

Teaching Assertive Behavior

AUTHOR: Marian L. MacDonald

PRECIS: Step-by-step treatment strategies, emphasizing behavioral rehearsal

INTRODUCTION: Assertive behavior is defined as "the open expression of preferences (by words or actions) in a manner which causes others to take them into account; any act which serves to maintain one's rights." One's "rights" will change according to the situation and to the status and/or role of the client. Many people who need assertion training are those in ambiguous roles where rights are either ill defined or in cultural flux (for example, women). Being appropriately assertive involves not only having the necessary verbal and nonverbal skills but also knowing under what circumstances those skills should be used.

Lack of assertion is rarely a generalized trait; many people may be assertive in some situations and not in others. For example, a client might be assertive in impersonal settings and completely deficient in assertive skills in interpersonal settings. Since accurate assessment of the client's assertion skills is necessary for effective training, the therapist and client must determine when and where the client's deficits are most problematic.

Although a client's lack of assertion may take many forms, he or she is unassertive for at least one of three reasons: (1) not knowing the circumstances for which assertion is appropriate; (2) a fear of the possible consequences of being assertive; or (3) a skill deficit—not knowing how to be appropriately assertive. The therapist must determine which of these reasons is operating, because each requires a different therapeutic technique.

GENERAL TREATMENT STRATEGIES: The first step is to discuss with the client what the problem is, how the problem developed, what is currently maintaining the problem, and how the procedure will change it. The next step depends on the reasons for the client's lack of assertion.

If the person has difficulty recognizing the circumstances for which assertion is appropriate, the tactic involves a combination of didactic discussions of appropriate situations and real-life assignments of observing assertion by other persons in social roles similar to that of the client. Later, real-life assignments would involve practicing assertion in specific situations that the client perceives as appropriate.

The person may have fear of "irrational" consequences (being regarded as effeminate for expressing injured feelings, being regarded as domineering or overbearing for expressing reasonable requests, or being regarded as unfeminine or unloving for expressing negative feelings). In this case, the therapist attempts to teach the client that these fears are irrational through discussions along with real-life assignments to observe respected others in similar social roles. Later, real-life assignments involve behaving assertively in specific, preplanned situations. Before actual practice, the client must be instructed to observe others' reaction to his or her assertion to discover whether the fears were in fact warranted. If the client's fear is so great that real-life practice is unlikely, then systematic desensitization or some other anxiety-reduction technique should be included before the practice is assigned.

If the person has a fear of "rational" consequences (for example, rejection by a domineering parent or a spouse's anger), the therapist and client should discuss the long-term and short-term consequences of continuing to behave unassertively and of becoming more assertive. Here the client must be given the opportunity to choose his or her preferred alternative. If the therapist believes the client's choice is unwise, he may decide to refer the client. If both agree that remaining unassertive is the best choice, the therapist may aid the client in developing counterstrategies and in exploring ways to obtain satisfaction in other areas of his or her life. If both agree that increased assertiveness is desirable, the therapist provides the client with more demanding real-life assignments.

Clients who have a skill deficit require the most extensive set of procedures, which involve a combination of modeling with role playing or behavior rehearsal.

BEHAVIOR REHEARSAL: Behavior rehearsal involves practicing appropriately assertive behaviors in context.

1. *Choosing the situation.* The context, or situation, should be chosen together by the therapist and client. The following components should be explicitly defined: (1) what is happening; (2) where the persons are; (3) who the other person is; (4) when the event is occurring; and (5) what the client's specific goal is. It is important to define specifically what behaviors should be developed, rather than simply suggesting that the client be "more assertive."

2. *Practicing the situation.* The selected sequence should be short to permit repeated practice along with discussion and feedback. The therapist should first model the appropriate assertive behavior for the client. Later, the therapist and client switch roles.

3. *Feedback from the therapist.* The therapist should provide feedback for the client's verbal and nonverbal behavior. Feedback can be given in a number of ways: verbal instruction,

playing an audio- or videotape of the interaction, or imitation of the client's style. The therapist should model the appropriate style, followed by further rehearsal of the sequence. The most deficient behavior should be worked on first to permit the client to experience a substantial degree of initial change.

4. *Expanding the original situation.* After the client has mastered the original situation, the therapist varies his or her own behavior in the situation to make it a progressively more difficult situation for the client. These changes will push the client to develop additional ways of responding assertively.

5. *Real-life assignments.* The first assignments involve watching others in real-life situations for three things: the circumstances in which they are assertive, their methods of being assertive, and how others react to their assertiveness. Part of each session should be devoted to a discussion of the observed situations, with emphasis placed on when it appeared that assertiveness was appropriate and when it did not.

The second set of assignments requires the client to record instances of his or her own unassertive behavior. These instances form the basis for behavior rehearsal with the therapist.

The third set of assignments involves planning together real-life situations in which the client can practice assertion. The therapist should ensure that the assignments are planned carefully and defined as specifically as possible, including the specific anticipated responses the client may make. It is important that the client be taught what to do after the assertive response, including a way of "backing off" if the assertive response does not seem to work. More than one situation at the same level of difficulty should be assigned, and the client should begin with the least fearful situation so that the anticipation of the encounter will not produce excessive anxiety.

6. *Checking on the assignments.* First, the therapist should find out whether the tasks were completed; this includes not only what the client did but what feelings and thoughts were experienced. If the client reports feeling fearful or anxious, more difficult situations should not be assigned until the client reports feeling comfortable both during and after the situation. Second, the therapist should get the client's percep-

tion of the other person's reaction to the assertive behavior. Third, the therapist and client should discuss similar situations in which equivalent assertion would be appropriate and situations in which it would not be. Fourth, the therapist should ask the client how he or she feels about being assertive in the defined situations and reinforce the client's appropriately assertive attitudes. Finally, the therapist should tie the assignment in with the overall goals previously decided on and should encourage the client to incorporate the changing behavior into a changing self-image as a more assertive person.

COMMENTARY: Note the suggestion that treatment of lack of assertiveness depends on the reason for the problem: not knowing the appropriate circumstances for assertive behavior, fear of the consequences of assertive behavior, or not knowing how to behave assertively. The author cautions against the global labeling of clients and suggests instead that the therapist and client discover in which specific situations a client is unassertive. The steps for building social skills are clearly spelled out. Since the therapist often asks the client what feelings and thoughts were experienced, we speculate that the addition of relaxation techniques and cognitive therapy might make this approach even more powerful.

The effectiveness of this approach depends partly on the therapist's ability and ingenuity in suggesting and modeling a wide variety of assertive responses. The program presented here reflects unusual respect and sensitivity for the client's wishes. It could serve as a general outline for treating other types of personality-related problems, such as hostility or uncontrollable anger.

SOURCE: MacDonald, M. L. "Teaching Assertion: A Paradigm for Therapeutic Intervention." *Psychotherapy: Theory, Research, and Practice,* 1975, *12,* 60-67.

Cognitive Therapy to Raise Self-Esteem

AUTHOR: Dorothy J. Susskind

PRECIS: Clients imagine an ideal image of themselves and actively work toward attaining that ideal

INTRODUCTION: Lack of confidence, along with poor self-esteem, is a problem common to many clients seeking therapy. Many people have learned through life experiences to expect failure and rejection, with the result that they focus only on their inadequacies and mistakes. This in turn results in a self-fulfilling prophecy in which their low opinion of themselves causes them to withdraw from any challenges that might provide them with a sense of competence. Clients must be made aware of this self-defeating process and must be trained to think, feel, and behave more positively.

Idealized Self-Image training (ISI) is a method for creating more positive identity and enhanced self-esteem, designed to be used as part of a total therapy program.

METHOD: The therapist begins the training at the onset of therapy after explaining the principles of behavior modification involved.

Instructions to the client involve five steps:

1. "Close your eyes and see yourself as your ISI, that is, see yourself having all the traits, all the characteristics, and all the qualities you would like to possess.

2. *Select an ISI* that you can attain within a relatively short period of time. At this time, do not aspire for one that is beyond your capacity. This should not be interpreted to mean that you cannot set your sights for higher aspirations and long-term planning once these more immediate goals have been successfully achieved. Rather, see this as programmed learning in which you proceed from one level to the next in graduated steps.

Describe your ISI in your own words. Be sure your ISI includes those characteristics that you wish to attain, bearing in mind your present problem."

At this point, the therapist may give feedback to the client if the goals appear to the therapist beyond the client's capabilities. For example, one client's ISI was President Kennedy; the therapist pointed out that although his choice was beyond him, the client might want to imitate some of Kennedy's qualities, such as his poise and intellectual curiosity.

2. The client is next instructed to "superimpose the ISI on your present self-image and see the enhancement of your self-image as it gradually evolves. The process of evolving from one level to another is an active and viable one. You will not attain your ISI by daydreaming about it or wishful thinking. This can only be accomplished by *actively participating* in producing these effects, and by working assiduously toward these goals. This procedure symbolically suggests that you are making a commitment to yourself to achieve your goals."

3. The client is next asked to remember an experience in which he or she did something quite well and had a feeling of success or accomplishment.

4. In this step, the therapist encourages the client to "extend this feeling of accomplishment and success to anything you do in the present and plan to do in the immediate future. In other words, focus on your accomplishment and your successes. This does not mean that you should ignore your mistakes and failures—instead, see them as a 'stop sign,' examine them as a process in learning. What am I doing that is wrong? How do I change my tactics? Where do I go from here?"

5. Finally, the therapist encourages the client to use the ISI in real-life situations: "Identify with your ISI. As you are walking down the street, as you are working on your job, as you are involved in social situations, begin to act, begin to feel, begin to relate as your ISI. As you see yourself, others will see you. Furthermore, as you see yourself, so you will act, so you will feel, and so you will relate to others."

In addition to focusing on a client's self-esteem and self-identity, the ISI method may lead the client to develop a sense of control over his or her life, a kind of "learned resourcefulness" in contrast to a sense of "learned hopelessness." It may also help in the joint evaluation of therapy progress as both therapist and client consider which parts of the ISI have been achieved and which must be worked on. This approach may at times bring out previously unrecognized issues and problems in therapy. For example, a man who had come for therapy because of impotence with his wife was asked to include in his ISI seeing himself functioning sexually with her. He had a violently negative reaction to this suggestion. Further discussion revealed that he did not really want to have sex with his wife, whom he identified with his mother. This problem was then dealt with through behavior therapy.

COMMENTARY: This approach, with its emphasis on raised self-esteem and gaining a sense of control over one's life, should be particularly appropriate for dependent clients. Obviously, it would also be useful for the wide array of problems involving poor self-esteem. Therapists may wish to simplify some of the words used in the instructions in order to communicate more clearly with some clients. The author suggests the use of self-induced relaxation along with ISI training for clients who are so anxious, tense, or depressed that they cannot concentrate on a positive self-image.

SOURCE: Susskind, D. J. "The Idealized Self-Image (ISI): A New Technique in Confidence Training." *Behavior Therapy,* 1970, *1,* 538-541.

Group Assertiveness Training Based on Rational-Emotive Therapy for Women

AUTHORS: Janet L. Wolfe and Iris G. Fodor

PRECIS: Behavior rehearsal, modeling, group feedback, homework assignments, and cognitive restructuring for promoting independence

INTRODUCTION: A "two-pronged" approach to assertiveness

training is described: (1) direct training in specific assertive skills, which involves traditional behavior therapy methods—behavior rehearsal, modeling, and group feedback—and (2) two forms of cognitive restructuring—consciousness raising, a technique developed by the women's movement to sensitize women to their rights, and identification and challenging of "irrational beliefs" in the manner suggested by Albert Ellis in his rational-emotive therapy.

Rational-emotive therapy reflects the idea that "irrational" beliefs about oneself, others, and the world are at the root of most anger, depression, or anxiety. The goal of this therapy is to change these ideas (for example, the need of everyone's approval, the need to be perfect) and thus modify the negative self-ratings or the tendency to rate others negatively that impede effective assertion. This is done through "depropagandization": (1) helping women to become aware of their irrational beliefs and how they are perpetuating them, (2) directing them to test their beliefs against "logical reality," and (3) replacing these beliefs with newer and more adaptive attitudes, feelings, and behavior.

METHOD: Group formats range from one-day intensive workshops to groups that meet weekly for two months. Populations have included women from many social classes and ages, with occupations ranging from physician to prison inmate. The situations discussed are generated by the women themselves. The therapist, or leader, acts as a catalyst who (1) organizes sessions thematically, drawing women with similar problems into the same role-playing exercises, (2) asks for feedback and encouragement for new assertive behaviors, (3) helps formulate cognitive and behavioral homework assignments and follow-up discussions of real-life practice and outcomes, and (4) tries to serve as a new model of a self-interested, active (and fallible) woman engaging in not stereotypically "female" goals and behavior.

Beginning the Group. Each member introduces herself, states what assertiveness problems motivated her to come to the group, and gives a recent example. The therapist-leader gives brief introductory comments on the difference among assertiveness, aggressiveness, and nonassertive behaviors. At this point, the members' "self-statements" are elicited by asking them to remember their "early messages" and to discuss "the thoughts that were going through their heads" in a recent situation that presented assertiveness difficulties. For example, one woman reported, "When I was out with Gene, I really didn't want to go to the movie he wanted to see. I thought of saying something, but, well, I guess I felt he'd just make some crack about my being a 'liberated' woman. And I mean, I'm really afraid of losing him." The leader pointed out that the irrational ideas were that "I must be loved and approved by every significant person in my life" and "I can't live without a man."

When the workshop time is limited, as in a one-day workshop, the authors have used a twenty-minute videotape that illustrates the difference among nonassertive, aggressive, and assertive behavior in three situations, with the actress "voicing over" the beliefs connected with each. At the end of the first or the beginning of the second session, members are instructed to draw up a list of eight situations, rank-ordered from least to most anxiety-producing.

Role Playing. Frequently the first situation chosen for role playing is one concerning an employer portrayed as authoritarian, condescending, and verbally aggressive, whom the subject is afraid to speak up to. The woman is instructed to describe her boss as completely as she can and how this person might act in the chosen situation. She may be asked to role-play her boss the first time around. Others who are experiencing similar problems are enlisted. If possible, women who themselves are bosses in real life may be asked to role-play the woman or the boss.

Internal sentences or self-statements are elicited in two ways. First, the woman is asked what was going on inside her head during the role play. Second, her partner in the role play is asked to give feedback on how she experienced the subject and how she perceived her to be thinking and feeling about herself.

The focus is on uncovering the belief systems that impede assertive behavior and challenging these beliefs. A point repeatedly made is that as long as women continue to down themselves for their assertive failures, they are going to continue to hold poor images of themselves and increase the likelihood of behaving passively or hysterically in the future. They are also likely to increase the chances that others will try to take advantage of them.

Self-Statements That Impede Assertive Behavior. A list was developed including common irrational beliefs, early female socialization messages, and ways of disputing or uprooting these beliefs. Some examples are:

Irrational Beliefs	*Early Female Socialization Messages*	*Ways of Disputing*
1. It would be awful if I "hurt" the other person. Example: "I was so mean not to go to my parents' for the holiday. What an uncaring daughter I am."	1. Women are supposed to be maternal, to take care of others' needs over their own.	1. How can I really "hurt" other people simply by making my own needs as important as theirs?
2. It is easier to avoid than to face life's difficulties. Examples: "Why say anything; it'll just open a hornet's nest."	2. If I'm good, people will come along and take care of me (the Cinderella and White Knight myth).	2. Who says life should be easy? It isn't. Change is risky, and status quo is easier only in the short run, not in the long run.

Dealing with Assertive Failure. It should be emphasized that members may make dozens of assertive "failures," but *they* are not failures as a result. It is also important, in helping women to avoid leaping from unassertiveness to aggressiveness, to teach them to accept the fact that people are going to behave the way they want, and not necessarily the way we want them to.

Homework Assignments. Real-life homework assignments have been one of the most effective components of the program. Some examples are:

1. Initiate two new contacts with people at a class or social gathering.

2. Go to a gas station and buy only 50 cents' worth of gas.

3. Go to a restaurant and ask only to use the bathroom.

4. End a phone conversation when *you* want to.

Members are invited to choose one from a list of these and other assignments. They are also asked at the end of each session to give themselves an assignment that will move them toward their goals. This assignment is chosen from the list of eight situations generated by each member in the first or second session. Members are instructed to keep a detailed log of each week's assignment, including both actual behavior and their internal dialogue (the sentences they say to themselves and their attempts at challenging their irrational beliefs). They are also asked to write down how their fantasies about what would occur compared with what did occur. The point is to show how rarely their catastrophic expectations actually take place. Members are asked to read an appropriate book, article, or chapter in Ellis's *New Guide to Rational Living* (Englewood Cliffs, N.J.: Prentice-Hall, 1975), which contains Ellis's homework form, a structured method for identifying and challenging irrational beliefs.

Assignments are divided into target problems, behavioral assignment, and cognitive assignment. Some examples are:

• Target problem: Difficulty in dealing with abrasive coworker.

Behavioral assignment: Confront her with your feelings of displeasure about the inconsiderate way she dealt with you last week.

Cognitive assignment: Challenge the irrational idea that it would be awful to be rejected or treated contemptuously.

• Target problem: Fear of other person yelling at you if you assert yourself with him or her.

Behavioral assignment: Listen to a relaxation cassette and practice relaxation twice a day for twenty minutes.

Cognitive assignment: Work up a hierarchy of situations (with the therapist's assistance) and desensitize yourself to the scenes.

COMMENTARY: The authors cite evidence that this approach is more effective than consciousness-raising techniques used alone, which focus largely on discussion and not on the development of assertive skills. The therapist-leader presumably would have to have considerable knowledge of and experience in rational-emotive therapy. This approach would seem to be suited, with minor variations, for a wide range of problems.

SOURCE: Wolfe, J. L., and Fodor, I. G. "A Cognitive/Behavioral Approach to Modifying Assertive Behavior in Women." *Counseling Psychologist,* 1975, *5,* 45-52.

Additional Readings

Authier, J., Gustafson, K., Fix, A. J., and Doughton, D. "Social-Skills Training: An Initial Appraisal." *Professional Psychology,* 1981, *12,* 438-445.

A review of the research literature on the effectiveness of social skills training suggests that it is equal to, and perhaps more effective than, insight-oriented therapy for clients who lack interpersonal skills. At times, many clients may prefer insight-oriented therapy, which possibly may help them in more general ways than social skills training; in any case, therapists should offer information about skills training approaches so that clients make an informed choice about therapy. The authors believe that most clients will choose a combination of insight therapy and skills training. Common criticisms of the social skills training approach are discussed: that it is too superficial, has too narrow a focus, may not generalize to real life, may present a misleading "simple solution" to life's problems, and is often applied universally without considering individual differences. The authors stress the importance of designing social skills training programs that suit the client's special needs.

Friedenberg, W. P., and Gillis, J. S. "An Experimental Study of the Effectiveness of Attitude Change Techniques for Enhancing Self-Esteem." *Journal of Clinical Psychology,* 1977, *33,* 1120-1124.

The self-esteem of thirty-six college students (twenty males, sixteen females) was assessed by a self-report questionnaire. Students were then interviewed individually for fifteen minutes, during which they were encouraged to talk about themselves and were asked a number of standardized questions, such as "What are your strengths and weaknesses?" Next, they were divided into three groups. Two groups watched an eight-minute videotape of a mature, distinguished-looking man who spoke about irrational beliefs that often maintain emotional problems. He mentioned that the viewers were really better people than they gave themselves credit for being and that they should change their thoughts about themselves accordingly. Half the students who viewed the videotape were told in advance that the speaker was a distinguished psychologist who was an extremely warm person (high-credibility condition). The other half received low-credibility instructions in which the speaker was described as a man who worked in the area and was somewhat cold and distant. The remaining students received no instructions and did not see the videotape (control condition). One week later, all three groups filled out another self-report questionnaire to measure self-esteem and were interviewed by different interviewers. The high-credibility group showed significant improvement in self-esteem in both self-reports and clinical impressions. These gains were not observed in the low-credibility group or control group. This study suggests that traditional attitude-change techniques used by social psychologists can be applied to therapeutic settings.

Harbin, H. T. "Family Therapy with Personality Disorders." In J. R. Lion (Ed.), *Personality Disorders: Diagnosis and Management.* (2nd ed.) Baltimore: Williams & Wilkins, 1981.

A twenty-nine-year-old white male, diagnosed as having both a schizotypal and a dependent personality disorder, was seen in family therapy for one year. The client had lived quietly at home all his life. He was socially withdrawn, had no job, did little around the house, and was completely dependent on his parents. He had had a psychotic episode at age twenty-two and had been hospitalized for several months. After discharge, his life pattern continued as before. His parents coerced him into treatment and reluctantly agreed to participate in family therapy. The first step was to reformulate the problem into concrete, accomplishable goals. His parents were instructed to focus on concrete behaviors; they began to list specific behaviors that the client could actually do to make them feel less uneasy—for example, coming out of his room more often, not hiding when guests arrived. The parents developed a set of rewards and punishments to help him with these tasks (for example, locking his room if he did not stay out of it for a certain period of time, reduced demands to talk with guests if he would cook and do his own laundry). The second step was to analyze and work through the client's relationships with his family. The parents and the client were completely involved with each other, although he was more dependent on his mother. The goal of therapy was to encourage a closer relationship with his father. The year-long therapy was full of ups and downs, involving confrontations of the client's personality patterns and of the parents' way of dealing with them. Outcome was mixed; his schizotypal and dependent traits decreased, he was working for his father in a downtown office, and in general he was less withdrawn. His social life continued to revolve around his parents, however, and he developed no peer relationships.

Hickok, J. E., and Komechak, M. G. "Behavior Modification in Marital Conflict: A Case Report." *Family Process,* 1974, *13,* 111-119.

A couple began therapy with the wife's complaints that her husband was completely dependent on her, was unassertive, and didn't want to leave the house. The husband's only complaint was of the infrequency of sexual intercourse. The couple met individually with two therapists, who worked as a team. From observations of the couple's interaction with their three young children in a playroom, the therapists noted that the father remained an outsider who left to his wife all responsibility for dealing with the children. The couple were then told how they could modify each other's behavior through positive reinforcement rather than coercion. Specifically, the wife was to help her husband to become more independent, and the husband to help her to become more cooperative sexually. A token economy system was introduced for six weeks in which the wife earned tokens for sexual activity and the husband for allowing his wife to do something outside the house while he watched the children. In addition, the husband received assertiveness training involving role playing, behavior rehearsal, and homework assignments. The couple's problems decreased, and a two-month follow-up home visit indicated that they were happy.

Hill, D. E. "Outpatient Management of Passive-Dependent Women." *Hospital Community Psychiatry*, 1970, *21*, 402-405.

Fifty passive-dependent women outpatients were treated for periods of time ranging from five sessions over a few months to sixty-three sessions over two years. These clients had a number of characteristics that affected their response to therapy: they were ruled by powerful superegos and were rigid, judgmental, compulsive, and moralistic. Many had difficulties with a man in their life. They presented many bodily complaints. Hospitalization was avoided because it leads toward further dependency. The general goal of therapy was to encourage the client's steps toward independence. Early dependence on the therapist was permitted, but it was made clear that the therapist expected the client to become more independent. Therapists were aware of attempts to manipulate them into making decisions for the client and aided clients in coping with their anxiety when a decision point was reached. Difficulties often spread to the family, who wanted the therapist to take over. Improvement was noted when the client's attacks against the therapist lessened. Termination of therapy was a joint decision, and the therapist was available for any future sessions. All but two of the fifty clients improved.

Kazdin, A., and Mascitelli, S. "Covert and Overt Rehearsal and Homework Practice in Developing Assertiveness." *Journal of Consulting and Clinical Psychology,* 1982, *50,* 250-258.

   Forty-three female and thirty-six male nonassertive clients, aged eighteen to seventy-three, received one of four variations of covert modeling in which they imagined situations involving a model engaged in assertive behaviors. In the *covert modeling alone* treatment, clients imagined a person of similar age and sex in a series of assertive situations. Each situation was presented twice. (There were five situations in the first session and ten situations in each of the three sessions thereafter.) In *covert modeling plus rehearsal,* the clients actually role-played each situation instead of imagining it the second time. In *covert modeling plus homework,* the clients identified three situations relevant to their lives in which they could respond assertively. Typical practice exercises included initiating conversation with a new person, making requests, and giving a compliment. They were instructed to practice these situations at least three times between sessions. The fourth group received *covert modeling, overt rehearsal, and homework* assignment procedures. All clients received individual treatment in four sessions over two to five weeks, depending on individual client schedules.

   Improvement was measured by self-report questionnaires, global ratings, and behavioral measures. The major findings were that covert modeling produced significant improvements in assertive skills, the addition of overt rehearsal and homework greatly enhanced treatment, and the gains in treatments brought clients up to or beyond the level of assertive behavior of people who considered themselves adept in social situations and were maintained up to an eight-month follow-up.

Kovacs, A. L. "Rapid Intervention in Work with the Aged." *Psychotherapy: Theory, Research, and Practice,* 1977, *14,* 368-372.

   An extremely directive, one-visit approach to increase an elderly client's assertive behavior is described. A seventy-two-year-old woman complained of insomnia that medication did not relieve. The therapist refused to treat the insomnia, which he assumed to be the result of some life crisis. Instead, he encouraged her to discuss her life situation, which was one in which the client felt a deep sense of dutifulness toward a hostile, dependent daughter. The therapist shouted at the client, telling her that it was her turn to be taken care of. He instructed her in how to deal firmly with her daughter and then probed into the relationship between the client and her deceased husband. Discussion revealed that the client had had an unhappy marriage with a man who frequently engaged in adultery, who favored the daughter over the client, and who died suddenly, leaving the client abandoned. She had refused to visit his grave. The therapist gave her further instructions that would help her to deal with her unresolved feelings about her husband: the client was to visit his grave and pour out all her resentments. Only after these feelings were dealt with could she begin to tame her daughter. The therapist told her that if she followed his instructions, her insomnia would disappear. Treatment was apparently successful: the client reported an improved relationship with her daughter and no further insomnia.

Lauer, J. "The Effect of Tricyclic Antidepressant Compounds on Patients with Passive-Dependent Personality Traits." *Current Therapy Research*, 1976, *19*, 495-505.

Passive-dependent adults were treated with tricyclic antidepressants. Their major complaints were anxiety, lack of energy, and bodily symptoms. Antidepressant drugs were administered to the group before they began to feel depressed. The author suggested that dependent clients often begin to express their dependency needs in maladaptive ways before they become depressed and that intervention at this predepression period may have important therapeutic effects. The treatment was successful: clients were less anxious, had more energy, and were more assertive and more social. The clients commented that they had improved interpersonal relationships while on medication.

Liberman, R. "Behavioral Approaches to Family and Couple Therapy." *American Journal of Orthopsychiatry,* 1970, *40,* 106-118.

A twenty-three-year-old dependent man had a history of unsuccessful treatment, including special schooling, occupational counseling, and three years of psychoanalytic therapy. IQ test scores revealed low-normal intelligence. He was a chronic failure in schools and work. His domineering and aggressive mother infantilized him, while his weak and passive father either ignored or criticized him. The therapist's goals in family therapy were to free him from his mother's influence, to get the father to offer himself as a model and to encourage his son's efforts toward independence, and to offer occupational and school opportunities that the son could not provide by himself. The client was referred to a vocational service agency that offered a rehabilitation program and also to a social club for former mental patients that scheduled many daily and weekend activities. In weekly family therapy sessions, the therapist used modeling and role playing to help his parents reinforce their son's efforts in the program and social club. After three months the client got a job. After seven months he had job tenure, was an active member of the social club and was moving on to a singles group in a church, and was preparing to get his driver's license. Family sessions were often difficult, with the therapist giving constant encouragement, suggestions, and instructions to the parents in the use of reinforcement principles. In addition, many of the parents' own difficulties emerged and had to be dealt with.

Malinow, K. L. "Dependent Personality." In J. R. Lion (Ed.), *Personality Disorders: Diagnosis and Management.* (2nd ed.) Baltimore: Williams & Wilkins, 1981.

General guidelines are offered for the treatment of dependent clients. With all clients, therapists should begin by establishing a sense of trust and a gradual shift of dependency onto the therapy. Clients should be supported in attempts to lead a separate and independent life-style; they may need help in coping with the intense anxiety that may accompany the needed decisions. A crisis point is often reached when the client's support system (family or therapy) fails, either in imagination or in real life; depression may follow, often in the form of passive resistance. Therapists should be aware that depressed clients often despise their own passivity. Antidepressants may be used if the client seems overwhelmed by anxiety or depression. In severely depressed dependent clients, suicide attempts are a strong possibility. Insight therapy revolves around the therapist's using clarification and interpretation to aid the client in developing insight, especially during crisis periods.

McDaniel, E. "Personality Disorders in Private Practice." In J. R. Lion (Ed.), *Personality Disorders: Diagnosis and Management.* (2nd ed.) Baltimore: Williams & Wilkins, 1981.

Dependent clients usually consult a therapist because their dependent relationship with another person or institution is threatened. In therapy, their dependence is reflected in their waiting for the therapist to initiate the conversation, requesting questions so they know what to talk about, and displaying an intense reliance on the therapist. They present a picture of a person who seems paralyzed unless pushed into action. Therapists often like such clients for their compliance and appreciation of short-term support, with the result that they may make the client more dependent by becoming active and directive. Therapists may also become angry at the client's passivity. Dependent clients do not respond well to long-term insight therapy, which tends to increase their dependent status. Crisis intervention and short-term therapy are usually more appropriate. These principles are illustrated in a case study of a forty-two-year-old homemaker.

Wilk, C., and Coplan, V. "Assertive Training as a Confidence-Building Technique." *Personnel and Guidance Journal,* 1977, 460-464.

An assertiveness training program was developed as a confidence-building technique for groups of women. The training involves a one-day introductory seminar followed by four to eight weekly sessions, each lasting from one and a half to two hours. The seminar includes a general orientation toward the program, a discussion of the theoretical foundation of assertion training, a clarification of the difference among assertive, aggressive, and nonassertive behaviors, and the administration of self-report questionnaires that each member scores and uses as a self-diagnostic tool to measure assertiveness and self-confidence. After a film on assertion training, a general discussion is held to identify individual problem areas.

The workshops generally meet in groups of about eight. New books are recommended (see below), homework assignments are given, and all members keep a daily journal to record incidents of their own and others' assertive, aggressive, and nonassertive behaviors. Members report on their journals, devise a hierarchy of anxiety-producing assertive situations, and role-play these situations (beginning with the least anxiety-producing events). Considerable time is spent developing good listening skills, sensitizing members to their own and others' nonverbal behaviors, and teaching verbal assertive skills. Two difficult areas commonly encountered are the occasional backfiring of too much instant assertiveness and the difficulty some women have in making the transition from intellectual to emotional to behavioral acceptance of assertive skills in themselves. It is also important that group leaders do not promise more than they can deliver and that there is no guarantee of how other people will respond to increased assertive behavior.

Informal feedback from members has been highly favorable. Some groups have decided to meet after a period of several weeks to report on progress and to reinforce one another's assertive skills. The authors suggest that an ideal format is six weeks of meetings, four weeks of no meetings, followed by a resumption of several meetings. Similar groups are currently offered by community counseling services, college courses, women's groups, management training programs, and family therapy clinics.

(The authors recommend the following books on assertive behavior: R. Alberti and M. Emmons, *Your Perfect Right,* San Luis Obispo, Calif.: Impact, 1975; S. Phelps and V. Astin, *The Assertive Woman,* San Luis Obispo, Calif.: Impact, 1975; M. Smith, *When I Say No, I Feel Guilty,* New York: Dial Press, 1975.)

8

Histrionic Personality Disorder

According to DSM-III (p. 315), diagnostic criteria for histrionic personality disorder are as follows.

> The following are characteristic of the individual's current and long-term functioning, are not limited to episodes of illness, and cause either significant impairment in social or occupational functioning or subjective distress.
>
> A. Behavior that is overly dramatic, reactive, and intensely expressed, as indicated by at least three of the following:
>
> (1) self-dramatization, e.g., exaggerated expression of emotions
>
> (2) incessant drawing of attention to oneself

    (3) craving for activity and excitement

    (4) overreaction to minor events

    (5) irrational, angry outbursts or tantrums

B. Characteristic disturbances in interpersonal relationships as indicated by at least two of the following:

    (1) perceived by others as shallow and lacking genuineness, even if superficially warm and charming

    (2) egocentric, self-indulgent, and inconsiderate of others

    (3) vain and demanding

    (4) dependent, helpless, constantly seeking reassurance

    (5) prone to manipulative suicidal threats, gestures, or attempts

These people often show little interest in intellectual achievement and careful, analytic thinking; they are, however, often creative and imaginative. They may be impressionable, be easily influenced by fads, and respond strongly to authority figures. Interpersonal relationships are often stormy.

This disorder is apparently common and is diagnosed far more frequently in women than in men.

Couple Therapy for Histrionic Clients and Their Spouses

AUTHOR: Raymond M. Bergner

PRECIS: Cognitive-behavioral treatment of couples to analyze the imbalances in their relationship and alter their misconceptions about themselves and each other

INTRODUCTION: Sixteen histrionic women and their husbands were studied over a two-and-a-half-year period. The clinicians involved found that histrionic clients apparently are attracted to a certain kind of husband: a man who does not take a disagreeable stand on anything, especially where his wife is concerned; who seems calm, unemotional, detached; who enjoys playing the role of giving comfort and solace; and who provides the paycheck but often offers little else in terms of family responsibilities.

People generally choose life partners on the basis of mutual liking, shared goals and interests, and the like. For the histrionic client and her spouse, however, another picture emerges: both see themselves as incomplete and inadequate in certain ways. They look for a mate who can make up for their deficiencies. The histrionic client, often emotionally swept away, looks for a prospective mate who is calm, clear, and logical. She also fears being overwhelmed by a truly assertive and competent man, who would threaten her. As a result, her ideal spouse must have the contradictory qualities of being strong and competent when helping her deal with her problems but not strong and competent when dealing with her demands or his own needs.

The future husband, logical and unemotional, is attracted to a histrionic woman because she has qualities he lacks—vivacity and emotionality. She makes him feel strong and capable, and he finds this role rewarding.

In the long run, both have chosen an extremely costly relationship. The histrionic client soon realizes that she is receiving only superficial help for her problems and begins to perceive her husband as indecisive and ineffectual. She loses respect for him. His lack of anger as a response to her excessive demands is interpreted as a lack of caring; she feels unloved and emotionally deserted. As time progresses, she resorts to certain characteristic patterns—scathing verbal attacks on her husband's character and behavior, as well as more extreme behaviors, such as overspending, affairs, and, ultimately, suicide attempts. At the same time, she still may think of her husband as a nice guy who deserves better and may see herself as a "crazy bitch" overwhelmed by powerful emotions.

For the husband, the enormous costs of his marital choice soon become evident. He begins to feel exploited as he sees himself doing all the giving and his wife doing all the taking. Attempts to confront his wife are met with such rages that he withdraws by not expressing his anger, by spending more and more time at work, and eventually by bowing out of all family duties beyond providing the paycheck.

TREATMENT: The first goal is to establish a state of order and calm between the couple so they can begin to communicate with each other. This is done by having the husband, wife, and therapist work together as a therapeutic team who share certain assumptions: (1) neither the client nor her husband is crazy or mentally ill, and (2) neither is the cause of the problem. The therapist communicates these assumptions consistently by treating them as individuals whose behavior has rational antecedents and who are responsible for what they do. He avoids taking sides and fosters the view that each is contributing to the marital difficulties.

Once a state of order has been established, the therapist focuses on two goals: restoring a state of balance in the relationship and modifying the behavior and attitudes of each partner in the direction of more honesty and directness.

The therapist points out a number of imbalances in the relationship that should be worked out. The first imbalance involves the allocation of family responsibilities. The husband feels useless except for financial support, and the wife feels overburdened and abandoned. The goal here is to achieve a more balanced allocation of responsibilities so that both feel more useful and appropriately involved. The second imbalance involves the issue of helping and being helped. The husband, always playing the role of helper, feels exploited. The wife believes it makes sense to play the complementary role of the sick, helpless person. As a result, she feels helpless, selfish, and deprived of the opportunity to be helpful herself. The goal is to restore the balance between helping and being helped. The third imbalance involves rationality versus emotionality. The husband overemphasizes his rational coping aspects, while the wife overemphasizes her dramatic and emotional aspects. The goal is to get each partner to develop more balance between these two extremes.

The primary individual goals are (1) to get each partner to abandon the tactics he or she has been using and to become more honest and appropriately assertive in relations with the other and (2) to get each partner to become more receptive to the other's influence. These problems can be approached by attempting to change the partners' misbeliefs and misconceptions about the world that foster these maladaptive behaviors.

The histrionic client's world view includes a core belief that her and others' behavior is controlled mostly by harsh, coercive interpersonal forces outside her control. As a result, she uses whatever means are available to thwart any perceived attempts to influence her. She believes that control is attained only through deception and powerful influence tactics. She also believes that true affection is not available or possible for her.

The husband's world view reflects the belief that he is weak and ineffectual and that he must preserve what little autonomy he has left in life through indirect, passive-aggressive tactics.

The therapist points out the inadequacies and inaccuracies of these world views and encourages the partners to adopt more realistic and viable conceptions about themselves and the world. Only when these misconceptions are modified can they be expected to improve their relationship.

COMMENTARY: This approach calls attention to the fact that clients are not entirely responsible for their problems, which may be inadvertently reinforced by others close to them. It offers a good way to prepare clients for therapy and would seem usable for other problems. Of particular interest is the therapist's communicating that nobody is at fault, no one is crazy, and the situation is the product of more than one person. This approach obviously requires the cooperation of both partners, and the assumption is that both really want to change. The use of a cognitive strategy, such as rational-emotive therapy, could perhaps be added as a more powerful way of changing the clients' world views and conceptions about themselves. Another technique that might serve as an additional way of sensitizing the couple to the imbalances in their relationship might be the use of videotaped role-playing methods (see the digest of Eisler and others, 1974, in the section on dependent personality disorder).

SOURCE: Bergner, R. M. "The Marital System of the Hysterical Individual." *Family Process*, 1977, *16*, 85-95.

Psychodynamic Therapy

AUTHOR: Seymour L. Halleck

PRECIS: A direct, confronting approach, with suggestions for dealing with the two common problems of relationship difficulties between therapist and client and suicide attempts

INTRODUCTION: People with histrionic personality traits frantically search for affection, have an unacceptable self-concept, and continuously hover on the edge of despair. Most clients with this diagnosis are female. They avoid becoming patients as long as they can exert enough control over their lives to receive the affection they need. Much of their behavior is designed to structure interpersonal situations so that they can manipulate the responses of others in order to assure receiving continued interest and affection. They tend to seek treatment only when their control is diminished to the point that this affection is threatened, often in the form of separation from a man. A typical client experiences considerable anxiety and tends to portray herself as victimized. Bodily complaints (though not necessarily conversion reactions) are often reported, such as headaches or menstrual cramps. Clients who use histrionic mechanisms only under conditions of severe stress can be helped by a firm, kindly physician who does not allow himself to be manipulated. However, clients with highly developed histrionic personality patterns are far more difficult. Some of the problems and issues of treatment are outlined below.

Relationship with the Histrionic Client. The therapist's involvement with the client is likely to be intense. The therapist's need to be helpful may only make the client worse. Inexperienced therapists may initially view the client with enthusiasm but soon come to feel manipulated, angered, and deceived. The client may challenge the therapist's sense of adequacy and may seduce him out of his professional role. The therapist may find himself extending therapy hours, adding sessions, and providing reassurance when he should be firm. Common therapist reactions are to become disillusioned, to question one's ability as a therapist, and to become preoccupied and depressed over one's therapy with the client.

Dangers of Supportive Therapy. Therapists may respond to the client's attempts at manipulation by offering "supportive therapy," which may help the client to continue functioning but also assures that she will remain in therapy indefinitely. When the therapist uses drugs, electric shock therapy, reassurance, flattery, and encouragement, he is reflecting the belief that the client cannot help herself and that she is a victim. Subtle flirtations may develop. This supportive therapy may sustain the client for a long time, especially if the therapist is charming, has a need to give to dependent people, and has a capacity to tolerate infringements on his time and energy. However, this approach can be expected to produce little or no change in the client.

Therapy That Produces Change. Another way of responding to the client's attempts at manipulation is to face them head
on with rigid honesty. The client should be told that the purpose of therapy is to understand herself and that permanent relief from her difficulties will come only if she is able to change
her style of living. If she insists that she will change when she
feels better, the therapist should counter with the suggestion
that she will not feel better until she changes. No exaggeration,
no histrionic outburst, no attempt at sexual seductiveness must
pass unnoticed. The client must be told to take responsibility
for all her thoughts and actions. The therapist must attack every
defensive effort to blame external circumstances for her situation. At the same time, he must not drive the client away with
this seemingly harsh position; he must also communicate that
he cares about the client, that he is willing to accept some of
her dependency needs, and that he wants her to feel better.

The first few months of therapy are often stormy, with
many direct encounters between therapist and client. Some clients will leave, unable to tolerate this approach. Those who remain may do so because they are fascinated with the therapist's
honesty and a growing awareness that they, too, can be honest
without endangering themselves. Once some of the more extreme histrionic traits have been examined and attacked, the client can begin to acknowledge the depth of her needs for affection and attention. At this point she can relax and enjoy a relationship in which she can be honestly dependent. The therapist
then focuses on the relationship with him and the working
through of the various maladaptive defenses she has developed
in her life.

The therapist should present himself as an ordinary person who has many of the same existential problems she has; he
is vulnerable and not all-powerful. If therapy is eventually successful, the client is able to find gratifying relationships with a
man other than her therapist—relationships with an active, honest interest in sex and a mature willingness to accept herself as a
worthwhile person.

Suicide Threats. Threats of suicide, often encountered
with histrionic clients, may drive the therapist into a pattern of

unprofessional concern that reduces his therapeutic effectiveness. Two approaches are especially useful in times of crisis: couple therapy (if the client is married or attached) and the use of two therapists. In couple therapy, the husband's presence may diminish the client's tendency to see the therapist as the only answer to her problems. The client can share her anxiety about the suicide attempt with her spouse. It may also help the husband to understand his wife's needs and to learn how he may have unwittingly reinforced her histrionic behavior. The use of two therapists may discourage the development of sticky romantic transference. The support that the therapists give each other may counteract the client's manipulative use of suicide threats.

COMMENTARY: This article reflects the psychoanalytic tradition of emphasizing the importance of countertransference and helps alert therapists to what they should watch for in their own emotional reactions to clients. With histrionic clients, therapists must avoid mistakes resulting from their need to be helpful; charm, support, and indiscriminate reassurance may only extend therapy indefinitely. Instead, therapists must be rigidly honest, should point out every attempt at manipulation, must attack every defensive effort to blame external circumstances for the problem, and should avoid being seduced out of their professional role. At the same time, they must communicate that they care about the clients and want them to feel better. These guidelines are not limited to the treatment of histrionic clients but apply to issues that commonly arise in many therapist/client interactions.

The comment that a therapist's need to be helpful to dependent people makes matters worse is also applicable to clients with a dependent personality disorder. The two approaches suggested for dealing with suicide threats (couple therapy and the use of two therapists) are also applicable to clients with depressive symptoms.

In general, this article is rich with warnings to therapists about common pitfalls that they encounter with a wide range of clients.

SOURCE: Halleck, S. L. "Hysterical Personality Traits: Psychological, Social, and Iatrogenic Determinants." *Archives of General Psychiatry*, 1967, *16*, 750-757.

======================

Group Behavioral Treatment

AUTHORS: David J. Kass, Frederick M. Silvers, and Gene M. Abroms

PRECIS: A short-term, intensive educational program in which five hospitalized women pointed out one another's histrionic behaviors and were taught to modify one another's behaviors through rewards and penalties

INTRODUCTION: Histrionic behavior is seen from an operant conditioning viewpoint: histrionic clients typically display demanding, theatrical, and manipulative behaviors because these behaviors have paid off in the past. The treatment strategy is to structure a total situation in which histrionic behaviors no longer pay off. Thus, these behaviors, instead of gaining attention or relieving the client of responsibilities, now lead to penalties, such as negative feedback, lack of attention, increased demands, or loss of privileges. At the same time, more adaptive behaviors are modeled and reinforced.

A group of hospitalized histrionic clients interacted under the supervision of the staff, who served primarily in an advisory capacity. The clients, who lived together in a large room, were given three basic tasks: (1) to notice and list one another's specific histrionic behaviors, (2) to schedule situations in which those specific behaviors were most likely to occur, and (3) to provide feedback for one another's behaviors through rewards, penalties, and support. The goal was to replace histrionic behaviors with more adaptive ones. The staff's job was to ensure that the clients understood and properly used behavioral techniques. To the extent that the clients took responsibility for these procedures, the staff avoided the common problem of being targets for the clients' hostile, dependent, or antiauthority feelings.

The program involved five white single women between ages seventeen and twenty-five who had been diagnosed as hysterical personality disordered. All volunteered for the program. Four of the five had been admitted to the emergency room because of attempted suicide, the most common reason for hospitalization of histrionic clients.

TREATMENT PROGRAM: Clients were required to adhere to a tightly structured schedule, which required the ability to meet the kind of adult responsibilities that histrionic clients often lack. The mere requirement that the schedule must be followed often provoked the kind of manipulative, responsibility-avoiding behaviors that are characteristic of the disorder. The schedule included general daily events, such as recreational therapy and meal times, and more specific activities that involved techniques designed to call attention to and to modify the clients' communication and behavior problems. If a client wished to change the schedule, the staff encouraged her to do so through direct confrontation of the staff rather than through indirect manipulation and/or avoidance.

A typical schedule included the following activities designed especially for this group.

Group Meeting (9:45 A.M. to 10:30 A.M.). The clients met with staff advisers for exposure to various behavioral techniques, including positive and negative feedback, self-assertion training, and role playing in which clients offered to display their hostile, manipulative, or seductive behaviors. Videotaping was also used as a means of pointing out clients' covert hostility, histrionics, and shallow emotional reactions. Limits, rewards, and penalties were decided by the clients themselves, with the staff intervening only if it appeared that a client was in danger of being harmed in some way or was about to leave the ward. Penalties, which included relinquishing such things as makeup, cigarettes, or desserts, were imposed only for schedule breaking. Other histrionic behaviors, such as physical complaints, seductiveness, or histrionics, were noted by the group members but did not receive a formal penalty. Members were asked to read Wolpe and Lazarus's *Behavior Therapy Techniques* (New York: Pergamon Press, 1966).

A general goal of these group meetings was to teach the members to recognize one another's feelings and to express these feelings without being hostile or destructive.

Staff and Client Meeting (10:30 to 11:30). All clients and staff met in a group to discuss the progress and possible revisions in each client's program. Plans were made for specific activities, such as videotaping or desensitization exercises.

Recreational Therapy (1:00 to 2:30). Clients gave feedback to one another on possible assertive, aggressive, or histrionic behaviors observed during the scheduled activities.

Individual Contact with Client from the Ward (2:30 to 3:00). Each client discussed with another patient from the ward (but not in the histrionic group) some specific problems she had encountered during the day.

Contact with Group Member (3:00 to 3:30). Each client met with another group member for various behavioral exercises, such as role playing or systematic desensitization.

Frequency-Chart Compiling (3:30 to 3:45). Members met to record the frequency of nonassertive behaviors during the previous twenty-four hours: instances of pouting, playing the victim, sarcasm, and so on. The client's own score sheet could be supplemented by examples provided by other group members.

Feeling Recognition and Assertion Training (3:45 to 4:00). Members discussed their feelings in various situations and practiced verbalizing them to one another and/or to imagined other persons.

Group Schedule Meeting (4:30 to 5:30). All members, with staff assistance, reviewed the events of the previous day and then set up therapy plans for the next day. Group members helped one another to set up stressful situations designed to bring out their typical problems. In some cases, the client was tested or challenged in real-life situations, such as going for a job interview or hunting for an apartment. Group members accompanied the client if possible in order to provide feedback to the client and to the staff.

Stressful Situation (6:30 to 8:30). Clients tested themselves in stressful situations either in the ward or outside the hospital.

Group Meeting with Staff (8:30 to 9:30). Rewards, penalties, and scheduling were discussed.

Negative Practice (10:30 to 11:00). Clients practiced an unwanted behavior in order to understand it more clearly. For example, in a fifteen-minute role-playing session, a client might behave as nonassertive and passively hostile as possible.

This schedule is intense but not necessarily complex. The rules are easily understood, explicit, consistent, and flexible enough to allow for needed changes.

The program was successful for four of the five women. (The fifth had participated only with reluctance and left after three weeks.)

CASE STUDY: One of the five women was a twenty-two-year-old college student with a history of numerous suicide attempts in response to being jilted by a boyfriend. Instead of being depressed, she appeared pouty and angry; the nursing staff saw her as an icy bitch. When confronted, she would ignore the other person, change the subject, or become hostile, yelling and cursing. She threatened suicide often. She volunteered for the program because she was aware of the deterioration of her academic and social life.

Her schedule required that she attend college classes and accept the goal of achieving a C+ average for the semester. Therapeutic techniques included videotaping, operant conditioning, desensitization, negative practice, and role playing. She worked specifically on nonassertive behavior and the indirect or misdirected expression of anger.

Her suicide threats, the major indicator of her problems, were initially high in frequency and then became extremely high during the middle period of the program. (This crisis period was noted in all the clients—a pronounced peaking of maladaptive behaviors during this period, followed by a dramatic drop in these behaviors.) Before her discharge, these threats were dramatically reduced.

The client was discharged at the end of the fifth week. She had completed her midterm examinations with a B+ average. She enrolled in outpatient group therapy for six months. In the following year, her social and academic life improved. Eighteen months later, she had received her B.A. degree, had enrolled in graduate training in social work, maintained a part-time job, and was engaged to be married.

COMMENTARY: The intensive short-term approach described here was apparently successful with clients diagnosed as having a histrionic personality disorder, a condition recognized as extremely difficult to treat. The use of a structured schedule as the vehicle through which the clients' problems were worked out is an innovative approach that might be suitable for other types of personality disorders, such as those involving narcissistic or antisocial problems. The program, designed for use in a hospital ward, might be modified for use in an outpatient clinic providing intensive weekend and nightly therapy sessions.

SOURCE: Kass, D. J., Silvers, F. M., and Abroms, G. M. "Behavioral Group Treatment of Hysteria." *Archives of General Psychiatry,* 1972, *26,* 42-50.

Goal-Oriented Therapy

AUTHORS: Allen M. Woolson and Mary G. Swanson

PRECIS: Individual therapy with four histrionic women to teach them to clarify their goals and to use operant conditioning principles to reach them

INTRODUCTION: The basic problem of four histrionic women

was their difficulty in finding and maintaining a satisfactory relationship with a man. In addition, they all described themselves as uncontrollably tense much of the time and had thought of suicide. Treatment involved teaching the women in individual sessions to use reward and reinforcement in their relationships with others by giving them information about operant conditioning theory. The focus at the beginning of treatment was on clarifying the client's goals, finding out why she was not attaining those goals, and then investigating various methods of attaining them. All four women were on the way to attaining their goals at the end of four months of therapy. In all four cases, their behavior was more acceptable and they had a greater capacity for affection, were less frigid sexually, and felt more self-assurance in interpersonal relationships.

TREATMENT:

Relationship with the Therapist. The therapist, hoping to avoid a conventional therapist/patient relationship, presented herself as an expert with information helpful in teaching the client how to clarify and attain her goals. The therapist's job was to help the client to see herself realistically in relation to her goals, to provide feedback about what might work and what might be impractical, to point out additional possibilities, and to provide a level of organization that the client might not have.

Clarifying the Client's Goals. The therapist focused on the client's own knowledge, resourcefulness, competence, and ability for growth in helping her to define her goals. Typical goals included wanting to feel calm, to deal better with anger, to resolve ambivalence about the client's second husband, to have a better marriage.

If the client's goals appeared destructive to herself or others, the therapist encouraged the client to see that they were secondary goals that reflected her anger over having failed to attain a more basic goal.

Seeking Reasons for the Client's Problem Behavior. The therapist introduced questions of why the client was not the kind of person she wanted to be. She was asked to examine two types of information: childhood experiences that she felt had either handicapped or helped her and factors in her present life that she felt were either contributing to her unhappiness or helping her. The client was encouraged to have fantasies about how it would feel if she changed her life according to her stated goals.

Trying New Behaviors. The therapist had four objectives: (1) to get the client to adopt more acceptable ways of interacting with people, at least on a trial basis; (2) to teach her to observe and behave empathically, to note other people's empathic verbal and nonverbal behavior, and to emphasize the long-term value to her of such behaviors; (3) to teach her to adjust her own behavior to the demands of the situation; and (4) to keep her aware that she is testing in real life what she has learned about operant conditioning principles and to encourage her to observe and discuss the effect of this learning on her.

The client was persuaded to try substitute behaviors for three to four weeks. These behaviors were designed to help her attain her goals of attention and affection through socially acceptable means. The therapist taught her principles of operant conditioning to use on herself and other people. Some common behavior problems, along with their suggested substitutes, were provocation of jealousy as a means of getting affection (substitute: supporting husband's self-esteem and meeting his emotional needs), withholding sex as a means of control (substitute: cooperating more generously sexually as a means of improving the relationship), nagging, scolding, complaining as a way to change husband's behavior (substitute: noticing and rewarding husband's favorable behavior).

The therapist avoided moralizing when suggesting these new behaviors. Instead, they were introduced simply as a more practical and effective way of attaining the clients' goals. The women were enthusiastic about how their changed behaviors were causing improvements in the way their husbands and children were treating them.

Three Common Problems with Histrionic Clients. In general, histrionic clients share three basic problems: fear of loss of love, frigidity, and ambivalence about acceptance of male domination. Any therapy that brings about improved behavior but does not deal with these problems will probably be too superficial to have long-term effects.

All four clients believed that loving was dangerous because love might be easily lost; they had learned that people who were attracted to them initially rejected them later. The therapist attempted to change their concept of love by emphasizing that loving is safe if a person behaves acceptably, that love is not magical, and that a person cannot necessarily expect to be loved by everyone. However, the clients could be taught to maintain the initial relationship, in most cases, if they were empathic, observed the other person's needs, and tried to satisfy those needs to a reasonable degree.

The topic of frigidity was discussed by the therapist's asking what the client wanted in her sexual relationships. Three of the four women for whom this was a long-standing problem had had close sibling relationships in childhood. When it became apparent in therapy that the women were repeating these early patterns in relationships with their husbands, their sexual relationships improved.

The therapist encouraged the clients to discuss their feelings about acceptance of male domination. The therapist mentioned that women in most cultures accept a considerable degree of male domination and that what goes along with such an arrangement is the advantage of being considered feminine and attractive. Rather than using passive-aggressive means of manipulating men, the clients were encouraged to exercise will over their lives through the use of selective, subtle, and frequent reward for behavior they liked.

The clients showed surprisingly little resistance to the therapist's attempts to change their behaviors, possibly for the following reasons. First, the client was encouraged to set up therapy goals for what she wanted to feel rather than for what she wanted to do. Second, she was given information about operant conditioning that would generalize to real-life situations and would help her to sustain herself in the transition period toward more acceptable behavior. Third, the client initially tried new behaviors for a specified trial period only, and she was not committed to them until she found out how well they worked. Last, her improved behavior apparently led to new insights. (This is in contrast to a common belief that behavior change cannot occur unless preceded by the client's insight.)

COMMENTARY: This approach was successful apparently because the therapist took the pragmatic stance of presenting the new behaviors as good methods of attaining the client's goals. Although considerable attention was placed on the client's formulating her own goals, the therapist took an active role in the treatment by teaching operant conditioning principles, discussing and examining childhood events, and presenting a philosophical position about love and women's relationships with men. The approach thus seems similar in some respects to other cognitive-behavioral approaches, such as rational-emotive therapy. The therapist focused on attaining the client's basic goals rather than trying to change them; this is in contrast to feminist therapy, which would attempt to change the client's goals, especially in regard to relationships with men.

SOURCE: Woolson, A. M., and Swanson, M. G. "The Second Time Around: Psychotherapy with the 'Hysterical Woman.' " *Psychotherapy: Theory, Research, and Practice,* 1972, *9,* 168-175.

_____

Additional Readings

Harbin, H. T. "Family Therapy with Personality Disorders." In J. R. Lion (Ed.), *Personality Disorders: Diagnosis and Management.* (2nd ed.) Baltimore: Williams & Wilkins, 1981.
     Families and spouses of histrionic clients may become involved in therapy after the client's emotional outbursts, which may have included self-destructive threats. A common situation is a histrionic wife who regresses during marital separation or divorce. The loss of a stable dependent figure is often a major

catastrophe and may lead to increased emotional outbursts, attention seeking, seductiveness, and/or promiscuity.

A therapist may use the following guidelines to evaluate these situations for marital therapy: (1) if the client and her spouse are separated but still seeing each other, they should be included in evaluation and short-term therapy, with the goals of reducing the client's histrionic behaviors and clarifying the relationship, and (2) if a definite divorce is planned and the couple are separated, the client may want the husband to come in for an evaluation session, followed by a few sessions in which the therapist helps the client to accept this as a permanent situation, deal with children, and so on.

More general principles are demonstrated in a case study of a couple who originally entered family therapy to deal with their teenage daughter and who remained in therapy to focus on their own problems. The husband, forty-five years old and successful, displayed compulsive personality features: irritability, stubbornness, an overvaluation of work and undervaluation of interpersonal relationships, and perfectionism that led to a hypercritical view of his wife and daughter. His thirty-nine-year-old wife often had dramatic outbursts of anger or depression and was alternately seductive and detached. They had difficulty communicating with each other, the wife's emotional outbursts causing the husband to withdraw more and more. The therapist saw these circular patterns emerging in therapy whenever important issues arose. His goal was to break this unproductive pattern. The therapist began by encouraging the husband to talk about himself and his background with the goal of discovering issues that would evoke strong emotions. The therapist prevented the wife from intervening or attacking but encouraged her to listen so that she could realize that her husband could be vulnerable and experienced the same painful emotions as she. When the husband became tearful, the therapist encouraged the wife to be supportive. Later the therapist focused on the wife by attempting to get her to be more analytical and intellectual. The therapist repeatedly called attention to their tendency to exaggerate each other's disagreeable traits. He pointed out how the wife's histrionic behaviors actually encouraged the husband's compulsivity and, in turn, how his compulsivity made his wife more histrionic. Emphasis was placed on breaking this vicious cycle of interaction. (See the digest of Bergner, 1977, for a description of couple therapy with a histrionic client.)

Klein, D. F. "Psychopharmacological Treatment and Delineation of Borderline Disorders." In P. Horticollis (Ed.), *Borderline Personality Disorders: The Concept, the Syndrome, the Patient.* New York: International Universities Press, 1977.

Guidelines are offered for the pharmacotherapeutic treatment of histrionic clients, who are often depressed because of their sensitivity to rejection: (1) imipramine should be avoided with these clients because of serious side effects; (2) MAO inhibitors may reduce the client's vulnerability to depression by dosages of phenelzine, 45 to 90 mg daily, for a prolonged period; (3) sedative neuroleptics should not be used, but nonsedative neuroleptics may be administered in combination with MAO inhibitors; (4) alcohol decreases feelings of apprehension and may aid clients in becoming less fearful, although there may be some danger of abuse and habituation. (See digests on antidepressant drugs in the section on depression.)

Luisada, P., Peels, R., and Pittard, E. A. "The Hysterical Personality in Men." *American Journal of Psychiatry,* 1974, *131,* 518-521.

Current literature suggests that women are more likely to be diagnosed as histrionic than men. The authors state, however, that this disorder is more common in men than is generally recognized. They summarize the case reports of twenty-seven hospitalized men, aged fifteen to twenty-five, who met the criteria for DSM-II diagnosis of hysterical personality disorder. Most had a history of suicidal gestures, an unassertive father, occupational and marital instability, heavy drug or alcohol use, and a pattern of impulsive acting out. Contrary to common opinion, they did not all present a pattern of exaggerated femininity—some were strikingly effeminate, some were strikingly masculine, and others were neither.

Treatment included group therapy and, when necessary,

phenothiazines for calming. Men placed in a maximum security unit improved more than those placed in a more permissive setting.

Considerable evidence exists that the incidence of histrionic personality disorder is about the same in both sexes at age twenty but increases with age for women and sharply decreases in men. This may be due partly to men's tendency, because of social pressure, to hide their histrionic traits and also to a sex bias in diagnosis, with male therapists more likely to diagnose women as histrionic than men.

McDaniel, E. "Personality Disorders in Private Practice." In J. R. Lion (Ed.), *Personality Disorders: Diagnosis and Management.* (2nd ed.) Baltimore: Williams & Wilkins, 1981.

Histrionic clients often seek therapy because of an emotional crisis. In the initial session, the client is often warm, charismatic, and quick to speak of her distress. The therapist soon notices, however, that the client's associations are hard to follow, that there is an unclear presentation of exactly why the client is there, and that the client has an intense desire to please the therapist. In subsequent sessions, the client's impulsivity, lack of internal controls, and great concern for interpersonal relationships emerge. The client often has a distorted self-view because of denial. Payment and session schedules may be ignored. The therapist is often seen as a benevolent parent figure. There may be strong sexual overtones, which the therapist must immediately point out. The client may become more impulsive and demanding if her wish to be taken care of is not satisfied. The therapist must recognize that these behaviors represent a conflict over dependency; the relationship need not turn into a power struggle unless the therapist makes it so. Therapists must be aware of their own countertransference reactions of irritation or of oversupport.

Insight-oriented therapy is suggested for clients with high motivation for therapy, relatively little use of denial and repression, and fairly accurate perception of reality. For clients with poor ego strength and more extensive use of denial and repression, family therapy, marital therapy, or supportive individual therapy is the preferred choice. Once therapy is undertaken, compulsive traits often emerge. These principles are illustrated by a brief case study.

9

Narcissistic
Personality
Disorder

According to DSM-III (p. 317), diagnostic criteria for narcissistic personality disorder are as follows.

> The following are characteristic of the individual's current and long-term functioning, are not limited to episodes of illness, and cause either significant impairment in social or occupational functioning or subjective distress.
> A. Grandiose sense of self-importance or uniqueness, e.g., exaggeration of achievements and talents, focus on the special nature of one's problems.
> B. Preoccupation with fantasies of unlimited success, power, brilliance, beauty, or ideal love.
> C. Exhibitionism: the person requires constant attention and admiration.

D. Cool indifference or marked feelings of rage, inferiority, shame, humiliation, or emptiness in response to criticism, indifference of others, or defeat

E. At least two of the following characteristic of disturbances in interpersonal relationships:

(1) entitlement: expectation of special favors without assuming reciprocal responsibilities, e.g., surprise and anger that people will not do what is wanted

(2) interpersonal exploitativeness: taking advantage of others to indulge own desires or for self-aggrandizement; disregard for the personal integrity and rights of others

(3) relationships that characteristically alternate between the extremes of overidealization and devaluation

(4) lack of empathy: inability to recognize how others feel, e.g., [inability] to appreciate the distress of someone who is seriously ill.

Individuals with this diagnosis may show features of other disorders, such as histrionic, borderline, and antisocial personality disorders. Depression is frequent. They often are painfully self-conscious, or preoccupied with appearance and remaining young, and may be intensely envious of others. They may be concerned with bodily aches and pains.

This disorder is more commonly reported now than in the past. There is no information on relative prevalence in men and women.

Brief Training to Increase Empathy

AUTHORS: Paul A. Payne, Stephan D. Weiss, and Richard A. Kapp

PRECIS: Teaching specific empathic responses through audio-taped verbal instructions, models, and feedback from a supervisor

INTRODUCTION: A technique is described in which counselors are trained to become warm, empathic, and genuine—characteristics that are thought to be related to various measures of client improvement.

BRIEF EMPATHY TRAINING: A group of male college students was trained to respond empathically to another student's problems. Training involved the following steps:

Audiotape. Subjects met in groups of ten to twenty to listen to a thirty-minute tape recording on empathy. Empathy was defined, and then two interviews were presented, one with a high-empathy counselor and one with a low-empathy counselor. A commentator on the tape then described the differences between the two counselors, and the interviews were presented again.

Individual Training Sessions. After the initial small-group session, subjects received individual training sessions with an assigned supervisor. They listened to three tapes in which a college student discussed a variety of problems—problems with grades, roommate, parents, professors, or loneliness. Each tape had six statements, each followed by a thirty-second pause during which the subject responded on dictation equipment as if he were counseling the student. After the first and again after the second tape, the subject was given a fifteen-minute supervision interview.

During this interview, the supervisor tried to establish an empathic relationship with the subject. In addition, he commented on the subject's techniques in counseling and how successful he thought the subject had been in his responses to the tape. The supervisor gave specific examples of responses that would have been more empathic than the ones given by the subject. For example, he might say, "I think your last comment about things not going well at home was conveying some understanding for the client's feelings. An even higher level of empathy would have been 'Your parents' nosy questions make you really furious.' "

The subject responded to a third tape. His responses to all three tapes were subsequently rated for empathy by two independent judges. Each set of six responses was given an overall rating of empathy.

The training appeared to be an effective means of increasing the subjects' level of empathy: empathic responses were significantly increased between the first and second tapes and remained high for the third tape. This method—called "modeling didactic"—involves exposure to both a model who demonstrates empathy (the tape) and a supervisor who gives corrective feedback and examples to the subject. The empathy levels of this group were superior to those of other groups of subjects who had been exposed to either modeling or didactic supervision alone. They were also superior to the empathy levels of a group who had been exposed to a supervisor who displayed empathic behavior toward the subject but did not give corrective feedback.

COMMENTARY: Two elements of training were found to be especially important in teaching a group of adults to develop empathic responses: exposure to an empathic model plus corrective feedback from a supervisor. Modeling, a common element in most social skills training approaches, has generally been found to be effective. What is noteworthy in this study is that the effectiveness of modeling was increased by providing the client with corrective feedback. The implications for therapy are that therapists can increase the effectiveness of modeling techniques by providing corrective suggestions to their clients who are attempting to copy the model through role playing.

As the authors point out, the training period was brief and there was no follow-up. However, we believe this method is usable for narcissistic clients who have a deficit in the ability to display empathic responses. The method could also be modified for use with a number of other problems involving lack of social skills, such as hostility, angry outbursts, and dependency.

SOURCE: Payne, P. A., Weiss, S. D., and Kapp, R. A. "Didactic, Experiential, and Modeling Factors in the Learning of Empathy." *Journal of Counseling Psychology,* 1972, *19,* 425-429.

===

Similarities Between Psychoanalytic and Client-Centered Therapy for the Treatment of Narcissism

AUTHOR: Robert D. Stolorow

PRECIS: Empathic acceptance and understanding, positive regard and admiration, genuineness and reflection of feelings in treating narcissistic clients

INTRODUCTION: Rogers's client-centered therapy is ideal for the treatment of narcissistic personality disorders, which have been discussed mainly in the psychoanalytic literature. The techniques, therapeutic processes, and ideal outcomes are strikingly similar for client-centered therapists and psychoanalytic therapists. The understanding and treatment of such disorders may provide an unexpected point of communication between the two groups.

DESCRIPTION OF THE TYPICAL CLIENT:
Typical Narcissistic Personality. According to Kohut, a person suffering from a narcissistic disturbance is an individual who has failed to develop the internal structures necessary for maintaining a cohesive, stable, and positive self-representation

and self-image. Lacking these internal structures, the person attempts to bolster a precarious sense of self through interpersonal relationships. As a result, he or she cannot relate to or appreciate others as separate persons in their own right. Rather, relationships with others are substitutes for the missing or defective parts of his or her own psychic structure.

Typical Client-Centered Client. Rogers's description bears a strong resemblance to the above description of the narcissistic individual: The client feels no sense of self. He or she feels that the only sense of self and self-esteem consists in trying to do what others believe should be done. In Rogers's terms, the client has no "internal locus of evaluation." Relationships with others are based on a need to bolster a precarious self-structure; as a result, no real understanding of the other person exists. Thus, like the narcissistic person, the client is incapable of true empathy.

COMPARISON OF CLIENTS' DEFENSES: Rogers often describes the client as lacking in self-unity and as being extremely vulnerable to experiences that contradict and jeopardize the current organization of the self. The ultimate threat, to Rogers, is the danger of disintegration or dissolution of the self-structure. The client's defenses are aimed at protecting his or her self-image.

From a psychoanalytic perspective, these same clients would be described as suffering from extreme narcissistic vulnerability. They are seen as being urgently occupied with "narcissistic reparation"—restoring and sustaining the unity, stability, and positive emotional coloring of their self-representation.

ESTABLISHING THE THERAPEUTIC ALLIANCE: Establishing a relationship between therapist and client in the initial phase of treatment is often especially difficult with extremely vulnerable narcissistic clients, who may experience any interpretation from the therapist as a shattering injury. The therapist must demonstrate an attitude of complete acceptance and unwavering empathic understanding of the client's narcissistic needs. Especially relevant is Rogers's discussion of the critical importance of the therapist's communication of three basic attitudes: total acceptance of the client, empathic understanding, and genuineness.

TREATMENT:

Psychoanalytic Approach. Kohut suggested that narcissistic people may attempt to solidify and sustain their sense of self-structure through two possible ways: (1) by merging themselves with an idealized, all-powerful other ("idealized parent image") or (2) by maintaining self-representation through another person who continuously mirrors back reflections of the person's own wishful self ("grandiose self"). In therapy, the narcissistic client may see the therapist as the idealized parent ("idealizing transference") or may experience the therapist as an extension or duplicate of his or her own grandiose self ("mirror transference"). Therapy involves establishing conditions that encourage the unfolding and gradual resolution of one or the other of these two types of transference.

The author elaborates on techniques for the development of mirror transference: The therapist must reflect back the client's emerging grandiose wishes of self-glorification. The client needs to feel special and to be admired and appreciated by the therapist, who must communicate an attitude of complete nonjudgmental empathic acceptance and noninterference. The therapist must demonstrate a finely tuned empathic understanding of the narcissistic vulnerability that makes the continuous mirroring of the client's grandiosity necessary. Immersion in this narcissistically sustaining mirror transference gradually strengthens the client's precarious self-representation. The therapist must not confront the client with the unrealistic quality of his or her needs and fantasies, which must be permitted to unfold within the accepting therapeutic atmosphere. The gradual tempering of these needs and fantasies is to be achieved by the client's own efforts at "reality testing." The unfolding and tempering of the grandiose self in the relationship to the therapist result in a gradual working through of the mirror transference. The client's self-representation gradually becomes internalized and becomes part of the client's own psyche. Since the client now possesses structural stability to maintain his or her own self-system, it is no longer necessary to use others for that purpose. The client will be capable of relating empathically to others as separate persons in their own right.

Client-Centered Approach. Similarly, Rogers suggests that the therapist avoid any attitudes that imply that the therapist knows more than the client. The therapist reflects the client's experiences with an attitude of "unconditional positive regard" and acceptance. It appears that Rogers is discouraging the development of idealizing transference and is encouraging the unfolding and working through of mirror transference. The therapist must reflect total empathy with the client's internal frame of reference, thus demonstrating the client's ultimate significance or value to him. The therapist who follows Rogers's recommendations accepts and promotes his own role as an impersonal function substituting for missing or defective segments in the client's own self-structure.

The goal of client-centered therapy, according to Rogers, is the consolidation of an undistorted, firmly and clearly articulated self-structure, which is congruent with the client's actual self-experience. In successful client-centered therapy, similar to successful psychoanalytic treatment of narcissism, the client achieves a lasting stabilization of his or her self-esteem through internalization of the therapist's attitude of unconditional positive regard and gradual realistic tempering of his or her "ideal self" (or, in Kohut's words, "grandiose self"). The client has gained an internal locus of self-evaluation (internal regulatory structures), is less self-preoccupied and vulnerable in relationships, and is capable of an empathic understanding of others as separate persons.

COMMENTARY: The general stance suggested for dealing with narcissistic clients is one that involves a typical Rogerian attitude: the therapist should be empathic, genuine, and nonjudgmental and should encourage the client to develop a stable sense of self that can accommodate and accept the complete range of the client's experiences. The major point of the article is that this approach is similar to that suggested by the psychoanalytic position of Kohut: the therapist should encourage the development of a strong therapist/client relationship in which the therapist accepts the client completely and encourages the client to experience the therapist as an extension of his or her own ideal self. In both cases, the crucial focus is on the establishment of the therapeutic alliance. This approach may be applicable for any other personality disorders that involve some elements of narcissism, such as antisocial and borderline disorders.

By suggesting that Rogers's client-centered therapy is appropriate for the treatment of narcissistic personality disorders, Stolorow has provided a service to two groups of therapists whose approaches are generally viewed as dissimilar. As the author points out, therapists of both persuasions may mutually benefit from exposure to therapeutic techniques formerly thought to be outside their domain.

SOURCE: Stolorow, R. D. "Psychoanalytic Reflections on Client-Centered Therapy in the Light of Modern Conceptions of Narcissism." *Psychotherapy: Therapy, Research, and Practice,* 1976, *13,* 26-29.

Cooperative Treatment by Two Therapists

AUTHORS: Jack S. Winberg and Robert L. Sheverbush

PRECIS: Unstructured psychodynamic therapy to treat a student's narcissistic problems and structured behavior therapy to deal with his study problems

INTRODUCTION: A twenty-two-year-old medical student had reached an impasse in his unstructured, long-term psychoanalytic therapy: his inability to study, thought best dealt with in a structured manner, was threatening to disrupt both his academic efforts and his treatment. He appeared to be struggling with two diverse needs: the dealing with issues arising in his ongoing psychotherapy (which both client and therapist agreed were important) and the need to focus in a structured way on his study difficulties. These needs were dealt with separately by two therapists: the original therapist, who continued his psychoanalytic approach, and a second therapist, who followed a structured behavioristic approach.

CASE STUDY: The student (G.) initially contacted the health service in which the original therapist (J.W.) was a psychiatric consultant. He was a first-year medical student in an unstructured program, which made him anxious because of his concern about his ability to cope with the demands of school and his personal life. G. was treated with support and reassurance, some mild medication (Librium capsules 10 mg t.i.d., p.r.n.), and the invitation to return as needed. He returned twice during the following year.

A year later, he requested ongoing treatment: he was anxious, depressed, and somewhat confused and rambling. The diagnostic impression of G. was that of a narcissistic personality disorder, with arrogance, grandiosity, and difficulty in interpersonal relationships.

Psychoanalytic Treatment. G. sought treatment because of the rage directed at him on all sides as a result of his arrogant, argumentative behavior. As transference developed, he became argumentative and angry at his father, his mother, and the therapist. G. claimed to be studying well for the National Board Examinations, but he failed them for the second time, a severe narcissistic blow in the therapist's opinion. He decided to drop out of school for a year to focus on his treatment and to decide what to do with his future.

When G. was confronted with his arrogant and provocative behavior, he retreated in a childish manner and displayed a great deal of anxiety. Gradually, however, a positive transference developed. At the end of a year he decided to reapply to medical school and was reaccepted as a second-year student. For the first time, he was concerned about how his behavior would affect school and his personal life. He began to recognize that his difficulty with controlling rage was not solely the result of external forces. He also began to gain perspective about the magnitude of his earlier arrogance. G. did well on college examinations but failed the National Board Examinations for the third time. He blamed the therapist for this failure. At this point he began to see another therapist for his study difficulties, while continuing therapy with J.W.

The two therapists agreed that the role of each would be tightly defined, the original therapist continuing his psychoanalytic approach and the second therapist (R.S.) focusing on behavioral interventions.

Behavioristic Counseling. Sessions were structured in the following sequence: (1) recognizing G.'s self-defeating behavior in academic situations, (2) helping him to find appropriate alternatives, (3) allowing him to define these alternatives in clear behavioral terms, and (4) offering him the choice of accepting or rejecting these behavioral changes while making sure that he did not shift the responsibility and consequences of the alternatives he chose. This involved teaching G. good structuring skills, which allowed him to set specific academic goals such as a specified number of hours of study each week.

The second therapist found that G. was initially very resistant to the idea of improving his study skills and habits, although he agreed that he would need to do so in order to achieve his goal of becoming a physician. G. attempted to use each therapist for the other's intended purpose; these attempts were firmly discouraged. The therapists discussed their first few sessions with G. in order to get a clear idea about what each was trying to do.

By the third session G. was beginning to improve: he had kept a daily log of activities, which made him aware of how much time he spent in a manner he considered unproductive. The therapist discovered that G. had been an excellent student in his early years; he used this information to help G. to gain more confidence in his academic ability.

G. had difficulty turning to others for help, even when he needed it. The therapist introduced him to a student, a former client, who had also failed and subsequently passed the Boards. G. was able to relate to this student and came to the following session excited about the insights he had gained into the subject matter that the two of them had discussed. G. bought some study guides and eventually joined a study group.

Within three months, G. passed the Board examination, did well in other aspects of his academic performance, got along better with peers and supervisors, and performed well in clinical situations.

COMMENTARY: The successful outcome of this approach was apparently due to a number of formal and informal factors. Formally, the client was exposed to psychoanalytic and behavior therapies; informally, to a model (the student) and a study group. Since narcissistic personality disorders are notoriously difficult to treat, as the authors point out, this method, using therapists of different theoretical backgrounds and approaches, along with different therapy methods, would appear to offer encouraging possibilities.

An important aspect of the treatment is that both therapists agreed that their roles should be tightly defined, and they were careful not to infringe on each other's territory. The approach was truly "cooperative" in that the therapists discussed the first few sessions with each other in order to clarify what they were doing with the client.

This cooperative approach provides a model for a way of dealing with a client who has a problem the therapist is not equipped to handle: the therapist can work with a second therapist, who focuses on this problem.

The client had a number of characteristics that possibly could have been dealt with by other techniques: anger control techniques and social skills training for his arrogance, argumentativeness, and anger; relaxation techniques for his anxiety.

SOURCE: Winberg, J. S., and Sheverbush, R. L. "Cooperative Treatment of Narcissistic Personality Disorder by Two Therapists." *Psychotherapy: Theory, Research, and Practice,* 1980, *17,* 105-109.

Psychoanalytic Treatment of Narcissistic Disorders

AUTHOR: Normund Wong

PRECIS: Seven-year psychoanalytic treatment with combined individual and group therapy

INTRODUCTION: Narcissism is defined and treated differently by psychoanalytic theorists Kohut and Kernberg. The current treatment approach combines theoretical contributions from both authors.

It is necessary to use individual therapy to prepare the narcissistic patient for a group. The alliance with the therapist is fostered by following Kohut's recommendation that clients' tendencies to idealize the therapist and see him as a mirror of their own personality be permitted to develop unimpeded. (Readers are referred to the digest of Stolorow, 1976, for a discussion of Kohut's position.) The client's emerging hostility and ambivalence toward the therapist are then dealt with.

Group therapy, combined with individual therapy, serves as a transitional object to reduce the client's fears of being swallowed up by the therapist and lessens anxieties about feelings of retaliation against the therapist. It also allows the issue of separation/individuation to be explored.

The group is especially valuable in helping work through the client's grandiose and aggressive concerns and in easing the therapist's countertransference difficulties. Later, it also provides a variety of role models and possibilities for the client, who is working through feelings of separation and abandonment on the way to the establishment of a mature, integrated sense of self.

CASE STUDY: Alice, a woman in her early twenties, was referred after unsuccessful treatment with five therapists over the previous two years. She continued to pursue therapy, hoping to find the perfect therapist who could change her life.

An illness, followed by an endocrine disorder, had transformed her life in college from one of glamour and attention to one of rejection and depression. She underwent psychiatric care and was able to graduate from college. She then returned home to her family, with whom she lived for the next five years. She was full of self-pity and feelings of helplessness. Although she continued to see a therapist, she remained a recluse, morose and bitter. Her appearance and habits continued to deteriorate. Her family's attempts to reach out to her were met with disdain and anger. Over a two-year period Alice was unable to maintain a relationship with any of her therapists. She was hospitalized several times and received shock treatment.

Alice's state of ego integration was precarious, and she showed the features of a borderline personality disorder. This aspect was treated in individual therapy for two and one-half years before focusing on Alice's narcissistic characteristics later in combined individual and group therapy.

First Year. Alice showed a high degree of self-references in her interactions with others, a great need to be admired and loved, little empathy for others, and a contradiction between her inflated self-concept and an insatiable need for acknowledgment. Her haughty, grandiose, and controlling behavior was used as a defense against her suspicious, angry fears of being rejected.

Therapy began with family sessions to reinforce her grasp of "reality." Alice and the therapist agreed that the family was to dispense all medications under the therapist's directions. A daily routine was constructed. She was, for example, no longer permitted to stay in bed all day. The therapist was available to her at all times for real emergencies. During the first few months he saw her every day for at least a few minutes.

The first year was used to allow Alice to develop an "idealizing transference" that contained elements of an idyllic situation she had had with her grandmother. This was fostered by the therapist's reasonable availability during periods of great anxiety and his attempts to empathize with her over narcissistic insults, which occurred frequently during the day.

Second Year. Alice's ambivalence toward the therapist was revealed through abrupt shifts in which she depreciated the therapist and overvalued herself. She simultaneously loathed and needed the therapist. She alternately undervalued or over-idealized the therapist in accordance with her failures and successes outside therapy. In a noncritical fashion, the therapist attempted to clarify, confront, and interpret to her in the "here and now" the disappointment, rage, and anger directed toward him. Working through this negative transference helped her to separate out parts of herself from the therapist, reduced her acting out in real life, and lowered her anxiety following her attacks aimed at the therapist. She also had cosmetic surgery, and her physical appearance was improved. During the second year, she required only one brief hospitalization following a suicide attempt.

Third and Fourth Years. Alice's feelings were accepted, worked through, and interpreted by the therapist. She was able to gain a sense of humor and could say, "If I think you're so great, how come I'm not better by now?" Her aggression could appear as "Who needs you anyhow? All you care about is my money," only to be followed by "You seem so dangerous and angry with me today. I guess I'm still so confused, I don't know which is you and which is me."

At this point, Alice was placed in a beginning group in order to weaken the intense and frightening symbiotic tie with the therapist. Though improved socially, she had been fired from several jobs and had engaged in disastrous relationships with men. A beginning group was chosen to decrease the discomfort she might experience when entering an established group and to lessen the shock upon realizing that she was not the therapist's only patient.

Although Alice initially charmed the group, her insensitivities were soon noticed. The group attacked her for her lack of commitment to the group and her self-centeredness. She identified with Janet, another narcissistic member of the group. Although she gained some insight into the group's reactions to Janet, Alice continued to react negatively when the group confronted her with her lack of empathy and need to monopolize. After two years, Alice left the group with the excuse that she had been accepted into law school and had no time for group therapy.

Fifth Year. Remaining in individual therapy, Alice continued to struggle with her negative and positive feelings toward the therapist. She had derived some benefits from the group through group confrontation and her seeing the pitfalls of Janet's behavior. Achievement in law school, in social life, and in therapy appeared to raise her self-esteem, and she was less needy.

Sixth and Seventh Years. Alice realized that some of her problems experienced in the group were similar to unresolved problems in her relationships at school; she asked to join another group, an ongoing group of members who functioned like people in her life.

In this group Alice worked out feelings of abandonment, rejection, separation, and autonomy that had surfaced during her individual treatment. She moved out of her parents' home and gradually reduced her individual sessions to once weekly. She was more sensitive toward others. She tried on different personalities until she shifted into the role of "doctor's assistant." Her primitive grandiosity and need to be exhibitionistic were more under control, and she was taking on the caretaking role of the therapist.

Alice remained in the group for two more years and then ended all therapy. She graduated from law school and passed her bar exam. Eventually she became a trial lawyer and married. She has maintained a reasonable career and marriage.

COMMENTARY: The author points out that therapists working with such patients should be aware of three areas in which treatment may fail unless the combined individual and group approach is used: (1) narcissistic clients may be unsuited, uncooperative, or disruptive to the group unless their narcissistic needs are dealt with in individual therapy; (2) the therapist must avoid prolonged, unproductive confrontations with the narcissistic group member that are the possible result of his or her own countertransference feelings toward the member; and (3) over a long period, a narcissistic client may assume a number of different roles in the group. The significance of these changing roles can be understood and appreciated more completely if the therapist knows the client through both individual and group therapy.

SOURCE: Wong, N. "Clinical Considerations in Group Treatment of Narcissistic Disorders." *International Journal of
Group Psychotherapy*, 1979, *29*, 325-345.

Additional Readings

Ayllon, T., and Michael, J. "The Psychiatric Nurse as a Behavioral Engineer." *Journal of the Experimental Analysis of Behavior*, 1959, *2*, 323-334.

In an early study that served as a model for many later
studies, a hospitalized woman's attention-seeking behaviors
were sharply reduced by the complete and sudden removal of
all positive reinforcements for such behaviors. An analysis of the
situation had revealed that her continued visits to the nurses'
ward station were reinforced by the attention she received from
the nurses. When the attention was withdrawn, ward visits decreased from sixteen to two daily. These procedures offer promise for use by therapists, family members, or spouses when dealing with a narcissistic client.

Horowitz, M. *Stress Response Syndromes*. New York: Jason
Aronson, 1976.

In this book on stress response syndromes in various personality disorders, a supportive approach is recommended for
narcissistic clients. Therapists must be aware of clients' need to
be admired and must proceed slowly and tactfully in order to
help them repair their injured self-esteem and rebuild their self-
image. Therapists must accept the fact that they will often be
spurned by clients, who are basically unable to acknowledge
others as fully human.

Narcissistic clients have a number of characteristic defects
or styles that the therapist must counter in therapy. Among
them are (1) concern with praise and blame, countered by the
therapist's refusal to praise or blame the client, (2) denial of unpleasant information about themselves, countered by tactful

timing and working to point out the denial, (3) an inability to identify who is responsible—the self or others—for acts, motives, and beliefs, countered by clarifying who is responsible, (4) tendency to interpret all events in terms of self-enhancement, countered by the therapist's pointing out other possible meanings and tactfully decreasing the client's grandiosity; and (5) reduced problem-solving ability because of extensive use of denial to maintain self-esteem and obtain fantasy gratifications, countered by the therapist's tactfully pointing out distortions in perceptions, supporting the client's self-esteem through genuine interest, encouraging an appropriate sense of responsibility, and discouraging unrealistic gratification from therapy.

Leaff, L. A. "Psychodynamic Aspects of Personality Disturbances." In J. R. Lion (Ed.), *Personality Disorders: Diagnosis and Management.* (2nd ed.) Baltimore: Williams & Wilkins, 1981.

Kernberg and Kohut, two major theorists in the field of psychoanalytic treatment for narcissism, have different explanations of the disorder and different recommendations for treatment, although their descriptions of clients are similar. Their viewpoints, however, invite a compromise position.

Kernberg sees narcissistic clients as defending themselves against disturbances in early parental relationships, while Kohut focuses on developmental difficulties and arrests in the normal growth of narcissistic development. Thus, Kernberg's goal in therapy is to work through the client's envy and rage. For Kohut, therapy should permit the client to complete the process of growth from primitive to mature narcissism.

According to Leaff, therapists dealing with narcissistic clients must deal with both these aspects. In addition, they should provide the client with a "corrective growth experience" that will aid the client in becoming more mature, more integrated, and less defensive. Severely disordered narcissistic clients often control, exploit, and manipulate others without apparent guilt, thus resembling sociopathic individuals. They need a steady supply of attention and admiration; when it is not forthcoming, they feel empty, lonely, and depressed. Therapists need to understand that these clients need others; however, the harshness of their childhood deprivation has led them to expect only rejection, with the result that they see others with suspicion, distrust, envy, and greed.

McDaniel, E. "Personality Disorders in Private Practice." In J. R. Lion (Ed.), *Personality Disorders: Diagnosis and Management.* (2nd ed.) Baltimore: Williams & Wilkins, 1981.

Narcissistic clients generally seek a therapist in private practice because of some blow to their self-esteem, such as rejection by a friend or denial of a promotion. Though often highly successful in their jobs, these clients rarely can sustain satisfying interpersonal relationships. In the initial interview they often express rage and hurt and overreact to perceived criticism by becoming angry or withdrawing. Once these clients have regained a sense of self-esteem, they become unruffled, superficially self-confident, and self-righteous. They tend to use primitive defenses, such as denial and projection, and use people mainly as a means of building up their own self-esteem. The therapist is initially perceived as a magical provider of nurturance and help and subsequently attacked and scorned if these expectations are not met. Countertransference feelings can be intense, and therapists must guard against their fear of being a disappointment to the client. Two approaches to therapy are suggested: short-term supportive therapy for crisis situations and long-term insight therapy to reduce clients' vulnerability and to increase their self-esteem. Success depends on clients' desire to change and willingness to continue therapy. A case study of a thirty-five-year-old male college teacher is presented to illustrate these principles.

10

Paranoid
Personality
Disorder

According to DSM-III (p. 309), diagnostic criteria for paranoid
personality disorder are as follows.

> The following are characteristic of the individual's
> current and long-term functioning, are not limited to
> episodes of illness, and cause either significant impair-
> ment in social or occupational functioning or subjec-
> tive distress.
> A. Pervasive, unwarranted suspiciousness and mis-
> trust of people as indicated by at least three of the
> following:
>   (1) expectation of trickery or harm
>   (2) hypervigilance, manifested by continual scan-

ning of the environment for signs of threat, or taking unneeded precautions

(3) guardedness or secretiveness

(4) avoidance of accepting blame when warranted

(5) questioning the loyalty of others

(6) intense, narrowly focused searching for confirmation of bias, with loss of appreciation of total context

(7) overconcern with hidden motives and special meanings

(8) pathological jealousy

B. Hypersensitivity, as indicated by at least two of the following:

(1) tendency to be easily slighted and quick to take offense

(2) exaggeration of difficulties, e.g., "making mountains out of molehills"

(3) readiness to counterattack when any threat is perceived

(4) inability to relax

C. Restricted affectivity as indicated by at least two of the following:

(1) appearance of being "cold" and unemotional

(2) pride taken in always being objective, rational, and unemotional

(3) lack of a true sense of humor

(4) absence of passive, soft, tender, sentimental feelings

D. Not due to another mental disorder such as Schizophrenia or a Paranoid Disorder.

These people often have a strong fear of losing independence or power, have an excessive need to be self-sufficient, and avoid participation in groups unless they are in a dominant position. They are keenly aware of who is in power, tending to be envious of those with authority and disdainful of those without it. They are often interested in mechanical devices and electronics and uninterested in art or esthetics.

People with a paranoid personality disorder rarely seek therapy. They may be overrepresented among leaders of esoteric religious groups and of pseudoscientific and quasi-political groups.

Men are more likely to receive this diagnosis than women.

Treatment Approaches for
Older Paranoid Clients

AUTHORS: Karen Sommer Berger and Steven H. Zarit

PRECIS: Drugs, supportive therapy, behavioral shaping, and careful medical diagnosis

INTRODUCTION: Late-life paranoid clients are likely to be female, single or widowed, and living alone; to have few children; to have failed in their more intimate relationships in early life; and only rarely to have reached a stage of full and satisfying sexuality. Such clients are often in good health except for problems with vision or hearing.

Two factors have been found to be associated with late-life paranoid states: social isolation and sensory losses. Social isolation often appears to be a consequence of poor lifelong social adjustment. Sensory losses, especially of hearing, are common. Onset of deafness typically is in middle age or earlier. These sensory losses may lead to a sense of social isolation: inattention and lack of sympathy from others, depression, feelings of loss, bitterness, suspicion, persecutory ideas, and anger against one's fate. These changes, in turn, result in further social isolation.

Paranoid symptoms may depend on whether sensory loss or long-standing personality style is involved. Among nondeaf clients, paranoid states frequently occur in people who have always been emotionally cold, incapable of forming intimate relationships, and uncomfortable with sexuality. By contrast, clients who became deaf in their middle years often do not have these long-standing characteristics; their paranoid behaviors appear to result mainly from social isolation associated with hearing loss.

In general, then, people are more likely to display paranoid symptoms if they have been socially isolated, are deaf, and have had difficulties in interpersonal relationships. Current events that may trigger paranoid reactions are stresses that increase feelings of insecurity, inadequacy, loss of control, and loneliness. These feelings are usually dealt with through projection and displacement. For example, an elderly woman complained that the nurses were stealing her things and that her daughter was not paying enough attention to her. This was seen as an example of both projection of her anger and an attention-getting device. When the staff worked with the daughter to give more attention to her mother, the paranoid symptoms decreased.

This example suggests that paranoid behavior may be maintained through secondary gains, such as attention from others. The therapist must be aware of these consequences, both in order to suggest more appropriate behaviors to the client and to ensure that treatment is not undermined through continued reinforcement of the paranoid behaviors.

ASSESSMENT OF PARANOID STATES: The first step is to assess the client's physical and mental status to determine whether medical conditions, such as acute or chronic brain disease, are involved. If the client has difficulty with language or shows other signs of acute brain disease, possible causes must be considered: tumors, malnutrition, toxic drug reaction, physical illness, a recent fracture, or reaction to recent stress. Treatment of the underlying problem will lead to a gradual diminishing of paranoid symptoms in one to four weeks. With chronic brain syndrome, two approaches are suggested. First, the client often uses paranoid symptoms to cover up increasing memory difficulties. Family members or the therapist should respond to and emphasize other areas of the client's competence so that she will feel less need to present herself as unimpaired in memory. Second, paranoid thoughts usually decrease as intellectual impairment increases. Family members can be told that paranoid symptoms will not persist and may be directed to encourage other behaviors that compete with paranoid behaviors.

The second major step in assessment is to determine whether the client is paranoid or depressed. When depression is a significant symptom, antidepressant drugs may be effective.

Third, the therapist should get a careful family and personal history, identifying the client's typical pattern of functioning, available social resources, and current consequences of the paranoid behavior.

Finally, the therapist must look for losses and other immediate precipitating factors in the client's life.

TREATMENT: The therapist must develop a trusting relationship with the client by showing care, expressing regret over the difficult time the person is going through, and accepting uncritically any accounts of paranoid behaviors and delusions. Establishing the relationship has two goals: encouraging the use of medication when appropriate and facilitating support and trust that can decrease the paranoid symptoms.

Phenothiazines have eliminated or reduced paranoid symptoms in older clients. Medication must be presented to a paranoid client in an uncritical and supportive way. For example, the therapist might say, "Your nerves have been affected by all these experiences, and the tablets that are about to be prescribed will place you in a better position of resisting these onslaughts against your health." Though useful, phenothiazine therapy must be carefully monitored because of the possibility of side effects, especially with aged clients.

Supportive therapy can complement drug therapy or be used alone with a client for whom drug therapy is contraindicated or who refuses it. Supportive therapy has a number of functions: (1) The therapist's acceptance and warmth may compensate for the client's sense of social isolation. (2) The therapeutic relationship may help the client to explore earlier stresses and losses, their meaning, and alternative ways of dealing with them. The therapist should not confront the client about his or her delusions, but rather should respond empathically to the client's feelings indicated by the delusion or through discussions of the client's life circumstances prior to and separate from the paranoid issues. (3) When feelings of lack of control and vulnerability arise, the therapist can help the client to develop a greater sense of control both in the therapy and through involvement of community agencies and family members. Many older clients are worried about the future, and the assurance that agency services will be available when needed often reduces the client's feelings of vulnerability. (4) The therapist can develop and reinforce appropriate social skills in the client. (5) The therapist should respect the client's preference for personal space, since some paranoid clients prefer a somewhat distant relationship.

CASE STUDIES: The following case examples illustrate the use of different approaches: supportive therapy in the first and the shaping of positive behaviors in the second.

Case One. Mrs. X, a seventy-two-year-old woman living alone, requested help from a family service agency. She believed her neighbor was doing damage by putting gas in her cupboards and so on. She wanted a caseworker to prove she was right, since no one believed her. She had moved to the United States from Europe when she was middle-aged in order to be near her two children. Her husband had left her when she was twenty-five, and she did not remarry. Her son moved out two years before therapy began. After he left, her relationship with him was poor. Her daughter and grandchildren visited her regularly. Mrs. X was able to take care of herself. She was both friendly and aloof with the caseworker. She did not see herself as sick and refused to see a psychiatrist. The family service consultant had suggested an institution, but the caseworker ignored this advice and attempted to develop a trusting relationship and to keep Mrs. X in her own home. The caseworker listened to Mrs. X's stories and never told her she did not believe her. Mrs. X appeared to sense that her stories were not fully believed but accepted the caseworker anyway. The caseworker visited Mrs. X in her home every two weeks for approximately six months. Mrs. X continued her paranoid behaviors but became calmer and more willing to go out. When the caseworker left the agency, Mrs. X declined further treatment, saying that the worker did not believe her stories. However, her symptoms diminished, and she was able to function in her home.

Case Two. Miss S, an eighty-two-year-old woman, was referred to a senior daycare center by a family service agency. She felt she was being poisoned by disinfectant because the superintendent or doorman of her apartment hotel wanted to force her out of her apartment. She had held jobs and supported herself but had never married or made many close friendships. Her closest friends were her brothers and sisters. Her symptoms be-

gan when one brother died and another, who visited her regularly, became ill.

The daycare staff decided on a program of shaping: listening politely to her complaints and initiating conversation
about other, more appropriate activities. Miss S gradually began
talking about other things, mixing with other daycare members,
and making some friends. She began to dress with more care.
The staff visited her building, where there was a faint disinfectant odor but no apparent attempt to get her to move. They
told her that they had asked the building manager to watch over
her to prevent the spraying from happening again. Over six
months her paranoid complaints diminished, although they
were not completely eliminated.

The two women were similar in many ways: both had a
lifelong history of social isolation, both responded to attention
and interest in them, and both were capable of self-care activities. The therapy reduced their distress and allowed them to
continue in a community setting rather than be placed in an institution.

In general, the issues of hospitalization and medication
for paranoid clients are difficult. Clients who refuse treatment
are making a choice that they prefer their current situation in
spite of the distress involved. Many paranoid symptoms interfere little with the person's functioning, and especially with
older clients, fairly severe degrees of impairment are often toler-
ated in community settings. Paranoid clients should be coerced
into treatment only when their situations become dangerous to
themselves or others.

COMMENTARY: The authors point out the importance of discovering possible physical or medical factors, especially hearing
loss, that may be related to paranoid symptoms in older clients.
The implication is that paranoid clients with a hearing loss may
be more responsive to therapy than clients with no hearing loss
but with a long-standing pattern of emotional coldness and lack
of social involvement. Presumably, the first step for therapists
dealing with hearing-impaired clients would be to help them
find a good hearing aid. The two case studies involved women

with life histories of relative social isolation. The therapist's goal with both women was to keep them out of an institution rather than to completely eliminate their paranoid symptoms. This goal was accomplished by providing a sympathetic listener in the first case and by asking the staff to reinforce nonparanoid comments in the second. A factor that appeared to be especially important in both cases was the fact that staff members and therapists responded to the clients with attention and interest. The case studies suggest that what is called "paranoia" may be, for some clients, a well-thought-out action designed to get attention. Therapists might look for clients' needs for attention and then aid in getting it in appropriate ways.

SOURCE: Berger, K. S., and Zarit, S. H. "Late-Life Paranoid States: Assessment and Treatment." *American Journal of Orthopsychiatry,* 1978, *48,* 528-536.

Cognitive-Behavioral Treatment

AUTHOR: Kenneth Mark Colby

PRECIS: Altering feelings of inadequacy, anxiety, shame, and humiliation in paranoid clients

INTRODUCTION: In general, therapists claim little success with paranoid clients. One reason is that therapists have used theories that are inadequate in explaining, and subsequently treating, the wide range of paranoid behaviors. Cognitive therapy in which the therapist attempts to correct the client's misbeliefs and misperceptions offers a promising approach for the treatment of paranoid clients, whose major symptoms revolve around a "paranoid style" of thinking.

According to this approach, paranoid clients emerged from their childhood with the belief that they were dumb, crazy, worthless, or dishonest. This profound belief in their own inadequacy and the resulting feelings of shame and humiliation can be easily activated by interpersonal encounters. For example, if the question "How far did you go in school?" activates feelings of being dumb, the person's shame results in a high level of distress. He or she attempts to deal with this distress by trying to find its cause. The paranoid way of dealing with this discomfort is to conclude that the distress comes not from within the person but from some other person in the situation. By blaming the other person for the distress, the paranoid person can reduce the feelings of shame and humiliation by convincing himself or herself that the other person is inadequate. As this strategy is used over time, the paranoid client acquires beliefs about situations in which the distress was experienced and attributed to others. The client soon develops a generalized strategy in which others are blamed more and more for the distress.

Signs and symptoms of paranoia include persecutory delusions, accusatoriness, rigid and false beliefs, hypersensitivity, excessive fear and anger, and, in men, concern about homosexuality. All make sense if viewed as a result of shame and humiliation resulting from deep feelings of personal inadequacy.

Common life events that often trigger paranoid reactions or states can also be understood from a shame/humiliation point of view: social isolation and language differences, false arrests in men, birth of a deformed child in women, increasing deafness, results of a severe accident, failures in work, school, and sexual relations, and any severe assault on self-esteem, such as being embarrassed in public.

TREATMENT, MANAGEMENT, AND PREVENTION STRATEGIES: Treatment would involve attempting to modify the intense shame posited to be the core process in paranoid disorders. Therapists using cognitive approaches would explore topics involving shame, self-esteem, and eventually self-blame. The therapist should attempt to change the client's belief in his own inadequacy. He must proceed cautiously, since the client may not openly acknowledge these feelings and beliefs. Behavior therapy, involving the use of graded hierarchies of imagined distress situations and countering self-instruction procedures, has been successful in reducing clients' anxiety. Similar techniques might be used to desensitize paranoid clients to shame experiences. Because the client is extremely sensitive to shame and humiliation, the therapist should introduce techniques that the client can practice alone.

The client's tendency to overgeneralize should be countered through cognitive therapy techniques. For example, the therapist may focus on the client's tendency to infer self-references when none were intended. The paranoid strategy of blaming others must be dealt with through cognitive techniques that focus on the client's own beliefs and emotional reactions as the cause of the distress.

Management of a paranoid client revolves around removing him from situations that may trigger humiliation. If he is living in a situation that repeatedly subjects him to feelings of insufficiency and defeat, he should be helped to change or get out. Common examples are social or linguistic isolation or exposure to people who ridicule him. Physical handicaps, such as hearing loss, can make such situations worse.

In terms of prevention, child-rearing techniques that use shaming should be avoided. Parents often instill in a child a sense of shame, which is used as a later strategy for self-control. Though effective, the use of shaming often leads to a sense of global self-criticism that may lay the foundations for a later paranoid style.

COMMENTARY: This approach, which emphasizes modification of the client's feelings of shame and inadequacy, would appear to be a helpful strategy in dealing with a major characteristic of paranoid clients: their extreme fear of dependency because it signifies weakness. An innovative suggestion is the use of desensitization techniques to reduce clients' anxiety associated with shame and humiliation, along with environmental intervention to remove the client from stressful situations. Paranoid clients rarely enter therapy willingly, and if they do, therapists must proceed with great caution. A sense of trust must be established before the therapist can begin to focus on the issues described here. (See the Additional Reading by Millon regarding the building of trust.)

SOURCES: Colby, K. M. "Clinical Implications of a Simulation Model of Paranoid Processes." *Archives of General Psychiatry*, 1976, *33*, 854-857.
Colby, K. M. "Appraisal of Four Psychological Theories of Paranoid Phenomena." *Journal of Abnormal Psychology*, 1977, *86*, 54-59.
Colby, K. M. "Cognitive Therapy of Paranoid Conditions: Heuristic Suggestions Based on a Computer Simulation Model." *Cognitive Therapy and Research*, 1979, *3*, 55-60.

Managing Threatening Paranoid Clients

AUTHOR: G. A. Williston Di Bella

PRECIS: Teaching therapists and staff members to recognize paranoid thinking and behavior, to manage their own reactions, and to have a knowledge of practical techniques of managing violence

INTRODUCTION: A three-step process is outlined for training therapists and hospital staff to deal with threatening paranoid patients: recognition of symptoms, self-management, and practical techniques.

Recognizing Symptoms. The first step in helping therapists and staff to deal with potentially violent patients involves helping them to recognize symptoms of paranoid behavior and thinking, a process too often neglected in training. The following vignettes provide examples of seven types of paranoid thinking.

1. *Projective thinking.* After knocking a ward psychiatrist to the floor, a patient said, "God told me to beat him up."

2. *Suspiciousness.* In response to a friendly approach, a patient says, "Don't come off like you are my friend when I know you just want me to stay locked up in this miserable jail."

3. *Viewing the world as a hostile place.* Often indicative of imminent violence, and frightening to the staff, is the "paranoid stare"—a peculiar, penetrating, unblinking look with raised upper and lower eyelids.

4. *Fear of loss of autonomy and control.* A patient, refusing to get involved in activities, said, "Activities are for children."

5. *Feeling of self as a pivotal point of events.* When the patient's refrigerator was cleaned, the food was shifted from one shelf to another. Without really looking, the patient became violently angry, saying, "I knew they were out to get me; they took my food."

6. *Grandiosity.* One patient condescendingly lectured on the "one true way" of socialism. He tried to show that he was a staff member rather than a patient by helping to manage other patients or doing other ward work.

7. *Delusions.* A patient hated medications and believed they were poisons.

Self-Management. Therapists and staff members often react to threatening patients with fear, anxiety, anger, and frustration. They must become aware of, and master, their own feelings before they can manage a patient. The first step is to reassure the staff that strong reactions to hostile paranoid patients are common. The next step is to discuss some expected emotional reactions and subsequent defense mechanisms used to cope with these reactions.

• *Denial.* Denial is a mechanism commonly used by the staff, who may "forget" the patient's violent episodes. Before being beaten up by a patient, one staff member had said, "He is just misunderstood; he would never hit me."

- *Withdrawal.* Staff members may stay away from a patient because they are afraid. Others may neglect hostile patients. Others may fail to carry out certain crucial interactions, such as setting firm, fair limits.
- *Reaction formation.* Some staff members take the attitude of not hating or fearing the patient, but rather wanting to mother or rescue him. In some cases, such an attitude may only further agitate a paranoid patient.
- *Displacement of anger.* Staff members may displace their anger onto other staff authority figures. For example, staff members protested the setting of limits and thus encouraged patients' paranoid attitudes. "Of course the patient is angry. . . . Why wouldn't he be? All he needs is to be free." Paranoid patients often induce divisiveness among staff members and their own families.
- *Acting out.* Punitive retaliation against difficult patients is not uncommon. Paranoid patients tend to push therapists and staff members into such acting out. When therapists act out punitively, they are confirming the paranoid patient's predetermined view of the world. Therapists and staff members should not have to deal with these reactions alone, but should be provided with opportunities to discuss them with supervisors and in conferences.

Practical Techniques. The therapist must be scrupulously frank, honest, and straightforward. He or she must take a structured approach in therapy. The therapist should not be too warm or friendly or try to get close too quickly and should be cautious about touching the patient. Therapists and staff members should not approach the patient suddenly and rapidly.

Paranoid patients are often extremely sensitive to admitting deficiencies and often will not seek help. The staff must take the initiative in offering their resources to paranoid patients.

Violence must be controlled early in therapy. The patient must be encouraged to take responsibility for his or her actions, to become aware of dangerous levels of mounting anger, and to have appropriate ways of dealing with this anger. The therapist must tell the patient that in no circumstance is violence acceptable. The patient must also be told exactly what will happen if he or she is violent and that in such instances the patient will be firmly controlled by the staff. Patients often fear and exaggerate unknown penalties and may break the rules just to find out what the penalties are.

The patient's family should be involved in therapy and instructed how to avoid provoking the patient. Paranoid patients are often more violent toward family members than toward others.

Paranoid clients often refuse to take medication because they think it is poison. The therapist should ask patients how they feel about medication and should help them to deal with their resentment and/or the feeling that taking drugs relieves them of responsibility for their behavior. A long-acting injectable medication, such as fluphenazine decanoate, might be preferred over oral medication.

Therapists must be sensitive to signs of impending violence. Paranoid patients rarely explode without warning; there is almost always a period of mounting tension, turmoil, and excessive angry brooding. Intervention should occur at this point. If violence occurs, the staff must be trained in how to restrain a patient. Violent episodes should be discussed openly and thoroughly with the patient. In addition, therapists and staff members should discuss the episode as soon as possible in order to ventilate their feelings and to discuss what to do in the future. The episode must also be discussed with the rest of the patients on the ward.

COMMENTARY: The issue of possible violence from clients is rarely discussed, even in articles dealing with therapy for paranoid clients. Although the clients in this instance were so seriously disturbed that they were hospitalized, the author's guidelines might be helpful to any therapist, who must be sensitive to signs of possible violence from a client. Particular emphasis is placed on the importance of a therapist's ability to manage his or her own reactions in order to deal with such clients.

SOURCE: Di Bella, G. A. W. "Educating Staff to Manage Threatening Paranoid Patients." *American Journal of Psychiatry*, 1979, *136*, 333-335.

Paradoxical Therapy

AUTHOR: Allen Fay

PRECIS: Reducing paranoid delusions by instructing the spouse to agree with and exaggerate the client's distortions

INTRODUCTION: Many people cannot recognize their own irrational thoughts, but when these thoughts are mirrored back to them, occasionally with an element of benevolent mimicry or humor, they can begin to see them as inappropriate. By agreeing with and exaggerating the deviation, a therapist or family member can incite the client to take a stand against the irrationality of the imitator. This "paradoxical" method is useful for therapists of differing theoretical orientations. It is generally used along with other approaches. The introduction of humor into therapy often aids in bringing the client and therapist into a closer, freer, more spontaneous relationship. Clients may gain some perspective on their problems by learning to laugh at themselves. In addition, identification with a therapist who can laugh at his own irrationality as well as that of the client may be a good way to get paranoid clients to face the inappropriateness of their delusional systems. This method has been used successfully with over thirty patients seen in private practice.

CASE STUDIES:
    Case One. A man of sixty-one who had been moderately paranoid for forty years became worse after losing his job as a buyer in a department store. He tried working as a salesperson but left after a few weeks. He was convinced that the depart-

ment store had agents spying on him and was about to press criminal charges against him because on one occasion his cash register was three dollars short. During his first session with the therapist he was extremely anxious and spoke only of this topic. Before leaving, he said he could not keep his next appointment because he was about to be arrested. Ignoring this prediction, the therapist asked that his wife attend the next session with him.

His wife was exhausted by her constant efforts to reason with him and to get him to "face reality." For example, when he would say, "They are after me," she would try to convince him that he was wrong, that a big department store would not worry about such a small amount, that if they really wanted him, they would have had him arrested long before now, and so on.

The therapist suggested, in the client's presence, that she respond as follows:

Patient: They are after me.

Wife: They certainly are. Not only are they after you from that store, but they have notified other stores in the area as well. A citywide alert is out for you. The police have been notified, and the conspiracy has already extended to the FBI. Countrywide agencies are focused on you and are trying to get you. Not only is the conspiracy nationwide, but Scotland Yard and other international police organizations are interested in this case. There is no question that you are going to be arrested very soon.

One week later the client said he was feeling much better. Although he had an occasional paranoid thought, he did not express the same delusional ideas. By the fourth session he was doing well. Follow-up sessions at three and six months indicated that his symptoms did not return.

Case Two. A woman of thirty was jealous of her husband. If she answered the phone and an unknown caller hung up, she would accuse her husband of having a lover. In the client's presence, the therapist suggested that her husband should avoid becoming locked in a struggle in which he defended himself by denying her accusations. Instead, the therapist recommended an alternative response in which the accused partner agrees with the deviation and amplifies it: "You know, I have been thinking about confessing for a long time. You are absolutely right. That was my lover on the phone, and we were supposed to go out tonight, but I told her to hang up if you answered. Not only do I have one lover, but I have five. Do you remember last week when you wondered where I was? I was with one of my lovers from eight to nine and with another from nine to ten."

In this case, as in others, destructive games between the couple were stopped, and they began to communicate more directly with each other.

COMMENTARY: It would appear that the personality of the therapist is an important ingredient in this approach: he or she must be empathic and have a sense of humor that is shared by the client. As the author points out, this treatment is not used alone but generally along with other intervention strategies. Therapists should be aware of the danger of humor that develops a sarcastic edge, which a paranoid client might perceive as an attack. It is important to note, given paranoid clients' suspiciousness and lack of trust, that the therapist was careful to avoid manipulating the client in any way and always gave the instructions for paradoxical therapy in the client's presence.

SOURCE: Fay, A. "Clinical Notes on Paradoxical Therapy." *Psychotherapy: Theory, Research, and Practice,* 1976, *13,* 118-122.

Difficulties with Paranoid Clients

AUTHOR: Monna Zentner

PRECIS: The value of understanding rigidity, fear of the unexpected, guardedness, and other features of how paranoid clients think

INTRODUCTION: When we identify clients as paranoid, we are often referring to the specific content of their thoughts: unwarranted fears, expectation of being fooled, chronic anticipation of danger from others, and so on. From a treatment point of view, however, it may be more helpful to focus on how a paranoid client thinks rather than on what he thinks.

PARANOID STYLES OF THINKING: Thinking styles characteristic of paranoid individuals are as follows: they view information with great bias and will accept as truth only that which confirms their suspicions, scan their environment actively and with great intensity, dislike the unexpected, attribute to others their own unacceptable feelings and motives, and are guarded and controlled, with little spontaneity.

Rigidity and Narrow Focus. Paranoid clients have an ax to grind, an idea to be supported, an all-consuming concern; the result is that they view the world with a rigid, narrow focus. Rather than allowing their perspective to be modified by observed facts and events, they seem to impose their own convictions on whatever they observe. They accept as truth only that which confirms their suspicions. Paranoid clients' often considerable intelligence is used to mold the world to fit their own prejudices. This is often noticeable in therapist/client interactions. For example, when the therapist tries to persuade the client to abandon her paranoid thoughts, the client may not only retain a paranoid style of thinking but also begin to view the therapist with suspiciousness. The following case example illustrates a paranoid client's rigidity and inability to attend to information that does not support her idea: Jane, a twenty-six-year-old graduate student, insisted that Dr. Smith take her immediately for an examination. The social worker told her that his secretary had offered her an appointment for next week and that the doctor could see no one, except for an emergency, for the next few days. Jane replied, "He just doesn't want to see me because I am a feminist." The worker said that she didn't know about the doctor's opinion on feminists but that Jane had been offered an appointment for a later date. She asked whether this was an emergency. Jane said it didn't matter. "I know damn well why he doesn't want to see me. You are just defending him because you don't like me being a feminist either."

Active and Intense Scanning. Paranoid clients are often difficult to work with because their observations, though biased, are often accurate. They actively scan the environment with great intensity and often make detailed observations of events unnoticed by others. The client may notice small details about the therapist's appearance or objects in the office that the therapist had not noticed. In long-term treatment the therapist notices that the client's careful scrutiny and well-directed attention are not triggered by fear of a specific danger but seem to be a fundamental way of operating. The client is ever vigilant and seems incapable of being passive or casual, even when dealing with problems involving such things as daily activities or courses in school.

Fear of the Unexpected. Paranoid clients often have difficulty dealing with unexpected events, which seem, by virtue of their newness, to be threatening. It is as if their alertness were so finely drawn that the smallest touch caused an extreme reaction.

Projection. Paranoid clients rely extensively on projection—the attribution of one's own unacceptable feelings, motives, and impulses to others. They bring scrupulous attention and scrutiny to the object of their projection. They observe the other person, convinced that there is a hidden intent that can be discovered. The specific intent to be looked for will depend on the client's particular concern.

Guardedness, Control, and Lack of Spontaneity. Paranoid clients often appear to be in a constant state of anticipation for crisis. They lack spontaneity; they observe themselves and others carefully. Even social behaviors that are automatic in most people seem to be consciously controlled in these clients. Feelings of concern or tenderness are often regarded with contempt if they appear in someone else; if experienced internally, they are regarded as a sign of weakness. Even sensuality is suspect, since opening oneself to pleasure may mean letting down one's guard. The underlying concern of this mode of functioning seems to be one involving independence and mastery and the related fears of being weak and dependent. Very paranoid clients are often arrogant, secretive, and almost ashamed. They seem to have a general sense of self-contempt and a fear of vulnerability to others, as if control over themselves and events would disappear at a touch. They do not trust others or themselves. They have an inordinate fear of being subjugated by others, that someone will force them to submit to his or her power. Thus, they are extremely sensitive to authority and power, are always aware of who is in command and who is an underling, and tend to value those in power more than themselves. Paranoid clients are fearful of any kind of rejection from those in power. In therapy, it often happens that the therapist's attention awakens in the client a sense of humiliation. It is as if the client were being looked at before he or she was ready to be looked at. This internal sense of vulnerability leads to more rigidly sustained suspiciousness.

CASE EXAMPLES: The following case example demonstrates a paranoid client's problems related to the expression of affection for the therapist.

Mrs. S had an intense dislike for her social worker. She had spent her sessions complaining that the caseworker was ruining her life and was against her. Despite this, her life in general was improving. During one session, Mrs. S told the caseworker hesitantly that perhaps she was being helpful and that she was beginning to have some positive feelings toward her. Soon after, Mrs. S began to worry about what the caseworker "really thought" of her. She felt that once she had opened herself up to the caseworker by stating positive feelings, she was placed in a vulnerable position; the caseworker would take advantage of her weakness. Although she continued to do well in real life, the next several sessions reflected her concern that the caseworker was rejecting her, making fun of her, or trying to hurt her in some way. Apparently, Mrs. S viewed her affection and declaration of it as a possible self-destructive act, an exposure to shame, and an invitation to invade and hurt. By asking the social worker to help, Mrs. S was giving up a certain amount of autonomy.

In another case, a nurse had a long-standing concern that taking orders from her superiors might place her in a humiliating position. A new supervisor arrived, whom she admired. In a relatively short time, however, the supervisor was perceived as a dangerous person. The nurse had responded to her admiration of the supervisor in a paranoid way: positive feelings were a sign of weakness or a threat to her self-mastery. The supervisor was seen as dangerous because to admire the supervisor was to be infantile and passive.

COMMENTARY: This article may be a useful addition to the DSM-III criteria for paranoid personality disorder: by focusing on how a paranoid client thinks, the therapist may be able to devise a workable therapeutic approach while avoiding inadvertently reinforcing the client's paranoid symptoms. Of particular interest is the author's discussion of paranoid clients' difficulties related to the expression of affection and positive feelings. For example, therapists who try to foster the expression of positive feelings by paranoid clients may not realize how threatening these feelings may be. Because of paranoid clients' tendency toward projection and guardedness, therapists must be honest and straightforward in discussing the goals for therapy. In order not to feed into the client's paranoid system, therapist and client must continually share, clarify, and be in agreement on therapeutic goals. Another possible therapeutic strategy would be to emphasize the potential value of some of these paranoid thinking styles—for example, to focus on the client's intelligence, to point out the importance of accurate, detailed observation and to shape the use of detailed scanning in appropriate situations, and to discuss the fear of the unexpected as it occurs in many of us. Therapy might be aimed at helping clients to develop a better sense of discrimination in the use of these thinking styles.

SOURCE: Zentner, M. "The Paranoid Client." *Social Casework: The Journal of Contemporary Social Work,* 1980, *61,* 138-145.

Additional Readings

Davison, G. C. "Differential Relaxation and Cognitive Restructuring in Therapy with a 'Paranoid Schizophrenic' or 'Paranoid State.' " In *Proceedings of the 74th Annual Convention, APA.* Washington, D.C.: American Psychological Association, 1966.

A patient reported that pressure points he felt above his right eye were signs that a spirit was attempting to help him make decisions. A cognitive restructuring approach was used in which the therapist explained that unusual events or experiences are often interpreted as supernatural; however, there can be another explanation for such experiences. The therapist demonstrated how feelings of pressure could be the result of muscle tension and then instructed the client in relaxation training to ease the discomfort. The client was reported to be greatly improved at a six-week follow-up.

Harbin, H. T. "Family Therapy with Personality Disorders." In J. R. Lion (Ed.), *Personality Disorders: Diagnosis and Management.* (2nd ed.) Baltimore: Williams & Wilkins, 1981.

Although many paranoid clients seen by family therapists are married, their extreme mistrust and hypervigilance often lead to marital problems. The therapist tries to discover the interaction patterns between client and spouse that seem to maintain the paranoid behaviors. Marriage is viewed as a potentially rehabilitative relationship. The therapist must be clear and open with the client, who will closely monitor the therapist's behavior, and must avoid playing into the client's suspiciousness. Any attempts of the spouse to form an alliance with the therapist that excludes the client must be blocked. Once a relationship has been established with the client, the therapist can support the spouse in challenging the client's mistrust. After expected initial angry reactions, the client often becomes less paranoid. The therapist must be aware of possible physical violence and should confront the client only when aggression is under control.

A case study is presented: A twenty-six-year-old white male was hospitalized for the second time for acute paranoid psychosis. After his psychotic symptoms decreased, he showed symptoms of a paranoid personality disorder, with some aspects of a dependent personality disorder. As marital therapy progressed, the dynamics of their relationship became clearer: the wife was domineering, critical, and secretive, while the client was paranoid and passive. His paranoid behaviors could be seen as an attempt to assume a more dominant position in their relationship. Therapy revealed the wife's long-standing pathological jealousy and mistrust, which led to a worsening of the client's own jealousy. The therapist repeatedly challenged the wife's guardedness, thus revealing her vulnerability. The client, seeing that his wife was also insecure, became less mistrustful. Both began to improve as they became more open with each other. After six months of outpatient marital therapy, the client's paranoid and dependent behaviors had decreased, and the couple reported that their marriage was happier than before his hospitalization.

Kaffman, M. "Monoideism in Psychiatry: Theoretical and Clinical Implications." *American Journal of Psychotherapy*, 1981, *35*, 235-243.

A number of psychiatric disorders, including paranoid states, share the common element of an incessant preoccupation with a repeated disturbing thought or idea. The repetition of this idea leads to a kind of self-induced hypnotic state in which the person becomes more and more suggestible to the idea. This process, called "monoideism," has a constricting effect on what the person says to himself, which in turn affects his thoughts, emotional reactions, and interpersonal relationships. This pattern is often reinforced by family members and/or friends, who mutually reinforce each other either by agreeing with the client or by denying, criticizing, and arguing with the client, who is then forced to supply additional evidence that strengthens his belief system.

The goal of therapy is to break this self-perpetuating pattern by replacing it with a continuous suggestion pattern provided by the therapist. People involved with the client are instructed to stop their counterarguments with the client, to pay no attention to his obsessive ruminations, and to look for more acceptable ways of interacting with the client. The therapist should consistently point out how ineffective the preoccupation with the disturbing thoughts has been. The client is encouraged to take some "psychic rest." Thus, the therapist attempts to redirect the client's language and communication strategies, as well as looking for alternative ways of behaving and thinking.

Kennedy, T. "Treatment of Chronic Schizophrenia by Behavior Therapy: Case Reports." *Behaviour Research and Therapy,* 1964, *2,* 1-6.

The staff used reinforcement techniques to decrease the number of delusional statements made by three hospitalized chronic paranoid schizophrenics. The staff responded with strong positive verbal reinforcement to nonparanoid statements and strong negative verbal reinforcement to paranoid statements. In all three cases, delusional references decreased or disappeared; two of the three patients showed continued improvement at a six-month follow-up.

Millon, T. *Disorders of Personality: DSM-III: Axis II.* New York: Wiley, 1981.

In a chapter on paranoid personality, Millon describes a general approach for dealing with paranoid clients. Therapy revolves around building trust through a series of slow and progressive steps. The therapist must show genuine respect for the client, must accept but not confirm the client's beliefs, and must proceed at a pace that is comfortable for the client. The initial goal is to free the client of his mistrust of others by showing him that he can share his anxieties with the therapist without being humiliated or badly treated. It is hoped that the client can begin to see the world as others do. Through trust, the client begins to relax, to loosen his defenses, and to open himself to new attitudes. Specific therapy techniques are less important than developing a sense of trust. However, drugs may be helpful to reduce acute anxiety or acting-out episodes. Institutionalization may be required if the client shows psychotic symptoms. Stressful situations should be reduced if possible with outpatients. Behavioral or psychoanalytic approaches cannot be used unless a sense of trust has been developed with the therapist. In any case, therapy is likely to control or moderate but not change the client's basic personality pattern.

Strange, R. E. "Personality Disorders in the Military Service." In J. R. Lion (Ed.), *Personality Disorders: Diagnosis and Management.* (2nd ed.) Baltimore: Williams & Wilkins, 1981.

Personality disorders frequently appear in military personnel and account for betweeen 56 and 63 percent of all diagnosed psychiatric problems. Among young men, the most commonly encountered diagnoses are borderline, passive-aggressive, schizoid, and antisocial disorders. Particularly difficult is the management of personality disorders in older personnel, who are often of relatively high rank. A relatively common diagnosis is paranoid personality disorder: the client is a previously competent, conscientious officer who displays paranoid characteristics of rigidity, hypersensitivity, suspiciousness, grandiosity, and hostility. As the client is given more responsibilities, these characteristics become more and more detrimental to his career. A case study of a thirty-eight-year-old paranoid commander is described.

Weintraub, W. "Compulsive and Paranoid Personalities." In J. R. Lion (Ed.), *Personality Disorders: Diagnosis and Management.* (2nd ed.) Baltimore: Williams & Wilkins, 1981.

The following comments represent a consensus about therapy with paranoid clients. Therapists must be absolutely honest with the client, and the therapy contract must be spelled out in great detail so there is no chance of misunderstanding. Any messages from friends or relatives should be shared. Therapists should be cautious in giving interpretations, which should be concrete and brief. They must avoid taking sides when the client makes accusations against other people. Therapists must be aware of their own fear of a client's hostility, disappointment in a slow rate of progress, and intolerance of the client's dependent needs. Paranoid clients may be provocative and threatening; therapists who are uncomfortable with their own aggressive feelings should not try to treat them. Common therapist errors are to withdraw and to argue with the client. A case example is presented in which a client's spouse called to tell the therapist that the client was coming to the office armed, with the intention of "finishing things." The therapist met the client in the corridor, told him of his wife's call, and demanded he turn over the weapon. Although the client denied any intention to harm the therapist, he subsequently handed over a knife after the therapist had persisted and threatened to call the police. The therapy session was held as scheduled.

Paranoid clients, often basically insecure and dependent, will make excessive demands for advice and guidance once rapport is established. Therapists must avoid the extremes of either taking over the client's life or permitting him to flounder. Denial and projection should not be challenged directly but should be handled through patient listening to complaints, refusing to take sides, and focusing attention on the client's hurt feelings.

Paranoid clients are often extremely sensitive to signs of hostility in others. Therapists should be quick to admit whether and when they have been angered, reassuring the client that the relationship can survive even if there is anger.

When medication is involved, therapists must be honest and firm and should involve the client in decisions about drug dosage. Clients often resist medication, although they may request it if threatened by psychotic symptoms.

11

Schizoid
Personality
Disorder

According to DSM-III (p. 311), diagnostic criteria for schizoid personality disorder are as follows.

> The following are characteristic of the individual's current and long-term functioning, are not limited to episodes of illness, and cause either significant impairment in social or occupational functioning or subjective distress.
>
> A. Emotional coldness and aloofness, and absence of warm, tender feelings for others.
>
> B. Indifference to praise or criticism or to the feelings of others.
>
> C. Close friendships with no more than one or two persons, including family members.

D. No eccentricities of speech, behavior, or thought characteristic of Schizotypal Personality Disorder.
E. Not due to a psychotic disorder such as Schizophrenia or Paranoid Disorder.
F. If under 18, does not meet the criteria for Schizoid Disorder of Childhood or Adolescence.

These individuals are often unable to express hostility or anger, are indecisive, absent-minded, and "in a fog," and may daydream excessively. Males rarely date and marry, because of their lack of social skills; females may passively accept courtship and marriage.

The prevalence of this disorder is unknown, but it is thought that a large proportion of people working in jobs that involve little contact with others or living in skid-row sections of cities may experience this disorder.

People with this disorder are distinguished from those diagnosed as having a schizotypal personality disorder, which includes bizarre and eccentric behavior and is thought to be related to borderline schizophrenia. Schizoid personality disorder is different from avoidant personality disorder in that schizoid individuals have no desire or ability to relate to others, while people with an avoidant personality disorder have a capacity for emotional involvement with others in spite of their shyness and oversensitivity.

Short-Term Intensive
Social Skills Training

AUTHORS: Jean B. Goldsmith and Richard M. McFall

PRECIS: Teaching male inpatients to handle difficult interpersonal situations in three sessions

INTRODUCTION: Social skills training is a general approach aimed at increasing competence in critical interpersonal situations. Rather than emphasizing elimination of maladaptive behaviors, it focuses on the positive, educational aspects of treatment. Past research has suggested that social skills training is effective in laboratory settings; the purpose of this study was to apply this training to actual clinical patients in a clinical setting. Of particular interest was the extent to which the training would generalize to real-life situations.

METHOD: On the basis of many interviews with staff members and psychiatric inpatients (with diagnoses including personality disorders, neuroses, and schizophrenia), fifty-five problem situations were developed. The general situational contexts most frequently reported were dating, making friends, having job interviews, relating to authorities, relating to service personnel, and interacting with people perceived as more intelligent or attractive or people who were different in some way (for example, physical appearance, race). The most common crucial moments within these situations were beginning and ending interactions, making personal disclosures, handling conversational silences, responding to rejection, and being assertive. In addition to these common problem situations, the experimenters developed a list of competent responses for dealing with these situations, specific principles about effective behaviors, and a manual for scoring responses in these situations. These materials were used in the assessment procedures and training program described below.

Thirty-six male inpatients on the psychiatric ward of a Veterans Administration hospital volunteered for the study.

Their mean age was thirty-five, half were black and half white, and half were diagnosed as schizophrenic and half as neurotic or personality-disordered.

Initial Assessment. The competency of the patients in social situations was assessed by giving them a number of tests. All instructions and stimuli were presented on audiotape. The first two measures were administered to patients in groups of four. First, using 9-point scales, each patient rated his difficulty in meeting and talking to people, his expected future ability to handle social interactions outside the hospital, and his feeling of self-worth. Second, each was given a questionnaire listing the fifty-five situations mentioned above. For each situation, the patient indicated on a 5-point scale how competent or incompetent he thought he would be. A role-playing test was then administered to each patient individually: for each of twenty-five tape-recorded simulated interpersonal situations, the patient role-played his response, using the actual words he would use in real life. The situations were chosen from the fifty-five situations to be the most relevant to the patient populations. The patients' responses were tape-recorded for subsequent scoring.

After the patients' social competency was measured, they were randomly assigned to one of three groups: assessment only, interpersonal skill training, or pseudotherapy.

Assessment Only. These patients received only the pretreatment and posttreatment assessments. They were told that the role-playing test was a new form of treatment involving "response practice." They were praised for their efforts and instructed to return a week later for another "practice session."

Interpersonal Skill Training. These patients were seen in three one-hour training sessions over a five-day period. The first fifteen minutes was devoted to covering eleven problem situations (chosen from the twenty-five situations in the role-playing test). For the next thirty minutes, the patient received interpersonal skill training, which involved coaching, modeling, behavioral rehearsal, recorded response playback, and corrective feedback. Instructions and training stimuli were prerecorded on audiotape.

The step-by-step training sequence was as follows: (1) the

patient listened to a taped description of the situation; (2) he was coached about the principles of effective behavior in that situation; (3) he heard a competent response by a male model; (4) he heard a review and summary of the training material, including a description of the likely consequences of various response alternatives; (5) the experimenter stopped the tape recorder and made sure that the patient understood the material and was willing to try the suggested behavior; (6) the situation was played again; (7) the patient rehearsed his response, which was recorded; (8) his response was played back and evaluated, first by the patient and then by the experimenter, who gave corrective feedback; rehearsal was repeated until both patient and experimenter agreed that the response was acceptable on two consecutive tries; (9) training then advanced either to the presentation of a new coaching segment for the same situation or to a new situation (some situations were broken down into small segments to facilitate training). The last fifteen minutes was devoted to a review of the training.

Pseudo Therapy. These patients were also seen in three individual one-hour sessions over a five-day period. The same eleven situations were presented on the same time schedule as for the skill-training patients. However, the experimenter gave no training or suggestions, but encouraged the patient to explore his feelings about the problem situation and to seek insight into the psychological and historical reasons for those feelings.

Posttreatment Assessment. One day after the last treatment session, each patient was readministered the role-playing test. This was followed by a real-life tape-recorded simulation test: he was asked to meet with a male stranger (a confederate) and to initiate the conversation, ask the stranger to lunch, and terminate the interchange after ten minutes. The confederate was instructed to confront the patient with three "critical moments": not hearing the patient's name when introduced, giving an excuse for not accepting the lunch invitation, and saying, "Tell me about yourself," at the first pause. Afterward, the patient rated his skill and comfort in that encounter on a 5-point scale. The confederate evaluated the patient in a similar way.

On the following day, patients were seen in groups of four and were readministered the self-report measure using 9-point scales and the fifty-five-item questionnaire.

The skill-training patients were superior on every measure: global self-rating scales, self-report measures of specific interpersonal comfort and competence, behavioral measures of performance in specific problem situations, and the simulated encounter approximating a real-life situation. There was also evidence of treatment generalization: skill-training patients improved not only in situations for which they had been trained but also in situations for which no training was given. The training was equally effective for patients in all three diagnostic categories—neurotic, personality-disordered, and schizophrenic. This may be because the training procedures were broken down into small units, were placed according to each patient's progress, and were highly repetitive. In addition, a follow-up measure taken eight months later—the patients' readmission rate—suggested that there had been a positive transfer of training to real life.

COMMENTARY: When male psychiatric inpatients were given only three hours of interpersonal skill training, they showed significantly greater improvement in their ability to handle difficult interpersonal situations than patients receiving either three hours of pseudo therapy or patients in a control group. The relative success of this program may be due partly to the fact that a great deal of time was spent developing training situations that had real meaning for the patients. If the skills being taught do not offer real solutions to the patients' life problems, then any program may fail regardless of the particular training methods used.

The authors point out some ways in which the program could be made more effective: giving patients more time to practice each new behavior, providing more training sessions covering more situations, allowing patients more flexibility to focus on problems related to their own lives, and developing better methods for assessing long-term, real-life changes. The program may provide a useful method for treating a wide range of problems.

SOURCE: Goldsmith, J. B., and McFall, R. M. "Development and Evaluation of an Interpersonal Skill-Training Program for Psychiatric Inpatients." *Journal of Abnormal Psychology,* 1975, *84,* 51-58.

Social Skills Training

AUTHORS: Martin E. Gutride, Arnold P. Goldstein, and G. F. Hunter

PRECIS: Using videotaped modeling, actual role playing, and social reinforcement to increase social behaviors in a group of asocial inpatients

INTRODUCTION: In the past, two major approaches have been used for increasing social behaviors in withdrawn, asocial people: milieu therapy, in which clients are part of a total environment that promotes interaction through group activity and group pressure, and token economy programs, in which clients' social behaviors are gradually shaped through the use of operant conditioning. A third approach is a variation of social skills training called "structured learning therapy." This approach consists of (1) modeling, in which the client is exposed to specific, detailed, and vivid examples of appropriate social behavior, (2) role playing, which involves behavior rehearsal or practice of the modeled behaviors, and (3) social reinforcement, including positive feedback, approval, or rewards for desired behaviors.

Forty-two asocial inpatients received this training. Part of the group suffered chronic illness, with more than two prior hospitalizations and longer than one year in the current hospital. The remainder were acute patients with less than two prior hospitalizations and less than one year in the current setting. The patients received diagnoses of schizoid personality disorder, inadequate personality, schizophrenia, or psychotic depression.

TREATMENTS: In addition to the group of patients who received social skills training, another group received only individual or group therapy for the same period of time. Still another group received both structured learning therapy (social skills training) and psychotherapy. There was also a control group who received neither training nor psychotherapy.

Social Skills Training. Each patient's level of social functioning was assessed by ward psychiatrists' ratings and various self-report questionnaires filled out by the patient. Next, the patients participated in a four-week structured learning therapy program. The staff explained the program's goals to all patients, whose active participation was invited.

The training involved the use of four modeling videotapes, arranged in order from the more simple, less threatening, and less demanding to the more complex, potentially threatening, and demanding. The first tape showed how a person can interact with another person who approaches him or her, the second showed how one person can initiate interaction with another, the third involved interaction with a group, and the fourth showed how a person can resume relationships with various people in real-life situations.

The patients met in groups of five to eight three times a week for four weeks. Group leaders were undergraduate volunteers who had had twelve hours of training in the use of modeling, role playing, and social reinforcement. Each session began with the presentation of the videotape, during which the group leaders drew attention to the modeled behaviors. The sound was frequently turned off for discussion of the importance of the nonverbal aspects of social behaviors, such as leaning forward, eye contact, and smiling. After each tape, the group discussed ways in which the taped behaviors and circumstances could relate to each patient's own problems and situations. The rest of the session was devoted to role playing. Group leaders and members participated in the role-playing scenes, and the patient was encouraged to approximate the videotaped model's behaviors. Each patient was videotaped, and these tapes were played back for group comments and corrective feedback.

One week after the training was completed, all patients

were brought into a waiting room and given questionnaires to fill out. An accomplice, posing as a patient, was already seated in the room, apparently waiting to complete the testing. The accomplice was instructed to behave in a standard manner by asking the patient a number of questions, such as "Were you in the program?," "How many people were in your group," and "Would you go through this again?" Each patient was observed through a one-way mirror by raters trained to observe specific social behaviors, such as eye contact, forward leaning, physical contact, and the initiation of conversation. Each patient was also observed in a natural setting, mealtimes, by a rater for ten minutes. Raters noted specific behaviors, such as eye contact and sitting alone or with others, and also evaluated each patient according to general social skill and social impact on others.

Compared with the control group, structured learning therapy yielded significant improvement in most, though not all, specific social behaviors in the waiting-room situation. It did not have an effect on mealtime behaviors. Patients who had received psychotherapy showed only slight improvement in the mealtime setting and none in the waiting-room setting. An unexpected finding was that patients who received both training and psychotherapy, though slightly improving in some aspects, showed little improvement in general. The possibility should be considered that the structured learning therapy and psychotherapy, when used together, may have a mutually inhibiting effect on patients' social behaviors. Each approach, when used alone, may be effective, structured learning therapy being the more powerful. It is interesting to note that both chronic and acute patients responded to the skills training approach, although it was more effective with acute patients, whose social skills were more intact.

COMMENTARY: Since schizoid clients appear to have no desire for social interaction, the major goal of therapy is to keep them from isolating themselves entirely from human support and to prevent them from withdrawing into their own fantasy world. The approach described here offers a method that may help schizoid clients to gain social skills that they lack, although it is difficult to evaluate how successful this procedure would be with clients in an outpatient clinic who are not part of a total environment provided by the hospital ward and staff. Treatment might have generalized more if the training videotapes had included a broader range of situations.

Although we have often suggested that a particular approach could be augmented by other approaches, this article calls attention to the possibility that two approaches are not always better than one. In this case, structured learning therapy and psychotherapy, while successful in some areas separately, were not as effective when used together. This unexpected finding might have been more easily understood if the authors had specified what was meant by *psychotherapy,* which was defined here simply as "individual or group therapy."

SOURCE: Gutride, M. E., Goldstein, A. P., and Hunter, G. F. "The Use of Modeling and Role Playing to Increase Social Interaction Among Asocial Psychiatric Patients." *Journal of Consulting and Clinical Psychology,* 1973, *40,* 408-415.

======

A Multifaceted Approach
for Severe Withdrawal

AUTHORS: Michel Hersen, Barry A. Edelstein, Samuel M. Turner, and Susan G. Pinkston

PRECIS: Using drugs, social skills training, and vocational training to improve social and work behavior of a hospitalized man

INTRODUCTION: In this case study, the multifaceted treatment included adjustments of drug levels, token economy, social skills training, and job retraining. This case shows that unless specific therapeutic and vocational interventions are used, clients' specific presenting symptoms may be reduced, but their social functioning is unlikely to improve.

CASE STUDY: A twenty-seven-year-old black male was admitted to a Veterans Administration hospital with a diagnosis of schizophrenia, catatonic type, withdrawn. He was partly mute, unkempt, unresponsive, hallucinating, and drowsy. He had been an outpatient and was taking daily doses of Thorazine 500 mg and Stelazine 8 mg.

His history revealed a long-standing pattern of withdrawal and borderline functioning. Although he obtained passing grades in high school, he had few friends, did menial work on a chicken farm, and had been discharged from the army during duty in Vietnam because of a schizophrenic episode. For the next two years, he resumed his job on the chicken farm. He then lost his job and became progressively more withdrawn, remaining at home with his mother. He was hospitalized a year later; on discharge he was maintained for the next three years on phenothiazines and supportive outpatient therapy. He remained withdrawn and inactive, relating poorly to family members, his only social contacts. He did not work; instead he spent his days watching television and taking a daily half-mile walk. The gradual deterioration of his behavior over the three-year period resulted in his being readmitted to the hospital by his mother.

Initial Treatment. For the first twelve days drug levels were adjusted to control the patient's hallucinations and drowsiness. He was then placed in a token economy program and attended group therapy and occupational therapy. After one month he failed to improve: he was still unkempt, hallucinating, and withdrawn. He was removed from the group because of his complete lack of participation. During the next six weeks, drug dosages were further adjusted to control hallucinations, and his personal hygiene was dramatically improved through a token economy program designed specifically for him.

Social Skills Training. An intensive training program was begun nine weeks after admission. The first step was to list the patient's specific deficits: failure to maintain eye contact when spoken to, responding to questions with long pauses (latency), not initiating conversation or making requests, and being generally unassertive.

The training included eight simulated interpersonal situations in which the patient was instructed to make an appropriately assertive response. His verbal and nonverbal behavior was videotaped while he was seated next to a female assistant who assumed various roles—lady, friend, cashier, waitress, and so on. The scenes were described over an intercom from an adjoining room by another assistant. Specific social skills training consisted of instructions, behavior rehearsal, feedback, and real-life modeling on four of the eight scenes (Training Series). On the remaining four scenes (Generalization Series), no training was given the last phase of the study.

An example of a Training Series scene is "You are standing in line to buy a ticket to a movie that has just come to town. This is supposed to be a good movie and the theater is crowded. Then a lady cuts in line in front of you." Lady (assistant): "You don't mind if I cut in line here, do you?" Other scenes involved being asked for a loan by a friend, being short-changed, and being given a paycheck that was less than it should have been.

An example of a Generalization Series scene is "You have just bought a new shirt and when trying it on for the first time discover that several buttons are missing. You return to the store and approach the sales clerk who sold it to you." Clerk (assistant): "May I help you, sir?" Other scenes included being charged for services that had not been requested, receiving the wrong order in a restaurant, and having a friend refuse crucial help for an apparently trivial reason.

The training consisted of daily thirty- to forty-five-minute training sessions over a period of five weeks, with a different phase each week.

Week one: The patient's initial competencies were assessed by asking him to make videotaped responses to the four training and four generalization scenes.

Week two: Treatment was directed toward increasing eye contact. At the end of each daily session, he was asked to respond to the eight scenes again.

Weeks three and four: Treatment was additionally focused on latency of response and requesting the partner to change her behavior.

Week five (generalization): The patient was told to apply

what he had learned during the training scenes to the Generalization Series scenes. In addition to the training, the patient also resumed group therapy, where his behavior was observed through a one-way mirror.

The training resulted in considerable improvement. He displayed increased requests, eye contact, and overall assertiveness and decreased speech disturbances. He initiated more conversations in group sessions. There was some decrease in social competency during the fifth phase, which suggests that the generalization instructions may have confused him.

Job Retraining. It was clear that a return to the patient's home setting would result in a rapid readmission unless he received some kind of vocational placement and retraining. The patient was placed at Goodwill Industries in a two-week training program as a trucker's helper. He returned to the hospital each night. His progress was monitored at Goodwill Industries, and his social relationships improved to the extent that he was initiating conversations with fellow trainees. At the end of two weeks, the patient requested discharge so he could obtain higher pay. He found a job assembling lighting parts in a factory near his home. However, the therapist found it necessary to tell the foreman that he would be responsible for the patient, who was not dangerous. The patient was then given a two-week leave of absence to aid him in readjusting to home and work situations. He was still taking daily dosages of Stelazine and Cogentin.

An extensive multiple-check follow-up period up to twenty-two weeks revealed gradual improvement in both work and social situations. The patient returned to the hatchery, where he received higher pay and could see old friends. He reported he was pleased with his job. He reported eating and sleeping well, and his appearance and personal hygiene continued to improve.

COMMENTARY: In this case, after drug levels had been properly adjusted, careful attention to a chronic patient's social and vocational deficits resulted in his functioning in a natural setting after hospital discharge. The report also calls attention to the importance of gradually fading the patient back into his natural environment. For example, if the Goodwill Industries training had been omitted, the patient might have had more difficulty adjusting to the pressures of living outside the hospital. Though not specifically planned, the patient's interactions with the female assistant may have had a positive effect, since he became fond of her and appeared eager to please her.

SOURCE: Hersen, M., Edelstein, B. A., Turner, S. M., and Pinkston, S. G. "Effects of Phenothiazines and Social Skills Training in a Withdrawn Schizophrenic." *Journal of Clinical Psychology,* 1975, *31,* 588-593.

=====

Additional Readings

Alden, L., Safran, J., and Weideman, R. "A Comparison of Cognitive and Skills Training Strategies in the Treatment of Unassertive Clients." *Behavior Therapy,* 1978, *9,* 843-846.

Twenty-seven men and women who wanted assertion training were recruited from the community and a college campus. They were randomly assigned to skills training, cognitive behavior modification, or a no-treatment control group. Treatment involved groups of four to five who met for six two-hour sessions led by two cotherapists.

Skills training included modeling, behavioral rehearsal, therapist and group feedback, and homework in real-life situations.

Cognitive behavior modification focused on awareness of irrational beliefs, identification of negative self-statements, and real-life practice of cognitive coping strategies between sessions.

On the basis of self-report measures and videotaped role-playing sessions, both the skills and the cognitive treatments produced significantly more improvement than in the control group. Both treatments appeared equally effective. It was hypothesized that both methods worked because they provided the clients with a greater sense of personal competence in assertion settings. The two approaches are similar in that they provide clients with something to do in awkward social situations, thereby increasing their sense of control.

Marzillier, J. S., Lambert, C., and Kellett, J. "A Controlled Evaluation of Systematic Desensitization and Social Skills Training for Socially Inadequate Psychiatric Patients." *Behaviour Reseach and Therapy*, 1976, *14*, 225-238.

Social skills training and systematic desensitization were compared in a study with socially inadequate patients. Target behaviors included social anxiety, social skills, social activities and contacts, and general clinical improvement. Groups receiving either treatment improved more than control groups. Social skills training resulted in a significant increase in the number of social activities and contacts, with less effect on clinical improvement. The group receiving systematic desensitization for social anxiety also had greater social contacts but a high dropout rate. The final conclusion was that social skills training, with its broader focus, was generally more effective than systematic desensitization, which involved the treatment of social anxiety alone. It would appear that a combination of both methods may be the best approach for socially withdrawn clients.

Schierloh, V. C., and Bernal, M. E. "Operant Conditioning of Verbal Behavior in a Withdrawn Patient by a Patient Peer." In M. D. Lebow (Ed.), *Approaches to Modifying Patient Behavior*. New York: Appleton-Century-Crofts, 1976.

A patient with a diagnosis of paranoid schizophrenia was taught to use reinforcement techniques with her similarly diagnosed withdrawn roommate. Both were asked to discuss magazine pictures, and their interaction was videotaped. Every time the patient initiated conversation, her peer responded by smiling, nodding her head, or laughing. Initiations of conversations increased as predicted. When the peer was instructed to ignore these responses, they decreased. When social reinforcement was again introduced, the behaviors reappeared quickly. Studies such as this demonstrate the possibility of family members' using operant conditioning techniques with schizoid clients.

Siever, L. J. "Schizoid and Schizotypal Personality Disorders."
In J. R. Lion (Ed.), *Personality Disorders: Diagnosis and Management.* (2nd ed.) Baltimore: Williams & Wilkins, 1981.

Schizoid clients may initially seek help but often resist it when treatment is begun by keeping the therapist at a distance. Therapists must be especially tactful and sensitive when working with these clients and should be continuously available in spite of the client's apparent withdrawal from therapeutic interaction. They must be aware of their own reactions to clients and use these reactions to understand the client's feelings of being cut off, which are used as a defense against painful emotions and fears of intimacy. Occasionally another person will succeed in breaking through a schizoid client's defensive barrier, and an intimate relationship develops. In such cases, schizoid clients, unable to cope with overwhelming fears of intimacy that are stirred up, may seek therapy because of their intense anxiety. Short-term crisis intervention is recommended, with the goal of restoring the client's equilibrium; in-depth interpretation is likely to frighten the client away from therapy.

Moderately schizoid clients may benefit from group therapy along with short-term individual therapy. Severely disordered clients, with their dread of self-disclosure, may be unable to tolerate group experiences.

Pharmacological treatment is not recommended for chronic treatment, although minor tranquilizers may be helpful when clients are anxious or socially inhibited. Antidepressants may relieve depressive episodes, and phenothiazines may be used for clients with psychotic symptoms.

The relationship among schizoid, schizotypal, and borderline personality is discussed, and guidelines for differential diagnosis and therapeutic approaches are offered. Both schizoid and schizotypal clients are extremely difficult to treat, by either psychotherapy or pharmacotherapy.

Author Index

Subject Index

personality disorder, 463-466, 470-472; and social phobia, 145-147

Benzodiazapines: for antisocial personality disorder, 330; for generalized anxiety disorder, 235-236; for simple phobia, 197

Borderline personality disorder: adult therapies for, 333-369; and amphetamines, 367; annotated readings on, 364-369; and anxiety, 342-346; brief therapy for, 354-357; described, 333-335; diagnostic criteria for, 333-334; distinguishing features of, 367; dream interpretation for, 336-341; family therapy for, 367-368; lithium for, 358-360; medication for, 346-348, 358-360, 366-367, 432; and narcissism, 364; and organic brain syndrome, 365-366; psychotherapy for, 336-357, 361-364, 366-367, 368; relaxation for, 342-346; subtypes of, 346-348; and therapist relationship, 336-341, 349-357, 361-364, 369; tranquilizers for, 366-367; tricyclic antidepressants for, 367

Brevitol, for generalized anxiety disorder, 243

Brief Psychiatric Rating Scale, 121

Brief therapy: for borderline personality disorder, 354-357; for dependent personality disorder, 377-380, 388-391, 407-408; for depression, 19-22, 41-44, 79-80, 83-85; for histrionic personality disorder, 422-426; for narcissistic personality disorder, 437-439; for schizoid personality disorder, 485-489; for simple phobia, 190-192

Cancer phobia, implosive therapy with hypnosis for, 185-187

Carbon dioxide: and generalized anxiety disorder, 243; for obsessive-compulsive disorder, 290

Cardiac arrhythmia, and anxiety, 211

Cardiopulmonary disorders, and anxiety, 210-211

Causes, expanded view of, trend toward, 9-10

Chillicothe Correctional Institute, 323

China, exercise program in, 172

Chlordiazepoxide (CDP) (Librium): for antisocial personality disorder, 305, 326; for generalized anxiety disorder, 235-236; for narcissistic personality disorder, 444

Client-centered therapy, for narcissistic personality disorder, 439-443

Clients, informing, about therapy, trend toward, 8

Chlorimipramine (clomipramine), for obsessive-compulsive disorder, 270-273, 283-284, 287

Clorazepate, for generalized anxiety disorder, 236

Cogentin, for schizoid personality disorder, 495

Cognitive behavior therapy: for antisocial personality disorder, 316-319; for generalized anxiety disorder, 227-229, 237; for histrionic personality disorder, 415-418; for obsessive-compulsive disorder, 259-261; for paranoid personality disorder, 463-466. *See also* Behavior therapy; Cognitive therapy

Cognitive preparation, for antisocial personality disorder, 310-313

Cognitive restructuring: for agoraphobia, 95-102; for anger, 324-325; for paranoid personality disorder, 477

Cognitive therapy: for anxiety, 18; for compulsions, 18; for dependent personality disorder, 396-403; for depression, 17-19, 32-35, 44-47, 60-67, 72, 76-77, 79-80, 85-86; for generalized anxiety disorder, 204-207; for paranoid personality disorder, 18; for schizoid personality disorder, 496-497; for simple phobia, 178-181, 192-193; for social phobia, 135-138, 141-144, 147-149. *See also* Cognitive behavior therapy